Multicultural Education, Critical Pedagogy, and the Politics of Difference

SUNY Series, Social Context of Education
Christine E. Sleeter, editor

and

SUNY Series, Teacher Empowerment and School Reform
Henry A. Giroux and Peter L. McLaren, editors

Multicultural Education, Critical Pedagogy, and the Politics of Difference

edited by
Christine E. Sleeter
and
Peter L. McLaren

State University of New York Press

Published by
State University of New York Press, Albany

For information, address the State University of New York Press,
State University Plaza, Albany, NY 12246

Production by Christine Lynch
Marketing by Fran Keneston

Library of Congress Cataloging-in-Publication Data

Multicultural education, critical pedagogy, and the politics of
     difference / edited by Christine E. Sleeter and Peter L. McLaren.
          p.   cm. — (SUNY series, social context of education) (SUNY
     series, teacher empowerment and school reform)
          Includes bibliographical references and index.
          ISBN 0-7914,2541-X (acid-free paper). — ISBN 0-7914-2542-8 (pbk.
     : acid-free paper)
          1. Multicultural education—United States.   2. Critical pedagogy—
     United States.   3. Education—United States—Sociological aspects.
     4. Multiculturalism—United States.   5. Differentiation (Sociology)
     I. Sleeter, Christine E., 1948–   .   II. McLaren, Peter, 1948–   .
     III. Series.   IV. Series: Teacher empowerment and school reform.
     LC1099.3.M816 1995
     370.19'6'0973—dc20   94-32892
                                                                    CIP

CONTENTS

To El Erjército Zapatista de Liberación Nacional
and to struggles for liberation throughout the globe.

FOREWORD

MICHAEL PAVEL

The growing diversity in our society beckons that we move from excoriating diversity as a weakness to legitimizing it as a strength. As the world watched the racial unrest in Los Angeles during the summer of 1993, it became clear to many of us that our very survival depends on a transformation of our ideological perspectives and changes in our social, cultural, and institutional relations. The book you are about to read is an important contribution to the literature not simply because it recognizes that we must confront the challenge of diversity in our neighborhoods, our businesses, and our government offices as well as our classrooms. It is important because the voices that it brings together speak directly to our destiny as a democracy and the quality of all our futures. We should all be motivated to embrace diversity by a commitment to the principle that equitable access, widespread achievement, and social justice result in a provision of noncoercive choices. As the contributors illustrate, such a principle is given meaning and purpose by individuals who are able to question, investigate, and influence the role that difference and diversity play in determining the direction of United States society.

We need to understand the dynamics involved in the study of diversity and learn about ways to expand the context of the way we analyze multiculturalism. We should focus on the individuals—from the children yet unborn to the elders—and understand the myriad complex of social, historical, economic, and cultural relations that influence their learning and quality of life. Then it will be necessary to determine what social environments and relations can be designed to better fulfill our students' needs. Our attention must also be directed toward achieving a broader contextual understanding about the role played by education in a postindustrial, late capitalist society. In their introductory chapter, Christine E. Sleeter and Peter McLaren direct our attention to the interaction between these domains as a means of developing a praxis of social change.

1

All of us have at one time or another looked at difference from a deficit perspective. However, the contributors to Part I of *Multicultural Education, Critical Pedagogy, and the Politics of Differences* offer us the convincing position that if we do not promote an understanding of difference in its historical, racial, and gendered specificity, all us will suffer. Not engaging the sociohistorical and cultural perspectives of the politics of difference has been a serious problem. Such perspectives may provide new ways of overcoming problems that have been inherent and systemic in our society. The chapters by Peter McLaren, Stephen Haymes, Donaldo Macedo, Shirley R. Steinberg, and Joe Kincheloe explore the dimensions of those sociopolitical factors that impede our social transformation toward an appreciation of diversity and a fostering of respect for difference that moves beyond the neoliberal approach to multiculturalism as a mere celebration of difference. Simply celebrating difference is like a birthday party; once over, we need to wake up and face the reality that the coming year is a time to become wiser. These authors are wise to put us in a dialectical mode of questioning that asks: Diversity to what end? In whose interest? For what purpose? It is only through a criticalist approach to multiculturalism that we will be able work toward a democracy of many voices and diverse perspectives.

The contributors in Part II provide a conceptual framework in order to understand multicultural education, critical pedagogy, and politics difference as forms of political and historical agency. Geneva Gay, John Rivera, Mary Poplin, Sonia Nieto, Carl Allsup, Cameron McCarthy, Carmen Montecinos, and Mary Ritchie are resolute in their message that there are many collective memberships desiring to maintain their distinct culture and values yet wanting to participate in a broader, collective history. Multicultural education and critical pedagogy do not require that all collective communities share the same intellectual values, beliefs, and norms. For example, while it can be argued that various cultures share certain values concerning, let us say, the environment, clearly these values are interpreted somewhat differently by each culture. Still, we all need clean water to drink, fresh air to breath, and sacred lands to live on. In the highly differentiated world of human society, cultural respect can occur because of overlapping memberships in environments of shared concern—even if only provisional—leading to the construction of ideas and values important to developing the human spirit and conditions that promote the positive aspects of that spirit.

The trend toward recognizing and appreciating cultural diversity—where an increasing number of cultures are able to convey an ever-widening variety of ideas that are productive of liberation and social justice—can accelerate within our life time. We can change the context of cultural understanding from a dominant paternalistic culture transmitted along the one-way communication channel of a mainstream ideology toward a cultural understanding that results from a greater variety of interlocking cultures transmitted along many channels involving entities like schools, governments, and private enterprises. Those who promote a critical multiculturalism are deeply concerned with the empowerment of those who have no voice, those who toil, those who live unappreciated, and those who die in silence.

In Part III, Antonia Darder, Khaula Murtadha, Evelyn Newman Phillips, Janine Pease-Windy Boy, and Christine Sleeter remain unified by the conviction that multiculturalism—as a field of practice, focus of research, and topic of meaningful discussion—will succeed as a medium of cultural critique to stimulate transformative social change because its primary pedagogical aim is to produce critical self-awareness. Various groups, defined by the axes of race, class, gender, and sexuality, can satisfy their intellectual needs without discarding their identities as historical agents when the aim of multiculturalism is to recognize a common ground of struggle that can be engaged from various vantage points. In this respect, critical multiculturalism and multicultural education advocate that a contextual understanding of the sociohistorical production of oppression is a necessary precondition for transforming those relations more in line with a concept of democracy that the fledgling United States borrowed from the Great Iroquois Confederacy: That all people would have a voice and no decision would be made without considering how it affected the collective membership and ultimately the seven generations to come.

CHRISTINE E. SLEETER AND PETER MCLAREN————————

Introduction: Exploring Connections to Build a Critical Multiculturalism

We are in search of the true America—an America of multiple cultures, multiple histories, multiple regions, multiple realities, multiple identities, multiple ways of living, surviving and being human. And no where is this struggle for the true America more profoundly being waged than in the classrooms of public schools in the United States.

Darder

It is a curiously discomfiting paradox that during the early 1990s, the term "diversity" came into vogue at a time when groups that had been historically polarized by antagonisms centering on race, class, gender, and sexual orientation were being pushed farther and farther apart following the conservative restoration of the Reagan-Bush administrations. Multicultural education was no longer a new term that elicited the question, 'What's that?' when mentioned in conversation. The front pages of newspapers and popular magazines across the nation featured stories about the controversial *Children of the Rainbow* first grade curriculum in New York City, vociferous debates about history curricula, Afrocentric schools, bilingual education, and revisions of core curricula in universities such as Stanford. While some of the publicity surrounding multicultural education roundly condemned it, even that same publicity acknowledged its impact on schools.

Yet at the same time, evidence mounted that disparities among groups had widened markedly over the past two decades. Hacker (1992) amassed a wealth of data to argue that the U.S. was becoming two polarized nations: "Black and white, separate, hostile, unequal." Barlett and Steele (1992) opened their discussion of what went wrong with America by observing that "The wage and salary structure of American business, encouraged by federal tax policies, is pushing the nation toward a two-class society. The top 4% make as much as the bottom half of U.S. workers" (p. ix).

5

Faludi (1991) described the 1980s as an "undeclared war against American women," supporting this characterization with over 400 pages of data and examples. Kozol (1991) described the growing inequalities between the richest and the poorest schools in the U.S. as "savage."

Multiculturalism did not cause these widening disparities, contrary to what some tried to argue (e.g., Schlesinger 1992). In fact, multiculturalism has acquired a deepened resolve among its advocates as well as among increasingly counterhegemonic forces precisely because of the decidedly Euro-American emphasis the antimulticulturalists place on sharing common values—an emphasis which is grounded in white supremacist, patriarchal discourses of difference and democracy. We juxtapose the growing attention to diversity with widening chasms among various socio-cultural groups to frame our discussion of the politics under-girding multicultural education and critical pedagogy. A proliferation of political and economic disparities among groups gave rise to multicultural education and critical pedagogy during the late 1960s. By the 1990s, oppressive relations had intensified, and the Radical Right's capturing of the slogan "family values" turned it into a code word for segregation, intolerance, white priv-ilege, and white Christian schools. However, this reality is often obscured in uncritical celebrations of difference and the push to increase the nation's global competitiveness.

Mainstream schooling reinforces the dominant culture's way of producing subjectivities by rationalizing and accommodating agency into existing regimes of truth. In other words, dominant forms of pedagogy accommodate existing modes or forms of intel-ligibility and their distributive effects which are part of the ritual-ized conversation of becoming a citizen. Most mainstream teaching practices, therefore, could be characterized as "membership-oriented" pedagogy which requires that teachers assist students in acquiring those necessary interpretive skills and forms of cultural capital that will enable them to negotiate contemporary zones of contest—the often complex, complicated, and conflictual public and institutional spaces within the larger society. The dominant culture of schooling mirrors that of the larger culture in so far as teachers and students willingly and unwittingly situate themselves within a highly politicized field of power relations that partake of unjust race, class, and gender affiliations. Within such a culture, individuals are differentially enabled to act by virtue of the social, cultural, and institutional possibilities afforded them on the basis of their race, class, gender, and sexual orientation. Such a "culture of silence" teaches students to harmonize a world of incongruity and fractious antipathy and to domesticate the unruly and unpleasant and messy features of everyday life in which costs are imposed for being different and rewards given for 'fitting in' compliantly.

Multicultural education and critical pedagogy bring into the arena of schooling insurgent, resistant, and insurrectional modes of interpretation and classroom practices which set out to imperil the familiar, to contest the legitimating norms of mainstream cultural life, and to render problematic the common discursive frames and regimes upon which "proper" behavior, comportment, and social interaction are premised. Together, they analyze extant power configurations and unsettle them when such configurations serve to reproduce social relations of domination. Critical and multicultural pedagogy defamiliarize and make remarkable what is often passed off as the ordinary, the mundane, the routine, and the banal. They ambiguate the complacency of teaching under the sign of modernity, under which meaning too often is seen as ahistorical, neutral, and separated from value and power.

In their essence, neither multicultural education nor critical pedagogy consist of lists of items to add onto school practices, although one can find simplistic prescriptions for both. Multicultural education initially referred to demands for school reform articulated first by African Americans, then by other groups of color, followed by women, people with disabilities, and gay rights advocates (Banks 1989, p. 5). Critical pedagogy "challenges teachers and students to empower themselves for social change, to advance democracy and equality as they advance their literacy and knowledge" (Shor 1993, p. 25). Strictly speaking, any course in any discipline can be taught from a critical or a multicultural perspective and could justifiably be called critical pedagogy or multicultural education. This is perhaps why the terms "critical pedagogy" and "multicultural education" are now more frequently used in courses taught across the curriculum. However, we wish to be clear that we do not consider either critical pedagogy or multicultural education to consist simply of a set of methodological formulations. Rather, both refer to a particular ethico-political attitude or ideological stance that one constructs in order to confront and engage the world critically and challenge power relations. One could perhaps argue—although it is not within the scope of this introduction to do so—that these are both standpoint epistemologies as well as ethical imperatives, that they advocate a preferential option for certain types of actions and social interests. Critical educators adopt the stance of the *cultural worker*, an individual who may work in schools but who may also work in other public spheres such as the arts, medicine, law, social work, or community work.

This book attempts to build a coalition that enables dialog, to identify terrains for mutual support, and to articulate common concerns and agendas. It attempts to enable such dialog around three themes: contexts for pedagogy, theories of pedagogy, and pedagogies in action.

CONTEXT

Of course, particular meanings, stereotypes and myths can change, but the presence of a *system* of racial meanings and stereotypes, of racial ideology, seems to be a permanent feature of US culture.

Omi and Winant

The American Indian has struggled with accessing an accurate past image, and is bombarded by the media's contrived and inaccurate images...These intrude and damage individual visions of past, which so significantly influence "today."

Pease-Windy Boy

This book would not have been conceivable at this present historical conjuncture were it not for the precipitous theoretical and political convergence of critical pedagogy and multicultural education over recent years. While we would not advocate that their distinctions become conceptually blurred out of existence in one transdisciplinary stroke, we do think it is productive to see these two formerly discrete fields as representing a common political project that may be distinguished less by their substantive interests than by their current emphases. Critical pedagogy and multicultural education are complementary approaches that enable a sustained criticism of the effects of global capitalism and its implication in the production of race and gender injustices in schools and other institutional settings.

We locate the current struggle in our schools in the larger efforts of white supremacist, patriarchal capitalism to condition the public's consciousness of everyday life, to create the borders of what is considered the meaningful universe of its citizens, and to tacitly privilege the manner in which everyday life is framed and coded. Macedo's insightful discussion in this volume of how media framed the Gulf War, for example, challenges that conditioning and the teaching of "literacy for stupidification."

Global capitalist hegemony has become increasingly ambiguous, elliptical, ironic, and seductive. Domination is no longer only signalled by overt class exploitation, legalized racial and sex discrimination, or the fascist instrumentalization of everyday life. Structures of domination are, today, much less tangible and more difficult to decode, in part because of their hegemonic entrenchment. Spaces for commodification are endless and now include the very critics of capitalist commodification as, for instance, in the burgeoning book industry that deals with criticisms of contemporary incarnations of global capitalism and the demythologization of the advertising establishment. The motor force of capitalist domination rests on the tacit collusion of the oppressed in their own lived subordination; oppressed and oppressors alike are conditioned to accept the current economic and racial tensions as inevitable and to recode potentially oppositional anger into popular cultural forms (i.e., radio, film, and video), domesticating the modes of address that articulate the debates over public life and social justice and eclipsing the original referent system of revolutionary struggle. The transformation of Malcolm X from a revolutionary leader into an object of consumption is but one example. Hegemony no longer requires a uniform, monolithic reading of the social world but, in fact, successfully conscripts the self-reflexive and socially conscious citizen into its ranks, as witnessed in advertising's appeals to "liberated" women and men dedicated to environmental concerns and career advancement for all regardless of race, class, or gender. Hegemony has become 'sexier' but not less violent.

The new conservative agenda has been officializing a concept of democracy that conflates it with nationhood, making it inhospitable to the struggle of social justice. In effect, the right has attempted to emplace a white supremacist, capitalist, and patriarchal subjectivity that would channel resistance into a substratum of popular culture and make acculturation into the logic of consumption as penetrative as possible for the majority of citizens. Even the emphasis placed by liberals on the concept of pluralism demands an unhealthy allegiance to a set of discourses and social practices which serve to legitimize the imperatives of white patriarchal capitalism. Faced with the ominous threat of Gingrich and his minions, we need to brace ourselves for an all-out war against difference. Here the term "democracy" becomes whatever it is necessary for it to mean given the interests of the groups that it serves— a type of *objet petit a* that can never be pinned down, a universal referent that can never be fully realized in the concreteness of everyday, situated existence, a signifier that is just free-floating enough to provide the ambiguity necessary to keep the symbolic order from imploding.

Critique of the political-economic context of schooling must be ongoing. Although schools are situated in increasingly embedded systems of domination, the particular ways in which forms of domination are encoded and played out shift over time and space, in order to appear benign, virtuous or simply normal. Even multiculturalism is being domesticated as diversity becomes fashionable, necessitating a continuous critical examination of multicultural practice. San Juan, Jr. (1992), for example, criticizes many contemporary literary texts that attempt to broaden the canon as resting on "a foundational scheme of inventing America as the model poly-ethnic nation with 'a shared sense of destiny' and ethnicization as a form of modernization" (p. 38)—peaceful coexistence within an historical trajectory of progress for all. One of the problems we need to face is that the academy encourages black academics to engage in the articulation of a theory of multiculturalism as long as it remains contextually tied to issues of racism and sexism, that is, issues dealing mainly with the private sphere. They are not encouraged to engage in criticisms of the wider public spheres dealing with the global implications of late capitalism or white supremacy (Gilroy, 1993).

Analyses of oppression in education must always be situated historically and on vigilant guard against cooptation. Thus, the first chapters in this book analyze the context of education in the early 1990s in terms of how differences are commodified and sold and relations of power are muted by appealing to exoticized images of difference.

PEDAGOGY AND THEORIES

Until recently, nobody had ever asked me if I was an Indian: it was obvious I was not; neither was I asked if I was a "minority" or a "Hispanic." I never had to talk about myself in those terms. It was only after I came to the United States that I had to learn the many ways in which those terms were socially constructed by diverse groups in this country.

Montecinos

Differences between multicultural education and critical pedagogy
are more context than content, semantics than substance,
and oratorical than essential.

Gay

Education critics often identify themselves according to a
particular theoretical or disciplinary allegiance to multicultural
education, critical pedagogy, or feminist pedagogy, and these
perspectives are often conflated within the critical educational
tradition in both the practice of theory and in actual classroom
praxis. As chapters in this volume by Gay, and by Rivera and
Poplin argue, multicultural education, critical pedagogy, and feminist pedagogy are mutually informing frameworks or constructs
that differ not so much in their overall political project of self and
social transformation as in the emphases they place on theoretical
approaches to class, gender, race, and sexual relations.

E. San Juan, Jr. (1992) argues that there is "no single master
narrative" for liberation (p. 7). Rather, there must be multiple narratives as different groups of people define their own identities,
analyze the circumstances of their own oppression, and chart
strategies for empowerment. To complicate the situation further,
groups are not discrete, freestanding entities, since all of us are
racialized, genderized, and so forth; we all belong to multiple collec-
tivities and define ourselves accordingly, although groups are
constituted overwhelmingly within asymmetrical relations of power.

Multicultural education and critical pedagogy can each be
traced historically to specific struggles; each has further been elaborated as its main precepts have proved useful in specific contexts.
While there is no single narrative of liberation, a brief glance at the
historic roots of multicultural education and critical pedagogy illustrates that both developed from complementary struggles and,
further, that narratives of liberation can be pulled away from liberating projects and employed in the service of extant power relations.

Multicultural education is an offspring of the Civil Rights movement in the U.S. Gay (1983) notes that multicultural education

> originated in a socio-political milieu and is to some extent a
> product of its times. Concerns about the treatment of ethnic
> groups in school curricula and instructional materials directly
> reflected concerns about their social, political, and economic
> plight in the society at large. (p. 560)

African American scholars and educators, working in conjunction with the Civil Rights movement as a whole, provided much of the leadership of multicultural education (Banks 1992).

The prefix "multi" was adopted as an umbrella to join diverse groups of color. Nakagawa (1989), for example, explains that it was a leap for her to move from identifying with the struggles of Asian-Americans to those of oppressed racial groups as a whole. The term "multiethnic education" was used to bridge racial and ethnic groups; "multicultural education" broadened the umbrella to include gender and other forms of diversity. The term "culture" rather than "racism" was adopted mainly so that audiences of white educators would listen. As a result, however, many white educators have pulled multicultural education away from social struggles and redefined it to mean the celebration of ethnic foods and festivals; the field is sometimes criticized as having turned away from its initial critique of racism in education (Mattai 1992). It is important to locate multicultural education in the Civil Rights struggle for freedom, political power, and economic integration since its roots were in racial struggle.

The late 1960s and early 1970s witnessed several other movements that have connected loosely with multicultural education. The women's movement gained strength and impacted schools with passage of Title IX in 1972. Although the women's movement has had a White middle-class orientation, there has been continued effort on the part of some workers to link struggles against racism with struggles against sexism. Bilingual education was advanced in the late 1950s by Cubans fleeing Castro's revolution. While this was a relatively privileged minority, since then Mexican-Americans, Puerto Ricans, and Asian-Americans have advanced bilingual education legislation, theory, and practice. The history and development of bilingual education is somewhat separate from that of multicultural education, although the two have grown in a mutually reinforcing symbiosis. Also, during this time ethnic studies and women's studies departments were established on some university campuses, providing a basis for contemporary debates about multiculturalism in higher education.

Multicultural education frames inequality in terms of institutionalized oppression and reconfigures the families and communities of oppressed groups as sources of strength. By the early 1980s, this formulation was turned on its head in the dominant discourse about education. Discussions about education were framed mainly in terms of how to enable the U.S. to maintain international supremacy in the Cold War and the "trade war" (Shor 1986). The early 1980s saw a wave of educational reform reports, beginning with that by the National Commission on Excellence in Education, *A Nation at Risk* (1983). In this context, students of color, those from poverty areas, and those whose first language was not English were defined as "at risk" of failure, and their homes and communities were defined as culturally deprived and morally depraved.

Nevertheless, by 1985 demographic data reports were informing educators and the general public that people of color would become the majority during the twenty-first century, and multicultural education received renewed attention. At the K–12 level, workshops on multicultural education became "in" again, with many teachers interpreting it to mean teaching supplementary lessons about "other" cultures. Multicultural educators had made some substantive changes in curricula, however, which led to fierce battles in states such as California and New York (Cornbleth and Waugh 1993). In higher education, lively debates about the canon were met by conservative challenges against "political correctness." The roots of Western civilization were reconnected with Africa and Asia (Bernal 1987), a connection that was fiercely rejected by those who feared that the loss of European supremacy would mean loss of civilization.

However, as White teachers in K–12 classrooms developed "tourist" conceptions of multicultural education (Derman-Sparks 1989) and as desegregated schools demanded children of color go far more than halfway to bring about integration, many educators of color grew disillusioned with the fading promises of the Civil Rights movement and multiculturalism. At the center of this disillusionment has been the failure of white people and institutions to grapple substantively with our own racism at personal as well as systemic levels, concomitant with the escalated transfer of economic resources and the mobility of capital away from poor communities. Native American, African American, Chicano/a, Puerto Rican, and other communities of color responded with resurgent self-determination. Tribal schools and Afrocentric schools and programs are vibrant examples of this response, and are discussed here in chapters by Pease-Windy Boy, Murtadha, and Phillips. These efforts argue compellingly for the need to center oneself spiritually and culturally before one can connect meaningfully across cultural borders and illustrate the failure of white controlled multicultural schools to advance the interests and needs of communities of color.

One also finds "multicultural education" in other institutional arenas, although exactly what this means varies widely. Many corporations now offer multicultural (or "human relations") training as part of their in-service personnel agenda, primarily to maximize their own profits, although women and groups of color often define such training as part of a strategy for opening doors of opportunity. As a 1993 special issue of the *Labor Research Review* illustrates, organized labor is also beginning to use multicultural education as a way of bridging historical racial cleavages for the purpose of collective empowerment.

Multicultural education, initially born in liberation struggles, has become a free-floating signifier that is now used in widely differing contexts for conflicting purposes. Conservatives can be seen as wanting to exploit difference for its potential market value while liberals wish to celebrate difference under the sign of a unified, harmonious culture. In both cases difference is tolerated—even celebrated—as long as it does not contest white Anglo-European values that serve as the invisible referent against which difference is defined. In other words, difference becomes a marker for novelty while concealing the social, cultural, political, and economic conditions out of which difference becomes valued or demeaned. In this sense multicultural pluralism is understood as partly a detente between conservativism and liberalism in so far as its underlying unity is built upon commodity logic. We feel it is crucially important to fuse multicultural pedagogies with ongoing social critiques of oppression. Although critical pedagogy grew from different roots, linking critical pedagogy with multicultural education can strengthen this critical stance.

While critical pedagogy draws inspiration from liberation struggles in Latin America and elsewhere and invokes the example of individuals such as Farabundo Marti, Cesar Augusto Sandino, Rosa Luxemburg, and Che Guevara, it is most often associated with the literacy practices and brilliant exegetical work of Brasilian educator Paulo Freire. Freire's work is broad in theoretical sweep, but in most U.S. contexts educators have rather narrowly appropriated Freire's work as a methodology that will help them better understand the social physics of classroom life. Freire's work is best understood as problem-posing education rather than as a classroom tool kit for finding classroom solutions. Until recently, Freire's work dealt with mainly issues of education and social class discrimination although Freire has been directing his attention to questions dealing with race and gender in recent works. Freire's early emphasis on social class has to be seen in its historical context as far as radical work goes; in this respect it was, in fact, no different from the earliest exponents of North American criticalist work in education.

Influenced by the work of U.S. social reconstructionists, participatory research, ethnomethodology and hermeneutics, British advances in sociolinguistics and the sociology of knowledge, the Frankfurt School critique of the culture industry, and the work of radical Latin American educators such as Freire, criticalists in the U.S. gained a tremulous foothold in the early 1980s with the contributions of Henry Giroux, Michael Apple, Jean Anyon, Philip Wexler, Bill Pinar, Madeline Grumet, and others. These forerunners of critical pedagogy continue to break new theoretical ground, less isolated now in their endeavors perhaps but still relatively marginal actors when compared with those operating in mainstream educational arenas. What is promising in this present historical juncture is that a new generation of educators, working alongside the early pioneers of critical pedagogy or working independently at various sites across the country, are currently helping to steer the direction of scholarship in new directions. Today the critical enterprise has been subdivided into new categories: critical postmodernism, border pedagogy, neo and post-Marxism, feminist poststructuralism, ritology (study of ritual), border identity, postcolonial pedagogy, discourse analysis, historical genealogy, to name but a few. While theoretical differences certainly inflect the currently and often virulently contested field of critical pedagogy, there are also those who identify themselves as criticalists but who either eschew theory altogether or remain wary of criticalists who appropriate from the language of "high theory" to advance proposals for classroom reform. This book does not attempt to resolve such debates.

Since the conceptual beginnings of critical pedagogy in North America, there have been growing attempts among cultural workers to ground analysis in a more developed and sophisticated understanding of the role that race, gender, and class play in social formations and the production of historically and culturally specific modes of subjectivity. In addition, critical pedagogy has accomplished in more recent years a more detailed understanding of the production and disarticulation of women and people of color as the abjected other (*les autres*) through processes of ideological differentiation against invisible cultural markers consisting of Eurocentric, Anglocentric, and patriarchal assumptions and practices.

We acknowledge the need for critical pedagogy to study further the racializing of identity and social space, personal and institutional relations, and the public sphere, especially as these have shifted during the passage from what David Theo Goldberg (1993) calls "classical liberal modernity to postmodern bourgeois liberalism" (p. 206). We follow Goldberg in asking how we can turn the category of race from one of oppression to become "the site of a counterassault, a ground or field for launching liberatory projects or from which to expand freedom(s) and open up emancipatory spaces" (Ibid., p. 211).

Critical pedagogy is situated as a critical/tactical practice designed to contest and transform what Lefebvre (1990) calls "terrorism and everyday life" and the "bureaucratic society of controlled consumption." Everyday life, according to Lefebvre, is "maintained by terror" through the efficiency of classification techniques and the function of forms (and of institutions that develop out of these forms). Critical pedagogy seeks counterterrorist intervention. This does not refer to the transformation of existence only through the development of new theoretical vocabularies; to argue this position is to miss the point of critical pedagogy's emphasis on the language of theory. The answer is not a new metalanguage but rather, in Lefebvre's terms, the critical rediscovery, reorganization, and transformation of everyday life. Lefebvre (1990) writes:

> The answer is everyday life, to rediscover everyday life—no longer to neglect and disown it, elude and evade it—but actively to rediscover it while contributing to its transfiguration; this undertaking involves the invention of a language or, to be precise, an invention of language—for everyday life translated into language becomes a different everyday life by becoming clear; and the transfiguration of everyday life is the creation of something new, something that requires new words. (p. 202)

Critical pedagogy is firmly set against what Kristin Ross (1993) calls "the integral 'pedagogicizing' of society" by which she refers to the "general infantilization" of individuals or groups through the discourses and social practices of "the nineteenth-century European myth of progress" (p. 669). Ross is able to move away from essentialist conceptions of cultural identity informed by a symbolic model of experience and representation in which one part timelessly and ahistorically reflects the whole. According to this model, the plight of, say, white women in New York is supposed to capture the struggle of black women in Alabama. This is decidedly insufficient if not politically ludicrous. Rather than viewing this relationship as unmediated—as a relationship in which the plight of white women constitutes an authentic or transparent reflection of the plight of black women—Ross prefers to see this and similar relationships as allegorical. According to Ross:

> Allegory preserves the differences of each historically situated and embedded experience, all the while drawing a relationship

between those experiences. In other words, one experience is read in terms of another but not necessarily in terms of establishing identity, not obliterating the qualities particular to each. (p. 672)

E. San Juan, Jr. (1988) describes the power of allegory as follows:

Instead of inducing an easy reconciliation of antimonies, an existential leap of faith where all class antagonisms vanish and rebellious desire is pacified, allegory heightens the tension between signifier and signified, between object and subject, thereby foiling empathy and establishing the temporary distance required for generating critical judgment and, ultimately, cathartic action. (p. 46)

Since it is impossible to represent every cultural group in the curriculum, the task of critical pedagogy, in Ross's terms, is to construct identity allegorically in order that each group is able to see his or her cultural narrative in a broader and comparative relationship to others and within a larger narrative of social transformation.

It is especially urgent for students to recognize the historical and cultural specificity of their own lived experiences in allegorical relations to other narratives, given the persecutory and diabolic character of the New Right's assault on difference. As Ross (1993) puts it:

within a growing global homogenization the non-west is conceived in two, equally reductive ways: one whereby differences are reified and one whereby differences are lost. In the first, the non-West is assigned the role of the repository for some more genuine or organic lived experience; minority cultures and non-Western cultures in the West are increasingly made to provide something like an authenticity rush for blasé or jaded Westerners, and this is too heavy a burden for anyone to bear. In the second, non-Western experiences are recoded and judged according to how closely they converge on the same: a single public culture or global average, that is, how far each has progressed toward a putative goal of modernization. (p. 673).

We want to add here that allegories must be read historically and understood not simply in terms of the way they are produced but also in terms of the way they are read by specific reading publics— taking into account what Walter Benjamin (1969) referred to as "constellations."

Chapters in the second part of this book explore theoretical ramifications of linking multicultural education with critical

pedagogy. How do the two fields connect? What light does one shed
on the other? What problems must we guard against? In what way
is it an act of power to name the experience of another? These are
the central questions addressed by chapters in Part Two.

PEDAGOGIES IN ACTION

> The responsibility of a community for teaching its youths in its
> indigenous ways rests with each ethnic group...Asymmetrical power
> relationships existing between the African American community and
> the school system make this issue critical to the success and
> achievement of African American students.
>
> Phillips

> How does one involve a class of male and female White students from
> mainly middle class backgrounds in a critique of various forms of
> oppression, and at the same time help them to construct for themselves
> insights grounded in emancipation of *other people*?
>
> Sleeter

Critical pedagogy and multicultural education require action.
Both pedagogies attempt to contest the established historical order
through a series of counterhegemonic articulations, counternarra-
tives, and countermyths that exist within a matrix of pedagogical
discontinuities or ruptures. In other words, both address the
configuration of sociopolitical interests that schooling serves.
Criticalists do not believe that it is possible to provide value-free
pedagogical knowledge—knowledge that is not the expression of
the teacher's political or value commitments. All pedagogical
efforts are infiltrated with value judgements and crosshatched by
vectors of power serving particular interests in the name of certain
regimes of truth. Human agency is not a transparent reflection of
universal selfhood but rather is structurally located and socially
and historically inscribed.

Critical pedagogy and multicultural education question how
we name and construct ourselves as well as others. Naming brings
to visibility and existence that which was formerly hidden or kept
silent. For instance, naming as racist, sexist, or patriarchal certain
relationships in the classroom helps to provide for students a

context in which those issues can also be discussed in the outside community and larger society. While every act of naming is in some sense an act of violence that makes something the object of knowledge, we advocate providing a critical vernacular so that subaltern groups can name and eventually own their own struggle for visibility and legitimacy. According to Rey Chow (1993), "The act of naming is not intrinsically essentialist or hierarchical. It is the social relationships in which names are inserted that may lead to essentialist, hierarchical, and thus detrimental consequences" (p. 105). This is to assert that naming is a discursive phenomenon, a particular network of signifiers that produce particular effects, given the concrete context of utterance. Critical subjectivity is not accomplished by the act of naming alone but in transforming those unjust social relationships in which the act of naming occurs.

Fundamental to critical pedagogy and multicultural education is the importance of reshaping, reformulating, and reenchanting the discursive and ideological formations in which subjectivities are produced and the social and political contexts out of which they are generated. Neither approach is simply the practice of inviting minority voices to trace their signatures against the firmament of social justice, for this is the paternalistic move of the bourgeois liberal educator. Nor do they place an emphasis on unforced subjectivity, a democratic conversation that may be transformed into an ideal form of discursive engagement. Criticalists recognize that unforced subjectivity or nondistorted communication can only take place in an uncontentious sphere of transcendental truth. Subjectivities are produced in public and private arenas that are riven with material inequalities and social injustices and that reflect race, class, and gender privileges. Subjectivities constituted by dominant discursive formations invite speakers or agents to misrecognize or mistake themselves as the authors of their own identity, occluding the material relations of capitalist production. Criticalists ask themselves: What is the type of human subject that our pedagogical practices summon into existence? As McCarthy illustrates convincingly in chapter 8 of this volume, the race, class, or gender identity of such a subject is never monolithic or essentialist in the sense of guaranteeing a particular politics. Similarly, we want to emphasize that identities are produced out of competing discourses, as multiplex, as multilayered palimpsests, as superimposed doublings. Identities are neither preconstituted by discourses nor hopelessly decentered; they are capable of becoming more self-reflexive if individuals are given the opportunity to acquire a critical praxis (what Freire terms "conscientization").

The experiences of students and teachers are important sites for constructing a pedagogy of transformation and social justice. Yet such experiences should not be uncritically patronized since experience never speaks for itself and needs always to be problematized for the ideological interests that it inevitably carries (McLaren 1993; Giroux and McLaren 1992; Scott 1992). Experience as situated meaning is largely understood and made sense of through language, and language is a social phenomenon that is always already embedded within a system of institutionalized sign systems, ideological constraints, and overdetermined or preferred readings. We do not completely own our own thoughts since we inherit structures of signification or vocabularies for making sense of the world (Ebert, 1991). The questions we ask and the statements we make are preceded by historical frames which delimit the range of our inquiry. Meanings are not panhistorically undecidable but are created (ideologically "sutured") through historical struggle over social relations, regimes of signification, and modes of intelligibility—conflicts which occur not simply in the arena of empty abstractions but at the level of material culture. In other words, truth is not something to be "discovered" in or as some timeless essence or to be taken from the metaphysical deep freeze and thawed out for consumption as a unitary, motionless, and apodictic meaning. Rather, truth is conjunctural, not essential, and is constructed through dialog among individuals in social contexts.

The analysis of experience needs to be turned into a mode of cultural critique. This does not mean that we should ignore experience but rather that we should understand that experience is always an 'experience effect' and thus must be understood in the context of its production and reception. Once it is interrogated for the interests it serves, it can be employed critically. This means more than simply recreating or resymbolizing experience or putting new labels onto what we already know. Making experience critical means reading experience performatively rather than constructing experiences mimetically. To create experiences mimetically means repeating what already is and what we already know. To understand experience performatively means taking experience beyond its uncontested service to empire and its chiasmatic remaking of what already is by transforming experience through the act of self-reflection (what Freire calls an "act of knowing") into an insurgent instrument for contesting domination and bringing into existence ideas and social practices that do not already exist. In order to do this we need a critical language of social analysis embedded not in the circular economy of empty idealism but in a praxis of possibility and a language of hope (McLaren, 1995). Experience is not the 'limit text' of the real.

It is the attention given to the historical conflict over signs that distinguishes critical pedagogy's recent alliances with resistance postmodernism (Aronowitz and Giroux 1992; McLaren 1993). Resistance or critical postmodernism grounds its project in the fact that significations are struggled over in arenas of power and privilege. This position can be contrasted with "ludic" postmodernists who simply assert the infinite play of signifiers in a culture in which value referents have no anchors outside of their own rhetorical embeddedness (Ebert, 1991). We do not equate revolution with clever semiotic displays by careerist academics whose decentering strategies are as conceptually dazzling as they are politically reactionary. As editors we are less concerned with the mutability of meaning and the slippery side of human agency than we are with linking meaning to the social contexts in which it is generated. In making this assertion, we follow Raymond Williams's (1979) observation:

> However dominant a social system may be, the very meaning of its domination involves a limitation or selection of the activities it covers, so that by definition it cannot exhaust all social experience, which therefore always potentially contains space for alternative acts and alternative intentions which are not yet articulated as a social institution or even project. (p. 252)

We do not wish here to suggest that immanent to the multireferentiality of language is the seedbed of revolution, for that assertion too easily lets us off the hook. However, we refuse to jettison the important connections between language and socioeconomic interests even though these connections are not fixed or invariable. We also want to make clear that the process of interrogating the ideological and discursive dimensions of experience necessitates that teachers be reflexive about the rhetorical construction of their own disciplinary authority. This means taking seriously the issue of speaking for and with students and questioning the conditions under which this is advisable and/or possible.

We also want to emphasize that every dominant discourse is in some sense ambiguous; that is, it is by definition incapable of squeezing out all spaces of counternarrative. However, we do not believe that recognizing or celebrating the "hybrid" nature of all social texts is enough to secure liberation for subaltern peoples. In other words, liberation can never be won, as Rey Chow (1993) notes, by simply deconstructing "the rich and ambivalent language of the imperialist" (p. 35). Rather, the act of speaking or enunciation "itself

belongs to an already well-defined structure and history of domination" (p. 36). This means that we, as editors, recognize that we cannot
simply translate subaltern discourses into the language of academic
social criticism. In other words, we need to identify with the "other"
precisely at those points at which he or she is least like us.

Chapters in the third part of this book offer snapshots of contemporary practice in different sites: an African-centered school, a
community center, a tribal college, and a teacher education
program. This section is by no means exhaustive, but rather illus-
trative of the day-to-day work of critical multiculturalists.

WHITE SUPREMACY AND ELITISM

Both multicultural education and critical pedagogy challenge
various forms of oppression but usually do not directly address the
subjective identities and vested interests of activists and advocates
who are white, male, and/or members of the intellectual elite. In
chapter 3 of this book, Haymes critiques white peoples' construction of racism as a symbolic consumption of the "Other" and challenges whites to interrogate their own whiteness. As editors of this
book, both of us, being white academicians, benefit from white
supremacy and intellectual elitism. How, then, can we contribute
to a discourse of social justice?

Both of us acknowledge that we have always benefited from our
own locations in a racial and social class hierarchy, and, in Peter's
case, in a patriarchal hierarchy. Had doors of privilege not been
opened to us at points all the way through our lives, we might not
be in the position today to write and teach. When confronting this
fact, whites tend to bog down, wallowing in guilt. To go beyond
white guilt, we believe it is critical to ask what to do with the privileged positions we currently occupy. We cannot escape participating in a racialized order, nor in a materialistic and highly
individualistic society, nor in a patriarchal one. Like it or not, we
are a part of this society.

As educated whites, we can speak to an educated white audience and attempt to contribute to dialog and praxis oriented
around the deconstruction of white supremacy. It is likely that the
majority of readers of this book will be educated whites: we urge
such readers to examine our own collective positions of privilege,
identify actions we can take to share power with non-white people,
and work toward racial justice. In part, this involves learning to
share, listen, step aside and take a backseat, admit that we know
less than we usually take for granted, and take seriously the intelligence of people of color. It means learning to work in multiracial

coalitions and learning to link our own fates with humans whose coloring may be darker than ours. It means curbing our own appetites for material gain and power. In our chapters in this volume, each of us speaks to issues and actions that whites can take.

Collective action also means supporting the ideas, perspectives, and very careers of colleagues of color, both men and women, from various walks of life. Throughout the construction of this book, we asked: Who will benefit monetarily from the book? Whose ideas are rendered legitimacy? Whose careers are supported? Who gains audience? We acknowledge our own limitations, mistakes, and blinders in attempting to work through these questions. However, we put forth these questions as guides to white elite writers in an effort to direct attention to the effects of what we do, effects which go beyond what we say.

DIALOG AND COALITION BUILDING

This book is about dialog and coalition building for the purpose of strengthening collective work toward social justice. Marable (1992) describes the building of a "new majority for justice and peace" (p. 254). Building this majority requires bridges, debate and discussion, shared experiences, and distillation of common concerns. As he explains:

> As long as we bicker over perceived grievances, maximizing our claims against each other, refusing to see the economic, political, cultural and social common ground which can unite us, we will be victimized by capitalism, sexism, racism, national oppression, homophobia, and other systems of domination....No single group has all the answers....But together, the collective path to human liberation, self-determination and sovereignty will become clear. (Ibid., p. 255)

Social justice movements tend to experience fragmentation, and the histories of multicultural education and critical pedagogy point to some persistent fissures. Constructing a dialog requires articulating some of the tensions that divide positions represented in this book. Historically, multicultural education has had the most to say about issues of race, culture, and ethnicity; its theorists and advocates have been uneven in their interest in gender issues, using largely a liberal perspective about sexism and, at the K–12 level, remaining virtually silent about social class and capitalism. Because of its African American origins and its silence about social class in most schools of education, the white left has tended not to identify with its issues. This has led many educators

of color to distance themselves from the racism embodied in disin-
terest or disdain by members of the white left.

This schism between the white left and groups of color is not
new. Indeed, much of the history of the labor movement in the U.S.
is a history of white racism. "[M]ore than enough of the habit of
whiteness and of the conditions producing it survived [slavery] to
ensure that white workers would be at best uncertain allies of
Black freedom and would stop short of developing fully new
concepts of liberation for themselves as well" (Roediger 1991, p.
177). Bridging a division between the white left and educators of
color will require whites to address our own racism, and the benefits we derive from it. We cannot call for solidarity across racial
lines, and at the same time continue to promote our own interests
first. Bridging this division will also require middle-class people to
question the ideology of individual mobility and material acquisition that allows us to move to the suburbs and into corporate
offices, leaving the masses behind.

Ironically, because of multicultural education's appeal to white
educators, many radicals of color view it with disdain. The staffs of
public schools have been predominantly white since desegregation
and are becoming progressively whiter. To address the needs of
children of color, some educators work toward the establishment
of schools that are staffed by educators of color and centered
within the historical and cultural context of their own group, such
as African American independent schools (Rattaray 1992).
However, many multicultural educators appeal to white teachers
who are already in the schools and are attempting to educate them
to work more productively with their own children. This appeal is
often taken up in a way that avoids confronting racism. How to
address the huge problem of an institutionalized white, largely
female, teaching staff is a very important issue.

Multicultural education is also often dismissed by white feminists who tacitly accept racism, view gender as the main axis of
oppression, and distrust men of color. A fissure between white
women and groups of color has a long history, as at various times
white women have turned against Americans of color in order to
advance their own interests (Blee 1991; Davis 1981). This fissure
can be seen graphically on many university campuses that have
predominantly white women's studies faculties and predominantly
male ethnic studies faculties (Butler and Walter 1991). Bridging
this gulf requires white women to confront racism, men of color to
confront sexism, and both to acknowledge that our own marginalized positions fuel fears that bridge-building will cost us something.

In chapter 9, Allsup argues that scholarship by women of color provides the most insightful analyses of intersections of racial and gender oppression, scholarship that the rest of us should learn from.

Yet another gulf occurs between academicians, and practitioners and other cultural workers. For example, classroom teachers who work with critical pedagogy largely emphasize forms of pedagogical practice in which students are invited to problematize aspects of everyday life as it is lived out in the home, the classroom, the school, the community, and in larger institutional and social contexts. Here, the primacy of experience is emphasized both as a methodological tool to uncover the world of student meaning and as the ontological ground from which a politics of liberation must be waged. Theory, in this case, is often viewed as delusory and inherently elitist, an enterprise that is profoundly alienating to the rank-and-file educator. It is criticized for mainly assisting teachers in stepping outside of present pedagogical practices in order to control them, thereby helping to maintain the various interests of the dominant credentialing system that is housed in the schools and universities. Academicians, on the other hand, concentrate considerable energy working in transdisciplinary projects such as critical ethnography, action research, and the development of critical social theory, undertaken at the intersection of various fields such as women's studies, feminist pedagogy, ethnic studies, cultural studies, curriculum theory, literary and film criticism, and the philosophy and foundations of education. The result is a tremendous growth of new theoretical languages proliferating within the field of critical social theory. Who speaks for multicultural education and critical pedagogies and in what voice? This important issue is addressed in quite different ways in chapters by McLaren, Montecinos, and Ritchie.

We are concerned with developing a common ground of struggle that will not eliminate difference or merely exoticize it but will conscript difference into the construction of a new multicultural imaginary. We need to struggle towards a critical multiculturalism which can speak to the universal values of freedom and justice without such values becoming totalizing and which permit particular groups to articulate their own struggles. We are worried that struggles for universal values and struggles that support context-specific values are now being conceptualized and operationalized as mutually exclusive terrains.

As Ernesto Laclau (1992) has pointed out, Eurocentrism does not differentiate between universal, Western values and the particular individuals who incarnate them on a daily basis. On the other hand, particularist politics separates itself out from any appeal to universal values. We are currently confronted with a proliferation of particularisms—i.e., feminist, environmentalist, labor, gay and lesbian, and others—and Laclau argues that it is impossible to appeal to any one of these without at the same time appealing to a universal value. Yet, at the same time, we need to understand that no difference can be fully achieved just as no universal can be complete. Laclau argues that we should consider the universal to mean a "missing fullness" or an open horizon rather than a seamless truth. Concurrently, we should understand differential identities to be never closed (i.e., always open to further difference). If, then, we can "show that the concrete practices of our society restrict the universalism of our political ideals to limited sectors of the population, it becomes possible to retain the universal dimension while widening the spheres of its application—which, in turn, will redefine the concrete contexts of such a universality" (Ibid., p. 90). Paradoxically, because difference always fails to constitute itself as pure difference and because universal representation is inevitably contingent and partial, democracy is possible.

Rey Chow (1993) has posed a recent challenge to intellectuals which we feel has important implications for educators working in the fields of critical pedagogy and multicultural education. She asks, "How do intellectuals struggle against a hegemony which already includes them and which can no longer be divided into the state and civil society in Gramsci's terms, nor be clearly demarcated into national and transnational spaces?" (p. 16). Chow remarks that most oppositional university intellectual work derives from *strategies* as opposed to *tactics*. Strategies occur as part of the political projects of those who wish to solidify a place or barricade a field of interest. Michael Shapiro (1992) (after Michel De Certeau) describes strategies as belonging "to those (e.g., the police) who occupy legitimate or what is recognized as proper space within the social order" (p. 103). He further describes them as "part of a centralized surveillance network for controlling the population" (Ibid.)

What we need instead of strategies, argues Chow, are tactics that deal with calculated actions outside of specific sites. Tactics are described as belonging "to those who do not occupy a legitimate space and depend instead on time, on whatever opportunities present themselves" (Shapiro, p. 103). Describing tactics as "weapons of the weak", de Certeau is worth quoting at length:

[A] tactic is a calculated action determined by the absence of a proper locus....The space of a tactic is the space of the other. Thus it must play on and with a terrain imposed on it and organized by the law of a foreign power. It does not have the means to *keep to itself*, at a distance, in a postion of withdrawal, foresight, and self-collection: it is a maneuver "within the enemy's field of vision,"...and within enemy territory. It does not, therefore, have the option of planning, general strategy....It operates in isolated actions, blow by blow. It takes advantage of opportunities and depends on them, being without any base where it could stockpile its winnings, build up its own position, and plan raids....This nowhere gives tactic mobility, to be sure, but a mobility that must accept the chance offerings of the moment, and seize on the wing the possibilities that offer themselves at any given moment. It must vigilantly make use of the cracks that particular conjunctions open in the surveillance of proprietary powers. It poaches them. It creates surprises in them....It is a guileful ruse. (Cited in Conquergood 1992, p. 82)

Unlike tactics, Chow (1993) warns that strategic solidarities only repeat "what they seek to overthrow" (p. 17).

We believe that Chow raises some important points with respect to oppositional movements such as multicultural education and critical pedagogy that begin as tactics but turn into strategies that unwittingly yet ultimately secure and protect precincts of the privileged. She writes:

We need to remember as intellectuals that the battles we fight are battles of words. Those who argue the oppositional standpoint are not *doing* anything different from their enemies and are most certainly not directly changing the downtrodden lives of those who seek their survival in metropolitan and nonmetropolitan spaces alike. What academic intellectuals must confront is *not* their "victimization" by society at large (or their victimization-in-solidarity-with-the-oppressed), but the power, wealth, and privilege that ironically accumulate from their "oppositional" viewpoint, and the widening gap between the professed contents of their words and the upward mobility they gain from such words. (When Foucault said intellectuals need to struggle against becoming the object and instrument of power, he spoke precisely to this kind of situation.) The predicament we face in the West, where intellectual freedom shares a history with economic enterprise, is that "if a professor wishes to denounce aspects of big business,...he will be wise to locate in a school whose trustees are big businessmen." Why should we believe in those who continue to speak a language of alterity-as-lack while their salaries and honoraria keep rising? How do we resist the turning-into-propriety of oppositional discourses, when the intention of such discourses has been that of displacing and disowning the proper? How do we prevent what begin as tactics—that which is "without any base where it could stockpile its winnings" (de Certeau 1984, p. 37)—from turning into a solidly fenced-off field, in the military no less than in the academic senses? (p. 17)

In order to contest the opportunity for mainstream pedagogical and social practices to reset social boundaries in the interests of strategies for the privileged and the powerful (mainly white men), our proposed volume will develop a discourse of tactical insurgency and hope, linking multicultural theory and critical pegadogy in a manner that seeks to construct counterhegemonic pedagogies, oppositional identity formations, and social policies that refuse, resist, and transform existing structures of domination primarily in school sites but also in other cultural sites within the North American geopolitical arena. The task, as we see it, for critical multiculturalists is to create a collective praxis of liberation and social justice in a manner that will—in the particular concrete struggles of the oppressed—begin to challenge social, cultural and economic relations of exploitation and also shed new light on the construction of difference.

NOTE

The authors wish to thank Rudolfo Chavez Chavez for his very helpful comments on earlier drafts of this paper.

REFERENCES

Aronowtiz, S. and Giroux, H. 1992. *Postmodern Education.* Minneapolis: University of Minnesota Press.

Banks, J. A. 1989. Multicultural education: Characteristics and goals. In *Multicultural Education: Issues and Perspectives*, ed. J. A. Banks and C. A. M. Banks, pp. 2–26. Boston: Allyn & Bacon.

————. 1992. African American scholarship and the evolution of multicultural education. *Journal of Negro Education* 61(3): 273–286.

Barlett, D. L. and Steele, J. B. 1992. *America: What went wrong?* Kansas City: Andrews and McMeel.

Benjamin, W., ed. 1969. *Illuminations.* New York: Schocken Books.

Bernal, M. 1987. *Black Athena: The Afroasiatic roots of Western civilization.* New Brunswick, NJ: Rutgers University Press.

Blee, K. M. 1991. *Women of the Klan: Racism and gender in the 1920s.* Berkeley: University of California Press.

Butler, J. E. and Walter, J. C., eds. 1991. *Transforming the Curriculum: Ethnic studies and women's studies.* Albany, NY: SUNY Press.

Chow, R. 1993. *Writing diaspora: Tactics of intervention in contemporary cultural studies.* Bloomington and Indianapolis: Indiana University Press.

Conquergood, D. 1992. Ethnography, rhetoric, and performance. *Quarterly Journal of Speech* 78: 80–123.

Cornbleth, C. and Waugh, D. 1993. The great speckled bird: Education policy-in-the-making. *Educational Researcher* 22 (7): 31–37.

Davis, A. Y. 1981. *Women, race, and class.* New York: Random House.

De Certeau, M. 1984. *The practice of everyday life.* Trans. Steven Randall. Berkeley: University of California Press.

Derman-Sparks, L. 1989. *Anti-bias curriculum: Tools for empowering young children.* Washington, DC: National Association for the Education of Young Children.

Ebert, T. 1991. Writing in the political: resistance (post)modernism. *Legal Studies Forum xv* (4): 291–303.

Faludi, S. 1991. *Backlash: The undeclared war against American women.* New York: Doubleday.

Gay, G. 1983. Multiethnic education: Historical developments and future prospects. *Phi Delta Kappan* 64: 560–563.

Gilroy, Paul. 1993. *Small Acts: Thoughts on the Politics of Black Cultures.* London: Serpent's Tail.

Giroux, H. and McLaren, P. 1992. Writing from the margins: geographies of identity, pedagogy, and power. *Journal of Education* 174(1): 7–30.

Goldberg, D. T. 1993. *Racist Culture: Philosophy and the politics of meaning.* Cambridge, MA and Oxford, England: Blackwell Publishers.

Hacker, A. 1992. *Two nations: Black and white, separate, hostile, unequal.* New York: Charles Scribner's Sons.

Kozol, J. 1991. *Savage inequalities.* New York: Harper Perennial.

Laclau, E. 1992. Universalism, particularism, and the question of identity. *October* 61: 83–90.

Lefebvre, H. 1990. *Everyday Life in the Modern World.* Trans. Sacha Rabinovitch. New Bruswick and London: Transaction Publishers.

McLaren, P. 1995. *Critical Pedagogy and Predatory Culture: Oppositional Politics in A Postmodern Age*. London and New York: Routledge.

McLaren, P. 1993. Border disputes: Multicultural narrative, identity formation, and critical pedagogy in postmodern America. In *Naming silenced lives: Personal narratives and the process of educational change*, ed. D. McLaughlin and B. Tierney, pp. 201–235. London and New York: Routledge.

Marable, M. 1992. *The crisis of Color and Democracy*. Monroe, ME: Common Courage Press.

Mattai, P. R. 1992. Rethinking multicultural education: Has it lost its focus or it is being misused? *Journal of Negro Education* 61(1): 65–77.

Nakagawa, M. 1989. *Cooperative pluralism: From "me" to "we"*. Video. Spokane, WA: Spokane School District No. 81.

National Commission of Excellence in Education. 1983. *A nation at risk: The imperative for educational reform*. Washington, DC: U.S. Government Printing Office.

Omi, M. and Winant, H. 1986. *Racial formation in the United States*. New York: Routledge and Kegan Paul.

Ratteray, J. D. 1992. Independent neighborhood schools: A framework for the education of African Americans. *Journal of Negro Education* 61(2): 138–147.

Roediger, D. R. 1991. *The wages of whiteness*. New York: Verso.

Ross, K. 1993. The world literature and cultural studies program. *Critical Inquiry* 19: 666–676.

San Juan, E., Jr. 1988. *Ruptures, schisms, interventions*. Manila, Philippines: De La Salle University Press.

———. 1992. *Articulations of power in ethnic and racial studies in the United States*. Atlantic Highlands, NJ: Humanities Press.

Schlesinger, A., Jr. 1992. *The disuniting of America*. New York: Norton.

Scott, J. 1992. Experience. In *Feminists theorize the political*, ed. J. Butler and J. W. Scott, pp. 22–40. New York and London: Routledge.

Shapiro, M. J. 1992. *Reading the postmodern polity: Political theory as textual practice*. Minneapolis: University of Minnesota Press.

Shor, I. 1986. *Culture wars: School and society in the conservative restoration 1969–1984*. Boston: Routledge and Kegan Paul.

————. 1993. Education is politics: Paulo Freire's critical pedagogy. In *Paulo Freire: A critical encounter*, ed. P. McLaren and P. Leonard, pp. 25–35. New York: Routledge.

Williams, R. 1979. *Politics and Letters*. London: New Left Books.

1

PETER McLAREN ─────────────────────────────────────

White Terror and Oppositional Agency: Towards a Critical Multiculturalism*

> Nothing can be denounced if the denouncing is done within
> the system that belongs to the thing denounced.
>
> Julio Cortázar, *Hopscotch*

As we approach the year 2000, we are increasingly living simulated identities that help us adjust our dreams and desires according to the terms of our imprisonment as schizo-subjects in an artificially generated world. These facsimile or imitative identities are negotiated for us by financial planners, corporate sponsors, and marketing strategists through the initiatives of transnational corporations, enabling a privileged elite of white Euro-Americans to control the information banks and terrorize the majority of the population into a state of intellectual and material impoverishment. With few, if any, ethically convincing prospects for transformation—or even survival—we have become cyber-nomads whose temporary homes become whatever electronic circuitry (if any) is available to us. In our hyper-fragmented and postmodern culture, democracy is secured through the power to control consciousness and semioticize and zombify bodies by mapping and manipulating sounds, images, and information and by forcing identity to take refuge in forms of subjectivity increasingly experienced as isolated and separate from larger social contexts. The idea of democratic citizenship has now become synonymous with the private, consuming citizen and the increasing subalternization of the "other." The representation of reality through corporate sponsorship and promotional culture has impeded the struggle to establish democratic public spheres and furthered the dissolution of historical solidarities and forms of community, accelerating the experience of circular narrative time (cultural implosion) and the postindustrial disintegration of public space. The proliferation and phantasmagoria of the image has hastened the death of modernist identity structures and has

33

interpellated individuals and groups into a world of cyborg citizenry in which "other" individuals are reconstituted through market imperatives as a collective assemblage of "them" read against our "us."

THE DEBATE OVER MULTICULTURALISM

It is no secret, especially after the Los Angeles uprising—or what Mike Davis calls the "L.A. Intifada" (Katz and Smith 1992)—that the white-controlled media (often backed by victim-blaming white social scientists) have ignored the economic and social conditions responsible for bringing about in African American communities what Cornel West has called a "*walking nihilism* of pervasive drug addiction, pervasive alcoholism, pervasive homicide, and an exponential rise in suicide" (cited in Stephanson 1988, p. 276). They have additionally ignored or sensationalized social conditions in Latin and Asian communities, polemicizing against their value systems and representing them as teleologically poised to explode into a swelter of rioting and destruction. Such communities have been described as full of individuals who lash out at the dominant culture in an anarcho-voluntaristic frenzy in a country where there are more legalized gun dealers than gas stations. In this view, agency seems to operate outside of forces and structures of oppression, policing discourses of domination, and social relations of exploitation. Subalternized individuals appear politically constituted outside of discursive formations and are essentialized as the products of their pathological "nature" as drug or alcohol users and as gleeful participants in crime.

Furthermore, the white media has generated the racially pornographic term "wilding" to account for recent acts of violence in urban centers by groups of young African Americans (Cooper 1989). Apparently the term *wilding*, first reported by New York City newspapers in relation to the Central Park rapists, was relevant only to violence committed by black male youth since the term was conspicuously absent in press reports of the attack by white male youths on Yusef Hawkins in Bensonhurst (Wallace 1991). Thus, the postmodern image which many white people now entertain in relation to the African American underclass is one constructed upon violence and grotesquerie. They picture a population spawning mutant youths who, in the throes of bloodlust, roam the perimeter of the urban landscape high on angel dust, and with steel pipes in hand, randomly hunt whites. In addition to helping to justify police "attitude adjustments" inflicted upon black people in places such as L.A., Detroit, and Hemphill in Sabine County, Texas, this image of minorities has engendered hostility to their efforts to articulate their own understanding of race relations and to advance a conception of democracy in a way that is compatible with a critical multiculturalism.

FORMS OF MULTICULTURALISM

This paper attempts to advance a conception of critical multiculturalism by exploring various positions held within the debate over multiculturalism which I have termed conservative or corporate multiculturalism, liberal multiculturalism, and left-liberal multiculturalism. These are, to be sure, ideal-typical labels meant to serve only as a heuristic device. In reality the characteristics of each position tend to blend into each other within the general horizon of our social lifeworld. As with all typologies and criteriologies, one must risk monolithically projecting them onto all spheres of cultural production and instantiating an overly abstract totality that dangerously reduces the complexity of the issues at stake. My effort should be understood only as an initial attempt at transcoding and mapping the cultural field of race and ethnicity so as to formulate a tentative theoretical grid that can help discern the multiple ways in which difference is both constructed and engaged. This chapter is to be read as an *essai*, an exploration.

CONSERVATIVE MULTICULTURALISM

Conservative multiculturalism can be traced to colonial views of African Americans as slaves, servants, and entertainers, views which were embedded in the self-serving, congratulatory, and profoundly imperialist attitude of Europe and North America. Such an attitude depicted Africa as a savage and barbaric continent populated by the most lowly of creatures who were deprived of the saving graces of Western civilization.[1] It can also be located in evolutionary theories which supported U.S. Manifest Destiny, imperial largesse, and Christian imperialism. It can further be seen as a direct result of the legacy of doctrines of white supremacy which biologized Africans as creatures by equating them with the earliest stages of human development. Africans were likened by whites to savage beasts or merry-hearted singing and dancing children. The former stereotype led a ten-year-old black boy—Josef Moller—to be exhibited at the Antwerp Zoo at the turn of the century. Closer to home and less remote in time is the case of Ota Benga, a Pygmy boy exhibited in 1906 at the Monkey House in the Bronx Zoo as an "African homunculus" and as the "missing link" and encouraged by zoo keepers to charge the bars of his cage with his mouth open and teeth bared (Bradford and Blume 1992). In less sensational guise, this attitude continues right up to the present time. For instance, in 1992, the Secretary of Health and Human Services in the Bush Administration appointed Frederick A. Goodwin, a research psychiatrist and career federal scientist, as Director of the National Institute for Mental Health. Goodwin used animal research findings to compare youth gangs to groups of "hyperaggressive" and "hypersexual" monkeys and commented that "maybe it isn't just the careless use of the word when people call certain areas of certain cities, 'jungles'" (*Observer* 1992 p. 20).

Whether conceived as the return of the repressed of Victorian puritanism, a leftover from Aristotelian hierarchical discourse or colonial and imperialist ideology, it remains the terrible truth of history that Africans have been forcibly placed at the foot of the human ladder of civilization (Pieterse 1992). As Jan Nederveen Pieterse notes, America historically has been the "white man's country," in which institutional and ideological patterns of the supremacy of white over black, and of men over women, supplemented and reinforced one another" (Ibid., p. 220).

While I do not wish to lapse into either an essentialized nativism which sees non-Western indigenous cultures as homogeneous or a view of the West that sees it as all of one piece—a monolithic block—unaffected by its colonized subjects, or solely as an engine of imperialism, I need to affirm the fact that many conservative multiculturalists have scarcely removed themselves from the colonialist legacy of white supremacy. Although they would like to officially distance themselves from racist ideologies, conservative multiculturalists pay only lipservice to the cognitive equality of all races and charge unsuccessful minorities with having "culturally deprived backgrounds" and a "lack of strong family-oriented values." This "environmentalist" position still accepts black cognitive inferiority to whites as a general premise and provides conservative multiculturalists with a means of rationalizing why some minority groups are successful while other groups are not (Mensh and Mensh, 1991). This also gives the white cultural elite the excuse they need for unreflectively and disproportionately occupying positions of power. They are not unlike the inscripti of the right-wing Roman Catholic organization, Opus Dei, who attempt to intellectually and culturally sequester or barricade their members from the tools for a critical analyses of social life in order to shore up their own power to manipulate and propagandize. Or the

Heritage Foundation that creates a climate of legitimacy for books like *The Bell Curve.*

One particularly invidious project of conservative or corporate multiculturalism is to construct a common culture—a seamless web of textuality—a project bent on annulling the concept of border cultures through the delegitimization of foreign languages and regional and ethnic dialects, a persistent attack on nonstandard English, and the undermining of bi-lingual education (Macedo, 1995). Gramsci's understanding of this process is instructive, and is cogently articulated by Michael Gardiner (1992):

> For Gramsci, the political character of language was most apparent in the attempt by the dominant class to create a common cultural 'climate' and to 'transform the popular mentality' through the imposition of a national language. Therefore, he felt that linguistic hegemony involved the articulation of signs and symbols which tended to codify and reinforce the dominant viewpoint. Thus, Gramsci argued that there existed a close relationship between linguistic stratification and social hierarchization, in that the various dialects and accents found within a given society are always rank-ordered as to their perceived legitimacy, appropriateness, and so on. Accordingly, concrete language usage reflects underlying, asymmetrical power relations, and it registers profound changes which occur in the cultural, moral, and political worlds. Such changes were primarily expressed through what Gramsci termed "normative grammar"; roughly, the system of norms whereby particular utterances could be evaluated and mutually understood...which was an important aspect of the state's attempt to establish linguistic conformity. Gramsci also felt that the maintenance of regional dialects helped peasants and workers partially to resist the forces of political and cultural hegemony. (p. 186)

In addition to its position on common culture and bilingual education, there are further reasons why corporate multiculturalism needs to be rejected. First, conservative or corporate multiculturalism refuses to treat whiteness as a form of ethnicity and in doing so posits whiteness as an invisible norm by which other ethnicities are judged. Second, conservative multiculturalism—as in the positions taken by Diane Ravitch, Arthur Schlesinger, Jr., Lynne V.B. Cheney, Newt Gingrich, and others—uses the term 'diversity' to cover up the ideology of assimilation that undergirds its position. In this view, ethnic groups are reduced to "add-ons" to the dominant culture. Before you can be added on to the dominant U.S. culture, you must first adopt a consensual view of culture and learn to accept the essentially Euro-American patriarchal norms of the 'host' country. Third, as I mentioned earlier, conservative multiculturalism is essentially monolingual and adopts the position that English should be the only official U.S. language. It is often virulently opposed to bi-lingual education programs. Fourth, conservative multiculturalists posit standards of achievement for all youth that are premised on the cultural capital of the Anglo middle-class. Fifth, conservative multiculturalism fails to interrogate the high status knowledge—knowledge that is deemed of most value in the white, middle-class U. S.—to which the educational system is geared. That is, it fails to question the interests that such knowledge serves. It fails, in other words, to interrogate dominant regimes of discourse and social and cultural practices that are implicated in global dominance and are inscribed in racist, classist, sexist, and homophobic assumptions. Conservative multiculturalism wants to assimilate students to an unjust social order by arguing that every member of every ethnic group can reap the economic benefits of neocolonialist ideologies and corresponding social and economic practices. But a prerequisite to "joining the club" is to become denuded, deracinated, and culturally stripped.

Recent popular conservative texts set firmly against liberal, left-liberal, and critical strands of multiculturalism include Richard Brookhiser's *The Way of the Wasp: How it Made America, and How it Can Save it, So to Speak,* Arthur Schlesinger, Jr.'s *The Disuniting of America: Reflections on a Multicultural Society,* and Laurence Auster's *The Path to National Suicide: An Essay on Immigration and Multiculturalism.* According to Stanley Fish (1992), these texts, which appeal to national unity and a harmonious citizenry, can readily be traced to earlier currents of Christianity (which proclaimed that it was God's wish that the future of civilization be secured in the United States) and social Darwinism (U.S., Anglo-Saxon stock is used to confirm the theory of natural selection). Reflecting and enforcing the assumptions made by the authors (whom Fish describes as racist not in the sense that they actively seek the subjugation of groups but who perpetuate racial stereotypes and the institutions that promote them) is the SAT test used in high school for college admission. Fish notes that one of the authors of this test, Carl Campbell Brigham, championed in his *A Study of American Intelligence* a classification of races which identified the Nordic as the superior race and, in descending order, located the less superior races as Alpine, Mediterranean, Eastern, New Eastern, and Negro. This hierarchy was first expounded by Madison Grant in *The Passing of the Great Race* (Fish 1992) and reflected in earlier European works such as *Essai sur l'inégalité des races humaines*, a four-volume testament to the racial superiority of the Germanic race by Joseph Arthur (Comte de Govineau), and Edward Gibbon's *Decline and Fall of the Roman Empire*, a work which blamed miscegination for the decline of civilization (Pieterse 1992). Not surprisingly, this hierarchy is confirmed in Brigham's later comparative analysis of intelligence. The library at the Educational Testing Service compound still bears Brigham's name (Fish 1992). Also problematic, as Mike Dyson (1993) points out, are theories linking white racism to biological determinism, such as recent discussions of "melanin theory" in which black researchers view whiteness as a genetic deficiency state that leads whites to act violently against Blacks because of white feelings of color inferiority.

When we contrast Brookhiser's key WASP virtues with non-WASP virtues (those of the Asians, African Americans, or Latinos), we see the Western virtues of the former—conscience, antisensuality, industry, use, success, and civic mindedness—being distinguished as more American than the lesser virtues of the latter—self, creativity, ambition, diffidence, gratification, and group mindedness. This also reflects a privileging of Western languages (English, French, German, and ancient Greek) over non-Western languages (see Fish 1992). Supposedly, Western European languages are the only ones sophisticated enough to grasp truth as an "essence." The search for the "truth" of the Western canon of "Great Works" is actually based on an epistemological error that presumes there exists a language of primordial Being and Truth. This error is linked to the phenomenalist reduction of linguistic meaning which endows language (through analogy) with sense perceptions and thereby reduces the act of interpretation to uncovering the "true understanding" that reciprocally binds the truth of the text to the preunderstanding, tacit knowledge, or foreknowledge of the reader (Norris 1990). From this view of the mimetic transparency of language, aesthetic judgments are seen as linked directly to ethics or politics through a type of direct correspondence (Ibid.). Language, therefore, becomes elevated to a "truth-telling status" which remains exempt from its ethico-political situatedness or embeddedness. It is this epistemological error that permits conservatives to denounce totalitarianism in the name of its own truth and serves as a ruse for expanding present forms of domination. It is not hard to see how racism can become a precondition for this form of conservative multiculturalism in so far as Western virtues (which can be traced back as far as Aristotle's Great Chain of Being) become the national-aestheticist ground for the conservative multiculturalist's view of civilization and citizenship. The power of conservative multiculturalism lays claim to its constituents by conferring a space for the reception of its discourses that is safe and sovereignly secure. It does this by sanctioning empiricism as the fulcrum for weighing the "truth" of culture. What discursively thrives in this perspective is an epistemology which privileges the logic of cause and effect narrative construction (see Norris 1990). In this case, 'bell curve' quotients and test scores become the primary repository of authoritative exegeses in interpretations of successful school citizenship. Fortunately, as Foucault points out, subjectivity is not simply constituted through the discourses and social practices of subjugation. Liberal, left-liberal, and critical forms of multiculturalism envisage a different "practice of the self" and new forms of self-fashioning and subjectivity based on more progressive conceptions of freedom and justice.

LIBERAL MULTICULTURALISM

Liberal multiculturalism argues that a natural equality exists among whites, African Americans, Latinos, Asians and other racial populations. This perspective is based on the intellectual "sameness" among the races, that is, on their cognitive equivalence or the rationality imminent in all races that permits them to compete equally in a capitalist society. However, from the point of view of liberal multiculturalism, equality is absent in U.S. society not because of black or Latino cultural deprivation but because social and educational opportunities do not exist that permit everyone to compete equally in the capitalist marketplace. Unlike their critical counterparts, they believe that existing cultural social and economic constraints can be modified or "reformed" in order for relative equality to be realized. This view often collapses into an ethnocentric and oppressively universalistic humanism in which the norms which govern the substance of citizenship are identified most strongly with Anglo-American, cultural-political communities.

LEFT-LIBERAL MULTICULTURALISM

Left-liberal multiculturalism emphasizes cultural differences and suggests that the stress on the equality of races smothers those important cultural differences between races that are responsible for different behaviors, values, attitudes, cognitive styles, and social practices. Left-liberal multiculturalists feel that mainstream approaches to multiculturalism occlude characteristics and differences related to race, class, gender, and sexuality. Those who work within this perspective have a tendency to essentialize cultural differences, however, and ignore the historical and cultural "situatedness" of difference. Difference is understood as a form of signification removed from social and historical constraints. That is, there is a tendency to ignore difference as a social and historical construction that is constitutive of the power to represent meanings. It is often assumed that there exists an authentic "Female" or "African American" or "Latino" experience or way of being-in-the-world. Left-liberal multiculturalism treats difference as an 'essence' that exists independently of history, culture, and power. Often one is asked to show one's identity papers before dialogue can begin.

This perspective often locates meaning through the conduit of "authentic" experience in what I feel to be the mistaken belief that one's own politics of location somehow guarantees one's "political correctness" in advance. Either a person's physical proximity to the oppressed or their own location as an oppressed person is supposed to offer a special authority from which to speak. What often happens is that a populist elitism gets constructed as inner city teachers or trade unionists or those engaged in activist politics establish a pedigree of voice based on personal history, class, race, gender, and experience. Here, the political is often reduced only to the personal where theory is dismissed in favor of one's own personal and cultural identity. Of course, one's lived experience, race, class, gender, and history is important in the formation of one's political identity, but one must be willing to examine personal experience and one's speaking voice in terms of the ideological and discursive complexity of its formation.

Admittedly, when a person speaks, it is always from somewhere (Hall 1991), but this process of meaning production needs to be interrogated in order to understand how one's identity is constantly being produced through a play of difference linked to and reflected by shifting and conflicting discursive and ideological relations, formations, and articulations (see Giroux 1992; Scott 1992). Experience needs to be recognized as a site of ideological production and the mobilization of affect and can be examined largely through its imbrication in our universal and local knowledges and modes of intelligibility and its relationship to language, desire, and the body (an issue that I have explored elsewhere in McLaren 1990). As Joan Scott (1992) notes, "experience is a subject's history. Language is the site of history's enactment" (p. 34). Of course, I am not arguing against the importance of experience in the formation of political identity but rather pointing out that it has become the new *imprimatur* for legitimating the political currency and uncontestable validity of one's arguments. This has often resulted in a reverse form of academic elitism. Not only is the authority of the academic under assault (and rightly so, in many cases), but it has been replaced by a populist elitism based on one's own identity papers.

CRITICAL AND RESISTANCE MULTICULTURALISM

Multiculturalism without a transformative political agenda can just be another form of accommodation to the larger social order. I believe that because they are immersed in the discourse of "reform," liberal and left-liberal positions on multiculturalism do not go nearly far enough in advancing a project of social transformation. With this concern in mind, I am developing the idea of critical multiculturalism from the perspective of both a neo-Marxist and poststructuralist approach to meaning and emphasizing the role that language and representation play in the construction of meaning and identity. The poststructuralist insight that I am relying on is located within the larger context of postmodern theory—that disciplinary archipelago that is scattered through the sea of social theory—and asserts that signs and significations are essentially unstable and shifting and can only be temporarily fixed, depending on how they are articulated within particular discursive and historical struggles. From the perspective of what I am calling "critical multiculturalism," representations of race, class, and gender are understood as the result of larger social struggles over signs and meanings and in this way emphasize not simply textual play or metaphorical displacement as a form of resistance (as in the case of left-liberal multiculturalism) but stress the central task of transforming the social, cultural, and institutional relations in which meanings are generated.

From the perspective of critical multiculturalism, the conservative and liberal stress on sameness and the left-liberal emphasis on difference is really a false opposition. Both identity based on sameness and identity based on difference are forms of essentialist logic: in both, individual identities are presumed to be autonomous, self-contained and self-directed. Resistance multiculturalism also refuses to see culture as non-conflictual, harmonious and consensual. Democracy is understood from this perspective as busy—it is not seamless, smooth, or always a harmonious political and cultural state of affairs (Giroux and McLaren 1991; 1991a; 1991b).

Resistance multiculturalism does not see diversity itself as a goal but rather argues that diversity must be affirmed within a politics of cultural criticism and a commitment to social justice. It must be attentive to the notion of difference. Difference is always a product of history, culture, power, and ideology. Differences occur between and among groups and must be understood in terms of the specificity of their production. Critical multiculturalism interrogates the construction of difference and identity in relation to a radical politics. It is positioned against the neoimperial romance with monoglot ethnicity grounded in a shared or "common" experience of America that is associated with conservative and liberal strands of multiculturalism. Difference is intimately related to capitalist exploitation.

Viewed from the perspective of a critical multiculturalism, conservative attacks on multiculturalism as separatist and ethnocentric carry with them the erroneous assumption by white, Anglo constituencies that North American society fundamentally constitutes social relations of uninterrupted accord. The liberal view is seen to underscore the idea that North American society is largely a forum of consensus with different minority viewpoints simply accretively added on. We are faced here with a politics of pluralism which largely ignores the workings of power and privilege. More specifically, the liberal perspective "involves a very insidious exclusion as far as any structural politics of change is concerned: it excludes and occludes global or structural relations of power as 'ideological' and 'totalizing'" (Ebert in press). In addition, it presupposes harmony and agreement—an undisturbed space in which differences can coexist. Within such a space, individuals are invited to shed their positive characteristics in order to become disembodied and transparent American citizens (Copjec 1991; Rosaldo 1989), a cultural practice that creates what David Lloyd (1991) calls a "subject without properties" (p. 70). In this instance, citizens are able to occupy a place of "pure exchangeability." This accords the universalized white male, heterosexual, and Christian subject a privileged status. Yet such a proposition is dangerously problematic. Chandra Mohanty (1989/90) notes that difference cannot be formulated as negotiation among culturally diverse groups against a backdrop of benign variation or presumed cultural homogeneity. Difference is the recognition that knowledges are forged in histories that are riven with differentially constituted relations of power; that is, knowledges, subjectivities, and social practices are forged within "asymmetrical and incommensurate cultural spheres" (p. 181).

Homi K. Bhabha (1992) makes the' lucid observation that in attributing the racism and sexism of the common culture solely to "the underlying logic of late capitalism and its patriarchal overlay," leftists are actually providing an alibi for the common culture argument. The common culture is transformed in this instance into a form of ethical critique of the political system that supposedly fosters unity within a system of differences. The concept of cultural otherness is taken up superficially to celebrate a "range of 'nation-centered' cultural discourses (on a wide axis from right to left)" (p. 235). It is worth quoting at length Bhabha's notion of common culture as the regulation and normalization of difference:

> Like all myths of the nation's "unity," the common culture is a profoundly conflicted ideological strategy. It is a declaration of democratic faith in a plural, diverse society and, at the same time, a defense against the real, subversive demands that the articulation of cultural difference—the empowering of minorities—makes upon democratic pluralism. Simply saying that the "nation's cement" is inherently sexist or racist—because of the underlying logic of late capitalism and its patriarchal overlay—ironically provides the "common culture" argument with the alibi it needs. The vision of a common culture is perceived to be an ethical mission whose value lies in revealing, prophylactically, the imperfections and exclusions of the political system as it exists. The healing grace of a culture of commonality is supposedly the coevality it establishes between social differences—ethnicities, ideologies, sexualities—"an intimation of simultaneity across homogeneous empty time" that welds these different voices into a "unisonance" that is expressive of the "contemporaneous community of the national culture." (pp. 234–235).

Too often liberal and conservative positions on diversity constitute an attempt to view culture as a soothing balm—the aftermath of historical disagreement—some mythical present where the irrationalities of historical conflict have been smoothed out (McLaren in press). This is not only a disingenuous view of culture; it is profoundly dishonest. It overlooks the importance of engaging on some occasions in dissensus in order to contest hegemonic forms of domination and to affirm differences. The liberal and conservative position on culture also assumes that justice already exists and needs only to be evenly apportioned. However, both teachers and students need to realize that justice does not already exist simply because laws exist. Justice needs to be continually created and constantly struggled for (Darder 1992; McLaren and Hammer 1992). The question that I want to pose to teachers is this: Do teachers and cultural workers have access to a language that allows them to sufficiently critique and transform existing social and cultural practices that are defended by liberals and conservatives as unifyingly democratic?

CRITICAL MULTICULTURALISM AND THE POLITICS OF SIGNIFICATION

Since all experience is the experience of meaning, we need to recognize the role that language plays in the production of experience (McLaren in press a; Giroux and McLaren 1992). You do not have an experience and then search for a word to describe that experience. Rather, language helps to constitute experience by providing a structure of intelligibility or a mediating device through which experiences can be understood. Rather than talking about experience, it is more accurate to talk about "experience effects" (Zavarzadeh and Morton 1990).

Western language and thought are constructed as a system of differences organized *de facto* and *de jure* as binary oppositions—white/black, good/bad, normal/deviant, etc.—with the primary term being privileged and designated as the defining term or the norm of cultural meaning, creating a dependent hierarchy. Yet the secondary term does not really exist outside the first, but, in effect, exists inside of it, even though the phallocentric logic of white supremacist ideology makes you think it exists outside and in opposition to the first term. The critical multiculturalist critique argues that the relationship between signifier and signified is insecure and unstable. Signs are part of an ideological struggle that attempts to create a particular regime of representation that serves to legitimate a certain cultural reality. For instance, we have witnessed a struggle in our society over the meaning of terms such as "negro," "black," and "African American."

According to Teresa Ebert (1991a), our current ways of seeing and acting are being disciplined for us through forms of signification, that is, through modes of intelligibility and ideological frames of sense making. Rejecting the Saussurian semiotics of signifying practices (and its continuing use in contemporary poststructuralism) as "historical operations of language and tropes," Ebert characterizes signifying practices as "an ensemble of material operations involved in economic and political relations" (p. 117). She maintains, rightly in my view, that socioeconomic relations of power require distinctions to be made among groups through forms of signification in order to organize subjects according to the unequal distribution of privilege and power.

To illustrate the politics of signification at work in the construction and formation of racist subjects, Ebert offers the example of the way in which the terms *negro* and *black* have been employed within the racial politics of the United States. Just as the term *negro* became an immutable mark of difference and naturalized the political arrangements of racism in the 1960s, so too is the term *black* being refigured in the white dominant culture to mean criminality, violence, and social degeneracy. This was made clear in the Willie Horton campaign ads of George Bush and in the Bush and David Duke position on hiring quotas. In my view this was also evident in the verdict of the Rodney King case in Los Angeles. It is also evident in some of the media coverage of the O.J. Simpson trial and in the Gingrich demonization of the poor and powerless.

Carlos Muñoz, Jr. (1989) has revealed how the term *Hispanic* in the mid-1970s became a "politics of white ethnic identity" that de-emphasized and in some cases rejected the Mexican cultural base of Mexican Americans. Muñoz writes that the term *Hispanic* is derived from *Hispania* which was the name the Romans gave to the Iberian peninsula, most of which became Spain, and "implicitly emphasizes the white European culture of Spain at the expense of the nonwhite cultures that have profoundly shaped the experiences of all Latin Americans" (p. 11). Not only is this term blind to the multiracial reality of Mexican-Americans through its refusal to acknowledge "the nonwhite indigenous cultures of the Americas, Africa, and Asia, which historically have produced multicultural and multiracial peoples in Latin America and the United States" (Ibid.), but also it is a term that ignores the complexities within these various cultural groups. Here is another example of the melting pot theory of assimilation fostered through a politics of signification. We might ask ourselves what signifieds (meanings) will be attached to certain terms such as "welfare mothers?" Most of us know what government officials mean when they refer derisively to "welfare mothers." They mean black and Latino mothers.

Kobena Mercer (1992) has recently described what he calls "black struggles over the sign" (p. 428). Mercer, following Volosinov, argues that every sign has a "social multi-accentuality," and it is this polyvocal character that can rearticulate the sign through the inscription of different connotations surrounding it. The dominant ideology always tries to stabilize certain meanings of the term. Mercer writes that for over four centuries of Western civilization, the sign "black" was "structured by the closure of an absolute symbolic division of what was white and what was non-white" (Ibid.) through the "morphological equation" of racial superiority.

This equation accorded whiteness with civility and rationality and blackness with savagery and irrationality. Subaltern subjects themselves brought about a reappropriation and rearticulation of the "proper name"—Negro, Colored, Black, Afro-American—in which a collective subjectivity was renamed. Mercer notes that in the sixties and seventies, the term "ethnic minorities" connoted the black subject "as a minor, an abject childlike figure necessary for the legitimation of paternalistic ideologies of assimilation and integration that underpinned the strategy of multiculturalism" (Ibid., p. 429). The term "black community" arose out of a reappropriation of the term "community relations." The state had tried to colonize a definition of social democratic consensus designed to "manage" race relations through the use of "community relations."

The examples discussed above underscore the central theorectical position of critical multiculturalism: differences are produced according to the ideological production and reception of cultural signs. As Mas'ud Zavarzadeh and Donald Morton (1990) point out, "Signs are neither eternally predetermined nor pan-historically undecidable: they are rather 'decided' or rendered as 'undecidable' in the moment of social conflicts" (p. 156). Difference is not "cultural obviousness" such as black versus white or Latino versus European or Anglo-American; rather, differences are historical and cultural constructions (Ebert 1991a).

Just as we can see the politics of signification at work in instances of police brutality or in the way Blacks and Latinos are portrayed as drug pushers, gang members, or the minority sidekick to the white cop in movies and television, we can see it at work in special education placement where a greater proportion of black and Latino students are considered for "behavioral" placements whereas white, middle-class students are provided, for the most part, with the more comforting and comfortable label of "learning disabled" (McLaren 1989). Here, a critical multiculturalist curriculum can help teachers explore the ways in which students are differentially subjected to ideological inscriptions and multiply-organized discourses of desire through a politics of signification.

A critical multiculturalism suggests that teachers and cultural workers need to take up the issue of difference in ways that do not replay the monocultural essentialism of the "centrisms"—Anglocentrism, Eurocentrism, phallocentrism, Afrocentrism, androcentrism, and the like. They need to build a politics of alliance building, of dreaming together, of solidarity that moves beyond the condescension of, say, "race awareness week" that actually serves to keep forms of institutionalized racism in tact. A solidarity has to be struggled for that is not centered around market imperatives but develops out of the imperatives of freedom, liberation, democracy, and critical citizenship.

The notion of the citizen has been pluralized and hybridized, as Kobena Mercer (1990) notes, by the presence of a diversity of social subjects. Mercer is instructive in pointing out that "solidarity does not mean that everyone thinks the same way, it begins when people have the confidence to disagree over issues because they "care" about constructing a common ground" (p. 68). Solidarity is not impermeably solid but depends, to a certain degree, on antagonism and uncertainty. Timothy Maliqualim Simone (1989) calls this type of multiracial solidarity "geared to maximizing points of interaction rather than harmonizing, balancing, or equilibrating the distribution of bodies, resources, and territories" (p. 191).

Whereas left-liberal multiculturalism equates resistance with destabilizing dominant systems of representation, critical multiculturalism goes one step further by asserting that all representations are the result of social struggles over signifiers and their signifieds. This assertion suggests that resistance must take into account an intervention into social struggle in order "to provide equal access to social resources and to transform the dominant power relations which limit this access according to class privilege, race, and gender" (Ebert 1991, p. 294). Differences within culture must be defined as political difference and not just formal, textual, or linguistic difference. Global or structural relations of power must not be ignored. The concept of totality must not be abandoned but rather seen as an overdetermined structure of difference. Differences are always differences in relation, they are never simply free-floating. Differences are not seen as absolute, irreducible or intractable, but rather as undecidable and socially and culturally relational (see Ebert 1991a).

The theorists of resistance or critical multiculturalism do not agree with those left-liberal multiculturalists who argue that difference needs only to be interrogated as a form of rhetoric, thereby reducing politics to signifying structures and history to textuality (Ebert 1991a). We need to go beyond destabilizing meaning by transforming the social and historical conditions in which meaning-making occurs. Rather than remaining satisfied with erasing the privilege of oppressive ideologies that have been naturalized within the dominant culture or with restating dangerous memories that have been repressed within the political unconscious of the state, critical multiculturalist praxis attempts to revise existing hegemonic arrangements. A critical multiculturalist praxis does not simply reject the bourgeois decorum that has consigned the imperialized other to the realm of the grotesque but effectively attempts to remap desire by fighting for a linguistically multivalenced culture and new structures of experience in which individuals refuse the role of the omniscient narrator and conceive of identity as a polyvalent assemblage of (contradictory and overdetermined) subject positions. Existing systems of difference which organize social life into patterns of domination and subordination must be reconstructed. We need to do more than unflaggingly problematize difference as a condition of rhetoric, or unceasingly interrogate the status of all knowledge as discursive inscription, because, as Ebert notes, this annuls the grounds of both reactionary and revolutionary politics. Rather, we need a rewriting of difference as *difference-in-relation* followed by attempts to dramatically change the material conditions that allow relations of exploitation to prevail over relations of equality and social justice. This is a different cultural politics than one of simply reestablishing an inverse hierarchical order of Blacks over whites or Latinos over whites. Rather it is an attempt to transform the very value of hierarchy itself, followed by a challenge to the material structures that are responsible for the overdetermination of structures of difference in the direction of oppression, injustice, and human suffering. However, this is not to claim that individuals are oppressed in the same ways since groups are oppressed nonsynchronously in conjunction with systems such as class, race, gender, age, ethnicity, sexuality, etc. (McCarthy 1988). People can be situated very differently in the same totalizing structures of oppression. We need to analyze and challenge both the specific enunciations of microdifferences within difference and the macrostructure of difference-in-relation (Ebert 1991a). We need to refocus on structural oppression in the forms of patriarchy, capitalism, and white supremacy—structures that tend to get ignored by liberal multiculturalists and their veneration of difference as identity. As educators and cultural workers, we must critically intervene in those power relations that organize difference.

WHITENESS: THE INVISIBLE CULTURE OF TERROR

Educators need to critically examine the development of pedagogical discourses and practices that demonize others who are different (through transforming them into absence or deviance). Critical multiculturalism calls serious attention to the dominant meaning systems readily available to students and teachers, most

of which are ideologically stitched into the fabric of Western imperialism and patriarchy. It challenges meaning systems that impose
attributes on the "other" under the direction of sovereign signifiers
and tropes. This means not directing all our efforts at understanding ethnicity as "other than white," but interrogating the
culture of whiteness itself. This is crucial because unless we do
this—unless we give white students a sense of their own identity as
an emergent ethnicity—we naturalize whiteness as a cultural
marker against which otherness is defined. Coco Fusco warns that
"To ignore white ethnicity is to redouble its hegemony by naturalizing it. Without specifically addressing white ethnicity there can be
no critical evaluation of the construction of the other" (cited in
Wallace 1991, p. 7). White groups need to examine their own ethnic
histories so that they are less likely to judge their own cultural
norms as neutral and universal. The supposed neutrality of white
culture enables it to commodify blackness to its own advantage and
ends. It allows it to manipulate the other but not see this otherness
as a white tool of exploitation. Whiteness does not exist outside of
culture but constitutes the prevailing social texts in which social
norms are made and remade. As part of a politics of signification
that passes unobserved into the rhythms of daily life, and a "politically constructed category parasitic on 'Blackness'" (West 1990, p.
29), whiteness has become the invisible norm for how the dominant
culture measures its own worth and civility.

Using an ethnosemiotic approach as a means of interrogating
the culture of whiteness and understanding ethnicity as a rhetorical form, Dean MacCannell (1992), in his new book, *Empty
Meeting Grounds*, raises the question: "In their interactions with
others, how can groups in power manage to convey the impression
that they are less ethnic than those over whom they exercise their
power; in other words, how can they foster the impression that
their own traits and qualities are correct, while the corresponding
qualities of others are 'ethnic?' " (p. 121–122). Furthermore, asks
MacCannell, how does the consensus that is achieved in this
matter structure our institutions? His answer leads us to explore
the secret of power in discourse—that simply because language is
essentially rhetorical (i.e., free of all bias because it is pure bias) we
cannot escape the fact that rhetoric and grammar always intersect
in particular ideological formations which makes language
unavoidably a social relation. And every social relation is a structurally located one that can never be situated outside of relations
of power. MacCannell locates this power in the ability of the
speaking subject to move into the position of "he" without seeming

to leave the position of "I" or "you" (which are empty or "floating" signifiers that have no referent outside the immediate situation). The personal pronoun "he" refers to an objective situation outside of the immediate subjectively apprehended situation. MacCannell asserts that whites have mastered interactional forms that permit them to operate as interactants while seeming to be detached from the situation, to be both an "I" or a "you" and a "he" at the same time—both to operate within the situation *and* to judge it. Dominant groups will always want to occupy the grammatical power position: that is, assume the external objective and judgmental role of the "he" by suggesting that their use of language is free of bias. White culture, according to MacCannell, is an enormous totalization that arrogates to itself the right to represent all other ethnic groups. For instance, binary oppositions such as "white as opposed to non-white" always occupy the grammatical position of "him", never "I" nor "you," and we know that in white culture, "whiteness" will prevail and continue to be parasitic on the meaning of "blackness" (p. 131).

Cornel West (1990, p. 29) remarks that "'Whiteness' is a politically constructed category parasitic on 'blackness.'" He further asserts that "One cannot deconstruct the binary oppositional logic of images of Blackness without extending it to the contrary condition of Blackness/Whiteness itself." According to Jonathan Rutherford (1990):

> Binarism operates in the same way as splitting and projection: the centre expels it anxieties, contradictions and irrationalities onto the subordinate term, filling it with the antithesis of its own identity: the Other, in its very alienness, simply mirrors and represents what is deeply familiar to the centre, but projected outside of itself. It is in these very processes and representations of marginality that the violence, antagonisms and aversions which are at the core of the dominant discourses and identities become manifest-racism, homophobia, misogyny and class contempt are the products of this frontier (p. 22).

Of course, when binarisms become racially and culturally marked, *white* occupies the grammatical position of *him*, never *I* nor *you* and, notes MacCannell (1992), "always operates *as if* not dependent on rhetoric to maintain its position" (p. 131). Rhetoric is aligned with *non-truth*, and whiteness is perceived as neutral and devoid of interest. Of course, "whiteness" projects onto the term "blackness" an array of specific qualities and characteristics such as wild, exotic, uncontrolled, deviant, and savage. Whiteness is founded on the principle of depersonalization of all human relationships and the idealization of objective judgment and duty. MacCannell is worth quoting at length on this issue:

> To say that white culture is impersonal is not the same thing as saying that it does not function like a subject or subjectivity. But it is the kind that is cold, the kind that laughs at feelings while demanding that all surplus libido, energy and capital be handed over to it...White culture begins with the pretense that it, above all, does not express itself rhetorically. Rather, the form of its expression is always represented as only incidental to the truth. And its totalizing power radiates from this pretense which is maintained by interpreting all ethnic expression as "representative," and therefore, *merely* rhetorical. (Ibid., p. 130)

When people of color attack white ground rules for handling disputes, or bureaucratic procedures, or specific policies of institutionalized racism, these are necessary oppositional acts but insufficient for bringing about structural change because, as MacCannell notes, this work is "framed by the assumption of the dominance of white culture" (Ibid., p. 131). This is because white culture is predicated upon the universalization of the concept of "exchange values"—systems of equivalences, the transcribability of all languages, the translatability of any language into any other language, and the division of the earth into real estate holdings in which it is possible to precisely calculate and calibrate the worth of every person. MacCannell is quite clear on this. Within such a totalization brought about by white culture, indigenous groups can only belong as an "ethnicity." As long as white culture, as the defining cultural frame for white-ethnic transactions, sets the limits on all thought about human relations, there can be no prospect for human equality.

Richard Dyer (1988) has made some useful observations about the culture of whiteness, claiming that its property of being both "everything" and "nothing" is the source of its representational power in the sense that white culture possesses the power to colonize the definition of the normal with respect to class, gender, heterosexuality, and nationality. Perhaps white culture's most formidable attribute is its ability to mask itself as a category. Whites will often think of their Scottishness, Irishness, or Jewishness, and so on, before they think of their whiteness. Michael Goldfield (1992) argues that white supremacy has been responsible for holding back working-class struggle in the United States, as labor groups tragically failed to grasp the strategic importance for labor in fighting the system of white supremacy, missing an opportunity—especially during Reconstruction—for changing the face of U.S. politics.

In her recent book, *Black Looks*, bell hooks (1992) notes that white people are often shocked when black people "critically assess white people from a standpoint where 'whiteness' is the privileged signifier" (p. 167). She remarks that

> Their [white people's] amazement that black people match white people with a critical "ethnographic" gaze, is itself an expression of racism. Often their rage erupts because they believe that all ways of looking that highlight difference subvert the liberal belief in a universal subjectivity (we are all just people) that they think will make racism disappear. They have a deep emotional investment in the myth of "sameness," even as their actions reflect the primacy of whiteness as a sign informing who they are and how they think. Many of them are shocked that black people think critically about whiteness because racist thinking perpetuates the fantasy that the Other who is subjugated, who is subhuman, lacks the ability to comprehend, to understand, to see the working of the powerful. Even though the majority of those students politically consider themselves liberals and anti-racist, they too unwittingly invest in the sense of whiteness as mystery. (pp. 167–168).

Hooks discusses the representation of whiteness as a form of terror within black communities and is careful not simply to invert the stereotypical racist association of whiteness as goodness and blackness as evil. The depiction of whiteness as "terrorizing" emerges in hooks' discussion not as a reaction to stereotypes but, as she puts it, "as a response to the traumatic pain and anguish that remains a consequence of white racist domination, a psychic state that informs and shapes the way black folks 'see' whiteness" (Ibid., p. 169).

ARE YOU AN AMERICAN OR A LIBERAL?

Critical pedagogy needs to hold a nonreductionist view of the social order; that is, society needs to be seen as an irreducible indeterminacy. The social field is always open, and we must explore its fissures, fault-lines, gaps and silences. Power relations may not always have a conscious design, but they have unintended consequences which define deep structural aspects of oppression even though every ideological totalization of the social is designed to fail. This is not to affirm Schopenhauer's unwilled patterns of history but rather to assert that while domination has a logic without design in its sign systems and social practices, it does operate through overdetermined structures of race, class, and gender difference. Resistance to such domination means deconstructing the social by means of a reflexive intersubjective consciousness—what Freire terms "conscientizaçao." With this comes a recognition that ideology is more than an epistemological concern about the status of certain facts. It is also the way in which discourse and discursive systems generate particular social relations as well as reflect them. A reflexive intersubjective consciousness is the beginning—but only the beginning—of revolutionary praxis.

We also need to create new narratives—new "border narratives"—in order to reauthor the discourses of oppression in politically subversive ways as well as to create sites of possibility and enablement. For instance, we need to ask: How are our identities bound up with historical forms of discursive practices? It is one thing to argue against attacks on polyvocal and unassimilable difference and on narrative closure or to stress the heterogeneity of contemporary culture. However, in doing so we must remember that dominant discourses are sites of struggle and their meanings are linked to social antagonisms and labor/economic relations and then naturalized in particular textual/linguistic referents. Consequently, self-reflection alone—even if it is inimicably opposed to all forms of domination and oppression—is only a necessary but not nearly sufficient condition for emancipation. This process must go hand-in-hand with changes in material and social conditions through counter-hegemonic action (Hammer and McLaren 1991; 1992). The sociohistorical dynamics of race, clan, and gender domination must never be left out of the equation of social struggle or take a back seat to the sociology seminar room. We need a language of criticism as an antidote to the atheoretical use of "personal experience" in advancing claims for emancipatory action. Commonsense consciousness is not enough. However, this needs to be followed by the development of truly counterhegemonic public spheres. We need more than rhetorical displacements of oppression but rather strategic and coordinated resistance to racist, patriarchal capitalism and gender-divided labor relations. According to Teresa Ebert (in press), what is needed is an intervention into the system of patriarchal oppression at both the macropolitical level of the structural organization of domination (a transformative politics of labor relations) and the micropolitical level of different and contradictory manifestations of oppression (cultural politics).

Those of us working in the area of curriculum reform need to move beyond the tabloid reportage surrounding the political correctness debate, take the issue of difference seriously, and challenge the dimissive undercutting of difference by the conservative multiculturalists. First, we need to move beyond admitting one or two Latin American or African American books into the canon of great works. Rather, we need to legitimize multiple traditions of knowledge. By focusing merely on diversity we are actually reinforcing the power of the discourses from the Western traditions that occupy the contexts of social privilege. Second, curriculum reform requires teachers to interrogate the discursive presuppositions that inform their curriculum practices with respect to race, class, gender, and sexual orientation. In addition, curricularists need to unsettle their complacency with respect to Eurocentrism. Third, what is perceived as the inherent superiority of whiteness and Western rationality needs to be displaced. The very notion of the "West" is something that critical educators find highly problematic. Why is Toni Morrison, for instance, denounced as non-Western simply because she is African American? (This scenario is complicated by the fact that conservative multiculturalists often retort with the insinuation that any attack on Western culture is an attack against being American.) Fourth, curriculum reform means recognizing that groups are differentially situated in the production of Western, high-status knowledge. How are certain groups represented in the official knowledge that makes up the curriculum? Are they stigmatized because they are associated with the Third World? Are we, as teachers, complicitous with the oppression of these people when we refuse to interrogate popular films and TV shows that reinforce their subaltern status? Educators would do well to follow hooks (1992) in dehegemonizing racist discourses such that "progressive white people who are anti-racist might be able to understand the way in which their cultural practice reinscribes white supremacy without promoting paralyzing guilt or denial" (p. 177). In addition, curriculum reform means affirming the voices of the oppressed; teachers need to give the marginalized and the powerless a preferential option. Similarly, students must be encouraged to produce their own oppositional readings of curriculum content. Lastly, curriculum reform must recognize the importance of encouraging spaces for the multiplicity of voices in our classrooms and of creating a dialogical pedagogy in which subjects see others as subjects and not as objects. When this happens, students are more likely to participate in history rather than become its victims.

In taking seriously the irreducible social materiality of discourse and the fact that the very semantics of discourse is always organized and interested, critical pedagogy has revealed how student identities are differentially constructed through social relations of schooling that promote and sustain asymmetrical relations of power and privilege between the oppressors and the oppressed. It has shown that this construction follows a normative profile of citizenship and an epistemology that attempts to reconcile the discourse of ideals with the discourse of needs. Discourses have been revealed to possess the power to nominate others as deviant or normal. Dominant discourses of schooling are not laws. Rather, they are strategies—disciplined mobilizations for normative performances of citizenship. Ian Hunter (1992) has shown that the concept of citizenry taught in schools has less to do with ethical ideals than with disciplinary practices and techniques of reading and writing and with the way students are distributed into political and aesthetic spaces. We are being aesthetically and morally reconciled with the governing norms of a civic unconscious. The "unconscious" is not a semiotic puzzle to be opened through the discovery of some universal grammar but is rather an ethical technology designed to "complete" students as citizens. Pedagogically, this process is deceptive because it uses liberal humanism and progressive education to complete the circuit of hegemony. The liberal position on pedagogy is to use it to open social texts to a plurality of readings. Because we live in an age of cynical reason, this pedagogy provides a "knowing wink" to students which effectively says: "We know there are multiple ways to make sense of the world and we know that you know, too. So let's knowingly enter this world of multiple interpretations together and take pleasure in rejecting the dominant codes." Consequently, teachers and students engage in a tropological displacement and unsettling of normative discourses and revel in the semantic excess that prevents any meaning from becoming transcendentally fixed. The result of this practice of turning knowledge into floating signifiers circulating in an avant-garde text (whose discursive trajectory is everywhere and nowhere and whose meaning is ultimately undecidable) is simply a recontainment of the political. By positing undecidability in advance, identity is reduced to a form of self-indexing or academic "vogue-ing." Liberation becomes transformed into a form of discursive "cleverness," of postmodern transgressive-chic grounded in playfully high vogue decodings of always already constructed texts, of fashionable language gaming by academic apostates.

I would also like to argue, in conclusion, that students need to be provided with opportunities to construct border identities. Border identities are intersubjective spaces of cultural translation—linguistically multivalanced spaces of intercultural dialogue.

It is a space where one can find an overlay of codes, a multiplicity of culturally inscribed subject positions, a displacement of normative reference codes, and a polyvalent assemblage of new cultural meanings (see Giroux 1992; McLaren in press; in press a).

Border identities are produced in sites of "occult instability" and result in *un laberinto de significados*. Here, knowledge is produced by a transrepresentational access to the real—through reflexive, relational understanding amidst the connotative matrixes of numerous cultural codes. It is a world where identity and critical subjectivity depend upon the process of translating a profusion of intersecting cultural meanings (Hicks 1991; Giroux 1992). We need to remember than we live in a repressive regime in which identities are teleologically inscribed towards a standard end—the informed, employed citizen. There is a tension between this narrative which schools have attempted to install in students through normative pedagogical practices and the nonlinear narratives that they "play out" in the world outside of the school. However, students and even their often well-intentioned teachers are frequently incapable of intervening (McLaren, 1986).

Especially in inner-city schools, students can be seen inhabiting what I call *border cultures*. These are cultures in which a repetition of certain normative structures and codes often "collide" with other codes and structures whose referential status is often unknown or only partially known. In Los Angeles, for instance, it is possible that an inner-city neighborhood will contain Latino cultures, Asian cultures, and Anglo cultures. Students live interculturally as they cross the borderlines of linguistic, cultural, and conceptual realities. Students, in other words, have the opportunity to live multidimensionally. Living in border cultures is an anticentering experience as time and space experienced at school is constantly displaced. Often a carnivalesque liminal space emerges as bourgeois linear time is displaced. Because the dominant model of multiculturalism in mainstream pedagogy is of the corporate or conservative variety, the notion of sameness is enforced and cultural differences that challenge white, Anglo cultures are considered deviant and in need of enforced homogenization into the dominant referential codes and structures of Euro-American discourse.

I am in agreement with critics who assert that border identity cannot be subsumed under either dialectical or analytic logic (Hicks 1991). It is, rather, an experience of deterritorialization of signification (Larsen 1991) in a postnationalist cultural space—that is, in a postcolonial, postnational space. Border identity is an identity structure that occurs in a postimperial space of cultural possibility. The postcolonial subject that arises out of the construction of border identity is nonidentical with itself. It acquires a new form of agency outside of Euro-American, Cartesian discourses. It is not simply an inverted Eurocentrism but one that salvages the modernist referent of liberation from oppression for all suffering peoples. I am here stressing the universality of human rights but at the same time criticizing essentialist universality as a site of transcendental meaning. In other words, I am emphasizing the universality or rights as historically produced. Social justice is a goal that needs to be situated historically, contextually, and contingently as the product of material struggles over modes of intelligibility as well as institutional and social practices. I need to be clear about what I mean by a referent for social justice and human freedom. I mean that the project underlying multicultural education needs to be situated from the standpoint not only of the *concrete other* but also of the *generalized other*. All universal rights in this view must recognize the specific needs and desires of the concrete other without sacrificing the standpoint of a generalized other, without which it is impossible to speak of a radical ethics at all. Selya Benhabib distinguishes between this perspective—what she refers to as an "interactive universalism"—and a "substitutionalist universalism": "Substitutionalist universalism dismisses the concrete other behind the facade of a definitional identity of all as rational beings, while interactive universalism acknowledges that every generalized other is also a concrete other" (1992, p. 165). This position speaks neither exclusively to a liberal, humanist ethics of empathy and benevolence nor to a ludic, postmodernist ethics of local narratives or *les petits recits*, but to one based on engagement, confrontation and dialogue, and collective moral argumentation between and across borders. It takes into account both macro and micro theory (Best and Keller 1991) and some degree of normative justification and ajudication of choices. As Best and Kellner note (1991), "one needs new critical theories to conceptualize, describe, and interpret macro social processes, just as one needs political theories able to articulate common or general interests that cut across divisions of sex, race, and class" (p. 301). In this sense I take issue with ludic voices of postmodernism that proclaim an end both to self-reflective agenthood and to the importance of engaging historical narratives and that proclaim the impossibility of legitimizing institutions outside of "practices and traditions other than through the immanent appeal to the self-legitimation of 'small narratives'" (Benhabib 1992, p. 220). Rather, a critical multiculturalism must take into account the "methodological assumptions guiding one's choice of narratives, and a clarification of those principles in the name of which one speaks" (p. 226).

A border identity is not simply an identity that is anticapitalist and counterhegemonic but is also critically utopian. It is an identity that transforms the burden of knowledge into a scandal of hope. The destructive extremes of Eurocentrism and national-cultural identities (as in the current crisis in what was formerly Yugoslavia) must be avoided. We need to occupy locations between our political unconscious and everyday praxis and struggle but at the same time be guided by a universalist emancipatory world view in the form of a provisional utopia or contingent foundationalism (See Butler 1991). A provisional utopia is not a categorical blueprint for social change (as in fascism) but a contingent utopia where we anticipate the future through practices of solidarity and community. Such a utopian vision demands that we gain control of the production of meaning but in a postnationalist sense. We can achieve this goal by negotiating with the borders of our identity—those unstable constellations of discursive structures—in our search for a radical otherness that can empower us to reach beyond them.

Border identities constitute a bold infringement on normalcy, a violation of the canons of bourgeois decorum, a space where we can cannibalize the traces of our narrative repression or engage them critically through the practice of cultural translation—a translation of one level of reality into another, creating a multidimensional reality that I call the *cultural imaginary*, a space of cultural articulation that results from the collision of multiple strands of referential codes and sign systems. Such collisions can create hybrid significations through a hemorrhage of signifiers whose meanings endlessly bleed into each other or else take on the force of historical agency as a new *mestizaje* consciousness. Mestizaje consciousness (Anzaldúa 1987) is not simply a doctrine of identity based on cultural bricolage or a form of bric-a-brac subjectivity but a critical practice of cultural negotation and translation that attempts to transcend the contradictions of Western dualistic thinking. As Chandra Talpade Mohanty (1991) remarks:

> A mestiza consciousness is a consciousness of the borderlands, a consciousness born of the historical collusion of Anglo and Mexican cultures and frames of reference. It is a plural consciousness in that it requires understanding multiple, often opposing ideas and knowledges, and negotiating these knowledges, not just taking a simple counterstance. (p. 36).

Anzaldúa speaks of a notion of agency that moves beyond the postmodernist concept of "split subject" by situating agency in its historical and geopolitical specificity (p. 37). Borders cannot simply be evoked in an abstract, transcendental sense but need to be identified specifically. Borders can be linguistic, spacial, ideological, and geographical. They not only demarcate otherness but also stipulate the manner in which otherness is maintained and reproduced. A mestizaje consciousness is linked, therefore, to the specificity of historical struggles (Ibid., p. 38).

A critical multiculturalism needs to testify not only to the pain, suffering, and "walking nihilism" of oppressed peoples but also to the intermittent, epiphanic ruptures and moments of *jouissance* that occur when solidarity is established around struggles for liberation. As I have tried to argue, with others, elsewhere (McLaren and Hammer 1989; McLaren, 1995), we need to abandon our pedagogies of protest (which, as Houston Baker (1985) reminds us, simply reinforces the dualism of "self" and "other," reinstates the basis of dominant racist evaluations, and preserves the "always already" arrangements of white male hegemony [see Baker, 1985]) in favor of a politics of transformation. Those of us who are white need also to avoid the "white male confessional" that Baker (1985) describes as the "confessional *manqué* of the colonial subject" (p. 388).

White male confessionals simply "induce shame" rather than convince people to change their axiology, yet still employ the language and "shrewd methods of the overseers." It is the type of confessional that proclaims that oppressed people of color are "as good as" white people. It simply asserts that subaltern voices measure up to dominant voices and that African Americans are merely 'different' and not deviant. In contrast, Baker calls for a form of "*supraliteracy*" or "guerrilla action" carried out *within* linguistic territories. This constitutes an invasion of the dominant linguistic terrain of the traditional academic disciplines—an invasion that he describes as a "deformation of mastery." From this perspective, critical pedagogy needs to be more attentive to the dimension of the vernacular—"to sound racial poetry in the courts of the civilized" (Ibid., p. 395). Teachers need to include nonliterary cultural forms into our classrooms—such as video, film, popular fiction, and radio—and a critical means of understanding their role in the production of subjectivity and agency.

Concentrating on the reflexive modalities of the intellect or returning to some pretheoretical empirical experience are both bad strategies for challenging the politics of the white confessional. The former is advocated mostly by academics while the latter is exercised by educational activists suspicious of the new languages of deconstruction and the fashionable apostasy of the poststructuralists whose intellectual home is in the margins. Academic theorists tend to textualize and displace experience to the abstract equivalence of the signified while activists view "commonsense" experience as essentially devoid of ideology or interest. We need to avoid approaches that disconnect us from the lives of real people who suffer and from issues of power and justice that directly affect the oppressed.

Critical social theory as a form of multicultural resistance must be wary of locating liberatory praxis in the realm of diachrony—as something to be resolved dialectically in some higher unity outside of the historical struggle and pain and suffering to which we must serve as pedagogical witnesses and agents of radical hope. Yet at the same time, critical pedagogy needs to be wary of forms of populist elitism that privilege only the reform efforts of those who have direct experience with the oppressed. After all, no single unsurpassable and "authentic" reality can be reached through "experience" since no experience is preontologically available outside of a politics of representation.

As multicultural educators informed by critical and feminist pedagogies, we need to keep students connected to the power of the unacceptable and comfortable with the unthinkable by producing critical forms of policy analysis and pedagogy. In tandem with this, we must actively help students to challenge sites of discursive hierarchy rather than delocalizing and dehistoricizing them, and to contest the ways that their desires and pleasures are being policed in relationship to them. It is important that as critical educators, we do not manipulate students simply to accept our intellectual positions nor presume at the same time to speak for them. Nor should our critical theorizing be simply a service to the culture of domination by extending student insights into the present system without at the same time challenging the very assumptions of the system. We cannot afford to just temporarily disengage students from the *doxa*—the language of commonsense. If we want to recruit students to a transformative praxis, students must not only be encouraged to choose a language of analysis that is undergirded by a project of liberation but must affectively invest in such a project.

If we are to be redeemed from our finitude as passive suppliants of history, we must, as students and teachers, adopt more directly oppositional and politically combatative social and cultural practices. The destructive fanaticism of present day xenophobia is only exacerbated by the current ethical motionlessness among

many left constituencies. Insurgent intellectuals and theorists are
called to steer a course between the monumentalization of judgment and taste and riding the postmodern currents of despair in
a free-fall exhilaration of political impotence.

The present historical moment is populated by memories that
are surfacing at the margins of our culture, along the fault lines of
our logocentric consciousness. Decolonized spaces are forming in
the borderlands—linguistic, epistemological, and intersubjective—
and these will affect the classrooms of the future. Here saints and
Iwa walk together and the Orishas speak to us through the
rhythms of the earth and the pulse of the body. The sounds
produced in the borderlands are quite different from the convul-
sive monotones voiced in 'waspano' or 'gringoñol' that echo from
the schizophrenic boundaries of Weber's iron cage. Here it is in the
hybrid polyrhythms of the drum that the new pulse of freedom can
be felt. Within such borderlands our pedagogies of liberation can
be invested once again with the passion of mystery and the reason
of commitment. This is neither a Dionysian rejection of rationality
nor a blind, prerational plunge into myth but rather an attempt to
embrace and reclaim the memories of those pulsating, sinewed
bodies that have been forgotten in our modernist assault on difference and uncertainty. An attempt to begin an *asiento.*

NOTES

* Slightly altered versions of this paper will appear in Peter McLaren,
Rhonda Hammer, David Sholle, and Susan Reilly, *Rethinking Media
Literacy,* New York: Peter Lang Publishers and Peter McLaren, *Critical
Pedagogy and Predatory Culture.* London and New York: Routledge, in
press. Some sections of this paper have appeared in Peter McLaren,
"Multiculturalism and the Postmodern Critique: Towards a Pedagogy
oú Resistance and Transformation. " *Cultural Studies* 7(1), 1993, p.
118–146 and Peter McLaren, "Critical Pedagogy, Multiculturalism, and
the Politics of Risk and Resistance: Response to Kelly and Portelli,
1991. *Journal of Education* 173(3): 29–59. This paper was originally
published in *Strategies,* no. 7 1994, pp. 98–131, and *Multiculturalism:
A Critical Reader,* edited by David Theo Goldberg. Oxford: Blackwell,
pp. 45–74. See also Peter McLaren, "Critical Multiculturalism, Media
Literacy, and the Politics of Representation. In Jean Frederickson (Ed.)
*Reclaiming Our Voices: Bilingual Education, Critical Pedagogy and
Praxis.* Ontario, California: California Association for Bilingual Education, 1995, pp. 99–138, for an earlier version of this article.

1 Africa is still demonized as a land uncivilized, corrupt, and savage and
as a continent divided into countries that are viewed as not evolved
enough to govern themselves without Western guidance and steward-

ship. We shamefully ignore Africa's victims of war and famine in comparison, for instance, to the "white" victims of Bosnia. When the U.S. media does decide to report on Africa, many of the images it reinforces are of a land of jungle, wildlife, famine, poachers, and fierce fighting among rival tribal factions (Naureckas 1993). The white supremacist and colonialist discourses surrounding the recent intervention in Somalia by heroic U.S. troops and relief workers (referred to by General Colin Powell as sending in the "cavalry") is captured in comments made by Alan Pizzy of CBS when he described the intervention in "humanitarian" terms as "just a few good men trying to help another nation in need, another treacherous country where all the members of all the murderous factions look alike" (cited in Jim Naureckas, *Extra*, March 1993, p. 12). Described as a land populated by helpless and historyless victims and drug-crazed thugs high on khat (a mild stimulant) who ride around in vehicles out of a Mad Max movie, an implicit parallel is made between Somali youth and the cocaine-dealing gangs of toughs who participated in the L.A. rioting (Ibid.). This "othering" of Africa encouraged a preferred reading of Somalia's problems as indigenous and camouflaged the broader context surrounding the famine in Somalia and its subsequent "rescue" by U.S. marines. Occluded was the fact that the U.S. had previously obstructed U.N. peacekeeping efforts in Somalia, Angola, Namibia, and Mozambique because it was too costly (the U.S. still owes $415 million to the U.N., including $120 million for peacekeeping efforts)—a factor absent in nearly all the media coverage (Ibid.). From a U.S. foreign policy perspective, Somalia still plays an important role geopolitically, not simply because of its potential interest to Israel and the Arab nations but because of its rich mineral deposits and potential oil reserves. As Naureckas notes, Amoco, Chevron, and Sunoco are engaged in oil exploration there (Ibid.).

The media have rarely reported on other factors surrounding the famine in Somalia. For instance, they have virtually ignored the U.S. support (to the sum of $200 million in military aid and half a billion in economic aid) to the Siad Barre regime (1969–1991). The U.S. ignored its corruption and human rights abuses because the dictatorship kept Soviet-allied Ethiopia embroiled in a war. Naureckas also points out that until the 1970s, Somalia was self-sufficient in grain and its agricultural land productive enough to withstand famine. However, U.S. and international agencies like the IMF pressured Somalia to shift agricultural from local subsistence to export crops (Ibid.)

REFERENCES

Anzaldúa, Gloria. 1987. *Borderlands/La Frontera*. San Francisco: Spinsters/Aunt Lute.

Auster, Laurence. 1990. *The path to national suicide: An essay on immigration and multiculturalism*. American Immigration Control Foundation.

Baker, Houston A. 1985. "Caliban's triple play." In *"Race," writing, and difference*, ed. Henry Louis Gates, Jr., p. 381–395. Chicago, Illinois, University of Chicago Press.

Benhabib, Seyla. 1992. *Situating the self: Gender, community, and postmodernism in contemporary ethics*. London and New York: Routledge.

Best, Steven, and Kellner, Douglas. 1991. *Postmodern theory: Critical interrogations*. New York: The Guilford Press.

Bhabha, Homi K. 1992. A good judge of character: Men, metaphors, and the common culture. *In Race-ing justice. en-gendering power*, Ed. Tony Morrison, pp. 232–249. New York: Pantheon Books.

Bradford, Phillips Verner, and Blume, Harvey. 1992. *Ota Benga: The pygmy in the zoo*. New York: St. Martin's Press.

Brookhiser, Richard. 1991. *The Way of the WASP: How it made America, and how it can save it, so to speak*. New York: Free Press.

Butler, Judith. 1991. Contingent foundations: Feminism and the question of "postmodernism." *Praxis International* 11(2): 150–165.

Cooper, B. M. 1989. Cruel and the gang: Esposing the Schomburg Posse. *Village Voice* 34(19): 27–36.

Copjec, Joan. 1991. The unvermögender other: Hysteria and democracy in America, *New Formations* 14(Summer): 27–41.

Cortázar, Julio. 1963. *Hopscotch.* Trans. Gregory Rabassa. New York: Random House.

Darder, Antonia. 1992. *Culture and power in the classroom.* South Hadley, MA: Bergin and Garvey.

Dyer, Richard. 1988. White. *Screen* 29(4): 44–64.

Dyson, M. E. 1993. *Reflecting Black: African-American Cultural Criticism.* Minneapolis and London: University of Minnesota Press.

Ebert, Teresa. 1991a. Writing in the political: Resistance (post)-modernism. *Legal Studies Forum* 14(4): 291–303.

————. 1991b. Political semiosis in/of American cultural studies. *The American Journal of Semiotics* 8(1/2): 113–135.

————. In press. Ludic feminism, the body, performance and labor: Bringing materialism back into feminist cultural studies. *Cultural Critique.*

Estrada, Kelly, and McLaren, Peter. In press. A dialogue on multiculturalism and democracy. *Educational Researcher.*

Fish, Stanley. 1992. Bad company. *Transition* 56: 60–67.

Gardiner, Michael. 1992. *The dialogics of critique: M. M. Bakhtin and the theory of ideology.* London and New York: Routledge.

Giroux, Henry. 1992. *Border crossings.* London and New York: Routledge.

Giroux, Henry, and McLaren, Peter. 1991a. Media hegemony. Introduction to *Media Knowledge* by James Schwoch, Mimi White, and Susan Reilly. Albany, NY: State University of New York Press, pp. xv–xxxiv.

————. 1991b. Leon Golub's radical pessimism: Toward a pedagogy of representation. *Exposure* 28(12): 18–33.

————. 1991. Radical pedagogy as cultural politics: Beyond the discourse of critique and anti-utopianism. In *Theory/Pedagogy/Politics*, ec. D. Morton and M. Zavarzadeh, pp. 152–186. Chicago: University of Illinois Press.

————. 1992. Writing from the margins: Geographies of identity, pedagogy, and power. *Journal of Education* 174(1): 7–30.

————. In press. Paulo Freire, postmodernism, and the utopian imagination: A Blochian reading. In *Bloch in our time*, ed. Jamie Owen Daniel and Tom Moylan. Bloch in our time. London and New York: Verso.

Goldfield, Michael. 1992. The color of politics in the United States: White supremacy as the main explanation for the pecularities of American politics from colonial times to the present. In *The bounds of race*, ed. Dominick LaCapra, pp. 104–133. Ithaca and London: Cornell University Press.

Hall, Stuart. 1991. Ethnicity: Identity and difference. *Radical America* 23(4): 9–20.

Hammer, Rhonda and McLaren, Peter. 1992. Spectacularizing subjectivity: Media knowledges and the new world order. *Polygraph*, No. 5, 46–66.

Hammer, Rhonda, and McLaren, Peter. 1991. Rethinking the dialectic. *Educational Theory* 41(1): 23–46.

Hicks, D. Emily. 1991. *Border writing*. Minneapolis: University of Minnesota Press.

hooks, bell. 1992. *Black looks*. Boston: South End Press.

Hunter, Ian. 1992. *Culture and government: The emergence of literary education*. Houndmills, Basingstoke, Hampshire and London: MacMillan Press.

Katz, Cindi, and Smith, Neil. 1992. L.A. intifada: Interview with Mike Davis. *Social Text* 33: 19–33.

Larsen, Neil. 1991. Foreword to *border writing* by Emily Hicks, pp. xi–xxi. Minneapolis: University of Minnesota Press.

Lloyd, David. 1991. Race under representation. *Oxford Literary Review* 13(1–2): 62–94.

MacCannell, Dean. 1992. *Empty meeting grounds: The tourist papers*. London and New York: Routledge.

Macedo, Donaldo. 1995. *Literacies of Power*. Boulder, Colorado: Westview Press.

McCarthy, Cameron. 1988. Rethinking liberal and radical perspectives on racial inequality in schooling: Making the case for nonsynchrony. *Harvard Educational Review* 58(3): 265–279.

McLaren, Peter, and Hammer, Rhonda. 1989. Critical pedagogy and the postmodern challenge: Towards a critical postmodernist pedagogy of liberation. *Educational Foundations* 3(3): 29–62.

———. 1992. Media knowledges, warrior citizenry, and postmodern literacies. *Journal of Urban and Cultural Studies* 2(2): 41–77.

McLaren, Peter. 1985. Contemporary ritual studies: A post-Turnerism perspective. *Semiotic Inquiry* 5(1): 78–85.

———. 1986. *Schooling as a ritual performance: Towards a political economy of educational symbols and gestures*. London and New York: Routledge (Revised edition in press).

———. 1988. Culture or canon? Critical pedagogy and the politics of literacy. *The Harvard Educational Review* 58(2): 213–234.

———. 1989. *Life in schools*. White Plains, NY: Longman.

———. 1990. Schooling the postmodern body. In *Postmodernism, feminism, and cultural politics*, ed. Henry A. Giroux, pp. 144–173. Albany, NY: State University of New York Press.

———. In press a. Collisions with otherness: Multi-culturalism, the politics of difference, and the ethnographer as nomad. *American Journal of Semiotics*.

————. In press b. Border disputes: Multicultural narrative, critical pedagogy and identity formation in postmodern America. In *Naming silenced lives*, ed. J. McLaughlin and William Tierney. New York and London: Routledge.

————. 1995. *Critical Pedagogy and Predatory Culture*. London and New York: Routledge.

Mensh, E. and Mensh, H. 1991. *The IQ Mythology: Class, Race, Gender*. Carbondale, Illinois: Southern Illinois University Press.

Mercer, Kobena. 1990. Welcome to the jungle: Identity and diversity in postmodern politics. In Identify: *Community, culture, difference*, ed. Jonathan Rutherford, pp. 43–71. London: Lawrence and Wishart.

Mercer, Kobena. 1992. 1968: Periodizing politics and identity. In *Cultural studies*, ed. Lawrence Grossberg, Cary Nelson and Paula Treichler, pp. 424–449. London and New York: Routledge.

Mohanty, Chandra Talpade. 1989/90. On race and voice: Challenges for liberal education in the 1990s. *Cultural Critique* (Winter): 179–208.

————. 1991. Introduction: Cartographies of struggle: Third world women and the politics of feminism. In *Third world women and the politics of feminism*, ed. Chandra Talpade Mohanty, Ann Russo, and Lourdes Torres, pp. 1–47. Bloomington: Indiana University Press.

Muñoz, Carlos. 1989. *Youth, identity, power*. London and New York: Verso.

Murray, C. and Hernstein, R. 1994. *The Bell Curve: Intelligence and Class Structure in American Life*. New York: Free Press.

Naureckas, Jim. 1993. The Somalia intervention: Tragedy made simple. *Extra* 6(2): 10–13.

Nieto, Sonia. 1992. *Affirming diversity: The sociopolitical context of multicultural education*. White Plains, NY: Longman Publishers.

Norris, Christopher. 1990. *What's wrong with postmodernism?* Baltimore, Maryland: The John Hopkins University Press.

Observer 5(2), (March 1992).

Pieterse, Jan Nederveen. 1992. *White on black: Images of Africa and blacks in western popular culture.* New Haven and London: Yale University Press.

Rosaldo, Renato. 1989. *Culture and truth: The remaking of social analysis.* Boston: Beacon.

Rutherford, Jim. 1990. A place called home: Identity and the cultural politics of difference. In *Identity: Community, culture, difference,* ed. J. Rutherford, pp. 9–27. London: Lawrence and Wishart.

Schlesinger, Jr., Arthur M. 1991. *The disuniting of America: Reflections on a multicultural society.* Knoxville: Whittle Direct Books.

Scott, Joan W. 1992. Experience. In *Feminists theorize the political,* ed. Judith Butler and Joan W. Scott, pp. 22–40. New York and London: Routledge.

Simone, Timothy Maliqualim. 1989. *About face: Race in postmodern America.* Brooklyn, New York: Autonomedia.

Sleeter, Christine E. 1991. *Empowerment through multicultural education.* Albany, NY: State University of New York Press.

Stephanson, Anders. 1988. Interview with Cornel West. In *Universal abandon? The politics of postmodernism,* ed. Andrew Ross, pp. 269–286. Minneapolis: University of Minnesota Press.

Wallace, Michele. 1991. Multiculturalism and oppositionality. *Afterimage* (October): 6–9.

West, Cornel. 1990. The new cultural politics of difference. In *Out there: Marginalization and contemporary cultures,* ed. Russell Ferguson, et al., pp. 19–36. Cambridge, MA: MIT Press; New York: New Museum of Contemporary Art.

Willis, Paul. 1990. *Common culture*, Boulder, CO and San Francisco: Westview Press.

Young, Iris Marion. 1990. *Justice and the politics of difference*. Princeton: Princeton University Press.

Zavarzadeh, Mas'ud and Morton, Donald. 1990. Signs of knowledge in the contemporary academy. *American Journal of Semiotics* 7(4): 149–60.

2

DONALDO MACEDO

Literacy for Stupidification:
The Pedagogy of Big Lies*

> The great masses of people...will more easily fall
> victims to a big lie than to a small one.
>
> Adolf Hitler

Most Americans would cringe at the thought that they have repeatedly fallen victim to big lies by their government. In fact, they would probably instinctively point out that the manipulation of people through big lies would only occur in totalitarian, fascist governments such as Hitler's. Within the same breath, they might remind us that their ancestors gave their lives in the great wars so we could enjoy the freedom and democracy we now have. They might also hasten to recite our national slogans such as "live free or die," "freedom of speech," and "freedom of information," among others. While busily calling out slogans from their patriotic vocabulary memory warehouse, these same Americans dutifully vote, for example, for Ronald Reagan, giving him a landslide victory under a platform that promised to balance the budget, cut taxes, and increase military spending. This "unreason of reason" led George Bush to characterize Reagan's economic plan as voodoo economics—even though he himself later became entranced by the big lie of this same voodooism. What U.S. voters failed to do was to demand that Reagan tell the whole truth and nothing but the truth. In other words, they failed to require that Reagan acknowledge that, in order for his proposition to be true (and not a lie), the voters would have to give him and Bush a blank credit card with $4.3 trillion in deficit credit to create the false sense of economic prosperity enjoyed under their leadership. I say a false sense not only because of the present economic malaise but also because the Reagan economic boom was a bust. According to Samuel Bowles, David M. Gordon, and E. Thomas Weisskopf (1992):

71

output growth did not revive during the 1980's cycle. Far from
stimulating investment through massive tax cuts and conces-
sions to the wealthy, Reagan-Bush economic policy has dealt
investment a blow; compared with the previous business cycle,
the pace of real net productive investment declined by a quarter
during the most recent business cycle. (pp. 163–164)

Despite concrete evidence indicating that the Reagan-Bush
economic plan was a failure, U.S. voters swept Bush into office in
1988 with the same voodoo trickle-down economics, now ornamented with a thousand points of short-circuited lights. These
same voters ascended to Bush's morally high-minded call to apply
international laws against Saddam Hussein's tyranny and his
invasion of Kuwait. The great mass of voters who rallied behind
Bush, pushing his popular approval rating beyond 90 percent
during the Gulf War, failed to realize that these same international
laws had been broken by Bush a year or so before in Panama and
by his predecessor in Grenada, Libya, and Nicaragua. This
phenomenon begs us to question why we supposedly highly
literate and principled citizens of a great democracy frequently
demonstrate the inability to separate myth from reality. This
inability pushes us to perpetual flirtation with historical hypocrisy.
However, not all Americans suffer from the inability to separate
myths from reality and to read the world critically. For example,
David Spritzler, a 12-year-old student at Boston Latin School,
faced disciplinary action for his refusal to recite the Pledge of
Allegiance, which he considers "a hypocritical exhortation to patriotism" in that there is not "liberty and justice for all." According to
Spritzler, the Pledge is an attempt to unite the

> oppressed and the oppressors. You have people who drive nice
> cars, live in nice houses and don't have to worry about money.
> Then you have the poor people, living in bad neighborhoods and
> going to bad schools. Somehow the Pledge makes it seem that
> everybody's equal when that's not happening. There's no justice
> for everybody. (Ribadeneira 1991, p. 40)

Spritzler was spared disciplinary action only after the
American Civil Liberties Union wrote a letter on his behalf, citing a
1943 case, *West Virginia State Board of Education versus Barnett*,
in which the U.S. Supreme Court upheld a student's right not to
say the Pledge of Allegiance and to remain seated.

What remains incomprehensible is why a 12-year-old boy
could readily see through the obvious hypocrisy contained in the
Pledge of Allegiance while his teachers and administrators, who

have achieved much higher levels of education, cannot. As Noam Chomsky (1988) pointed out in reference to a similar situation, these teachers' and administrators' inability to see through the obvious represents "a real sign of deep indoctrination [in] that you can't understand elementary thoughts that any 10-year-old can understand. That's real indoctrination. So for him [the indoctrinated individual] it's kind of like a theological truth, a truth of received religion." (p. 681) These teachers and administrators should know that history shows us convincingly and factually that the United States has systematically violated the Pledge of Allegiance, from the legalization of slavery, the denial of women's rights, and the near genocide of Native Americans to the contemporary discriminatory practices against people who, by virtue of their race, ethnicity, class, or gender, are not treated with the dignity and respect called for in the Pledge. If we did not suffer from historical amnesia, we would easily recall that, once upon a time, the Massachusetts legislature promulgated a law that provided monetary rewards for dead Indians: "For every scalp of a male Indian brought in...forty pounds. For every scalp of such female Indian or male Indian under the age of twelve years that shall be killed...twenty pounds." (Cited in Zinn 1990, pp. 234–235) Even the abolitionist President Abraham Lincoln did not truly uphold the U.S. Declaration of Independence propositions of equality, life, liberty, and the pursuit of happiness, when he declared: "I will say, then, that I am not, nor ever have been in favor of bringing about in any way the social and political equality of the white and black races...I as much as any other man am in favor of having the superior position assigned to the white race." (Cited in Hofstadter 1974, p. 148)

One could argue that the above-cited incidents belong to the dusty archives of our early history, but I do not believe that we have learned a great deal from historically dangerous memories, insofar as our leaders continue to incite racial tensions, as evidenced in the Willie Horton presidential campaign issue or in Bush's opposition to job quotas on the pretext that it was a renewed invitation to racial divisiveness. This racial divisiveness actually has served the Republican Party's interest of splitting voters along class, racial, and ethnic lines. Our perpetual flirtation (if not marriage) with historical hypocrisy becomes abundantly clear if we imagine the juxtaposition of students reciting the Pledge of Allegiance in Charlestown High School in 1976 in classrooms ornamented with copies of the Declaration of Independence hanging alongside racial epithets scrawled on the walls: "Welcome

Niggers," "Niggers Suck," "White Power," "KKK," "Bus is for Zulu," and "Be illiterate, fight busing." (Lucas 1985, p. 281)

Our inability to see the obvious was never more evident than when a predominantly white jury found the four white policemen who brutally beat Rodney King not guilty. Even though the world was shocked beyond belief by the raw brutality and barbarism of the Los Angeles law enforcers, the jurors who saw concrete video shots of King struggling on his hands and knees while being hit repeatedly by the policemen's batons concluded that "Mr. King was controlling the whole show with his action" (*Boston Herald*, May 1, 1992, p. 2). The racist ideology of Simi Valley, California blinded these jurors such that they could readily accept that the savage beatings they had seen on the video were, as the defense attorneys claimed, nothing more than a mere "controlled application of fifty-six batons" in order to contain King, who had been portrayed as a dangerous "animal," like "gorillas in the mist" (Ibid., p. 2).

However, one of the jurors did not fully accept the view of reality suggested by the defense attorneys: "I fought so hard to hang on, and hang on to what I saw on the video....There was no way I could change the others. They couldn't see what I saw....[But] they could not take away from what my eyes saw: (Ibid., p. 2).

The real educational question and challenge for us is to understand why most of the jurors either could not see, or refused to see, what their eyes and the eyes of the entire world saw on television. Unfortunately in the present conjuncture of our educational system, particularly in our schools of education, it is very difficult to acquire the necessary critical tools that would unveil the ideology responsible for these jurors' blinders. A critical understanding of the savage beating of Rodney King and the subsequent acquittal of the four white police officers necessitates the deconstruction of the intricate interplay of race, ethics, and ideology—issues that schools of education, by and large, neglect to take on rigorously. Courses such as race relations, ethics, and ideology are almost absent from the teacher preparation curriculum. This serious omission is, by its very nature, ideological and constitutes the foundation for what I call the pedagogy of big lies.

At this juncture, I can easily frame my argument to demonstrate that many, if not all, of David Spritzler's teachers and administrators are either naive victims of a big lie or are cognizant of the deceptive ideological mechanisms inherent in the Pledge and consciously reproduce them, even if it means violating the very rights the oath proclaims. I argue that the latter is true. Even if we want to give such educators the benefit of the doubt, their naïveté is never innocent but ideological. It is ideological to the degree that they have invested in a system that rewards them for reproducing and not questioning dominant mechanisms designed to produce power asymmetries along the lines of race, gender, class, culture, and ethnicity. Those teachers who refuse such investments in the dominant ideological system usually think more critically, thus recognizing the falsehoods embedded in the various myths created by the dominant class. Critical teachers of this sort, instead of sending David to the principal's office, would seize the pedagogical moment to engage the entire class in a consciousness-raising exercise that would be both in line with the democratic ideals of the Pledge of Allegiance as well as with the development of critical thinking skills. For instance, the teacher could have given David the opportunity to have his voice heard as he discussed the enormous contradictions inherent in the Pledge of Allegiance. The teacher could also have engaged the other students by asking them if they agreed or disagreed with David's position. The teacher could have asked the following: "Do you agree that the Pledge is a hypocritical exhortation to patriotism'? Explain why." This question would enable other students to voice their opinions regarding their perception of the Pledge of Allegiance. Students could also be asked whether David was right in asserting that the Pledge of Allegiance is a mere attempt to unite the "oppressed and the oppressors" since "you have people who drive nice cars, live in nice houses and don't have to worry about money. Then you have the poor people, living in bad neighborhoods and going to bad schools." The teacher could continue to encourage an open dialogue by asking students if they knew people who were poor, "living in bad neighborhoods and going to bad schools." If many students were to confirm David's position, then the teacher could raise the following questions: "Why do you think that we have so many poor people living in bad neighborhoods? Do you think that poor people choose to live in bad neighborhoods? Who is responsible for the present inequality? Would you like to live in a bad neighborhood and go to a bad school? What would you do if you were forced to live in poverty and to go to a bad school?" I am sure that a multiplicity of responses would have been given by the students according to their own social class and race position, as well as their different levels of political awareness. This exercise could have provided great insights into the students' personal narratives. It would also help the students to understand that the Pledge of Allegiance cannot fulfill its ideals in light of the social disparities and inequalities in our society. This exercise would also have provided the students the opportunity to reflect on the meaning of the proposition "liberty and justice for all." This reflection could also have prepare these students to understand their civic responsibility and their role in a society that, while it promises "equality, liberty and justice for all," is replete with inequality and injustice for those groups of people who are from different racial, class, and ethnic backgrounds.

The above exercise is one of the many constructive and creative ways that a critical teacher could begin to problem-pose with the class as the students and the teacher collectively engage in a pedagogical process to deconstruct the myth sustained by the Pledge of Allegiance. However, in order to do so, the teacher not only has to be critical but he or she must also be willing to take great risks, including losing his or her job, since the doctrinal system does not reward dissent. This risk became obvious when Jonathan Kozol was fired from the Boston Public Schools in 1964 for having his all-black, segregated fourth grade class read Robert Frost and Langston Hughes. The reason for his dismissal is that he did not follow the curriculum. According to school officials, "Robert Frost and Langston Hughes were 'too advanced' for children of this age. Hughes, moreover, was regarded as 'inflammatory'" (Kozol 1991, p. 2). It did not matter that "one of the most embittered children in the class began to cry when she first heard the words of Langston Hughes"

> What happens to a dream deferred?
> Does it dry up
> like a raisin in the sun? (Ibid., p. 2)

It did not matter to the Boston School officials that this fourth grade girl was touched by the poem and went "home and memorized the lines." What mattered to Boston School officials in 1964 when they fired Jonathan Kozol and in 1992 when they attempted to expel David Spritzler for refusing to say the Pledge of Allegiance, was denying the fourth grade the opportunity to answer and understand "what happens to a dream deferred" and preventing David Spritzler from exposing the hypocrisy embedded in the Pledge of Allegiance. Boston School officials and educators of this sort have chosen to "live within a lie" so as to protect their privileged position and the rewards the doctrinal system provides them.

What I have described so far points to the intricate and complex web of lies that functions to reproduce the dominant ideology through cultural literacy. This will become clearer in my analysis of the role of literacy in cultural reproduction, in which I will show how collective experiences function in the interest of the dominant ruling elites, rather than in the interest of the oppressed groups that are the object of its policies.

Literacy for cultural reproduction uses institutional mechanisms to undermine independent thought, a prerequisite for the Orwellian "manufacture of consent" or "engineering of consent." In this light, schools are seen as ideological institutions designed to prevent the so-called crisis of democracy, another Orwellian concept, meaning the beginnings of democracy. (Chomsky 1988, p. 671)

In fact, this very perspective on schools was proposed by the Trilateral Commission, a group of international and essentially liberal elites, which included Jimmy Carter in its membership. This commission was created in response to the general democratic participation of masses of people in the Western world in questioning their governments' ethical behavior. Its major purpose, as many understand it, was to seek ways to maintain the Western capitalist cultural hegemony. The Trilateral Commission referred to schools as "institutions responsible for the indoctrination of the young" (Ibid.). Noam Chomsky states it simply: [the Trilateral Commission argues that schools should be institutions for indoctrination,] "for imposing obedience, for blocking the possibility of independent thought, and they play an institutional role in a system of control and coercion" (Ibid.). This becomes clear in the conservative call for the control of the so-called "excess of democracy." For example, according to Henry Giroux (1992), Boston University President John Silber, who prides himself on being an education "expert," "has urged fellow conservatives to abandon any civility toward scholars whose work is considered political" (p. 3). What Silber fails to realize is that the very act of viewing education as neutral and devoid of politics is, in fact, a political act. In order to maintain schools as sites for cultural reproduction and indoctrination, Silber prefers an educational system that brooks no debate or dissent. This is apparent in his urging of "his fellow conservatives to name names, to discredit educators who have chosen to engage in forms of social criticism (work that the New Right considers political) at odds with the agenda of the New Right's mythic conception of the university as a warehouse built on the pillars of an unproblematic and revered tradition" (Ibid.).

Although it is important to analyze how ideologies inform various literacy traditions, in this chapter I limit my discussion to a brief analysis of the instrumentalist approach to literacy and its linkage to cultural reproduction. I also argue that the instrumentalist approach to literacy does not refer only to the goal of producing readers who meet the basic requirements of contemporary society but also includes the highest level of literacy found in disciplinary specialism and hyperspecialization.

Finally, I analyze how the instrumentalist approach to literacy, even at the highest level of specialism, functions to domesticate the consciousness via a constant disarticulation between the narrow reductionistic reading of one's field of specialization and the reading of the universe within which one's specialism is situated. This inability to link the reading of the word with the world, if not combated, will further exacerbate already feeble democratic institutions and the unjust, asymmetrical power relations that characterize the hypocritical nature of contemporary democracies. The inherent hypocrisy in the actual use of the term "democracy" is eloquently captured by Noam Chomsky (1987) in his analysis of the United States. Chomsky writes:

> "Democracy" in the United States rhetoric refers to a system of governance in which elite elements based in the business community control the state by virtue of their dominance of the private society, while the population observes quietly. So understood, democracy is a system of elite decision and public ratification, as in the United States itself. Correspondingly, popular involvement in the formation of public policy is considered a serious threat. It is not a step towards democracy; rather, it constitutes a "crisis of democracy" that must be overcome. (p. 6)

INSTRUMENTALIST APPROACH TO LITERACY

Both the instrumental literacy for the poor, in the form of a competency-based skills banking approach, and the highest form of instrumental literacy for the rich, acquired through the university in the form of professional specialization, share one common feature: they both prevent the development of the critical thinking that enables one to "read the world" critically and to understand the reasons and linkages behind the facts.

Literacy for the poor is, by and large, characterized by mindless, meaningless drills and exercises given "in preparation for multiple choice exams and writing gobbledygook in imitation of the psycho-babble that surrounds them" (Courts 1991, p. 4). This instrumental approach to literacy sets the stage for the anesthetization of the mind, as poet John Ashbery eloquently captures in "What is Poetry":

In School
All the thoughts got combed out:
What was left was like a field. (Ibid., p. 46)

The educational "comb," for those teachers who have blindly accepted the status quo, is embodied in the ditto sheets and workbooks that mark and control the pace of routinization in the drill-and-practice assembly line. Patrick Courts correctly describes the function of these workbooks and ditto-sheets:

> Either you must fill in the blank (or does the blank fill you in?—they have lots of blanks) or you must identify the correct or incorrect answer by circling it, underlining it, or drawing an X through it. In addition to all this, students will find that learning to spell involves copying the same word five times and copying the definition; and learning the meaning of the word involves looking it up in the dictionary and copying the definition; and learning to write involves writing a sentence or two using the word they copied five times and looked up in the dictionary. Much of what they read in the first four or five grades, they will read-to-read: That is, they will be practicing reading in order to show that they can read, which much of the time means that they will be involved in "word-perfect" oral-reading activities, grouped as Cardinals (if they are good at it), or Bluebirds (if they are not). They will learn that reading has one of two functions: Either you read orally to show that you can "bark at print" well (delighting your teachers and boring your peers), or you read silently in order to fill in those blanks in the workbook. (Ibid., p. 48)

One would hope the students grouped as Cardinals, who survived reading-and-writing drill boot camp to become fully literate, were empowered with some sort of ability for independent critical analysis and thought. Unfortunately, these Cardinals continue in their literacy practices to experience the same fragmentation of knowledge, albeit with more sophistication. The fragmentation of knowledge via specialization produces an intellectual mechanization that, in the end, serves the same function as the fragmentation of skills in the literacy for the poor. It is not a coincidence that the defense lawyers for the white policemen in the Rodney King trial insisted on showing the jurors the video frame by frame over and over again, instead of running the video at the normal speed. The fragmentation of the Rodney King beating served two important functions: (1) by showing each frame separately, the jurors were not allowed to see and experience the total impact of the violence incurred in the beatings, and (2) by repeating the frames over and over again, the defense lawyers were able to anesthetize the sensibilities of the jurors and routinize the action captured in each frame. Although the fragmentation of skills and bodies of knowledge is not the same as the fragmentation of the video into separate frames, the underlying principle serves the same function: it creates, on the one hand, the inability to make linkages, and, on the other hand, it deadens the senses. This process leads to a de facto social construction of not seeing. My colleague Robert Greene (personal communication fall 1992) noted that this once again proves the old proverb that the eyes do not see; they only record while the mind sees. To the extent that the mind can be ideologically controlled, it filters in order to transform what the eyes record, as was the case in the transformation of Rodney King's brutal beating to a "systematic application of fifty-six batons." However, an African American colleague, Pancho Savery, correctly pointed out to me (personal communication, Fall 1992) that the defense attorney's manipulative mechanisms to prevent linkages and to deaden the jurors' senses could only work if jurors were already invested in the doctrinal system that imposed a willful blindness to realities that contradicted or questioned the system. In other words, the success of the ideological manipulation depends on the degree to which one invests in the doctrinal system and expects rewards from it. Savery argues that the fragmentization of the video frames and the playing of them over and over again would not deaden the senses of most African Americans. On the contrary, the more they would see the video of King's beating, even in fragmented frames, the more enraged they would become, as they are not invested in the racist doctrinal system of which they are the victims.

For some, the instrumentalist approach to literacy may have the appeal of producing readers who are capable of meeting the demands of our ever more complex technological society. However, such an approach emphasizes the mechanical learning of reading skills while sacrificing the critical analysis of the social and political order that generates the need for reading in the first place. Seldom do teachers require students to analyze the social and political structures that inform their realities. Rarely do students read about the racist and discriminatory practices that they face in school and the community at large. The instrumentalist approach has led to the development of "functional literates," groomed primarily to meet the requirements of our contemporary society. The instrumentalist view also champions literacy as a vehicle for economic betterment, access to jobs, and an increase in the productivity level. As it is clearly stated by UNESCO, "Literacy programs should preferably be linked with economic priorities. [They] must impart not only reading and writing but also professional and technical knowledge, thereby leading to a fuller participation of adults in economic life."

This notion of literacy has been enthusiastically incorporated as a major goal by the back-to-basics proponents of reading. It has also contributed to the development of neatly packaged reading programs that are presented as the solution to difficulties students experience in reading job application forms, tax forms, advertisement literature, sales catalogs, product labels, and the like. In general, the instrumentalist approach views literacy as meeting the basic reading demand of an industrialized society. As Henry Giroux (1983) points out:

> Literacy within this perspective is geared to make adults more productive workers and citizens within a given society. In spite of its appeal to economic mobility, functional literacy reduces the concept of literacy and the pedagogy in which it is suited to the pragmatic requirements of capital; consequently, the notions of critical thinking, culture and power disappear under the imperatives of the labor process and the need of capital accumulation. (p. 87)

A society that reduces the priorities of reading to the pragmatic requirements of capital necessarily has to create educational structures that anesthetize students' critical abilities, so as to "domesticate social order for its self-preservation" (Freire 1985, p. 116). Accordingly, it must create educational structures that involve "practices by which one strives to domesticate consciousness, transforming it into an empty receptacle. Education in cultural action for domination is reduced to a situation in which the educator as 'the one who knows' transfers existing knowledge to the learner as 'the one who does not know'" (Ibid., p. 114)

Paulo Freire's concept of banking refers to this treatment of students as empty vessels to be filled with predetermined bodies of knowledge, which are often disconnected from students' social realities. This type of education for domestication, which borders on stupidification, provides no pedagogical space for critical students like David Spritzler, who question the received knowledge and want to know the reasons behind the facts. His defiance of the rigid bureaucracy, his refusal to surrender his civil rights, are rewarded by a threat of disciplinary action. In other words, according to Freire, the real rewards go to the "so-called good student who repeats, who renounces critical thinking, who adjusts to models,...[who] should do nothing other than receive contents that are impregnated with the ideological character vital to the interests of the sacred order" (Ibid., p. 117). A good student is the one who piously recites the fossilized slogans contained in the Pledge of Allegiance. A good student is the one who willfully and unreflectively accepts big lies, as described in Tom Paxton's song:

> What did you learn in school today, dear little boy of mine?
> What did you learn in school today, dear little boy of mine?
> I learned that Washington never told a lie,
> I learned that soldiers seldom die,
> I learned that everybody's free,
> And that's what the teacher said to me.
> That's what I learned in school today,
> That's what I learned in school.
> I learned that policemen are my friends,
> learned that justice never ends,
> I learned that murderers die for their crimes
> Even if we make a mistake sometimes.
> I learned our government must be strong,
> It's always right and never wrong
> Our leaders are the finest men
> And we elect them again and again.
> I learned that war is not so bad.
> I learned about the great ones we have had.
> We've fought in Germany and in France,
> And someday I may get my chance.
> That's what I learned in school today
> That's what I learned in school. (Ibid., p. 117)

THE BARBARISM OF SPECIALIZATION OR THE SPECIALIZATION OF BARBARISM

Long before the explosion of hyper specialization and the tragedies of the Holocaust and Hiroshima, Spanish philosopher José Ortega y Gasset cautioned us against the demand for specialization so that science could progress. According to Ortega y Gasset, "The specialist 'knows' very well his own tiny corner of the universe; he is radically ignorant of all the rest" (Ortega y Gasset 1964, p. 111). I am reminded of a former classmate of mine, whom I met while doing research work at MIT. When she learned that I was working with pidgin and creole languages, she curiously asked me, "What's a pidgin language?" At first I thought she was joking, but soon I realized that her question was in fact genuine. Here we had a perfect case of a technician of linguistics doing the highest level theory available in the field without any clue about historical linguistics. It is not difficult to find other examples of such limited specialization in that, more and more, specialists dominate institutions of learning and other institutional structures of our society. The social organization of knowledge, via rigidly defined disciplinary boundaries, further contributes to the formation of the specialist class, i.e., engineers, doctors, professors, and so on. This sort of specialist is

> only acquainted with one science, and even of that one only knows the small corner in which he is an active investigator. He even proclaims it as a virtue that he takes no cognizance of what lies outside the narrow territory specially cultivated by himself, and gives the name 'dilettantism' to any curiosity for the general scheme of knowledge. (Ibid., p. 111)

This so-called "dilettantism" is discouraged through the mythical need to discover absolute objective truth. I remember vividly when I gave my linguist friend at MIT articles on pidgins and creoles to read. I later questioned her as to whether she had found the readings interesting and informative. Half apologizing but with a certain pride in her voice, she told me: "If I want to be a great theoretical linguist, I just can't be reading too much outside theoretical linguistics. I can't even keep up with all the reading in syntax alone." Obviously there are exceptions to this attitude, Noam Chomsky, bell hooks, Howard Zinn, Gayatri Spivak, and Henry Giroux being prime examples. However, it is quite frequent in specialization to divorce science from the general culture within which it exists.

Not only does specialization represent a rupture with philosophies of social and cultural relations, but it also hides behind an ideology that creates and sustains false dichotomies rigidly delineated by disciplinary boundaries. This ideology also informs the view that "hard science," "objectivity," and "scientific rigor" must be divorced from the messy data of "soft science," and from the social and political practices that generate these categories in the first place. For example, those linguists and psycholinguists who "believe that what they study has little to do with social values or politics in any sense" (Gee 1992, p. vii) fail to realize that their research results are "the product of a particular model of social structures that gear the theoretical concepts to the pragmatics of the society that devised...the model to begin with" (Fowler et al. 1979, p. 192). That is, if the results are presented as facts determined by a particular ideological framework, "these facts cannot in themselves get us beyond that framework" (Myers 1986, 48:111).

Too often, the positivistic overemphasis on "hard science" and "absolute objectivity" has given rise to a form of "scientism" rather than science. By "scientism" I refer to the mechanization of the intellectual work cultivated by specialists, which often leads to the fragmentation of knowledge, as accurately understood by Ortega y Gasset: "A fair amount of things that have to be done in physics or in biology is mechanical work of the mind which can be done by anyone, or almost anyone...to divide science into small sections, to enclose oneself in one of these, and leave out all consideration of the rest" (Ortega y Gasset 1964, p. 111). Specialists of this sort have often contributed to a further fragmentation of knowledge due to their reductionistic view of the act of knowing. They have repeatedly ignored that their very claim of objectivity is, in fact, an ideological act. Objectivity always contains within it a dimension of subjectivity; thus, it is dialectical.

Almost without exception, traditional approaches to literacy do not escape the fragmentation of knowledge and are deeply ingrained in a positivistic method of inquiry. In effect, this approach has resulted in an epistemological stance in which scientific rigor and methodological refinement are celebrated, while "theory and knowledge are subordinated to the imperatives of efficiency and technical mastery, and history is reduced to a minor footnote in the priorities of 'empirical' scientific inquiry" (Giroux 1983, p. 87). In general, this approach abstracts methodological issues from their ideological contexts and consequently ignores the interrelationship between the sociopolitical structures of a society and the act of reading and learning. In part, the exclusion of social, cultural, and political dimensions from literacy practices gives rise to an ideology of cultural reproduction that produces semiliterates. My linguist friend at MIT, who reads only the theoretical work in syntax and dismisses relevant literature that links linguistics to the social and historical context, serves as a prime example of the highest level of instrumental literacy. In other words, at the lowest level of instrumental literacy, a semiliterate reads the word but is unable to read the world. At the highest level of instrumental literacy achieved via specialization, the semiliterate is able to read the text of his or her specialization but is ignorant of all other bodies of knowledge that constitute the world of knowledge. This semiliterate specialist was characterized by Ortega y Gasset (1964) as a "learned ignoramus." That is to say, "he is not learned, for he is formally ignorant of all that does not enter into his speciality; but neither is he ignorant, because he is a 'scientist' and 'knows' very well his own tiny portion of the universe" (p. 112).

Because the "learned ignoramus" is mainly concerned with his or her tiny portion of the world disconnected from other bodies of knowledge, he or she is never able to relate the flux of information so as to gain a critical reading of the world. A critical reading of the world implies, according to Freire (1985), "a dynamic comprehension between the least coherent sensibility of the world and a more coherent understanding of the world" (p. 131). This implies, for example, that medical specialists in the United States, who have contributed to a great technological advancement in medicine, should have the ability to understand and appreciate why over thirty million Americans do not have access to this medical technology and why we still have the highest infant mortality rate of the developed nations. (The United States in 1989 ranked 24th in child mortality rate as compared to other nations.) (*Boston Globe* article February 7, 1992, p. 8)

The inability to make linkages between bodies of knowledge and the social and political realities that generate them is predominant even among those who recognize that a coherent comprehension of the world cannot be achieved through fragmentation of knowledge. For example, at a recent professional meeting, a concerned environmental scientist decried the absence of critical perspectives in his field of study. He eloquently called for an interdisciplinary approach to world environmental problems, particularly within the developing countries. His present research is linked with environmental concerns in Mexico. With a certain amount of pride he emphasized that his research breakthrough could be used as a commodity in Mexico, since that country is becoming more and more rigorous with respect to environmental laws. He failed, however, to ask a fundamental question: How can the U.S. package environmental technology for Mexico while we are establishing factories there that pollute the country because they can operate with less government regulation? This environmentalist was baffled that such a question should even be raised.

Although specialization may lead to a high level of literacy acquisition in a particular subfield of knowledge, it often produces a disarticulation of this same knowledge by dislodging it from a critical and coherent comprehension of the world that informs and sustains it. This disarticulation of knowledge anesthetizes consciousness, without which one can never develop clarity of reality. As suggested by Frei Betto, clarity of reality requires that a person transcend "the perception of life as a pure biological process to arrive at a perception of life as a biographical, and collective process." (Freire and Macedo 1987, p. 130) Betto views his concept

as "a clothesline of information." In other words, "on the clothesline we may have a flux of information and yet remain unable to
link one piece of information with another. A politicized person is
one who can sort out the different and often fragmented pieces
contained in the flux" (Ibid., p. 130). The apprehension of clarity of
reality requires a high level of political clarity, which can be
achieved by sifting through the flux of information and relating
each piece so as to gain a global comprehension of the facts and
their raison d'être.

We can now see the reasons why David Spritzler's teachers and
administrators, who had attained a higher level of literacy through
a banking model of transference of knowledge, could not relate
each piece of this knowledge to separate the mythical dimension of
the Pledge of Allegiance from factual reality. Part of the reason lies
in the fact that the teachers, who, like most specialists, have
accepted the dominant ideology, are technicians who, by virtue of
the specialized training they receive in an assembly line of ideas
and aided by the mystification of this transferred knowledge,
seldom reach the critical capacity of analysis to develop a coherent
comprehension of the world. In reality, there is little difference
between the pedagogy for school children described in Tom
Paxton's song and the prevalent pedagogy in universities as
described by Freire:

> Today at the university we learned that objectivity in science
> requires neutrality on the part of the scientist; we learned today
> that knowledge is pure, universal, and unconditional and that the
> university is the site of this knowledge. We learned today, although
> only tacitly, that the world is divided between those who know and
> those who don't (that is, those who do manual work) and the
> university is the home of the former. We learned today that the
> university is a temple of pure knowledge and that it has to soar
> above earthly preoccupations, such as mankind's liberation.
>
> We learned today that reality is a given, that it is our scientific
> impartiality that allows us to describe it somewhat as it is. Since
> we have described it as it is, we don't have to investigate the
> principal reasons that would explain it as it is. But if we should
> try to denounce the real world as it is by proclaiming a new way
> of living, we learned at the university today that we would no
> longer be scientists, but ideologues.
>
> We learned today that economic development is a purely tech-
> nical problem, that the underdeveloped peoples are incapable
> (sometimes because of their mixed blood, their nature, or climatic
> reasons).

We were informed that blacks learn less than whites because
they are genetically inferior. (Freire 1985, p. 118)

In short, this type of educational training makes it possible for
us to rally behind our political leaders who ritualistically call for
the protection of human rights all over the world without recognizing these same leaders' complicity in the denial of rights of
human beings who live under dictatorships that we support either
overtly or covertly. The selective selection of our strong support for
human rights becomes glaringly clear in the case of Haitians. In
fact, the *Boston Globe*, confident of readers' inability to link historical events, published a front page article on the U.S. Supreme
Court decision that allowed the administration to repatriate thousands of Haitian refugees. On page two of the same issue, the
Boston Globe also ran a story about groups organized in Miami to
search for and assist Cuban boat people in reaching their final
destination in Florida. (Wilson 1992, pp. 2–3, Boyd 1992, p. 2)

Although U.S. foreign policy is so glaringly contradictory, most
Americans are unable or unwilling to see it. For example, on the one
hand the U.S. has had a macho-man policy of nonnegotiation with
Cuba, Nicaragua under the Sandinistas, and Libya. On the other
hand, the U.S. has engaged in endless negotiations with the Haitian
military. According to Derrick Z. Jackson (1993), the U.S. vacil-
lating policy toward Haiti was evident when a U.S. naval vessel
carrying military engineers was not able to dock at Port-au-Prince.
However, the same naval force was fully equipped and ready to
intercept and send back any Haitian refugees it encountered in the
open sea. (p. 19) We now have learned from Robert Torricelli, a
Democrat Congressman from New Jersey, who is a member of the
House Intelligence and Foreign Affairs Committee, that since the
mid-nineteen-eighties until the overthrow of the democratically-
elected Aristide, the Central Intelligence Agency made payments to
Aristide's top military opponents. Derrick Z. Jackson reports that
the democrat Torricelli defended the payments as if they were
scholarships sponsored by the Cub Scouts.

> The U.S. government develops relationships with ambitious and
> bright young men at the beginning of their careers and often
> follows them through their public service...[it] should not
> surprise anyone that these include people in sensitive positions
> in current situations in Haiti. (Chomsky 1991, p. 8)

Sensitive positions in the official discourse is an euphemism
for death squads directed by Port-au-Prince chief of police Michel
François and Raoul Cedras, whose leadership is responsible for

over three thousand deaths during a period of two years since the coup. The callous U.S. insensitivity toward human misery and in overlooking massacres when it is convenient to its policies led Derrick Z. Jackson (1993) of *The Boston Globe* to conclude that

> [it] should not surprise anyone why the United States developed relationships with ambitious and bright young men whose idea of 'public service' was the overthrow of democracy. The United States was never comfortable with Aristide, Haiti's first democratically elected leader. (p. 19)

While the United States is most comfortable with brutal totalitarian leaders like the Duvaliers and the El Salvador military leaders with records of outlandish massacres, it is often very uncomfortable with any democratic movement whose major purpose is the institutionalization of a democratic vision that emphasizes agrarian reform, education, less military spending and more spending on social programs such as health care and social security. Contrary to the U.S. proselytizing about democracy in the Third World, a closer analysis of its foreign policy reveals a sad truth: the U.S. fatal attraction to undemocratic and cruel military dictatorships.

It is this lack of connectedness that helped Bush to prevail in erasing our historical memory file of foreign policy in order to garner support for his fabricated high-tech war in the Gulf. In what follows, I use the Gulf War as an example of how questions of literacy and ideology can be used to separate events from their historical contexts. This fragmentation serves to create a self-serving history that feeds the recontextualization of a distorted and often false reality, leading (sometimes) to a specialization of barbarism ipso facto. In other words, the high-tech management of the Gulf War celebrated technical wizardry while it dehumanized the ten of thousands of people who were victims of specialized technical prowess.

THE ILLITERACY OF LITERACY OF THE GULF WAR

It is not a coincidence that during the Gulf War we were saturated with information around the clock in the comfort of our homes, and yet we remained poorly informed. It is also not a coincidence that George Bush categorically and arrogantly stated there will be "no linkage" in any possible diplomatic settlements in the Gulf crisis. Bush's insistence on "no linkage" served to eclipse historicity so as to further add to a total social amnesia. How else could we explain that a highly developed society that prides itself on its freedom of information and high democratic values could ignore the clarity of the obvious? I say the "clarity of the obvious" because it is a well-known fact that the Reagan-Bush decade was characterized by a total disdain for the United Nations. The Reagan-Bush administration stopped paying the U.S. membership contribution to the United Nations and threatened to withdraw from the world body because the rest of the world was not, in their view, subservient enough to U.S. interests. And yet, during the Gulf crisis, the same George Bush found it convenient to hail the United Nations as the theater where "civilized" nations uphold international laws and high principles. If it had not been for the denial of linkage and the social amnesia, we could have easily referred to Daniel Patrick Moynihan's role as the ambassador to the United Nations. In his memoir, *A Dangerous Place*, Moynihan discusses the invasion of East Timor by Indonesia and sheds light on his role as the U.S. ambassador to the United Nations: "The U.S. government wanted the United Nations to be rendered ineffective in any measures that it undertook. I was given this responsibility and I filled it with no inconsiderable success" (Chomsky 1991, p. 8). Moynihan later recounts his success when he states that "within two months, reports indicated that Indonesia had killed about 60,000 people. That is roughly the proportion of the population that the Nazis had killed in Eastern Europe through World War II" (Ibid.). By not linking these historical events, the Bush administration was able to claim a moral high ground in the defense of international laws and the sanctity of national borders during the Gulf crisis.

The United States' defense of high principles and international laws that led to the Gulf War could only have moral currency if we were to obliterate our memory of recent history. Before proceeding, let me make it clear that Saddam Hussein's invasion of Kuwait was brutal, cruel and unforgivable. The violation of international laws and borders by other nations, including the United States, is no small matter. According to Noam Chomsky, the irony of the United States' opposition to such violation and defense of high principles can be summed up as follows:

- The U.S. invasion of Grenada.

- The U.S. invasion of Panama, where the United States installed a puppet regime of its choice with U.S. military advisors running it at every level.

- The U.S. mining of the Nicaraguan harbor. The World Court found the United States guilty and the U.S. reaction was to arrogantly dismiss the World Court.

- The Turkish invasion and virtual annexation of northern Cyprus that killed several hundred people and drove out thousands more. The United States was in favor of the action.

- The Moroccan invasion of the western Sahara, also supported by the United States.

- The Israeli invasion of Lebanon, where the United States vetoed a whole series of resolutions in the Security Council, which was trying to terminate the aggression. In human terms, at least 20,000 were killed, mostly civilians.

- The Indonesian invasion of East Timor in which 60,000 people were massacred. The Carter administration provided 90 percent of the armaments to the invaders. (Ibid.)

Against this landscape of violation of international laws and aggression perpetrated by the United States or by other countries with U.S. support how can we explain the ease with which Bush convinced a supposedly highly literate and civilized citizenry that Saddam Hussein's invasion of Kuwait was an isolated case of aggression against a weaker nation and had nothing to do with the historical record? The inability to link and treat the "clothesline" of the Gulf War had to do with ideological obstacles that too often obfuscate political clarity. We need to develop a more critical literacy along Freirian lines where, "as knowing subjects (sometimes of existing knowledge, sometimes of objects to be produced), our relation to knowable objects cannot be reduced to the objects themselves. We need to reach a level of comprehension of the complex whole of relations among objects" (Freire and Macedo 1987, p. 131). In his book *The Social Mind*, Jim Gee (1992) elegantly demonstrates that "to explicate the 'internal working' of the 'machine', and not the uses to which the machine is put in the world of value conflicts and political action," is to treat each piece of the "clothesline" separately so as to never allow us to reach a level of comprehension of the complex whole of relations among objects. (p. xv) This functions as a form of illiteracy of literacy, in which we develop a high level of literacy in a given discourse while remaining semiliterate or illiterate in a whole range of other discourses that constitute the ideological world in which we travel as thinking beings.

In an era in which we are more and more controlled by ever increasing technological wizardry—ephemeral sound bites, metaphorical manipulations of language, and prepackaged ideas void of substance—it becomes that much more urgent to adhere to Gee's posture that we acquire literacies rather than literacy. Given our tendency as humans to construct "satisfying and often self-deceptive 'stories,' stories that often advantage themselves and their groups," the development of a critical comprehension between the meaning of words and a more coherent understanding of the meaning of the world is a prerequisite to achieving clarity of reality. As Freire has suggested, it is only "through political practice [that] the less coherent sensibility of the world begins to be surpassed and more rigorous intellectual pursuits give rise to a more coherent comprehension of the world" (Freire and Macedo 1987, p. 132). Thus, in order to go beyond a mere word-level reading of reality, we must develop a critical comprehension of psychological entities such as "memories, beliefs, values, meanings, and so forth...which are actually out in the social world of action and interaction" (Ibid.). We must first read the world—the cultural, social, and political practices that constitute it—before we can make sense of the word-level description of reality.

The reading of the world must precede the reading of the word. That is to say, to access the true and total meaning of an entity, we must resort to the cultural practices that mediate our access to the world's semantic field and its interaction with the word's semantic features. Since meaning is, at best, very leaky, we have to depend on the cultural models that contain the necessary cultural features responsible for "our stories," and "often self-deceptive stories" (Gee 1992, p. xi). Let's look at the Gulf War again to exemplify how the role of cultural practices not only shapes but also determines metaphorical manipulations of language which are facilitated by the electronically controlled images and mes-sages through "the strategic use of doublespeak to disguise from television viewers the extent of the real terror and carnage of the military campaign against Iraq" (McLaren and Hammer 1992, p. 51). According to William Lutz (1989), doublespeak "is a language that avoids or shifts responsibility, language that is at variance with its real or purported meaning. It is a language that conceals or prevents thought; rather than extending thought, doublespeak limits it" (p. 1).

The Gulf War coverage represented the production of doublespeak par excellence. The success to which the media and the government used euphemisms to misinform and deceive can be seen in the transformation of the horrible carnage of the battlefield into a "theater of operation," where the U.S. citizenry became willfully mesmerized by the near-precision zapping of "smart bombs" during the aseptic "surgical strikes." The "theater of operation" positioned viewers to see "human beings become insentient things while weapons become the living actors of war. 'Smart' weapons that have eyes and computer 'brains' make decisions when and where to drop seven and a half tons of bombs, taking away the moral responsibility of the combatants themselves" (McLaren and Hammer 1992, p. 51).

The effective outcome of the doublespeak during the Gulf War was not only to give primacy to sophisticated weaponry with its newly acquired human attributes; it also functioned as a means to dehumanize human beings by removing them from center stage. The preoccupation of reporters and so-called "experts" was to narrate zealously the "accuracy" of the "smart bombs" while showing over and over again Star-Wars-like images of "surgical strikes." What these reporters did not show was that 92.6 percent of the bombs dropped were not "precision guided ordinances," which amounted to roughly 82,000 tons. Even the 7.4 percent of "smart bombs" dropped during the war had a widely varied reliability rate of between 20 percent and 90 percent. (Walker and Stambler 1991, p. 15) However, it would be considered unpatriotic and un-American to question the Pentagon-controlled deceit of the U.S. public. Even after the Gulf War was all but faded in our national consciousness, the Pentagon ordered Theodore Postal, an MIT professor and leading critic of the Patriot missile, "to cease all public discussion of his critique or face disciplinary action" (*Boston Globe*, March 18, 1992, p. 3). The Pentagon's gag order was summarized by Postal himself: "The Army and Raytheon are now using DIS [Defense Investigation Service] which appears to be more than an unwitting partner to suppress my speech on the subject of Patriot performance in the Gulf" (Ibid.). So much for independent thought, critical thinking, and freedom of speech. What the U.S. citizenry was less concerned with was the terror of war and the horrible carnage caused by the 82,000 tons of "delivered packages" that ended up as de facto carpet bombings. But then, the U.S. television viewers and newspaper readers had already been positioned in a "theater of operation" context as passive observers seduced and fascinated by the wizardry of exciting precision-guided missiles. The "theater" "overfloweth with computer graphics, night-vision lenses, cruise missiles and, best ever, the replay of the impact of laser guided bombs" (*Boston Globe*, January 20, 1991, p. 74). Missing from the "theater" center stage were the horrified human faces of tens of thousands of Iraqis, including women and children, who were decimated by the unparalleled bombing "sorties." The U.S. public's feelings were steered away from the reality of over 100,000 Iraqi casualties to the degree that the electronic management of the Gulf War vulgarly reduced human suffering and casualties to mere "collateral damage."

In "Media Knowledges, Warrior Citizenry, and the Postmodern Literacies," Peter McLaren and Rhonda hammer accurately characterize the Gulf War as "a gaudy sideshow of flags, emblems, and military hardware—a counterfeit democracy produced through media knowledge able to effectively harness the affective currency of popular culture such that the average American's investment in being 'American' reached an unparalleled high which has not been approximated since the years surrounding the post World War II McCarthy hearings." This unparalleled patriotism was cemented by the signifier yellow ribbon that functioned effectively to suffocate any truly democratic dialogue. The yellow ribbon ideologically structured the Gulf War debate so as to brook no dissent or dialogue. Criticizing the Bush administration's policies was viewed as not supporting the troops. In fact, the yellow ribbon did more to ideologically cage the American mind than all the speeches given by politicians. One could easily argue that the yellow ribbon patriotically tied American minds by making them sufficiently complacent so as to comply with the manufacture of consent for a fabricated war.

The complexity of networks of relations in our present telecratic society is making our sensibilities of the world increasingly less coherent—leading to a real crisis of democracy, to the extent that the present "propaganda approach to media coverage based on serviceability to important domestic interests. This should be observable in dichotomized choices of story and in the volume and quality of coverage." This political dichotomization became flagrantly obvious when, on the one hand, George Bush, in a John Waynean style, rallied "civilized" nations to uphold high moral principles against aggression when Saddam Hussein invaded Kuwait. On the other hand, Bush sheepishly watched and allowed thousands of Kurds, whom he had incited to revolt, to be exterminated by the same forces of aggression. So much for high moral principles. What is at stake here is our ability as democratic citizens and thinking beings to see through the obvious contradictions and discern myth from reality. However, our level of critical consciousness is being rapidly eroded to the degree that "today's cultural and historical events bombard our sensibilities with such exponential speed and frequency, and through a variety of media forms, that our critical comprehension skills have fallen into rapid deterioration." The deterioration of Americans' critical comprehension of the world became self-evident when they readily rallied behind the "Pentagon's vacuous military briefings, lists of aircraft types, missions, and losses [that] have become the sterilized equivalent of body counts recited in Saigon. Far more important elements—human and political—are being lost" (*Boston Globe*, January 20, 1991, p. 74). It is indeed a sad statement about the inability of the U.S. citizenry to make the necessary historical linkages so as to develop a rigorous comprehension of the world when, with the exception of a small minority, only Vice President Dan Quayle was able to read the Gulf War correctly by describing it as "a stirring victory for the forces of aggression" (*Boston Globe*, April 12, 1991, p. 15). President Bush became entrapped in a similar Freudian slip during an interview with Boston's Channel 5 TV news anchor, Natalie Jacobson. Referring to the Gulf War, Bush said, "We did fulfill our aggression," instead of the no doubt intended, "we did fulfill our mission" (Jacobson interview, January 16, 1992).

The seemingly misspoken words by both Bush and Quayle denude the pedagogy of big lies to the extent that their statements more accurately capture the essence of Ortega y Gasset's (1964) proposition that civilization, if "abandoned to its own devices" and put at the mercy of specialists, would bring about the rebirth of primitivism and barbarism. (p. 130) In many instances, the attainment of a high level of technical sophistication has been used in the most barbaric ways, as evidenced in the gassing of the Jews and the bombing of Hiroshima. It is certainly not an illuminated civilization that prides itself in reducing Iraq to a preindustrial age—killing tens of thousands of innocent victims, including women and children, while leaving Saddam Hussein, our chief reason for war, in power and with an unreduced capacity to perpetuate genocide against his own people. Ask the Africans who endured the chains of slavery, the Indians who were victims of a quasi-genocide, the Jews who perished in the Holocaust, or the Japanese who experienced first hand the destructive power of science to measure our so-called advanced Western civilization. If conservative academicians apply the same rigorous objective standards of science, intellectual honesty, and academic truth in their inquiry, their response would have to be unequivocally primitive and barbaric. Ortega y Gasset could not have been more insightful on this issue:

> It may be regrettable that human nature tends on occasion to this form of violence, but it is undeniable that it implies the great tribute to reason and justice. For this form of violence is none other than reason exasperated. Force was, in fact, the "ultima ratio." Rather stupidly it has been the custom to take ironically this expression, to methods of reason. Civilization is nothing else than the attempt to reduce force to being the "ultima ratio." We are now beginning to realize this with startling clearness, because "direct action" consists in inventing the order and proclaiming violence as "prima ratio," or strictly as "unica ratio." It is the norm which proposes the annulment of all norms, which suppresses all intermediate process between our purpose and it execution. It is the Magna Carta of barbarism. (Ibid.)

Ortega y Gasset's profound thoughts enable us to deconstruct Bush's policy of violence parading under the veil of reason and justice. In fact, Bush successfully made force not only the "ultima ratio," but also the "unica ratio." His total disregard for a multitude of proposals to negotiate a settlement in the gulf characterized the "norm which proposes the annulment of all norms, which suppresses all intermediate process between our purpose and its execution" (Ibid.). Flip-flopping from a defensive stance to the protection of our oil and the invocation of international laws and the sanctity of national borders, Bush simply refused to negotiate. When Saddam Hussein proposed to withdraw from Kuwait with the condition that an international conference be held to discuss the Middle East situation, Bush flatly refused the offer, which, incidentally, was very much in line with the U.N. General Assembly vote of 142 to 2 that called for an international peace conference in the Middle East. It was just such a conference that Bush and his administration aggressively promoted after the execution of the violence and terror that had reduced Iraq to a preindustrial age. Had Bush accepted Saddam's condition for an international conference, a condition passionately promoted after the war, he would have avoided the carnage that cost over 100,000 lives and an ecological disaster of enormous proportions. Bush's insistence on force led his administration to a constant double standard, which our uncritical citizenry, including the media and the intelligentsia, fail to see and question. While Bush often referred to the United Nations resolution of November 29, 1990, which gave "the U.S. a green light to use military means to expel Iraqi troops from Kuwait," he totally rejected a "U.N. General Assembly resolution, passed a week later by a vote of 142 to 2, which called for an international peace conference on the Middle East" (Lee and Solomon 1991, p. xxii). Bush's convenient selective selection of the United Nations as a forum for international dispute resolution and justice points to a systematic gunboat diplomacy that views force as the "unica ratio" in our foreign policy. We do not have to dig too far in our historical memory files to understand that, over and over again, the United States resorts to force to settle its so-called "national interest," which is, more appropriately, the interest of capital and the ruling elite. When we mined the Nicaraguan harbor, supported the Contras as our proxy army and were censored by the World Court, we arrogantly dismissed the much-hailed world body, the theater of justice, and the Mecca of international disputes and settlements. It is this same arrogance of power and force that justified and rationalized Desert Storm. Closer to home, it is this same arrogance of power and force that continues to justify and rationalize our war on drugs.

In order for us to better understand how our rationalization process works to transform force and violence into methods of reason, I will create two hypothetical scenarios. The first finds its parallel in the Gulf War, the second in the war on drugs. To begin the first scenario, let's imagine that the African countries, where over twenty million people die of hunger every year, decide to call the U.N. General Assembly to session to ask for permission to send a defensive armed force led by Ethiopia to the Canadian and Mexican borders with the United States to protect and guarantee the flow of grain in order to prevent the death of over twenty million people. These African countries would argue that the United States, being a major producer of food, should stop burning grain and paying farmers not to produce so prices will remain stable and profitable. The Africans would also passionately point out that the burning of grain and the limitation on production constitute a crime against humanity and that the twenty million Africans who are at risk of dying of hunger should be protected by international laws that view hunger as a human rights violation. If this hypothetical scenario were to occur in reality and a half million African troops were dispatched to the U.S. borders with Canada and Mexico, most of us would find the move so ridiculous as to be laughable. Well, Bush's initial rationale for sending troops to Saudi Arabia was to protect the flow of oil that otherwise would have disrupted the economies of the developed and industrialized nations. Even though Bush later recanted his earlier position by claiming that the fight was not about oil but about naked aggression, all evidence points to oil as the reason for the Gulf War. If Bush were defending the world order from naked aggression, he would first have had to bomb Washington, DC, since we had recently been engaged in a number of naked aggressions, mainly the invasion of Panama, the war against Nicaragua via a proxy army, the bombing of Libya, and the invasion of Grenada—to mention only a few of the most recent violations of the same international laws that Bush had so passionately wanted to protect during the Gulf War. In fact, the oil rationale made infinitely more sense, given the architecture of our foreign policy throughout history. The question that we should now ask of ourselves is: Would it be ridiculous for the African nations to send an army to protect the flow of grain that would save the lives of millions of people who might die of hunger but not ridiculous for the United States to send a half-million troops to the Persian Gulf to protect the flow of oil so industrialized nations might avoid economic chaos?

Let's turn to the second scenario, which finds its parallel rationale in the war on drugs. Let's imagine that the developing countries, composed mainly of Latin American nations but including some African nations as well, were to call for a regional summit where a decision is made to send troops to the United States to put a halt to the steady supply of armaments to support what they have characterized as the death industry in their countries. By death industry these nations are referring to the monies spent arming their military forces. Many developing countries, because of the never-ending military rule often supported by the Western powers, spend between 25 percent and 50 percent of their GNP on armaments. This militarization of their societies is not only destroying their economies but also leading to the killing of great numbers of people every year. Thus these developing countries would send their troops to strategically select locations in the United States where research and production of destructive armaments are contributing to economic chaos in their own countries and the killing of millions worldwide. Their troops would be trained to bomb and destroy all research laboratories and armament factories—such as Raytheon, General Dynamics, Boeing, and so forth—in the hope of stopping the flow of arms to their countries. All of this would have international approval, since this measure would constitute the national interests of these countries. If this hypothetical scenario were to be enacted, we can readily imagine the panic of all of those highly trained specialists who would be jobless once their factories and research laboratories had been destroyed. We can imagine as well the chaos that would ensue when these same specialists were left without a livelihood and abandoned to luck or perhaps to some form of social welfare. A turn to the latter for support would entail a reliance on a social structure that they no doubt had fought most of their lives to destroy or at least curtail to a bare minimum.

I see little difference in what we are doing to fight the drug war. The United States has militarized many Latin American countries, including Colombia, Peru, Bolivia, and Guatemala, to fight and destroy coca fields and drug laboratories, which constitute the only means of economic survival for millions of natives in these countries. By randomly destroying these people's only means of economic support in already poor countries with feeble economies, we are sentencing these native people to hunger and possibly death. However, we seldom think about the consequences and implications of the arrogance of power in the design of our drug war policy. That is to say, if we switch contexts and focus on our hypothetical scenario, we can clearly see through the infantile dimension and the lack of logic behind the imagined destruction of workplaces devoted to the production of armaments. I am arguing that it is the same infantile, illogical policy that we support when we ratify Bush's war on drugs. The only effective way to fight the war on drugs is to decrease demand. Even law enforcement officials and officials of these Latin countries have admitted that they are losing the drug war. In fact, by focusing only on the destruction of drug production while ignoring the social causes that breed a high demand for drugs, we are contradicting even our principle of capitalism. In other words, the best way to control production is to control demand. If we try to destroy production while leaving demand unchecked, production will resurface elsewhere—as is the case with drug production in Latin America that is finding its way to Europe and other safe ports.

These contradictions and instances of the unreason of reason are rarely understood and just as rarely questioned. If, by coincidence, we come to understand the blatant contradictions and question them, the ideological machine will tow us immediately into line. That is what happened to a reporter in San Antonio, Texas, who incessantly questioned Bush about the obvious failure of his drug war. He was immediately fired for being insistent and impolite to the president. Here politeness functioned as yet another mechanism to eliminate the possibility of knowing the truth. Since our society functions more and more on a pedagogy of lies, it depends on ideological institutions, such as schools and the media, to reproduce cultural values that work to distort and falsify realities so as to benefit the interest of the power elite. If schools were really involved in the development of critical thinking to arm students against the orchestrated distortion and falsification of reality, they would have to teach both the truth and to question. That includes, obviously, the deconstruction of the Pledge of Allegiance so as to make its hypocrisy bare and the rewriting of history books to keep alive dangerous memories so that slavery, the Holocaust, genocide, and Hiroshima could not be repeated under the guise and protection of Western civilization.

I believe that we can now return, with greater understanding, to our original question: Why is it that David Spritzler, a 12-year-old boy, could readily see through the hypocrisy in the Pledge of Allegiance while many of his teachers and administrators could not? According to Chomsky (1988), in discussing other educational situations, these teachers and administrators, having been indoctrinated by schools, are unable to understand elementary thoughts that any 10-year-old can understand. (p. 681) The indoctrination process imposes a willful blindness that views facts and contradictions as irrelevant. On the other hand, the more educated and specialized individuals become, the more vested interest they have in the system that provides them with special privileges. For this reason, we often see people whose consciousness has not been totally atrophied; yet they fail to read reality critically and they side with hypocrisy. In most cases, these individuals begin to believe the lies and, in their roles as functionaries of the state, they propagate the lies. That is why, for example, the majority of the educated population supported the war in Vietnam, while in 1982, according to a Gallup poll, over 70 percent of the general population were still saying that the Vietnam War was "fundamentally wrong and immoral, not a mistake" (Ibid., p. 673). This is another example that supports the contention that more education does not necessarily entail a greater ability to read reality.

As I have tried to demonstrate, both the competency-based skill banking approach to literacy and the highest level literacy acquisition via specialization fail to provide readers with the necessary intellectual tools to denude a reality that is often veiled through the ideological manipulation of language. It is safe to assume, given the way the educated class more often than not supports "theological truths" (or unquestioned truths), that the less educated one is, in the reproductive dominant model, the greater the chances to read the world more critically. Chomsky accurately captures this form of illiteracy of literacy when he states that

> the less educated...tend to be more sophisticated and perceptive about these matters, the reason being that education is a form of indoctrination and the less educated are less indoctrinated. Furthermore, the educated tend to be privileged and they tend to have a stake in the doctrinal system, so they naturally tend to internalize and believe it. As a result, not uncommonly and not only in the United States, you find a good deal more sophistication among people who learn about the world from their experience rather than those who learn about the world from a doctrinal framework that they are exposed to and that they are expected as part of professional obligation to propagate. (Ibid., p. 708)

It is indeed ironic that in the United States, a country that prides itself on being the first and most advanced within the so-called "first world," over sixty million people are illiterate or functionally illiterate. If Jonathan Kozol (1985) is correct, the sixty million illiterates and functional illiterates whom he documents in his book *Illiterate America* do not constitute a minority class of illiterate. (p. 340) To the sixty million illiterates we should add the sizable groups who learn how to read but are, by and large, incapable of developing independent and critical thought. In reality, the United States is in forty-ninth place among the 128 countries of the United Nations in terms of literacy rate. This ranking applies basically to the reading of the word and not the world. Our ranking, if applied to the reading of the world, would indeed be much lower.

Against this high illiteracy landscape, we can begin to wonder why a country that considers itself a model of democracy can tolerate an educational system that contributes to such a high level of illiteracy and failure. I am increasingly convinced that the U.S. educational system is not a failure. The failure that it generates represents its ultimate victory to the extent that large groups of people, including the so-called minorities, were never intended to be educated. They were never intended to be part of the dominant political and economic spheres. How else can we explain why we sit idly by and tolerate dropout rates that exceed 60 percent in many urban cities, with New York City at 70 percent? (Giroux 1992, p. 111) I believe that, instead of the democratic education we claim to have, we really have in place a sophisticated colonial model of education designed primarily to train state functionaries and commissars while denying access to millions, which further exacerbates the equity gap already victimizing a great number of so-called minority students. Even the education provided to those with class rights and privileges is devoid of the intellectual dimension of teaching, since the major objective of a colonial education is to further deskill teachers and students so as to reduce them to mere technical agents who are destined to walk unreflectively through a labyrinth of procedures. What we have in the United States is not a system to encourage independent thought and critical thinking. Our colonial literacy model is designed to domesticate so as to enable the "manufacture of consent." The Trilateral Commission could not have been more accurate when they referred to schools as "institutions responsible for the indoctrination of the young." I see no real difference between the more or less liberal Trilateral Commission position on schooling and Adolf Hitler's fascist call against independent thought and critical thinking. As Hitler noted, "What good fortune for those in power that people do not think."

NOTE

* An earlier version of this chapter was published in *The Harvard Educational Review*, Volume 63, Number 2, Summer 1993.

REFERENCES

Bowles, Samuel, Gordon, David M., and Weisskopf, E. Thomas. 1992. An economic strategy for progressives. *The Nation.* February 10, pp. 163–164.

Boyd, Christopher. Friends for Cubans who flee. *Boston Globe*, February 2, 1992, p. 2.

Chomsky, Noam. 1987. *On power and ideology.* Boston: South End Press.

———. 1988. *Language and politics. New York: Black Rose Books.*

———. On the Gulf policy. *Open Magazine*, Pamphlet Series, p. 8.

Courts, Patrick L. 1991. *Literacy and empowerment: The Meaning makers.* South Hadley, MA: Bergin and Garvey.

Fowler, Richard et al. 1979. *Language and control.* London. Routledge and Kegan Paul.

Freire, Paulo. 1985. *The politics of education.* South Hadley, MA: Bergin and Garvey.

Freire, Paulo and Macedo, Donaldo. 1987. *Literacy: Reading the word and the world.* South Hadley, MA: Bergin and Garvey.

Gee, James. 1992. *The social mind: Language, ideology, and social practices.* South Hadley, MA: Bergin and Garvey.

Giroux, Henry A. 1983. *Theory and resistance in education: A Pedagogy for the opposition.* South Hadley, MA: Bergin and Garvey.

———. 1992. *Border crossings: Cultural workers and the politics of education.* New York: Routledge.

Herman, Edward S. and Chomsky, Noam. 1988. *Manufacturing consent: The polical economy of mass media.* New York: Pantheon Books.

Jackson, D. Z. The wrong relations. *Boston Globe*, November 3, 1993, p. 19.

Jacobson, Natalie. 1992. Interview with President George Bush. Nightly News at 6:00 P.M. January 16.

Kozol, J. 1991. *Savage inequalities: Children in American's schools.* New York: Crown Publishers.

Lee, Martin A. and Solomon, Norman. 1991. *Unreliable sources: a guide to detecting bias in news media.* New York: Carol Publishing Group.

Lukas, Alan. 1985. *Common ground.* New York: Alfred A. Knopf.

Lutz, William. 1989. *Doublespeak.* New York: Harper Collins.

McLaren, Peter and Hammer, Rhonda. 1992. Media knowledges, warrior citizenry, and postmodern literacies. *Journal of Urban and Cultural Studies* 1: 41–64.

Meyers, Greg. 1986. Reality, consensus, and reform in the rhetoric of composition teaching. *College English* 48:111.

Ortega Y Gasset, Jose. 1930. Reprint. *The revolt of the masses.* New York: W. W. Norton, 1964.

Packaging the war. *Boston Globe.* January 20, 1991, p.74.

Quayle, in Boston, tells of U.S. relief effort for Iraq refugees. *Boston Globe*, April 12, 1991 p. 15.

Ribadeneira, Diego. Taking a stand, seated. *Boston Globe*, November 14, 1991, p. 40.

U.S. infant mortality hits low. *Boston Globe*, February 7, 1992, p. 8.

U.S. ordered a stop to Patriot criticism MIT professor says. *Boston Globe*, March 18, 1992, p. 3.

UNESCO. 1966. *An Asian model of education development.* Paris: UNESCO.

Walker, Paul F. and Stambler, Eric. The surgical myth of the Gulf war. *Boston Globe*, April 16, 1991, p. 15.

Wilson, Catherine. U.S. begins returning Haitian refugees. *Boston Globe*, February 2, 1992, pp. 2–3.

3

Stephen Nathan Haymes, Ph.D

White Culture and the Politics of Racial Difference: Implications for Multiculturalism*

In our society, one of the first things we notice about people when we encounter them (along with their sex/gender) is their race. We utilize race to provide clues about who a person is and how we should relate to her/him. Our perception of race determines our presentation of self, distinctions in status, and appropriate modes of conduct in daily and institutional life. This process is often unconscious, we tend to operate off of an unexamined set of racial beliefs.

Omi

Introduction

If Michael Omi's comment is in fact true, then we must be concerned about the dominance of mainstream white culture in organizing our perceptions with respect to racial difference. This is because the ideology of white supremacy undergirds many of the assumptions and ideas of the white mainstream culture. For instance, popular culture has been one site in which mainstream white culture has been able to "provide an ideological framework of symbols, concepts, and images through which we understand, interpret, and represent "racial difference" (Omit 1989, p. 114). One reason for this is that white wealth and power control the electronic media, In other words, this power exerts much influence over the production of popular culture and how we interpret racial difference, particularly as it relates to multiculturalism. The significance of this situation is that mainstream white culture plays a pivotal role in the formation of our cultural identities and therefore how we see ourselves in relationship to others. Its influence is not only in terms of how we think but also in how we construct our fears, pleasures, desires, and dreams. Although Alberto Melucci (1989) does not mention the signifying role of white culture in the electronic media, his insight is still apposite. He writes: "In the current period, society's capacity to intervene in the production of meaning extends to those areas which previously escaped control and regulation: areas of self-definition, emotional relationships and biological needs" (p. 46).

105

Through the electronic media, white supremacist assumptions and ideas penetrate every facet of daily life, suggesting that close attention must be paid to how educators, students, and communities interpret racial difference, particularly as related to popular culture. Omi (1989) implies this when he writes:

> Racial beliefs account for and explain variations in "human nature." Differences in skin color and other obvious physical characteristics supposedly provide visible clues to more substantive differences lurking underneath. Among other qualities, temperament, sexuality, intelligence, and artistic and athletic ability are presumed to be fixed and discernible from the palpable mark of race. Such diverse questions as our confidence and trust in others (as salespeople, neighbors, media figures); our sexual preferences and romantic images; our taste in music, film, dance, or sports; indeed our very ways of walking and talking are ineluctably shaped by notions of race. (p. 113).

Along with paying close attention to how racial difference is organized within popular culture, critical educators need to analyze the mediating role played by race in the social construction of gender, sex and class identities. This is necessary if critical educators are to take seriously student experience as a basis of learning and an object of inquiry in the classroom. If this is the case, critical educators must be attentive to how popular culture shapes the categories of racial meaning that students construct when interpreting their experiences, therefore prefiguring how they produce and respond to classroom knowledge. This suggests that popular culture, along with its categories of racial meaning, should be made an object of classroom study when inquirying into student experience. In addition to this, educators must confront critically how the racial meaning systems found within popular culture also shape them as racial subjects, consequently structuring how they think about and do multicultural education.

I would also add that multicultural education is practiced not only within schools but also in other sites such as community-based organizations. Within the context of community organizing, multicultural education has been at the center in terms of rethinking how to organize "culturally diverse" urban communities. However, like many urban public schools, community-based organizations are staffed and administered by middle-class whites. This factor has had a profound effect in terms of how multiculturalism is conceptualized and practiced, in that what shapes the implementation of multicultural education is mainstream white culture. I am reminded of the multicultural event sponsored by a major community-based organization on the northeast side of Chicago.

At this event the food and artistic expressions of different nonwhite ethnic groups were displayed, and there was no discussion about the politics of race and racism, only statements referring to the importance of "celebrating cultural diversity in the neighborhood". What was so interesting was that every ethnic group represented was nonwhite. So what was being defined as "diverse" or "different" were nonwhite people. The question I constantly raised to myself was, "In relation to what were nonwhites different, and what did this event have to say about mainstream white identity?" Finally, this event reaffirmed my belief that in order to develop nonwhite supremacist forms of multiculturalism, multicultural education must insist on the importance of white people rethinking their own collective whiteness. This suggests that multicultural education must move beyond the issue of schooling and that educators must take the lead in developing a critical theory of multiculturalism. The issue is that as long as there are multipedagogies practiced in multisites, educators must develop an awareness as well as solutions that addresses the multiple misuses of pedagogy in terms of race/gender/class.

One way educators interested in doing this can begin is by confronting their own racial formation as well as that of their students. This process means understanding that mainstream white culture's control over the signifying practices of the electronic media and the images and representations it produces, is best explored by analyzing how popular culture is constructed around a "politics of difference" or "politics of diversity". As a response to this situation, I want to argue a number of points. First, that mainstream white culture's politics of difference or politics of diversity reproduces white supremacist ideology, by making the nonwhite cultures markers for racial difference. Second, that the social construction of multiculturalism in relation to mainstream white culture results in whites being deracialized and nonwhites racialized. Third, that this particular version of multiculturalism avoids dialogue about the issue of race and makes race the problem of nonwhites and not whites. Finally, the cultural authority of the white mainstream constructs nonwhites as either exotic or dangerous by sexualizing their racial, physical characteristics. The implication is that nonwhite cultures are viewed as either sexually provocative or pathological.

Thus, the primary aim of this chapter is to examine how mainstream white culture constructs racial difference and the white supremicist assumptions and practices that have historically informed it. This is important because multiculturalism has mostly been focused on nonwhites, and in order to link multiculturalism to an antiracist worldview and pedagogy, the category *white* must be critically interrogated. Coco Fuso states: "Racial identities are not only black, Latino, Asian, Native American, and so on; they are also white. To ignore white ethnicity is to redouble its hegemony by naturalizing it. Without specifically addressing white ethnicity, there can be no critical evaluation of the construction of the other." (hooks 1990). The first issue is therefore to understand how is it that mainstream white culture constructs racial difference.

WHITE CULTURE AND RACIAL DIFFERENCE

The commodification of Otherness has been so successful because it is offered as a new delight, more intense, more satisfying than normal ways of doing and feeling. Within commodity culture, ethnicity becomes spice, seasoning that can liven up the dull dish that is mainstream white culture. Cultural taboos around sexuality and desire are transgressed and made explicit as the media bombards folks with a message of difference no longer based on the white supremacist assumption that "blondes have more fun." The real "fun" is to be had by bringing to surface all those "nasty" unconscious fantasies and longings about contact with the Other embedded in the secret (not so secret) deep structure of white supremacy. In many ways it is a contemporary revival of interest in the "primitive." (hooks 1993, pp. 21–22).

This quote by bell hooks links the culture of consumption to the white supremacist discourse of mainstream white culture. This means then that "the act of consuming [has become] as much an act of imagination as a real act" (Lefebvre 1990, p. 90). In part, this points to the fact that in "the commodification of language and culture, objects and images are torn free of their original referents and their meanings become a spectacle open to almost infinite translation"(Rutherford 1990, p. 11). One instance of this phenomenon is the use of black American popular culture to signify pleasure and desire. Thus, in the act of consuming, mainstream white sensibilities, tastes, or lifestyles are predicated on consuming black images which are ideologically linked with the white racist imagination: "Otherness is sought after for its exchange value, its exoticism and the pleasure, thrills and adventures it can offer" (Ibid.).

For example, Levis's blue jean ads attempt to make middle-class white youth identify with Levis jeans by using a "street cool" motif, which romanticizes the ghetto. Underpinning this motif "is a conception about acting in public spaces and how blacks accomplish this" (Goldman and Papson 1991, p. 83). Suggested is that "black males move without inhibition to the rhythm of the street; they signify soul, movement, expressiveness, the body unencumbered by tight, stiff middleclassness" (Ibid.). Also, accompanying the street cool motif is Levis's exotic appropriation of black urban music to signify sexual pleasure and desire. Black music is used to express the physical sensuality and movement associated with jeans. Thus, by stylizing the black ghetto, Levi ads create a mood that mobilizes desire in such a way that middle class white youth come to identify Levis blue jeans with sexual provocativeness.

White mainstream consumption of the "other" is therefore like tourism. In support of this notion, Dean McCannell (1989) asserts that "the [white] middle class scavenges the earth for new experiences to be woven into a collective, touristic version of other people and other places" (p. 13). It is this voyeuristic attitude that helps to shape how cultural difference and multiculturalism get taken up within the popular cultures of white consumer capitalism. Usually this touristic attitude is expressed when cultural difference is interpreted by white culture as the appreciation of diversity. In fact, the sign of the "cultured" or the "civilized" attitude, Homi Bhabha (1991) writes, "is the ability to appreciate cultures in a kind of musee imaginaire; as though one should be able to collect and appreciate them" (p. 208). Thus, the likeness of white middle-class consumption to tourism provides some insight into how this attitude views and regulates cultural difference. Dean MacCannell (1991) believes that for middle-class whites, tourism or "sightseeing" is a ritual performed to the differentiation of society":

> Sightseeing is a kind of collective striving for a transcendence of the modern totality, a way of attempting to overcome the discontinuity of modernity, of incorporating its fragments into unified experiences....This effort of the [white] middle class to coordinate the differentiations of the world into a single ideology is intimately linked to its capacity to subordinate other people to its values, industry and future design. The [white] middle class is the most favored now because it has a transcendent consciousness. Tourism, I suggest, is an essential component of that consciousness. (p. 13)

It is through language and culture that middle-class whites, within the parameters of consumer capitalism, coordinate and contain cultural difference, while celebrating and consuming black culture (West, 1989, p. 94). One way of understanding this contradiction is by looking at how white cultural identity is constituted through the politics of language, discourse, and difference. This approach presents a departure from the Cartesian view of the subject, which has dominated modern discourse in the West.

According to the Cartesian view, the "self" or subject is a unified, integrated ego and as such a repository of consciousness and creativity. The presumption made is that "the subject is constituted through the exercise of a rational and autonomous mode of understanding and knowing" (Giroux, 1991, p. 29) outside the politics of language and discourse (West 1983). Because of the influence of Cartesian views of the subject, individual identities are supposedly able to perfectly replicate themselves as mirror images, thereby neglecting the mediating role that language plays in their construction and representation. However, identity is not outside of representation because we use language to describe ourselves to ourselves and to others. In the words of Stuart Hall, (1991), "[i]dentity is a narrative of the self; it's the story we tell about the self in order to know who we are (p. 16).

It is in this context that mainstream white cultural authority imposes structures of meaning on black narratives, consequently regulating how blacks come to know who they are as blacks. Nevertheless, the structures of meaning imposed that regulate the formation of black identity have more to do with how whites come to know who they are as whites. The point I am underscoring is that to understand white consumer culture's images and representations of black people and black culture, we must first recognize the historically specific ways that *whiteness* is a politically constructed category that is parasitic on *blackness*. Thus as Stuart Hall's comments: "[whites] are racist not because they hate the blacks, but because they don't know who they are without blacks. They have to know who they are not in order to know who they are" (Ibid.).

Within the cultural logic of white supremacy difference is defined as the black "other." Black identity functions for white culture as a way to mark off difference and define white people as normal. In contemporary society this is how power passes itself off as embodied in the normal as opposed to the superior (Dyer 1988, p. 19). In support of this interpretation of power, Richard Dyer asserts that "this is common to all forms of power, but it works in a peculiarly seductive way with whiteness, because of the way it seems rooted, in commonsense thought, in things other than ethnic difference" (Ibid., p. 20). The argument suggest is that racial and ethnic differences must be understood in relation to other Western, Eurocentric discourses that define the conceptual meanings of white and black.

In Western culture, the concept white is represented in direct opposition to the concept of black. As Winthrop Jordon (1968) indicates "No other colors so clearly implied opposition...no others were so frequently used to denote polarization" (p. 7). The positioning of white and black as polar opposites is significant because as Jacques Derrida argues, Western metaphysics has always privileged one term in a binary opposition over the other (Sarup 1989, p. 40–42). In Eurocentric Western culture this has been consistent with the concepts white and black. As Winthrop Jordan (1968) asserts "white and black connoted purity and filthiness, virginity and sin, virtue and baseness, beauty and ugliness, beneficence and evil, God and the devil"(p. 7). What is important is how the concepts white and black in dominant representations have come to be naturally conflated as race and ethnic categories. How does this conflation of the categories white and black function to reproduce white privilege and domination in ways that white people "colonize" the definition of normal?

One way to pursue this question is to pair the concepts black and white with the idea of color. Hence, "black is always marked as a colour, and is always particularizing; whereas white is not anything really, not an identity, not a particularizing quality, because it is everything —white is no colour because it is all colours" (Dyer 1988, p. 20). Thus, within this binary logic, Eurocentric or white supremacist discourse constructs blackness as other by making whiteness invisible. The process is one of racializing blackness while deracializing whiteness. Kobena Mercer (1988) agrees when he says, "whiteness has secured universal consent to its hegemony as the norm by masking its coercive force with the invisibility that marks off the other as all too visible—coloured" (p. 32).

To expose the invisibility of whiteness is to unmake race and ethnic difference as something exclusive to blacks. Unfortunately, within mainstream approaches to multiculturalism, the focus is on the black other and not on whiteness and white people, a selective move designed to conveniently avoid the issue of white power and privilege. Similarly, Henry Giroux (1991) argues that the discourse of white supremacy creates "the self delusion that the

boundaries of racial inequality and ethnicity were always exclusively about the language, experience, and histories of the Other
and had little to do with power relations at the core of its own
cultural and political identity as the discourse of white authority"
(p. 220). Therefore, to talk about the marginalization, oppression,
and exploitation of black people, white identity and the power and
privilege it enjoys must be made visible (Carby 1989, p. 39).
However, the difficulty lies in the fact that whiteness itself is
masked as a category. The colorlessness of whiteness secures
white domination and privilege because white people do not recognize their own whiteness.

For example, Euro-Americans very rarely define themselves as
being white, but rather as being Irish, Jewish, Polish, Italian,
German, or English. In fact, popular films about Europeans or
Euro-Americans rarely represent them as white people. So, instead
of being about white people, the film *Brief Encounter* is about
English middle-class people and *The Godfather* about Italian-
American people, "but *The Color Purple* is about black people,
before it is about poor, southern U.S. people" (Dyer 1988, p. 16).
This illustrates the way in which white people take for granted their
whiteness. Dean MacCannell (1989), in support of this theory,
argues that white people's taken for granted attitude regarding their
whiteness, as well as the privileges they secure by being white, is in
part what defines the ideological terrain of "white culture".

He also asserts that the inability of whites to recognize their
own whiteness is to some extent related to white culture's "grammatical structure." That is, there is a tendency for whites to use
the third person pronoun to refer to themselves, bestowing upon
themselves a quality of omnipotence, which implies personal
detachment and objectivity. MacCannell (1989) is worth quoting at
length on this issue:

> White Culture is an enormous totalization which, within current
> social arrangements, corresponding to the being of the third
> person on the plane of language, and to white light in physics.
> Its arrogates to itself the exclusive right to totalize and represent
> all other hues 'in the proportion in which they exist in the visible
> spectrum.' As a cultural totality, 'whiteness is founded on a few
> simple principles: the principle of depersonalization of human
> relationships and the idealization of objective judgement and
> duty....To say that White Culture is impersonal is not the same
> thing as saying that it does not function like a subject or subjec-
> tivity. It is a subjectivity. But it is the kind that is cold, the kind
> that laughs at feelings while demanding that all surplus libido,

energy, and capital be handed over to it. White culture begins
with the pretense that it does not express itself rhetorically.
Rather, the form of its expression is always represented as only
incidental to truth. (p. 24)

Furthermore, nonwhite cultures are believed to be rhetorical
and therefore partial and not suitable for "discovering" truth.
Sometime this is implicitly understood when white's express feelings of culturelessness. Underlying this feeling is the presumption
that Western societies possesses reason and not culture. An
example of this idea is Allan Bloom's (1987) statement: "What is
most characteristic of the West is science, particularly understood
as the quest to know nature and the consequent denigration of
convention—i.e., culture or the West understood as a culture—in
favor of what is accessible to all men as men through their
common and distinctive faculty, reason" (p. 38). So what is implied
is that as the West, through its "scientific reason," discovers
nature, it transcends the particularlism of is own culture, making
itself invisible. As Renato Rosaldo (1989) in *Culture and Truth*
argues, "as the other becomes more culturally visible the [white]
self becomes correspondingly less" (p. 202).

The real issue here is how white feelings of supposed culturelessness may be linked to the ideology of white supremacy. It
appears that these feelings mistakenly assume that to be without
culture is to be rational and white, while to be culturally visible is
to be irrational and nonwhite (Rosaldo 1989). The culturelessness
that whites say they experience is related to MacCannell's view of
"White Culture", that it "corresponds to the being of the third
person on the plane of language, and to white light in physics."
White feelings of culturelessness are linked to white people's self-
perceptions as rational, ordered, and civilized, which are constructed against a notion of irrationality, disorder, and uncivilized
behavior that rely on black stereotypes. Therefore, black stereotypes serve as a referent for whites to construct their own identity,
linking white identity-formation to the process of differentiation.
The assumption is that we learn our identities or who we are by
differentiating ourselves from each other. That is, in the context of
white culture the process of differentiation must be understood in
relation to constructing blacks as pathological.

WHITE CULTURE AND THE PATHOLOGICAL BLACK

Historically, the narrative of pathology that informs the discourse
of white supremacy has been based on human sexuality, particu-

larly black sexuality (Gilman 1985). Black sexuality has been viewed by the Eurocentric West as being disruptive to the latter's productivist ideology, which sees capitalist growth as a precondition for human freedom. This recalls Max Weber's thesis that the "Protestant Work Ethnic" (i.e., hard work, patience, and delayed self-gratification) has played an integral role in the cultural development of Western industrial capitalism. The work ethic of the Eurocentric West has constructed sexual pleasure and desire as a threat to productivity, efficiency, economic growth, and material prosperity or well-being. In fact, the Italian communist, Antonio Gramsci (1980), recognized in the 1920s how industrialist sexuality was antithetical to productivity and profit. He stated: "The new type of man demanded by the rationalization of production and work cannot be developed until the sexual instinct has been suitably regulated and until it too has been rationalized" (p. 282).

Underlying work ethic ideology is the proposition that hard work, patience, and delayed self-gratification leads to material prosperity, translating into independence and control over one's life. Because sexual pleasure and desire are additionally perceived as undermining independence and control, sexuality is perceived as stimulating anxiety. This is because sexuality is associated with lacking control and disorder. Western capitalist culture has dealt with this anxiety by projecting it onto black people, therefore associating black sexuality with loss of control, disorder, and dependence, all of which are associated with pathological behavior (Gilman 1985). David R. Roediger, in *The Wages of Whiteness*, argues that the early construction of U.S. white working-class identity was based on whites differentiating wage labor from slave labor by associating the former with whiteness and the latter with blackness. Wage labor for white workers signified discipline and independence while slave labor signified laziness and dependence. The slave's dependency was somehow perceived as having to do with the slave's "preindustrial, erotic, careless style of life, which was associated with the slave's blackness" (Roediger 1992). This reinforced the notion that slavery was a natural condition of blacks in that they were like children, dependent on the white slave master to police their sexual desires. According to Jan Nederveen Pieterse (1993), this was "an important reason for the institutionization of slavery in America and the West Indies" (1992, p. 174).

Today black sexuality is still perceived by whites as dangerous and disruptive and in need of containment. White perceptions regarding black sexuality as threatening to the social and moral order is a particular characteristic of "pathological stereotyping," which relies "upon the illusionary image of the world divided into two camps, us and them," with "them" being either "good" or "bad." (Gilman 1985, p. 17). Pathological stereotyping therefore depends upon creating an illusion of absolute difference between the self and the other. The illusionary line drawn between the self and the other denotes a binarism in that it "operates as splitting and projection" (Rutherford 1990, p. 14). This is triggered "when the centre expels its anxieties, contradictions and irrationalities onto the subordinate term, filling it with the antithesis of its own identity" (Ibid., p. 22). White insecurities about the future of their privileges and power, the result of demands for social justice by the underprivileged, are projected onto blacks, whose sexual behavior is stereotyped by whites as the cause for disorder and loss of control in their lives. Gilman refers to the particular formation of these fears and anxieties on the part of the privileged as status anxiety:

> When a group makes demands on society, the status anxiety produced by those demands characteristically translates into a sense of loss of control. Thus a group that has been marginally visible can suddenly become the definition of the Other. But stereotypes can also be perpetuated, resurrected, and shaped through texts containing fantasy life of the culture, quite independent of the existence or absense of the group in a given society. (1985: 21)

The projection by whites of their fears and anxieties onto blacks can lead to aggressive white behavior towards blacks, which Gilman equates with the pathological personality. Also, because white fears and anxieties have tended to demonize blacks by sexualizing them, white aggression towards blacks has historically taken on sexual overtones. Wilhelm Reich in his interpretation of Nazism argues that race and class oppression interfaced with sexual repression. Similarly, Franz Fanon had argued that "if one wants to understand the racial situation psychoanalytically...as it is experienced by individual consciousness, considerable importance must be given to sexual phenomena" (Young 1990). What this means is that the raping of black women by white men, particularly during slavery, can be read as the interfacing of race and class oppression with sexual repression. In agreement, bell hooks states: "Rape as both right and rite of the white male dominating group was a cultural norm. Rape was also an apt metaphor of European imperialist colonization of Africa and North America" (Ibid., p. 57). In addition, the lynching of black men in the Southern United States also indicated a close link with sexual repression in that lynching was frequently accompanied by castration. Commenting on the sexualization of racial oppression, James Earl Jones observed: "When a white feels so personally involved with a Negro that he takes the time to cut off his penis and torture him, then it has to be something sexual, the result of repressed sex. Everywhere in the world men kill each other, but nowhere do they cut off penises and lynch each other" (Pieterse 1992, p. 176–177). What got a black man lynched was not the accusation of murder but rape, linking the myth of the black rapist of white women to the status anxieties of white Southern males.

White fear of blacks even today continues to be based on race and sex. For example, former President George Bush had appointed Frederick A. Goodwin, a research psychiatrist and career federal scientist, to head the National Institute of Mental Health (NIMH). In a presentation to the National Advisory Council on Mental Health, the advisory board of the NIMH, Goodwin spoke about the new initiative of the NIMH in linking the behavior of inner city males with the behavior of primates in the jungle. The *Observer*, the national newsletter of the American Psychological Society, stated: "In speaking about a new intuitive on violence he used animal research findings to describe gang-related, inner-city violence. Goodwin compared youth gangs to groups of 'hyperaggressive' and 'hypersexual' monkeys and further said that 'maybe it isn't just the careless use of the word when people call certain areas of cities, "jungles"'" (American Psychological Society 1991, p. 1). Two decades ago Edward C. Banfield (1968), in *The Unheavenly City*, suggested that "to a greater extent [the slum] is an expression of his [the Negro's] taste and style of life." He further argued that the "subculture of the slum" rests on the premise that [the Negro's] bodily needs (especially sex) and his taste for action takes precedence over everything else." Banfield moves to describe the urban riots as "outbreaks of animal spirits" (1968, p. 297). Recently, Deborah Prothrow-Smith, M.D. (1991), in *Deadly Consequences*, rejects trends in contemporary research that link black male violence to high levels of testosterone. (p. 9)

White supremacist ideologies about black sexuality have been the basis for explaining not only black violence but also black poverty. In *The Promised Land: The Great Migration and How It Changed America*, journalist Nicholas Lemann (1991) tells us that the sexuality of the Southern black sharecropping families was responsible for urban black poverty in the North and that liberal welfare policies condoned and perpetuated loose sexual behavior. Brett Williams (1991) in the *Nation* responds to Lemann by arguing that his narrative is one that is "encouraged by the mass media's archetypes: the sexualized, dangerous reproducing poor black women, from sharecropper to slut to welfare dependent and her counterpart: the flailing, undomesticated poor black man" (p. 41). These sexualized images of poor blacks as dangerous and disruptive provided the Reagan and Bush Administrations with the rationale to support federal, state, and local initiatives to reform welfare, so as to instill discipline. Also supported were efforts to medically sterilize and castrate black women and black men, displace poor blacks from the central city through urban development, and intensify police repression and surveillance.

WHITE CULTURE AND THE EXOTIC BLACK

At the same time that whites view black sexuality as disruptive to the prevailing social and moral order, their exoticizing of black sexuality causes them also to be fascinated by it. This is because stereotypes are not rigidly constituted but are constantly shifting. Whites fluctuate from fearing to exoticizing and from hating to loving blacks. Gilman (1985) observes that even "the most negative stereotype always has an overtly positive counterweight." As any image is shifted, all stereotypes shift." Within popular culture this has been the case, particularly with Hollywood films. Cameron Bailey (1988) agrees that this combined fear and exoticizing of black sexuality has functioned as a powerful signifier in Hollywood films. He writes:

> Since the cavalry rode manfully across the crosscutting to save Lillian Gish from blackness in *Birth of a Nation*, since Barbara Apollonia Chalupiec became Pola Negri and took up a position as Hollywood's resident Other, black sexuality, indeed anything other than white sexuality, has been both a potent threat and a powerful attraction in American film. Adopting a centuries old signification system, Hollywood from its beginning linked racial difference to sexual danger. Danger, we saw, lurked in a capital-O Other: sexual transgression became Hollywood's darkest sin, and its surest box-office draw. (1988, p. 28)

Some cultural theorists argue that the racial aesthetics of early films such as *Birth of a Nation* foreground the use of black culture as a signifier or marker of exotica in contemporary North American white avant-garde and mainstream films (Bailey 1988, p. 40; Talyor 1991, p. 29). Clyde Taylor (1991), in his article "The Rebirth of the Aesthetic in Cinema" argues that in white American cinema, black culture "is not worshiped for itself but for the transcendental values it is believed to represent" (p. 22). He discusses how in the film *Birth of a Nation* D. W. Griffith used whites in blackface to exploit the emotional dynamics of white audiences. "Under the mask of racial and moral darkness, hidden desires could be exercised and indulged in public performance, even glamorized and applauded. The minstrel mechanism is one instance in which the ideological making of unspeakable knowledge requires an actual mask" (Ibid.). In reference to North American avant-garde films, bell hooks (1990) asserts that "[w]hile it is exciting to witness a pluralism that enables everyone to have access to the use of certain imagery, we must not ignore the consequence when images are manipulated to appear 'different' while reinforcing stereotypes and oppressive structures of domination" (p. 171).

The implication behind the black-as-exotic stereotype is that the black is more primitive or animal-like. Within North American film, the predominant physical stereotypes of blacks still hold sway—bulging eyes, thick lips, wide noses, and enlarged sexual organs. This stereotype transforms blacks into rampaging figures of excessive sensuality. The blacks' senses, Bailey (1989) observes, "admit more than is 'tasteful'; they are in bad taste because they are so obvious. In the white paradigm, blacks "consume too much (p. 33). Yet, still within this paradigm, there is a complex fusion of desire and aversion, projection and concealment. Cornel West (1989) implies the same: "Given the European and Euro-American identification of Africans and African Americans with sexual licentiousness, libertinism, and liberation, black music became both a symbol and facilitator of white sexual freedom" (p. 95).

I would also add that white culture's exotic interests in black culture may be a symbolic escape from the discipline of the work ethic. Roediger argues that urban white male workers, during the antebellum period, organized their leisure time, particularly popular celebrations, in terms of imitating black culture, which also involved blackening their faces. Roediger (1992) states: "Blackface served not only to identify the white crowd with the excellence of Black popular culture but also to connect its wearers with the preindustrial permissiveness imputed to African Americans. It reemphazied that the Christmas night or the militia day was a time of celebration and license, of looseness, drinking and promiscuity." (p. 106). He points out, too, that these public celebrations included white crowds violently attacking blacks. Blackfaced whites "both admired what they imaged blackness to symbolize and hated themselves for doing so" (Ibid.).

Black culture is therefore seen as providing substance or life to white identity, which defines itself as restrained, transparent, and neutral, and therefore lifeless. According to Dyer (1988), the desire to possess the other is derived from the Eurocentric belief that nonwhite cultures are more "natural" than white culture, and therefore represent "life."

> Life here tends to mean the body, the emotions, sensuality and spirituality; it is usually explicitly counterposed to the mind and the intellect, with the implication that white people's over-invest-ment in the cerebral is cutting them off from life and leading them to crush the life out of others and out of nature itself. The implicit counterposition is, of course, "death." (p. 56)

The mostly white dominated culture industry has made its fortunes by providing whites with access to "life", by exploiting black music, dance, art, fashion, sports, and linguistic codes. Recognizing white culture's exotic interest in black cultural prac-tices, the culture industry has played a pivotal role in the commod-ification of black culture, in order to expand its mainstream, white consumer market—except that what has been commodified has not been black culture per se but the sexualized exotic and prim-itivistic images and representations it evokes in the imagination of whites. Henceforth, stereotypical black images and signs are inscribed in and on mainstream American white popular music, dance, television, styles, fashions, advertising, and magazines. Through the luxury consumer market, mainstream whites can purchase a style of life, in which black cultural productions are the signifier, that permits them to imaginarily indulge in the exotic and sensual.

Insofar as the exchange value of white consumer goods is strongly influenced by black signifiers, the joining of black culture and consumer goods as a single, identical form has resulted in a separation of black cultural practices from the historical and social circumstances that gave them life (hooks 1992; West 1989, p. 87–96; Baudrillard 1981, p. 204–212). The circumstances that bore black cultural practices arose from a reality that Cornel West asserts was historically constructed through white supremacist practices—a reality marked by black insecurity and real necessity. So much so that the reality became infused with the strategies and styles of black cultural practices that Cornel West characterizes as kinetic orality, passionate physicality, and combative spirituality (1989, p. 96).

Similarly, Larry Neal (1989), a black cultural worker in the Black Arts movement of the 1960s, argued that the "ethos of the blues" is infused with the values and cultural codes that construct "black emotion" and hence blackness. He begins by asserting that the "blues are basically defiant in their attitude towards life" (p. 108). What Neal means is that the blues "are the expression of the larger will to survive—to feel life in one's innermost being, even though it takes place in an oppressive political context" (Ibid.). For him, "the blues are primarily the expression of a postslavery view of the world," referring to slavery's tendency to destroy the individual's sense of being a "person with particular needs and a particular style or manner of doing things" (Ibid., pp. 108, 112). Because under slavery "every aspect of one's life is controlled from the outside by others, the sense of one's individual's body is diminished" (Ibid., p. 112). Neal concludes, that "the intensely personal quality of the blues is a direct result of freeing the individual personality which was held in check by slavery" (Ibid.). Furthermore, because slavery was about white control and domination of the black body, the blues linked the emancipation of the individual black body and personality to a "politics of the flesh". This politics of the flesh refers to an effort to construct alternative forms of black pleasure and desire that are liberating to the black body and black personality, particularly in a white supremacist context that symbolically and physically degrades and demeans black people. Moreover, Paul Gilroy (1987) argues that black cultural practices embody anticapitalist themes that can be traced directly or indirectly to the formative years of slavery, themes which Paul Gilroy believes amount to a critique of productivism—an ideology that makes capitalist economic growth a precondition for human freedom and that sees wage work itself as a form of servitude:

> At best, it [wage work] is viewed as a necessary evil and is sharply counterposed to the more authentic freedoms that can only be enjoyed in nonwork time. *The black body is here celebrated as an instrument of pleasure rather than an instrument of labor.* The nighttime becomes the right time, and the space allocated for recovery and recuperation is assertively and provocatively occupied by the pursuit of leisure and pleasure. (p. 274)

In contrast to the ideology of white supremacist culture, black cultural practices therefore involve constructing forms of black pleasure and desire that in many ways are related to the notion of black joy. Distinguishing black pleasure from black joy, Cornel West writes:

> pleasure, under commodified conditions, tends to be inward. You take it with you, and it's a high individuated unit. But joy tries to cut across that. Joy tries to get at those non-market

values—love, care, kindness, service, solidarity, the struggle for justice—values the provide the possibility of bringing people together (quoted in Dent 1992 p. 1)

Black pleasure or black joy is therefore about how black cultural practices involve creating black public spaces, or as bell hooks would call them "homeplaces" that allow for black self-recovery. According to hooks, homeplaces refers to sites where one could confront the issue of humanization, where one could resist. Homeplace is where "all black people could be subjects, not objects, where we could be affirmed in our minds and hearts despite poverty, hardship, and deprivation, where we could restore to ourselves dignity denied us on the outside in the public world." In a sense, then, black cultural practices are essential for creating black joy and therefore black solidarity in order to be able to struggle for social justice.

By commodifying black culture and severing it from the social and historical circumstances in which it arose, commodity culture reduces black culture to a simulacrum or a copy without an original. This process allows black culture to be reinscribed into white fantasies about black sexuality. It therefore reduces black cultural practices to performance, and performance to the black body's imagined natural endowments, reducing black people to being primitives or animal-like. One result of this view is that the black body becomes either the basis of white envy or white fear. In this way, commodity culture and the white supremacist assumptions that underlie it have implicitly reinforced the racist idea that black cultural expressions are tied to the biology of the black body and not to black cultural resistance against white supremacist ideology and practices. This essentialist reading of black culture by white consumer culture in many ways has shaped the ways in which cultural difference gets interpreted in relation to multiculturalism.

> Culture is conceived along ethnically absolute lines, not as something intrinsically fluid, changing, unstable, and dynamic, but as a fixed property of social groups rather than a relational field in which they encounter one another and live out social, historical relationships. When culture is brought into contact with race it is transformed into a pseudobiological property of communal life (Gilroy 1987, p. 267).

CONCLUSION: TOWARDS A CRITICAL MULTICULTURALISM

Critical multiculturalism and its pedagogical assumptions must in part be about constructing a notion of multiculturalism that is antiracist by de-essentializing the cultures of nonwhites, which means critically deconstructing the category of whiteness itself. This deconstruction is particularly crucial in that supremacist notions of whiteness are constructed when nonwhites, in this case blacks, are essentialized. Thus, in constructing a new imagination about whiteness, white people have to construct along with blacks a new sense of blackness, a more liberating notion of blackness that is not contaminated by the discourse of white supremacy. This means that from the point of view of critical multiculturalism, Euro-Americans must engage black culture and black history from the perspective of understanding the political and ethical implications of their whiteness, particularly with respect to black oppression and exploitation. Bell hooks and Cornel West (1991) make the same point when addressing how whites should pedagogically engage black experiences and histories. Related to this, hooks argues that liberatory pedagogies should bring a kind of analysis of subjectivity "which says that studying 'the other' is not the goal, the goal is learning about some aspect of who you are" (p. 33).

For example, in a sociology of race and ethnicity freshman undergraduate course I teach at a predominantly white university, the first quarter of the course is spent examining whiteness as a racial category. This is done by having white students respond to the following questions regarding being white: (1) one thing you like about being white; (2) one thing you do not like about being white; and (3) one thing you do not like about other white people (Federation of Community of Work Training Group 1987). In addition to this, students review the documentary video *Being White*, which "shows white people from variety of backgrounds looking at what whiteness means from their particular standpoint: English, Irish, Jewish, working-class, middle-class, etc. (Federation of Community Work Training Group 1987). The intention of the questions and video is to discuss how difficult it is for Euro-Americans to think of themselves as white, raising the question why and the political and cultural implications of this for nonwhite people. White students generally respond by saying that "it is hard to think of themselves as being white"; "they take their whiteness for granted"; and "they do not think of themselves in racial terms." These questions illustrate to white students how mainstream white culture shapes their rhetorical responses to the questions and that mainstream white culture is about making whiteness invisible as a racial category.

The next question of the course is how does mainstream white culture make whiteness invisible? The intention here is to suggest that mainstream white culture does this by making blackness visible as a racial category. This is illustrated by using popular movie and music videos. In many of these videos, such as Madonna or "Something Wild" liberal-minded, white artistic producers or cultural workers unconsciously use stereotypes about blackness or black culture as a way to critique some aspect of mainstream white culture (hooks 1993; Bailey 1988). What this segment of the course tries to point out is that their particular appropriation and representation of black culture often reinforces the ideology of white supremacy, resulting in the entrenchment of white privilege and domination.

NOTES

*In this chapter I have expanded on some of the ideas from my dissertation.

REFERENCES

American Psychological Society. 1992. ADAMHA chief resigns, Becomes director of NIMH. *Observer* 5(2).

Bailey, Cameron. 1988. Nigger/Lover: The thin sheen of race in "Something Wild." *Screen* 29(4).

Baudrillard, J. 1981. *For a political economy of the sign.* St. Louis: Telos Press.

Banfield, Edward. 1968. *The unheavenly city revisited.* Boston: Little, Brown and Company.

Bloom, Allen. 1987. *The Closing of the American Mind.* New York: Simon and Schuster.

Carby, Hazel. 1989. The canon: Civil war and reconstruction. *Michigan Quarterly Review* 27(1).

Dent, Gina. 1992. "Black Pleasure, Black Joy: An Introduction." In Gina Dent (ed), *Black Popular Culture.* Seattle: Bay Press.

Dyer, Richard. 1988. White. *Screen* 29(4).

Ehrenreich, Barbara. 1989. *Fear of falling: The inner life of the middle class.* New York: HarperCollin Publishers.

Federation of Community Work Training Groups. 1987. *Being white.* Sheffield: Albany Video and Federation of Community Work Training Groups.

Gilman, Sander L. 1985. *Difference and pathology: Stereotypes of sexuality, race, and madness.* Ithaca, NY: Cornell University Press.

124

Gilroy, Paul. 1987. *There ain't no black in the union jack: The cultural politics of race and nation.* Chicago: University of Chicago Press.

Giroux, Henry A. 1991. *Postmodernism, feminism, and cultural politics: Redrawing the educational boundaries.* Albany, NY: State University of New York Press.

Goldberg, David Theo, ed. 1990. *Anatomy of racism.* Minneapolis: University of Minnesota Press.

Goldman, Robert, and Steve Papson. 1991. "Levis and the Knowing Wink." In Current Perspectives in Social Theory. Volume II.

Gramsci, Antonio. 1980. *Prison note books.* New York: International Publishers.

Hall, Stuart. 1991. Ethnicity: Identity and difference. *Radical America* 23(4).

Hall, Stuart and Jacques Martin. 1990. The new times: Manifesto for new times. in *New Times: The changing face of poltics in the 1990s.* ed. Stuart Hall and Martin Jacques. London: Verso.

hooks, bell. 1990. *Yearning: Race, gender, and cultural politics.* Boston: South End Press.

———. 1992. Representing whiteness in the black imagination, in *Cultural Studies,* ed. Lawrence Grossberg, Cary Nelson, and Paula Treichler. New York: Routledge.

hooks, bell and West, Cornel. 1991. *Breaking bread: Insurgent lack intellectual life.* Boston: South End Press.

Jordon, Winthrop D. 1968. *White over black.* New York: W. W. Norton.

Julien, Isaac and Mercer, Kobena. 1988. Introduction: De margin and de centre, *Screen* 29(4).

Kovel, Joel. 1984. *White racism: A psychohistory.* New York: Columbia University Press.

Lefebvre, Henri. 1990. *Everyday life in the modern world.* New Brunswick: Transaction Publishers.

Lemann, Nicholas. 1991. *The promised land: The great black migration and how it changed america.* New York: Vintage.

MacCannell, Dean. 1989. *The tourist: A theory of the leisure class.* New York: Schocken Books.

McLaren, Peter. 1991. Postmodernism, Postcolonialism and Pedagogy. *Education and Society* 9(2).

———. 1992. Collisions with otherness: 'Travelling' theory, postcolonial criticism, and the politics of ethnographic practice— the mission of the wounded ethnographer" *Qualitative Studies in Education* 5(1).

Melucci, Alberto. 1989. *Nomads of the present: Social movements and individual needs in contemporary society.* Philadelphia: Temple University Press.

Murray, Robin. 1990. Fordism and post-Fordism," in *New times: The Changing Face of Politics in the 1990s*, ed. Stuart Hall and Martin Jacques. London: Verso.

Omi, Michael. 1989. In living color: Race and American culture in *Cultural politics in contemporary America*, ed. Ian Angus and Sut Jhally. New York: Routledge.

Pieterse, Jan Nederveen. 1992. *White on black: Images of Africa and blacks in western popular culture.* New Haven: Yale University Press.

Roediger, David. 1992. *The wages of whiteness.* New York: Routledge.

Rosaldo, Renato. 1989. *Culture and truth: The remaking of social analysis.* Boston: Beacon Press.

Rutherford, Jonathan, ed. 1990. *Identity, community, culture, difference.* London: Lawrence and Wishart.

Smith-Prothrow, Deborah. 1991. *Deadly consequences: How violence is destroying our teenage population and a plan to begin solving the problem.* New York: Harper Collins.

Sarup, Madan. 1989. An Introduction Guide to Post-structuralism and Post-modernism. Athens: The University of Georgia Press.

Talyor, Clyde. 1991. The re-birth of the aesthetic in cinema. *Wide Angle* 13(3,4).

West, Cornel. 1989. Black culture and postmodernism in *Remaking history*, ed. Barbara Kruger and Phil Mariani. Seattle: Bay Press.

———. 1991a. The new cultural politics of difference, in *Out there: marginalization and contemporary cultures*, ed. Russell Ferguson et al. Cambridge: MIT Press.

———. 1991b. Princeton's public intellectual. *New York Times Magazine*, September 15.

Williams, Brett. 1991. Aliens in our midst. *Nation* 55(6).

Young, Loga. 1992. A nasty piece of work: A psychoanalytic study of sexual and racial difference in 'Mona Lisa'" in *Identity: Community, culture and difference*, ed. Jonathan Rutherford. London: Lawernce and Wishart.

4

Shirley R. Steinberg ———————————————————————

Critical Multiculturalism and Democratic Schooling: An Interview with Peter McLaren and Joe Kincheloe

Shirley: Why has the New Right come to dominate the public conversation about education in this country?

Peter: Shirley, I believe that the ascendancy of the New Right in this virulent period of recycled McCarthyism is truly frightening to those who believe in democracy and believe that democracy demands more than simply opening up the floodgates of social life to the current of free enterprise. Chester Finn may be waging a war on the very idea of "public" institutions, but in doing so he joins Ravitch, Gingrich, Schlesinger, Bennett, and others in putting their own ambition before the defense of freedom, and thereby masquerading reactionary power as democratic populism. As they rail against entrenched self-interest in patriotic hyperbole that is as self-congratulatory, self-indulgent, and self-glorifying as it is obscenely lacking in insight, they in fact are serving the interests of corporate capital and the status quo distribution of power and wealth which, let's face it, is the lynchpin of conservative policy. We have seen, over the last two decades, brutally effective measures to domesticate the working class (which Ravitch doesn't believe exists in the United States) and curtail or prevent labor militancy. In doing so, the new conservative cabal supports the goal of American enterprise, which is to keep the populace too busy to contemplate and organize resistance to the corporate empires that enslave them by supporting a consumer ethic that creates new demands, new desires, and new forms of discontent that can only be remedied with purchasing power, with becoming sexier, thinner, more muscular, more fashionable, and more powerful in the marketplace of a consumer and service-oriented, post-Fordist economy.

The repugnantly repressive moralism of the current conservative political regime, its recent counterattacks on cultural democracy, and its frenetic and at times savage attacks on the under-class and subaltern groups, as well as its militant antiunionism and foreign interventionist policies on behalf of capitalist interests, is reflective of the steady increase in the disproportionate level of cultural power and material wealth of Americans. We are encour-aged to blame the problems of America on the breakdown of family values when, in fact, the social and educational policies of conser-vatives actually foster such a breakdown. Witness the declining inner-city labor market, growing national unemployment rates, the drastic decline in the number of unskilled positions in tradi-tional blue-collar industries in urban areas, the increasing number of youths competing for fewer and fewer entry-level jobs, the automation of clerical labor, the shifting of service sector employment to the suburbs—and on a broader scale—the deregu-lation and globalization of markets, trade, and labor, and the deregulation of local markets.

And you've got a predominately right-wing media (best illus-trated by talk radio's Rush Limbaugh's influence on the 1994 elec-tion) that often, but not always, unwittingly promote the idea shared by conservatives that underclass minority youth are more prone to violence and drug use than the more "civilized" whites. These are the "wildings" that roam the streets high on angel dust, armed with steel pipes and hunting whites. These are the Rodney Kings who are presumed to be life-threatening even when lying face down on the ground in an arrest-ready posture, choking on dust and their own blood and vomit. And the answer to such violence and despair in their lives is to sound the lapidary phrase: "Just say no to drugs!" Can't you hear William Bennett hollering into the smoke-filled skies of Los Angeles, megaphone clutched in his beefy, manicured hand, crying: "Just say no to rioting!"

Shirley: What do Peter's ideas mean for those who are educa-tional leaders and are committed to principals of progressive, democratic reform?

Joe: Peter has much to say to educational leaders. Indeed, the ideas that Peter and I promote are concepts which many times have not been a part of the public conversation about education—a conversation dominated by the voices of Finn, Ravitch, Bloom, Hirsch, D'Souza, Bennett, and Alexander. Indeed, the most impor-tant new dynamic in the public conversation about education involves the publication of Richard Herrnstein and Charles Murray's *The Bell Curve: Intelligence and Class Structure in American Life*—a book designed to academically justify mean-spir-ited Republican policies against the poor. Educational leaders need to conceive of democracy as a fragile entity, a concept which cannot survive confrontation with unequal power relations. Educational reform conceptualized in an era which has seen an unprecedented growth in these unequal power relations must be carefully examined to see how it reflects antidemocratic tendencies. For example, when the Reagan and Bush administrations offered new strategies for education, they were conceived almost totally outside the social and economic context. Few of the conservative reformers think in terms of the impact of accountability-driven curricula on those who fall outside the dominant culture. As long as minority youth are positioned as outsiders to the dominant culture, as long as African American and Hispanic/Latino culture is viewed as an impediment to be erased, as long as the curriculum excludes the history and culture of such peoples, educational reforms will fail the test of democracy. We will continue to view intelligence as a form of male-centered, abstract rationality which has little to do with situated, contextual forms of thinking–cognitive styles which have traditionally been excluded from the definition of intelligence.

Shirley: When I read or listen to Chester Finn and Diane Ravitch write or talk about educational reform, I get the feeling that they have never considered such ideas. Is that a fair assessment?

Joe: I'm not sure where they are coming from. Wherever it is, they have captured the mood of the Reagan years with the denial that socioeconomic context must be considered in educational reform.

Shirley: But they are intelligent people; surely they have considered the socioeconomic context?

Joe: After studying their work, it seems to me that they are so caught up in the metanarratives of modernism (that is, the larger cultural stories we tell about who we are as a people and the purposes our institutions serve) that they are blind to the voices of the marginalized and the voices of those committed to economic justice. For example, Ravitch and Finn use evidence from researchers who view the improvement of standardized test scores as the raison d'être of teaching. No questions seem to have been asked here about where the knowledge on the tests comes from or whose interests it serves, what impact such tests have on the role of teacher, or the assumptions about the nature of knowledge embedded in it. Caught in the trap of objectivism, Finn and Ravitch cannot reflect on the political or epistemological presuppositions of this test-driven curriculum because they claim they don't exist. They never talk about the historical and social context which gave birth to such a curriculum. Thus, the dramatic negative effects such an education produces are swept under the neoconservative rug. In a number of ways it could be argued that Ravitch and Finn's work of the 1970s, 1980s, and early 1990s set the stage for a serious public and academic consideration of the pseudo science of *The Bell Curve*.

Shirley: There's a lot of discussion now among critical educators about using postmodern social theory to analyze schooling—something you and Henry Giroux pioneered at the Center for Education and Cultural Studies at Miami University of Ohio. It seems that those same educational critics who criticized you for being too esoteric are now writing from a postmodernist perspective. How does this perspective help you to challenge the onslaught of the New Right?

Peter: Some people blame me for introducing the term "postmodernism" into the educational debate. Frankly, I have no idea when it started and don't think its important who was first. I began writing about postmodernism in 1987 in an article I did on Paulo Freire for *Educational Theory*. Postmodernism had already been on the scene for some time outside the field of pedagogy. At that time I was worried about the cynicism that was associated with certain postmodern schools of thought, and I was trying to defend Freire's utopian thinking against such theoretical cynicism. Henry and I tried to expand on the idea picked up in cultural studies of a "resistance postmodernism" or "critical postmodernism"—something Henry has advanced brilliantly in his book, *Border Crossings*. This follows *Postmodern Education*, which he did with Stanley Aronowitz. My interest in postmodernism as resistance has led me to re-theorize difference as it is commonly used to refer to an excess of signs and their unrepresentability. While difference may well be a form of logocentric fiction it is not immanent to the laws of signification but rather located in class struggle, divisions of labor, and relations of consumption, production and exploitation in general. My work has also been about "borders" but as they relate to postmodern identity formation, the globalization of culture, and the production of desire. I've tried to counter conservative perspectives on national or civic identity by arguing that identities are always *multiply organized* as a series of often conflicting subject positions. On this basis, I am able to challenge the New Right perspectives on patriotism and civic duty as really being monolithic and linked to the imperatives of a service economy that produces good consumers.

Think about this, Shirley. Do you want your American citizenship shaped by corporate power and the big business establishment in collusion with the Educational Excellence Network? Do you want the future of your children to be mortgaged to a corporate business rationality that seeks to create a public sphere comprised of workers with an overabundance of technical skills so it can provide cheap labor? Think of the $200 million the America 2000 project will raise from the business community to create the New American Schools program. Think of the whole idea of selling school reform under the banner of choice. How can you really have choice when the government is prescribing the standards and forms of assessment? When it is regulating through national funds teaching standards and practices? This majoritarian control will lead to less cultural diversity, less creativity, less democracy.

Diane Ravitch, former assistant Secretary of Education, Gilbert Sewall of the American Textbook Council, Lynne Cheney, a consistent right-wing watchdog for any policy that addresses issues of social justice, and Chester Finn, a primary architect of America 2000, receive funding from conservative foundations such as the Olin Foundation and the Donner Foundation of New York. The right wing reform initiative invited Chris Whittle, who heads a corporation that uses place-based marketing, to supply television equipment free of charge in schools where his Channel One is shown in social studies, communications, or art classes. Daily broadcasts of twelve minutes reach approximately 8,000 schools. Channel One produces news segments that are interspersed with commercial messages, and Whittle Communications retains revenue for using them.

I am against corporate marketing in schools, and Whittle's Channel One sanctions the present role capitalism plays in democracy. It also is a question of privileging image over content and context. What gets ignored is how news stories and commercials get created and what constitutes their ideological imperative, which is to attract the largest numbers of corporate sponsors. Reality gets served up to students under the corporate banner of show business and profits. The media is already blurring the boundaries between news and advertising. Corporate ownership of the media is increasing commercial exploitation of student populations worldwide. Data systems of the world corporations will become the curriculum of the future. We have entered Paul Virilio's perceptual field of "instantaneous ubiquity" and Baudrillard's "hyperspace of simulation" and in the words of Larry Grossberg, which refer to the title of his book, *We Gotta Get Out of This Place.*

The whole argument that Channel One will overcome ignorance among students with respect to current events is silly and facile when you consider the way that the media articulates meaning. I'm not simply referring to the commercials that are part of the satellite broadcasts. Channel One fragments the viewer by eliminating self-reflection. While commercials construct the viewers as dependent consumers, viewers are invited to judge the validity of the advertisements. Viewers are framed monologically by providing them with the illusion that they exercise some power as interpreters of what they see and hear. Yet such a role is really illusory because self-reflection virtually collapses in television viewing. Advertisements flatter viewers into thinking they are self-constituting agents when in reality the self produced by media images is profoundly simulated. Channel One creates forms of consumer desire and models of and for citizenship in which the distinction between citizen and consumer is eliminated.

In saying this I want to make clear that I am not against the use of television, per se, in the classroom. Far from it. I think television is an inescapable and important medium. The most challenging, if not disturbing, aspect about living in a world of "virtual" realities brought about by postmodern electronics is that these new formation technologies or media knowledges instantaneously transform what Larry Grossberg calls our "mattering maps"—our affective investments in roles, goals, and meanings. Think of the implications for students living in a cyberspace of computers, Nintendo games, VCRs, and MTV to be suddenly wrenched back from this electronic cocoon into the nineteenth-century world of linear time and mostly print technology—which is what happens in most of our classrooms. Walter Benjamin, and later Harold Innis and Marshall McLuhan, anticipated the effect of these new media technologies. The new information technologies create what Australian educators Bill Green and Chris Bigum call "cyborg couplings." The boundaries between machines and humans are constantly becoming blurred in this age of new media technologies, creating what Donna Haraway refers to as the transformation of humans into cyborgs. Haraway refers here to an "informatics of domination" that reflects fundamental changes in the nature of class, race and gender in an emergent "information system." So whereas having television in the classroom may indeed be important in creating a postmodern curriculum for the new generation of young cyborgs that fill our classrooms, we need to be able to use such technology in ways that don't simply create what I have termed "corporate neocolonialism." Rather, as Henry Giroux and I have argued recently, helping students in the age of what Green and Bigum refer to as "technonature" or the new "digital ecosystem" in which contexts are always indeterminate and contingent instead of being anchored in biological or human time, means helping them to become media literate. When people ask me why I am stressing the idea of media literacy more and more in my writings, I have to admit to them that the effect of the new media technologies in forging identities for my students far outstrips what I am able to do in the classroom unless I begin to bring popular culture into the curriculum as a central focus. This, to me, is what the postmodern curriculum is all about. Providing young cyborgs with an understanding of how their identities are becoming constructed within the current proliferation of techno-cultures. What are the new postmodern pathologies that might emerge? Yes, I worry about this. But I also hold out some hope that students growing up in cyberspace may be able to educate us as to the possibilities of new cyber-identities, new postmodern narratives of the self that may bring about a better world. I am not overly optimistic, but I think it's a challenge we must not ignore. We need to be careful here and not assume that technology is the primary source of new inequalities created by post-Fordist economic arrangements. We can't forget that technological advances are grounded in material conditions linked to the exploitation of labor.

Shirley: Joe, you've written extensively on teacher education. What are the implications of Peter's comments on postmodernism for the professional education of teachers?

Joe: I would argue that these so-called educational innovations characterize a significant break with this country's educational past. Business involvement with education before Whittle was a bit embarrassed, taking place at a more covert level. With Channel One and initiatives by Disney (Teacher of the Year), Barbie (Learn-to-Read), McDonald's, et. al., we begin to see an unabashed merging of a public educational system with private economic interests. I get the feeling that the architects of these plans assume that any progressive opposition to their strategies would be so minimal that it would not merit serious consideration. I hope that assessment of critical progressivism is unfounded, but I do admit that I would like to see more outrage about the merging of these private and public institutions. Not only have schooling and business merged but education broadly defined (the learning that takes place both in schools and out of school) and business/corporate interests have never been so closely connected. Via technological innovation, business interests have constructed undreamed-of information monopolies that serve to transform information into a private commodity. As fewer and fewer corporations control the flow of information (two percent of publishers, for example, control 75% of the books published in the U.S.), public assessibility to information contracts.

Teachers, like most Americans, are too often incapable of analyzing the political interests of the information and the situations which confront them. A critical postmodern teacher education would prepare teachers to seek the origins of the "knowledge" with which they have to deal and to ask questions concerning who benefits from particular portrayals of reality. Such an analytical ability would alert teachers to the power interests involved in the schools. Critical postmodern teacher education teaches students much more than just how to "do it differently." Students learn how institutions operate, how bureaucracies produce goal displacement as they confuse form with substance. In the process, prospective teachers learn about how discursive conventions in general regulate what is deemed acceptable and unacceptable, while in particular they learn how dominant power shapes the discursive boundaries of the school. The right wing has been very successful in the promotion of the Great Denial in the professional preparation of teachers. This denial involves the right wing's refusal to acknowledge the political ramifications of teacher education. Much like the CIA, they maintain a stance of "plausible deniability" when confronted with the political nature of their mission.

Without using the term political, right-wing teacher educators frame their holy mission as a neo–White Man's Burden, a missionary struggle between forms of civilized high culture and the poor or "off-white" unwashed masses. Allan Bloom carries the flag as he portrays the culture of the masses as a disease to be cured with the magic of the traditional Western canon. Writing with latex gloves of the distasteful culture of the unwashed, Bloom turns up his nose at their music, their dancing, their television, and God forbid, their sexual impulses. After Bloom's death in 1992, William Bennett established himself as Bloom's heir as defender of Western values and virtues. *The Book of Virtues*, Bennett's toast to the trivialization of "doing-good," has celebrated Western values in the typical right-wing decontextualized manner—virtue is always simple and straight-forward, power relations and questions of commitment to principle never involve complex choices. Buoyed by Bloom's and now Bennett's call to arms, right-wing teacher education deploys prospective teachers on a search and destroy mission—the objective: pernicious youth culture and popular culture with their degraded use of multicultural forms and questionable non-Western values.

Shirley: Tell us some more about critical postmodern perspectives on teacher education.

Joe: Students in critical postmodern teacher education focus on the study of epistemology, the nature of knowledge. Not only do students learn how knowledge is produced and legitimated, but they learn that one of the most important features of a critical postmodern pedagogy involves the ability to create knowledge. Knowledge is not just created in the researcher's office or in the professor's study but in the consciousness produced in thinking, discussion, writing, argument, or conversation. It's created when teachers and students confront a contradiction, when students encounter a dangerous memory, when teacher-presented information collides with student experience, or when student-presented information collides with teacher experience. When teachers and students speculate on the etymology and deployment of knowledge, new knowledge is created. This ability to create knowledge forms the foundation of the type of teacher education that Peter and I promote. When we find ourselves in multicultural schools, this creation of knowledge takes on even more significance. When a critical postmodern teacher who doesn't share the culture, language, race, or socioeconomic backgrounds of students enters the classroom, she or he becomes not a Hirsch-like information provider but an explorer who works with students to create mutually understood texts. Based on their explorations, teachers and students create new learning materials full of mutually generated meanings and shared interpretations.

Feminist pedagogy theoretically contributes to our notion of critical postmodern knowledge production. Teachers who create knowledge must understand various ways of knowing (whether it be women's ways of perceiving or subjugated knowledges of oppressed peoples) and draw upon these perspectives when reconceptualizing the knowledge of school. These diverse ways of knowing will allow teachers to help students analyze events and interpret cultural meanings. Such ways of knowing will help teachers engage student experience in a way that allows it to be both affirmed and questioned, all the time keeping alive the possibility of self and social transformation.

It comes as no surprise that right-wing critics such as Bloom, Finn, Limbaugh, and Ravitch will decry such proposals on the grounds that they undermine the instruction of a core curriculum grounded on the great ideas of the Western tradition. Critical postmodern teacher education would produce students who are capable of engaging many of the ideas such critics hold dear. Students catalyzed by such encounters would, admittedly, be dangerous in the eyes of the cocky conservatives of post-1994-

elections America. Indeed, they would be the type of student who would be empowered to see through the cant of *The Bell Curve's* "new ground." They would understand the *absurdity* of Herrnstein and Murray's claim that African Americans are not as intelligent as white Americans. They would expose the racism and class bias that undergirds Herrnstein and Murray's argument that these low I.Q. African Americans receive too much attention in America's schools, thus taking time away from the cognitive elite (the gifted): "the students with the most capacity to absorb education should get the most of it" (Herrnstein and Murray, 1994, p. 418). Dangerous critical students would not allow such foolishness to go unchallenged. Of course, a critical postmodern curriculum would go beyond the boundaries of the West and engage ideas from Asia and Third World cultures as well.

The central point of critical postmodern teacher education, however, involves helping prospective teachers confront the epistemological shifts demanded by it. While a right-wing teacher education involves preparing prospective teachers to teach in a correct-answer-oriented curriculum with an unexamined realist epistemological base, critical postmodernism envisions a conceptually-oriented curriculum with a consciously examined, critical constructivist epistemological base. These critical curricular and epistemological perspectives change the purpose of teacher education programs and schools in general from vocational orientations with an emphasis on the provision of an essential body of knowledge and a set of narrow skills to one of intellectual development and an attempt to rewrite and transform the world.

Shirley: Peter, doesn't it strike you as odd that the conservative multiculturalists set themselves up as champions of diversity yet end up actually reinforcing the idea of a monolithic, singular culture?

Peter: Not at all, Shirley. Their language is very duplicitous. You need to be very careful not to take what they say at face value. That's what makes them so dangerous. The Native Americans knew this when they said early this century that white people speak with "forked tongues."

We create narrative spaces for individuals in our culture and classrooms to succeed as a condition of whiteness, of primarily white male values, values that stress boundaries, borders, and rationality. These are certainly linked to the ideology of the old "new" conservatives like Ravitch and Schlesinger who hide their thralldom to white culture in a measured discourse that calls for diversity and multiculturalism. That white values are held to be the apotheosis of civilization is camouflaged. In truth, it is not that the Whites are the most successful players in the interethnic struggle over identity and power, but the only group allowed to play. After all, it's the Whites who primarily set the rules for the game. Educators shouldn't let Ravitch and Schlesinger trick them into thinking that whiteness is constrained by a society premised on equality because in our society, whiteness and inequality are often coterminous—whiteness is often the force behind inequality.

Obviously white culture is not benign. It can be—and often is— a wrathful space of delirious greed; it spacializes the body and territorializes it in the service of capital. It is structured on race, class, and gender inequality. The new conservatives wrest their view of culture from the turbulence of such inequality while celebrating diversity and naturalizing the preferred structures of Western values of consumer individualism.

In saying this, let me emphasize something I think is crucial. We do not simply live in white or Latino or African American cultures. There is diversity within them, and also we must recognize there is cross-cultural sharing that occurs across the often permeable boundaries separating them. We are, in this country, transcultural citizens: we occupy points of identification with many cultures. To suggest that, for instance, African Americans lose their ethnic roots if they adopt aspects of white culture or that white people lose their ethnicity by engaging Afrocentric values is to actually reinforce the marginalization of African Americans by emphasizing the binary opposition: black vs. white. I am not trying to essentialize or romanticize differences between white and African American cultures or white and Latino cultures. White culture is not monolithic or homogeneous or thoroughly evil. I am, however, trying to suggest that there is a relationship among the culture of elite white men, an allegiance to capitalism, and the negation of the Other (women, minorities, and the poor). This relationship is not acknowledged by the conservative multiculturalists.

While its true that we no longer think of education as the same type of sorting mechanism that once served to separate out Eastern Europe and African American and Latino immigrants from those groups more easy identified as "Western," I do think schools still serve to conscript certain forms of difference into the service of the wealthy and the privileged, although today it's legitimized by different ideological methods and enhanced through privatization. One only has to read Jonathan Kozol's *Savage Inequalities*, to see how little things have really changed. Education is still the primary means for civilizing immigrants, for remodeling the so-called aberrant behavior of those groups whose flesh is unacceptable but who can serve as good scapegoats for building more jails and prisons instead of schools.

For too many minorities, schools have become cathedrals of death, agencies for reintegration, camps for ideological internment, factories for domestication. Schools are certainly not relevant to the way we conduct social life in this age of post-Fordist consumer culture. Far from it. However, they are profoundly necessary for conservatives in a world in which cultural meaning has been transformed into one big advertising montage. If we are going to divide the world of the "haves" and the "have-nots" into the "winners" and the "losers," then we need to keep control over who will win and who will lose. And if we can do this under the banner of "choice," then so much the better. We can give certain minorities the choice of which institutions will fail them and then blame their failure on personal lifestyle or lack of good old American family virtues. Fortunately, there are teachers and students out there fighting against this, along with marginal and interstitial groups. We need to build on these grassroots struggles, and for this reason the educational left must work together.

Shirley: Let's go ahead and address the issue of multiculturalism.

Peter: Well, first of all, America is not only a land of immigrants. African Americans were forced to come here as slaves and the Native Americans were already here. Minorities in this country have been and continue to be historically muted; subaltern groups continue to be oppressed, policed, and demonized within patriarchal imperialist ideological formations that exist as part of a capitalist technocracy. We are still witnessing the dissimulation of imperialism under the guise of creating a "common culture" that seeks unity and consensus in diversity. To me, we need to offer space for struggle, for conflict. The goal of a common culture is born out of a modernist legacy of trying to own knowledge, control knowledge, and is related to the Cartesian perspective of the autonomous, rational ego. It is born out of the legacy of imperialism that privileges the "high" culture of the Western Enlightenment. It's tied to the desire for objective knowledge. It's a symptom of the desire to contain and control the social by asserting a stable identity. Joe and I talk about this a great deal in our work.

The goal of a critical multiculturalism—which is how I identify my own pedagogy—is not to reverse the margins and centers of power but to displace their founding binarisms and dependent hierarchies. A critical multiculturalism foregrounds *whiteness* as an ethnic category parasitic on *blackness* so that whiteness ceases to serve as an invisible norm against which we measure the worth of other cultures. Such a move can help teachers and students question the received practical and disciplinary knowledge students bring with them to the classroom.

Joe and I talk about the importance of dislocating whiteness from its infusion into our national unconscious as a synonym for cultural and moral superiority. Western rationality associated with whiteness needs to be radically decentered as the source of pristine truth. In fact, Western rationality and values are murky: they are implicated in relations of power. Family values conceived without the realization that such values are socially construed within particular arenas of power and privilege lapses into a trivialization of a serious issue. The American government justifies its racist and sexist policy that created an underclass by turning social pathology into a question of personal choice. What gives the ruling elite the right to pass judgment on those groups who don't share their own economic and cultural privilege? Those who do not share these values are condemned as "relativists" who have *no* preferred values. Family values as defined by the right, in fact, are not only morally repugnant but intellectually dishonest. They are built upon an essentialist itinerary of white male hegemonic inteests. Right-wing spokespeople such as Gingrich and Rush Limbaugh are unaware of the structuring influence that ideology plays in producing the discursive field they exploit.

Diversity that somehow constitutes itself as a harmonious ensemble of benign cultural spheres is a conservative and liberal model of multiculturalism that, in my mind, deserves to be jettisoned because, when we try to make culture an undisturbed space of harmony and agreement where social relations exist within cultural forms of uninterrupted accord, we ascribe to a form of social amnesia in which we forget that all knowledge is forged in histories that are played out in the field of social antagonisms. As Joe mentioned earlier: Whose knowledge are we talking about? Whose interests does such knowledge serve? With the "diversity" the conservatives speak about comes a normative grid that contains cultural differences.

It is mentioning here that I see my work as part of much larger traditions within critical pedagogy and cultural studies that have been taking up the question of identity, difference, and human agency for some time. I'm thinking of people like Antonia Darder, Cameron McCarthy, Christine Sleeter, Jo Anne Pagano, Bill Pinar, Henry Giroux, and Paulo Freire in critical pedagogy and multiculturalism and Stanley Aronowitz, bell hooks, Homi Bhabha, Cornel West, Abdul JanMohammed, Larry Grossberg, Chandra Mohanty,

and Michele Wallace in cultural studies. While none of these traditions is homogeneous, I think it's important that we acknowledge
the theoretical trajectories out of which our work is forged.

Having said this, I think that the sites of our identity within
postmodern cultures are various and as seekers of liberation,
teachers need to recognize the heterogeneous character of their
inscription into colonial and neocolonial texts of history and
cultural discourses of empire. New sites of agency are erupting all
around us at the borderlines of cultural instability. I seek a pedagogy of insurrection, in the in-between spaces of cultural negotiation and translation. I look to the creation of hyphenated identities
that struggle against monolithic models of democratic citizenship
associated with Phil Gramm and the self-styled custodians of identity such as Ravitch and Schlesinger. That's why I admire and
support the struggles of Latino groups and African Americans in
the creation of new ethnicities that take seriously the politics of
difference and cultural justice. That's why my own work is
informed by feminist theory and post-colonial theory.

Henry Giroux wisely advises us to be "border crossers." We are
finished with the age of border guards and the naive psychologism
often associated with a total and autonomous self-identity. We
need, as teachers, to invent ourselves in new ways, to stop looking
for a natural language or a pure "ground" of being. We need to
develop new theories of social criticism and transformation and
not retreat from theory, as many conservatives and even some
leftist teacher activists are advocating. There is a danger in yielding
to the seduction of "plainspeak," because new social arrangements
demand more sophisticated theories of pedagogy, culture, identity-
formation, and liberation, and not the banal journalistic accounts
some teacher activists think is the antidote to the new continental
social theory. Diane Ravitch and Arthur Schlesinger, Jr., as historians of the mainstream, worry a great deal about multiculturalism turning into a vitriolic factionalism—self-interest groups
indulging in belligerent forms of ethnocentrism. The Committee of
Scholars in Defense of History, of which they are members, serves
as little more than an ideological bunker: a holding camp for
subjugated knowledges—those knowledges that threaten the
dominant culture's view of truth and justice. Hegemonic historians
who attempt to defend the lies of the empire—Ravitch, Schlesinger,
and others—fail to consider the privileging norms and articulatory
effects of their own positionality as white, Anglocentric theorists.

What we need as part of a multicultural curriculum is not only
a social, historical perspective that highlights the contributions

and struggles of subaltern groups but also one that provides us with an understanding of approaches to the study of history itself.

There's been a revolution in the social sciences that can help us to understand the ways in which historians construct the objects of their studies: how they create and often demonize their Others through the conceptual artifacts of their own methodologies and the ideological assumptions that inform the questions they ask and fail to ask. I think we need to understand that histories of minorities are too frequently textual constructions created by the winners who, not surprisingly, are usually white and Anglo. For example, Ravitch and Schlesinger use whiteness as a cultural marker against which otherness is defined by not interrogating their own privilege as white, hegemonic historians. Whiteness does not exist outside of culture but constitutes the prevailing social texts in which social norms are made and remade. Their own Eurocentric cultural norms and logocentric rationality pass unobserved in the discourses that structure their own research. The seeming pluralism and the lip service to diversity is belied by an allegiance to a monolithic view of citizenship steeped in a legacy of Western imperial high culture. It is almost as if whiteness depends on its legitimacy by being colorless and culture-less. It is this colonial invisibility that helps to create legitimizing norms defining "otherness" and racializing myths of difference. Whiteness is everything yet nothing, everywhere yet nowhere. Its slippery and formless and yet as intractable as hell when you brush up against it. Just ask people of color. I'm reminded of this each time I visit East L.A.

Shirley, I can see the ghost of Allan Bloom still pining for the former grandeur of Greek and Roman antiquity. Late Victorian highbrow culture could not be resurrected in the academy, so Bloom took it out on rock 'n' roll and non-Western thinkers whom he stigmatized as the inverted and debased image of the hyper-civilized metropolitan intellectual. To move away from Western knowledge and the radiantly civilized high culture of Hellenism is to descend into savagery and barbarism—into reason's Negative Other which, according to Bloom, is tantamount to Hell.

Shirley: Doesn't Diane Ravitch claim that the analysis of education in light of socioeconomic class is inappropriate in the study of education?

Joe: You're right. Ravitch claims that in an egalitarian society such as the U.S., class analysis doesn't really apply. I wish all the economically disadvantaged people in our country could hear her say that. Maybe this would alert us to the mind-set which has directed the educational reform movements of the last dozen years.

To personalize Peter's and my ideas about the moral failures of this neo-conservative perspective, I like to tell the story of some of the kids I grew up with in the rural Appalachian Mountains of east Tennessee. For example, my friend Larry was a kid whose parents finished no more than six grades of schooling. His mother worked in the home and his father cut firewood during fall and winter. Larry was brilliant. Before we started to school, Larry would take me into the woods behind his house and teach me the names and medicinal uses of many of the plants that grew in the hills. He was a storehouse of information. He also understood the workings of a car engine, having watched his father repair the old Ford perpetually parked out in the front yard. Sometimes when I was visiting he would take apart pieces of engine and show me how they worked. He was my teacher and I was a willing student. All of this changed when we started school. With his thick mountain accent, Larry had trouble understanding the language of the school. He frequently would ask me what the teacher meant. Growing up in a home with no magazines, newspapers, or books, Larry was poorly prepared for a curriculum grounded on one's familiarity with symbolic language. Moreover, because of his unfamiliarity with such linguistic conventions, he was deemed unintelligent by the evaluative instruments of school—no matter that he brought a wealth of knowledge with him, no matter that he had virtually no experience with symbolic language before coming to school. Larry's unique form of contextual understanding did not count in our school. It is the Larrys of the world that are victimized by the right-wing reforms. It is real live students from poor homes and the homes of the culturally different whose futures are undermined by the right-wing indifference to questions of social and economic context. The critical pedagogical tradition from which Peter and I come demands educational justice for Larry and students like him. This is why we work so hard to challenge the theoretical assumptions which undergird their perspectives—the modernist scientific tradition, unbridled free enterprise capitalism, socially decontextualized psychometrics, Eurocentrism, and patriarchy.

Shirley: But Bloom, Bennett, Finn, and Ravitch and let's not forget Rush attempt to frame your critique and your questions as some form of unreasonable assault on the sacred democratic success of schooling in America. How do you respond?

Joe: Part of the mythology that the right-wing has created to sustain its power involves the portrayal of a golden age of American education. It was a "simpler, more natural time" when students behaved, the basics were taught, and teachers were dedicated to their noble profession. Ronald Reagan built a career on creating nostalgia for this golden age; Rush Limbaugh and Phil Gramm are building their careers in the mid-1990s on a similar nostalgia created by Disney-identified political managers—Frontierland education from imagineers of simulacrum. If we would just get prayer back in the school, restore discipline like Joe Clark did in New Jersey, and teach reverence for American traditions, we could find our lost glory. Right-wingers make little attempt to hide the fact that it was the reformers of the "permissive" 1960s that defiled our grand traditions. It was a great story and it worked beautifully. Ward and June Cleaver are under siege, the right-wing argued, by the nontraditional destroyers of the family unit—the gays, the liberals, the feminists, and the militant Blacks. To regain Wally and Beaver's utopian childhood in mythical Mayfield, we must support an Ozzie Nelson-like president and his comforting homilies about the American past.

Shirley: Are you saying that the right-wing created a new history?

Joe: That's exactly what I'm saying. Reagan and his educational reformers erased our "dangerous memories." Vietnam became our finest hour in defense of freedom, and the quest for social and racial justice became the clambering of the special interest groups. William Bennett warned against using social studies to teach about racial issues; instead, he argued, we should be teaching the "great facts" of American history. These great facts became a code for the military and political exploits of white men— the Revolutionary War heroes, Zachary Taylor and Lewis Cass in the Mexican War, the commanders of the Army of the Potomac, Teddy Roosevelt at San Juan Hill, etc....

Such a history helps shape the consciousness of our students. It's amazing how well our memory of the "dangerous aspects" of the past has been erased. My students, for example, are virtually unacquainted with labor history or labor perspectives on history. They are shocked by stories of the "labor wars" of the late nineteenth century. They see Vietnam through the eyes of Ronald Reagan: a noble war undercut by a drug-crazed student anti-war movement and a liberal lack of resolve.

The Iranian Hostage Crisis is a dim vestige of a distant past where an innocent America was brutalized by non-Christian savages. Let's expand on this issue for a moment to illustrate my point. It is fascinating to watch my students respond to the questions: Why were the Iranian people so angry at the U.S.? What might induce millions of Iranians to march through the streets of

Tehran chanting death to the American devils? I rarely find a student who has learned in a school context that there was a historical dimension to the Hostage Crisis. They have been taught as if the crisis suddenly sprang out of history, completely out of context. Products of a media culture and schools which avoid perspectives unfavorable to the "national interest," my students are shocked when they hear and read about the role of the CIA in overthrowing the legitimate Iranian government in 1953. The government had to go, U.S. officials agreed, when it refused to allow U.S. military installations to be constructed on the Soviet border in the north of Iran. Shocked by such revelations, my students not only begin to empathize with the anger of the Iranian people, but they begin to ask about the information they have been fed by the schools and the media. My students are fascinated by the different perspectives on the situation brought by Iranian and other foreign students. Issues such as this one begin to stimulate an awareness of the ways that their consciousness has been constructed, an appreciation of how power legitimates itself in their own lives.

Shirley: Fascinating. Let's examine this concept of consciousness construction. What are we talking about here?

Joe: I use the term *critical constructivism* to help us understand the way our identity is shaped and our perception of the world is formed. A critical constructivist sees a socially constructed world and asks what the forces are that shape our construction. We need to abandon the naive notion that our view of reality is freely made and is unaffected by power interests in the larger society. In order to understand our constructions, we must familiarize ourselves with these power interests. In a critical pedagogy this attempt to familiarize our students with these power interests becomes a central goal. Thus, how we think becomes a political issue, not just a feature of the science of cognition. From our theoretical frames, we begin to examine cognition from a critical postmodern perspective—in the process questioning the assumptions of a cognitive science which has traditionally excluded consideration of power and social context. If critical constructivism was to be taken seriously it would revolutionize not only elementary and secondary schools but higher education as well. No educational institution would be unaffected; even colleges of education would be dramatically altered. A critical constructivist teacher education would transform colleges of education into serious academic institutions dedicated to an intense socio-psychological analysis of the effects of schooling. The ways that women and men construct their consciousnesses and the role that education plays in that process would become a guiding concern of teacher education—a concern which would necessitate interdisciplinary concerns and research alliances across the university.

In this context of revolutionizing the school through a critical constructivist awareness of how the "self" is produced, we are brought back to our concerns with multiculturalism. As travelers have discovered, the attempt to understand the cultural schemata of peoples from other countries often allows for a recognition of belief systems, cognitive styles, and social assumptions in oneself. When students widen their cognitive and epistemological circles by exposure to non-Western perspectives, they gain understandings which become extremely valuable in the media-saturated post-modern world. This is what critical postmodernist pedagogy refers to as learning via the power of difference. Peter and I find it phenomenal that our efforts to promote this power of difference in our advocacy of a critical multiculturalism is framed as an unwelcome threat to American traditions and values by the right-wing. Conservatives seem to conveniently forget that the American future will be marked by greater and greater non-Anglo populations. In this twenty-first century society the basic ability to live together and learn from one another in solidarity may be considered a survival skill. Instead of circling the Anglo wagons and attempting to save "civilization" by emphasizing our "true" heritage, Bennett, Bloom, Ravitch, and Finn might have to begin listening to our warnings.

Shirley: What is wrong with the New Right's concept of "citizen?"

Peter: We need to consider the concept of citizen in the context of the historically developed patterns of capital accumulation and their corresponding relations of production. We also need to view citizenship in terms of how people are inscribed within civil society on the basis of gender, age, race, and ethnicity, and how this occurs geopolitically in terms of locally and nationally structured identities. How are personal and public experiences, co-articulated within the framework of class, gender, race, and ethnic formations, linked to capital and forms of state regulation with respect to resources? Identity formation and the construction of the self is not simply a matter of what discursive categories are available to individuals but how interests are mobilized in the securing of certain discursive forms and material benefits. The New Right perversely hides how its own perspective on citizenship is linked to how the state obliges itself to produce specific dispositions in its youth: obedience to authority, deference to the symbols of nation-hood, respect for authority and state agencies, competitiveness and a desire to compete for material possessions, and the measurement of success in terms of material wealth. The New Right's uncritical appeal to a reified notion of "citizen" is dangerous. Much of the resurgence of ethnic identities we are seeing in Eastern Europe is the result of a reaction to bureaucratically-imposed homogenization and tyranny. But identity politics does not need to be cast as politics of *either* separatism *or* the more liberal form of pluralism in which citizenship is achieved at the price of becoming married to Dan Quayle's axiologically bourgeois vision of the suburban dream.

Society is not postconflictual. We need to recognize and appreciate difference. Our identities as citizens should not be premised on the happy idiocy of Quayle's partisan and silver-spooned vision of Mr. Rogers meets John Birch at a spelling bee where all the words are limited to two syllables.

Shirley: Is it fair to say that the right-wing equates good citizenship with a form of selfish, egocentric, socially unconscious profit-seeking?

Peter: I think that's well put, Shirley. I believe that too much emphasis on the profit motive is unhealthy for democracy and cooperative self-determination and social justice. In fact, I think racism and sexism have become an internal condition for current forms of capitalism. As I've said on occasion, the American public—and especially teachers—need to be wary of a conservative vision of democracy that partakes of a mixture of Sunday barbecue homilies, American gladiator jock talk, anti-immigrant sloganeering, and the ominous rhetoric of Conan the American's "new world order" jingoism. What kind of citizens do these conservative educators want produced by the schools? I think it's quite obvious that they want citizens who are committed to entrepreneurship, who will fight to keep English the official language of the country, who will give lip serve to democracy while really advocating a consumer culture, who will cherish and defend neocolonial imperatives of a new world order ruled by the United States. With the Cold War over, the New Right and its National Association of Scholars is attacking the so-called politically correct leftists in the academy. Those few professors who are openly speaking out against sedimented forms of racism, debilitating acts of patriarchy and homophobia, are being labeled as anti-Western and antidemocratic, as separatists and ethnocentric, as the return of the storm troopers, as leftist fascists. The left (which really doesn't exit in this country in the sense of an organized presence engaged to offer a socialist alternative to advanced capitalism) has been labelled a cadre of propagandists—"academic dragoons of newthink"—bent on silencing free expression and exercising censorship on behalf of a thought police resurrected from the universe of Orwell and Foucault's panopticon. Right-wing students and faculty who fear the appearance of the "New Inquisition" pine that they can no longer make jokes or unguarded statements about women, gays and lesbians, or racial minorities. Is it political opportunism or the promotion of tolerance and free speech when the New Right attacks affirmative action and minority group efforts to develop curricula and pedagogical practices that fight racism, sexism, and Eurocentric and white supremacist views of knowledge and identity? When I spoke at the University of Milwaukee, there were some protesters who came bound and gagged because they felt that leftist educators were taking away their right to freedom of speech. These are the same people who want to abolish "ethnic studies" programs.

When this same New Right ideology pits the search for truth against the so-called decline in academic standards brought on by lesbian, gay, and ethnic studies, not only is social amnesia invoked but an assumption that truth is immutable and seamless—that it is separate from forms of advocacy, that it ontologically resides in a metaphysical pasture in which academics can graze in order to become bloated with the truth. In other words, somehow knowledge lies outside the realm of social conflict and cultural interest. It is a knowledge that is premodern and holistic—a knowledge that existed before the advent of the social sciences and the logocentricity of the natural sciences. But truth is not something that can be investigated outside of its historical, geopolitical, or sociological situatedness or contextual specificity. Of course, the New Right needs an enemy after the collapse of communism—a Cold War substitute for the 1990s. A return of the Willie Horton campaign of 1988. It needs a scapegoat for the shrinking U.S. economy and expanding minority populations. So they pick on the 4.9 percent of all U.S. college professors who call themselves leftist.

We need to retreat from evoking metaphysical truths to ground our identities—from what Wlad Godzich calls a "metasocial guarantor"—some transcendental principle such as God or what the Marxists refer to as the "laws of history." The French Revolution sanctified reason as a metasocial guarantor, and Godzich calls this reason one "that in its universality required the conquest of the world in order to free it from its pre-rational state." I like to think of this quotation in terms of how it applies to the United States. It

seems to me that the conservative multiculturalists are still sanc-
tifying Western rationality which they equate with being Euro-
American. And non-Western people—people they associate with
the Third World—are seen as non-rational, "ethnic" peoples. They
prefer to see Toni Morrison, for instance, as non-Western. It seems
to me that we should be wary about fixing our identities through
such an appeal to a metasocial guarantor such as Western rationality because this tends to lead to a war against Otherness on
behalf of imperialist masculinity. It worries me. Right now the left
is a scapegoat for anti-Western sentiment.

Shirley: You mean Dan Quayle's "cultural elite?" Didn't he
manage to create his own Willie Horton in the leftist intellectual?

Peter: Absolutely! And they conflate expressions of anti-racism,
anti-sexism, and other progressive politics with intellectual
barbarism. This is not to suggest that marginalized minorities and
groups who are critical of the dominant culture are always immune
to dogmatism, but the "political correctness" controversy is really a
misunderstanding of the political economy of knowledge—of the
knowledge industry itself—and how certain knowledges become
legitimated over others under the guise of objectivity and neutrality.
All knowledge is situated knowledge, all knowledge is partial and
contingent, and all knowledge is embedded in context of production
and reception. People who are taking a progressively radical stand
on issues involving the production of meaning are suddenly branded
as propagandists and fascists of the mind. Here, in California,
Governor Pete Wilson is supporting real fascism through his conservative multiculturalist position in his support of the recently passed
Proposition 187, a hate-filled law which will deny illegal immigrants
schooling and medical care. What can we say about legislation
designed to legalize discrimination, to force doctors, nurses and
teachers to report suspected illegal immigrants to the INS? There will
be a legal harassment of Latino and black children. Let me mention
some statements I've made before in recent essays.

The New Right talks about diversity and difference in terms of
pseudo-equality wrapped up in a counterfeit democracy of flags and
emblems—as if diversity were simply accretive, benevolently
allowing other voices to add themselves to the mainstream—voices
that have yet to share the benefits of the American dream. As Robert
Stam and others have noted, diversity is something altogether
different—it is not a collection of ethnic "add-ons" like different
flavored toppings on a vanilla ice cream sundae—rather, it is a form
of thinking from the margins, seeing Native peoples, Latinos, and
African Americans not as interest groups to be added on to a preex-

isting pluralism, but rather as being at the very core of the American experience from the beginning—each offering unique dialogical perspectives to both national and local experiences. The oppressed—because they are obliged by circumstance and the imperatives of survival to know both the dominant and marginal culture—are in a strong position to actively mobilize against the oppression brought about by corporate capitalist power.

As Chandra Talpade Mohanty notes, difference cannot be formulated simply as negotiation among culturally diverse groups against a backdrop of presumed cultural homogeneity. Difference is the recognition that all knowledges are given birth in the crucible of history.

But I would ask: Is knowledge ever constructed outside the realm of the political? Whose knowledge is most privileged? What vantage point do we take when we proclaim what "fits in" to the so-called preexisting pluralism and what does not. Why is it that Western values of reason, neutrality, and objectivity are privileged over Afrocentric ones? Does this have anything to do with preserving what Chomsky calls "the welfare state for the rich?" Does it mean creating a common culture that is colorblind? Does it really mean achieving racelessness or are the terms colorblind, racelessness, unity, and pluralism just pseudonyms for white.

Because I'm highly critical of dominant white cultures, I'm often assumed to be in support of a particularist, as distinct from a universalist, form of identity politics.

Does this mean I'm unqualifiedly for, say, Afrocentrism? My position here is close to that of Paul Gilroy and bell hooks. Much of Afrocentrism doctrine rewrites political assertions in terms similar to those associated with the Enlightenment assumptions of Western civilization. African "authenticity" and "anteriority" and "purity" ignores the fact that Africa has been influenced by the cultural forms of the diaspora. African tradition has not been frozen in a timeless vault of preslave social memory, for instance. The concept of self that emerges from centrist positions—Afrocentrism, androcentrism, phallocentrism, Eurocentrism, Anglocentrism, etc.,—is often (but not always) monadic, isolated, unitary and independent. Centrist selves are not dialogical selves but singular, unitary selves, authoritarian selves, absolutist selves. Within the new black nationalism there's more of an emphasis on high culture and the creolization process is ignored. Gilroy and hooks have located Afrocentrism within bourgeois white assumptions about the value of scientific discoveries (by black Egyptians) and within European notions of development, time and history which can be traced to Rousseau and Descartes and a masculinist epistemology based on the racialized axiology of black versus white. While I may be critical of curricula based on, say, a neo-black nationalism that de-emphasizes the role of black women, for instance, I need to emphasize that the most debilitating form of "centrist" curricula and identity politics is grounded in the dominant cultures of whiteness. White patriarchal techno-capitalism overdetermines our educational system—to name just one of many systems—in such a way that the very criterion of academic success is predicated upon the expulsion of non-white forms of ethnicity. Sometimes Afrocentrism is needed to defend against the larger thret of white supremacy.

Shirley: What do you feel are some of the problems facing radical teacher intellectuals committed to a critical multiculturalism?

Peter: We can't simply assume Latin American pedagogies of liberation—such as Paulo Freire's brilliant work—are transposable without taking into critical consideration their historical and cultural situatedness in Brazilian life. We need to be careful we don't betray the oppressed in our academic constructions of them as objects of our research that give our roles legitimacy. As intellectuals we can work in solidarity with the oppressed and also extend our work into nonacademic publics. But we must do so thoughtfully and conscientiously without assuming the role of the cultural expert. Teachers as cultural workers need to make links among academic and popular and public cultures. But in doing so, they need to remain cautious about administering new forms of authoritarianism.

Our conceptual encapsulations as academics tend to put minority cultures and oppositional cultures and subcultures in formaldehyde, turning them into frozen and lifeless artifacts fit for the cultural mausoleum. Or else we romanticize them and nominate them as candidates for the cultural vanguard or avant-garde. Furthermore, we too often mistake the cultural production of books, articles, and democratic classroom experiences as the most effective form of resistance to domination. The educational and academic spheres are only several of many oppositional public spheres.

We also need to question where the development of multicultural theory actually reinforces the distance between the margins and centers of power by our rhetorizing moves as theorists. But I must say that critical multiculturalism is, overall, a worthy endeavor and necessary to combat corporate multiculturalism. What we, as teachers, need to understand is that the view of multiculturalism proposed by Gingrich, Limbaugh, and others is really compatible with the corporate view which is designed to put local cultures into the service of the national elites and the global centers of power. It precipitates a conservative ideology of citizenship predicated upon possessive, consumer individualism, and political consensualism.

Now that the liberal cry for disinterested knowledge, objectivity, and a neutral pluralism is being superseded by the New Right's clarion cry for the politicization of all cultural knowledge under the triumphalist banner of Western civilization, we need, as educators and cultural workers, to engage in attempts to align our efforts as educators with progressive social movements. No, I'm not talking about constructing an ethically pure populism, but rather joining in efforts to create civic, personal, public, and institutional spaces of coordinated activism. I would call these spaces of critique and refusal, of possibility and provisional utopian dreaming, spaces of reconfigured modes of sociality and reterritorialized desire—desire uncoupled from its circuits of corporate interest—forms of desire that can be recoupled with discourses and social relations of freedom. We need to face the dark night of history that is upon us. We are living at a time in which the politics of greed and conquest haunts our best intentions as educators. As I say to my students— whom I love dearly because they are my brothers and sisters in struggle, my compañeros y compañeras of the heart—we need to trouble the ambivalent space that we call our classrooms, that space of creative emptiness where knowledge gets reduced to inventories of silence. Within this space we need to redraw the boundaries of our identity to include chance encounters with otherness that might provoke a better understanding of the outsider within us. Encounters not framed in advance by glorious demarcations of "us" and "them." I tell my beloved students that we need to avoid the narrow, vapid politics of bourgeois pluralism that only reproposes, recuperates and reinstalls domination at a higher level by recontaining dialogue within a discourse of politeness and consensus. We need to reinvent ourselves in opposition to all forms of oppression and domination and not succumb to a despondency of the heart and servitude of the will. As educators, we need to invite students not just to think differently, but to live differently.

I suppose that I'm an example of what the dominant culture of this age does not want, of what the cultural and educational authorities despise. All of our lives are allegories of something else and I've tried to leave the study of some of that "something else" to theologians and mystics. My concern has been—and still is—with the material and existential circumstances in which we find ourselves and with the metaphorical criteriologies and nomencla-tures we employ to make sense of these circumstances. How we presently are signifying our world not only leads to a misunder-standing of it but also disfigures and demonizes others whom we attempt to represent. And then we become the prisoners of those whom we, ourselves, have imprisoned, through ideologies and discourses of violence and conquest. All my life I have seen unnec-essary pain and despair and that's what I write about. I have admired those who bear up with great dignity under what appear to be intolerable conditions. This is the heroic agency I write about—an agency I perceive more in relation to others than to myself. To put yourself at risk in one's academic writings is one thing, to live as many of the young people in East L.A. and South Central live, to put your life at risk every day and to struggle at the same time for a better life for yourself and your family, that is what I tell my students comprises the truly revolutionary life. That is what teaching is at its best—living the revolutionary life. This helps us to understand Freire. And for me, this helps to explain why Ché, Marx, Cabral, Fanon, Memmi, Malcolm, Sandino, Horton, Subcommandante Marcos, Emma Goldman and Fridha Kahlo are such great teachers. Their praxis is in their bloodstream. Their hearts are reflected in their work. They put everyday life at risk by risking their everyday lives in the struggle against capitalist exploitation, against petrified ideologies, against hatred, against racism, against dehumanization—against all the vocations of the colonizer.

NOTES

A version of this interview appeared in *The International Journal of Educational Reform*, vol 1, no. 4, October 1992, pp. 392–405.

5

GENEVA GAY

Mirror Images on Common Issues: Parallels Between Multicultural Education and Critical Pedagogy

INTRODUCTION

Multicultural education shares many of the concerns, intentions, and emphases of other educational innovations designed to reform schooling so that its positive benefits and effects are more accessible, equitable, and effective for a wider variety of student populations. Among these innovations are intergroup education, progressive education, humanistic education, child-centered education, citizenship education, and the more recent developments in critical pedagogy. In this sense, multicultural education continues a long and honored tradition among some educators of seeking alternatives to traditional forms of schooling when they fail to serve well the needs of some groups of students. Furthermore, its intentions and expected outcomes are consistent with prior initiatives (such as desegregation and compensatory education) to improve the academic success of children of color and poverty, although its specific methodologies are different.

Similarities between multicultural education and other educational innovations need to be made explicit as future efforts are explored and new directions charted for improving the quality of educational opportunities and experiences for all children. The discussion in this chapter responds to this challenge by exploring the ideological, conceptual, and operational parallels between multicultural education and critical pedagogy. It recognizes that while these two movements are not identical, many of their concerns, perspectives, and proposals are analogous with respect to issues of educational access, equity, and excellence in a culturally pluralistic society and world. It builds upon the efforts to explicate connections between multicultural education and critical pedagogy that are being offered by such educators as Christine Sleeter and Carl Grant, Warren Crichlow, Cameron McCarthy,

155

Antonia Darder, Jesse Goodman, Etta Hollins and Kathleen Spencer, Michelle Fine, and Terence O'Connor.

The chapter is divided into four major sections. They move the discussion from the general to the specific and from the theoretical toward the practical. The first section develops some general conceptual parallels between critical pedagogy and multicultural education. Some complementary philosophical and ideological attributes of the two are discussed in the second part. The third part suggests some possibilities for translating the conceptual and theoretical ideas of multicultural education and critical pedagogy into classroom practices. The last section provides a few reflective thoughts on the overall messages embodied in the preceding discussions. It serves as a summary to the chapter, and as a final reminder of why multicultural education and critical pedagogy are mirror images on common issues and themes.

CONCEPTUAL PARALLELS

Differences between multicultural education and critical pedagogy are more context than content, semantics than substance, and oratorical than essential. At the level of philosophical principles, ideological emphasis, and outcome expectations, multicultural education is a form of critical pedagogy. However, the specific structural elements, rhetorical styles, points of reference, and constituent orientations they use to analyze current educational issues and identify reform possibilities are different.

Multicultural education and critical pedagogy are mirror images of each other. They represent different perspectives and variations on the imperative of achieving educational quality, access, and excellence, and social equity, freedom, and justice for culturally diverse groups. Both are at once a philosophy and a methodology. As philosophies they constitute a set of beliefs which value an educational process that celebrates and facilitates individual diversity, autonomy, and empowerment. As methodologies, multicultural education and critical pedagogy are means of designing and implementing educational programs and practices that are more egalitarian and effective for diverse student populations. Both employ a language of critique, and endorse pedagogies of resistance, possibility, and hope. These are grounded in principles of personal liberation, critical democracy, and social equality, and an acceptance of the political and partisan nature of knowledge, human learning, and the educational process (Aronowitz and Giroux 1985; Banks and Banks 1993; Nieto 1992; Parekh 1986; Sleeter 1991).

The foundational principles and analytical techniques of critical pedagogy and multicultural education emphasize economic, political, and ethical analyses of how schools routinely perpetuate inequalities among marginalized ethnic, social class, and cultural groups, and ignore or violate their rights, cultures, and experiences. Inherent in these is a concerted effort to link schooling with domination and liberation. Critical pedagogues see schools as "agencies of social and cultural reproduction, exercising power through the underlying interests embodied in the overt and hidden curricula, while at the same time offering limited possibilities for critical teaching and student empowerment" (Aronowitz and Giroux 1985, p. 143). Bhikhu Parekh (1986), a British multiculturalist, expresses similar sentiments. He explains that education is neither culturally nor politically neutral. Rather,

> Its intellectual content and orientation is permeated by the world-view characteristic of the dominant culture. It cultivates specific attitudes and values. In so far as these assist and conduce to the maintenance of a particular type of social and political order, it is also a political activity....All this means that although an educational system may avow the ideals of freedom, objectivity, independent thought, universality of knowledge, intellectual curiosity and so on, in actual practice it often does little more than initiate and even indoctrinate its pupils into the dominant culture (p. 20).

These analyses generate many general guidelines for how pedagogical priorities and practices should be reformed. They recognize that major problems of inequity exist which require bold and radical efforts for change. However, neither critical pedagogues nor multiculturalists consider these conditions beyond reform. Rather, a strong sense of hope and belief in the redeeming potential of change, along with a wide variety of attendant strategies, permeate both. This is why they can be rightfully called pedagogies of possibility.

Some of the essential components of multicultural education and critical pedagogy are analyses of disparities in educational opportunities and their consequences for culturally diverse students; personal empowerment; and the critical knowledge, moral and ethical values, and sociopolitical action for educational change and the realization of democratic ideals (Banks 1990, Banks 1991/92; Giroux 1993, 1988, 1992; Giroux and McLaren 1989; McLaren 1989). The philosophical beliefs and preferred practices of both are embodied in a language of critique and a pedagogy of possibility. The differences between them are more a matter of scale and specificity than ideology and intentions.

Critical pedagogues tend to be generalists in that their proposals for action apply to the universe of U. S. education without reference to any specific programs of study. Multiculturalists are more particularistic in that their advocacy tends to concentrate on changing curriculum content and classroom instruction to incorporate cultural pluralism. This emphasis is justified as a means of making education more relevant to and effective for children of both sexes and from ethnic minority, poverty, language minority, and other culturally diverse backgrounds.

Therefore, the ideological relationship between critical pedagogy and multicultural education is parallel and complementary. Their terrains are closely juxtaposed and frequently overlap. Yet, few efforts to date are being pursued to demonstrate how they intersect, and may be extensions of each other. The underlying philosophy of multicultural education is, in essence, a form of critical pedagogy (Nieto 1992). Its content and strategies can be perceived as a set of methodological tools for translating and contextualizing general principles of critical pedagogy to the specific educational needs of socially, culturally, ethnically, racially, and linguistically different students who historically have been marginalized and oppressed by schools. These general conceptual relationships can be further verified by a closer examination of the major descriptive attributes and praxis proposals of multicultural education and critical pedagogy.

COMPLEMENTARY ATTRIBUTES

Although critical pedagogy began to appear in educational scholarship a decade or so after the initiation of multicultural education, both schools share some fundamental concerns about methods of inquiry and visions for the future of U. S. education and society. Multicultural education and critical pedagogy are philosophies and approaches to education that are driven by critical analysis, multiple perspectives, cultural pluralism, social activism, counterhegemony, and sociocultural contextualism in instructional processes and expected learning outcomes. They demand that democratic principles (representation, equality, freedom, dignity, and justice), within a framework of cultural diversity, be applied to the curriculum content and classroom instruction offered to all students. Both have transformative and revolutionary potential for reforming education because they challenge the underlying value assumptions and cultural ethos which currently govern schooling in the United States. These challenges are framed in a spirit of hope, a belief in the inherent worth and promise of democratic ideals and a conviction that school practices can be transformed to better embrace and emulate the cultural, racial, social, and ethnic pluralism which characterizes society. Although these consensual commitments are rather clear, they are coded and articulated somewhat differently in the professional dialogues and scholarship of critical pedagogy and multicultural education.

Advocates of multicultural education generally agree that it is a concept, an educational philosophy, a pedagogical process, an educational reform movement, and a social ideal (Banks and Banks 1993; Bennett 1990; Grant 1977; Parekh 1986; Sleeter and Grant 1988). As a concept it is grounded in the notion that culture influences all dimensions of human behavior, including teaching and learning. Culture may be defined as an aggregation of beliefs, attitudes, habits, values, and practices that forms a view of reality or as "the modal personality of a unique group of people that provides rules and guidelines for appraising and interpreting inter-actions with events, people, or ideas encountered in daily life" (Shade and New 1993, p. 317). The fact that many students do not share the same ethnic, social, racial, and linguistic backgrounds as their teachers, may lead to cultural incongruencies in the class-room which can mediate against educational effectiveness. These incompatibilities are evident in value orientations, behavioral norms and expectations, and styles of social interaction, self-presentation, communication, and cognitive processing (Bennett 1990; Garcia 1982; Gay 1991; Grossman 1984; Shade and New 1993; Spindler 1987; Trueba, Guthrie, and Au 1981). Therefore, if educational equity and excellence are to be provided to all students, cultural pluralism must permeate every aspect of the schooling enterprise.

As a philosophy, multicultural education is a way of knowing, believing, and behaving which incorporates sensitivity to cultural diversity in making all educational decisions about the planning, implementation, and evaluation of programs, policies, and proce-dures. It values and celebrates the cultural pluralism that is endemic to the human condition and U. S. society. It accepts the fact that "there is no single criterion of human potential applicable to all. Instead, complex and varied sets of coherent values, motives, attitudes, and attributes—which determine behavior patterns—exist among cultural groups" (ASCD Multicultural Education Commission 1977, p. 2). A galaxy of conterminous and equally valid cultural groups and experiences should comprise the universe of teaching and learning (Garcia I 982).

These orientations are based on three major assumptions: (1) the fabric of U. S. society is a composite of contributions from a wide variety of ethnic and cultural groups; (2) the perspectives, contributions, and experiences of all these groups are essential to the search for scholarly truth and for achieving the societal ideal of an egalitarian democracy; and (3) the contributions of diverse groups to the common culture and their own unique ones are readily accessible and easily verifiable. The efforts of schools to actualize their ideological commitments to making quality education available to all students and to maximizing the learning potential of all individuals must be situated in the contextual realities of the cultural pluralism which characterizes U. S. society.

Consensus prevails among advocates of multicultural education that it is more than teaching cognitive content about diverse cultural groups in separate curricular areas, such as social studies and language arts. Rather, it is an ongoing process of changing the environmental, cognitive, and pedagogical contexts in which teaching and learning occur. Essential contextual factors to be considered for change are classroom interactions between students and teachers, value assumptions underlying teacher attitudes and expectations for performance, how students are organized for instruction and learning activities, the variety of messages transmitted through the hidden and symbolic curricula, and the social interactions among students in the formal and informal realms of schooling (Hernandez 1989). All of these aspects of the educational enterprise, along with the content taught in various subjects, administrative leadership, counseling and guidance, and performance appraisal, must be changed to reflect cultural diversity at their most fundamental level. Anything less than comprehensive, pervasive, and systemic reform is inadequate for the effective implementation of multicultural education. As Garcia (1982) suggests, efforts to achieve educational excellence for diverse students must be contextualized within multiple cultural perspectives, and be very cognizant of "the ethnic factor" (p. 3).

These characterizations of multicultural education are further crystallized by Nieto (1992). According to her comprehensive description, multicultural education is a process of comprehensive school reform; basic education for all students; a confrontation with and rejection of racism and all other forms of discrimination and oppression in schools and society; an affirmation of ethnic, racial, linguistic, religious, economic, and gender pluralism; and a value and substantive presence throughout the entire educational process. It permeates all curriculum and instructional operations used in schools, school-community and parent-teacher relationships, and the very way that schools conceptualize the nature of teaching and learning.

Furthermore, multicultural education values diversity as imperative to educational quality and a condition of social equality and vitality. It contends that U. S. education and society can never be all that they might for anyone (and especially individuals from different racial, economic, and linguistic backgrounds) until they incorporate pluralistic cultures, experiences, heritages, and perspectives into their values, procedures, and structures on a regular basis. Multicultural approaches to education have the potential for relating abstract academic information to the personal experiences of culturally diverse students in ways that make learning easier and more lasting, as well as enabling more children to be better decision-makers and more effective citizens in a pluralistic world (Banks 1991; Gay 1988; Williams 1987).

These various descriptions of multicultural education suggest that it operates on multiple levels of conceptual complexity and practical application. However, its ultimate goals remain the same across the various forms and conceptions. They are to make education more equitable for and representative of the social, ethnic, and cultural pluralism which characterizes U. S. society; to make high quality learning more accessible to a wider variety of students; and to contribute to the creation of a society in which the democratic principles of equality, freedom, justice, and human respect are realized for culturally diverse people. Since minor modifications in the existing order of schools and society are not sufficient to accommodate these demands, some major changes must occur. Consequently, educational transformation and social reconstruction are recurrent themes in multicultural education theory (Banks 1990, 1991/92; 1992; Bennett 1990; Gay 1993; Hernandez 1989; Nieto 1992; Sleeter 1991; Sleeter and Grant 1988). These emphases make it a radical, visionary, and revolutionary enterprise, yet one that is very consistent with democratic ideals.

The philosophical underpinnings of critical pedagogy, like those of multicultural education, are central to the debate over reforming schools to achieve greater equity and excellence. They are concerned with connecting educational reform to the struggle for democracy, the ethics and politics of social relations, the demands for critical citizenship, and the politics and potentials of cultural differences (Giroux and McLaren 1989). While multicultural education gives priority to reforming curriculum content and classroom instruction, the centerpiece of critical pedagogy is how the institutional ideology and cultural ethos of schools reflect and perpetuate the oppressive practices of society. It argues that the fate and future of public education cannot be separated from the social problems facing the larger society, especially those having to do with political exploitation, and social and cultural domination. These problems have political and pedagogical consequences directly related to who has access to what kinds of wealth, knowledge, power, and learning. Therefore, "any discussion of public schooling has to address the political, economic, and social realities that construct the contexts that shape the institution of schooling and the conditions that produce the diverse populations of students who constitute its constituencies" (Giroux 1992, p. 162).

Resistance, oppression, reproduction, representation, transformation, power, domination, liberation, voice, and empowerment are major themes in critical pedagogy. They are the conceptual screens through which critical pedagogues articulate their critiques, and transmit their proposals for school reform. (Giroux 1981, 1992; Kreisberg 1992; McLaren 1989). Utmost among the purposes of these critiques is exposing the myths and fallacious assumptions that U. S. schools, as they currently exist, are egalitarian institutions, embodiments of a democratic social order, and major sites of social and economic mobility. Rather, they routinely engage in politics and practices of reproduction wherein the existing social order of mainstream society is replicated, complete with its established patterns of discrimination against individuals and groups on the basis of race, ethnicity, class, gender, and language. According to McLaren (1988), critical pedagogy "seeks to establish new moral and political frontiers of emancipatory and collective struggle, where both subjugated narratives and new narratives can be...voiced in the arena of democracy" (p. 76). In other words, it assumes that true democracy is unattainable until all people are free and their contributions to the human story are duly acknowledged and respected.

This clarion call for education for equality and democratic living among critical pedagogues is sounded equally as loudly and persistently by multiculturalists. For example, Banks (1990) argues that citizenship education for the twenty-first century must help students "become literate and reflective citizens who can participate productively in the workforce...care about other people...and...take personal, social, and civic action to create a humane and just society" (p. 211). Gay (1988) explains that the educational goals of equity and excellence are of equal significance in a culturally pluralistic society and are so closely interwoven that one cannot be achieved without simultaneously attending to the other. Multicultural inclusion is seen as a necessary condition for achieving citizenship, equity, and excellence (Asante 1991/92; Banks 1990; Bennett 1990; Crichlow et al. 1990; Darder 1991; Hilliard 1991/92). The cultures of diverse learners must be incorporated into "the academic and social context of schooling in ways that facilitate and support academic learning and cultural identity and promote personal, human, and social development" (Hollins and Spencer 1990, p. 90).

From the vantage point of critical pedagogy, the inclusion of critically informed versions of cultural studies in the educational process offers "a theoretical terrain for rethinking schooling as a form of cultural politics...the opportunity to challenge hegemonic ideologies, to read culture oppositionally, and to deconstruct historical knowledge as a way of reclaiming social identities that give collective voice to the struggles of subordinate groups" (Giroux 1992, pp. 164–165). The spirit of hope in the redemptive potential of schooling embedded in multicultural education and critical pedagogy is also apparent in persistent demands for the reform, not the replacement, of schools and in the belief that effective education can help students become better members of their own ethnic and cultural communities, as well as more effective citizens of the national culture.

Giroux and Simon's (1989) suggestion that educational policy, theory, and practice must be informed by the differences which constitute the everyday lives of students and McLaren's (1989) observation that "the critical perspective allows us to scrutinize schooling more insistently in terms of race, class, power, and gender" (p. 163) establish another clear ideological and operational connection between multicultural education and critical pedagogy. Both believe that current educational conditions and practices which give unfair advantages to the cultures, traditions, and experiences of middle-class, European Americans are not immune to change. Although pervasive and persistent, the mechanisms of domination and injustice in schools and society are not inevitable to human nature; nor are they immutable. They are social phenomena and human creations that can be transformed by human action informed by critical thinking, ethical principles, and the democratic imperatives of freedom, justice, and equality

(Kreisberg 1992; Goodman 1989; Giroux and McLaren 1989). Collective struggle and the acceptance of cultural pluralism are absolutely fundamental to achieving these goals. They "give desire wings" and allow thought to be "lifted beyond the limitations of the present moment in order to be transformed into dreams of possibility" (McLaren 1988, p. 76).

The social critique, community of political struggle, and the real location of power through access to knowledge that are central themes in critical pedagogy are also characteristic features of multicultural education. The movement to legitimize cultural pluralism and to recognize that U. S. culture—and its corollaries in schooling—is a synergy of multiple contributions "originated within a context of social activism, and has always drawn its main energy and inspiration from struggles against oppression" (Sleeter 1991, p. 9). Multicultural education is an outgrowth of the civil rights movement of the 1960s with its demands that human dignity, individual freedom, full citizenship rights, and representative democracy be extended to disenfranchised and oppressed groups. It assumes that the principles of power sharing, equal access to opportunities, and the empowerment of the disenfranchised are as apropos to educational institutions as to the civic arena.

Contrary to the notions of many educators that pedagogy is an impartial, neutral, and technical process, critical pedagogues and multiculturalists contend that it is a social, political, and cultural process. It reflects the cultural orientations of teachers and is always designed to achieve some kind of advocacy and opposition. Giroux and Simon (1989) describe pedagogy as a form of cultural politics in which deliberate attempts are made to influence what knowledge is valued and learned, the quality of learning experiences students have, and the ways our social and natural worlds are understood. Because "pedagogy is simultaneously about the practices students and teachers might engage in together and the cultural politics such practices support,…to propose a pedagogy is to construct a political vision" (p. 239). It involves much more than technical questions about how students learn. It is a host of political practices and cultural assumptions about how knowledge is produced and learned, how teaching and learning are linked to self and social empowerment, and the intellectual, emotional, and ethical investments educators make about how to best negotiate, accommodate, and transform social conditions (Giroux 1992).

Whether by deliberate intent or implicit assumption, whether in content or process, conventional pedagogy is a particular form of cultural reproduction which endorses, models, and transmits Eurocentric cultural values and ignores or denigrates other cultural heritages. Multicultural education and critical pedagogy are alternative ways of conceptualizing the pedagogical process so as to counteract these trends. They are anchored in such beliefs as the indisputable right of all children to a high-quality education, uncompromised citizenship privileges, and uncontested human respect; the moral imperatives of social justice and educational equity; and a vision of knowledge as a social construction comprised of equal status contributions from multiple cultural sources and groups. Therefore, multicultural education and critical pedagogy are, at once, types of philosophy, politics, and teaching.

Critical pedagogues operate on the premise that schools are "contested public spheres" characterized by ongoing struggles for control and contradictions among competing cultural structures and orientations (Aronowitz and Giroux 1985; Stanley 1992). Multiculturalists describe them as social systems that are often plagued by tensions due to the cultural incompatibilities among different ethnic, racial, social, and national origin groups of students and teachers (Garcia 1982; Gay 1991; Shade 1989; Spindler 1987). The cultural capital dispensed in them is too often hegemonic and debilitating to large numbers of students. It serves to constrain and delimit rather than to emancipate and elevate intellectual, social, and human potential.

However, schools can be agents of emancipation for individuals and society. They can become what John Dewey envisioned as laboratories of learning for democratic living where all forms of knowledge are ventilated and the experiences of all cultural groups are legitimated as worthy contributions to the life and culture of the United States, global society, and humankind (Goodman 1989). Schools also can and should be social and political forums in which culturally diverse students are enabled "to exercise power in the interest of transforming the ideological and material conditions of domination into social practices which promote social empowerment and demonstrate democratic possibilities" (Giroux and Simon 1989, p. 237). By establishing an inextricable linkage between education, ethics, morality, and politics, critical pedagogy and multicultural education resurrect the Jeffersonian idea that the maintenance of a democratic political system requires the active participation of an educated citizenry and places it within the operational context of cultural pluralism. They also offer a means for "enhancing and ennobling the meaning and purpose of education by giving it a truly central place in the social life of the nation, where it can become a public forum for addressing the needs of the poor, the dispossessed, and the disenfranchised" (Giroux and McLaren 1989, p. xxii).

Similar problems plaguing society which demand a radical rethinking of the educational process and its potential are highlighted by critical pedagogues and multiculturalists. Among these are exploitation and oppression, moral bankruptcy, social apathy, individual alienation, unconsciousable consumerism, and an insatiable hunger for power which have devastating consequences for every segment of the society. McLaren (1989) explains that historical neglect of social ethics, community, and consciousness has created a present era "where hope is held hostage, where justice is lashed to the altar of capital accumulation, and where the good works of our collective citizenry have been effaced by despair, we desperately need a new vision of what education should mean" (McLaren 1989, p. 21). Education must be re-visioned to help stem the tide of these destructive trends. Schools must become places where everyone learns how their destinies are inextricably linked, inequities and injustices are examined candidly and critically, and a commitment to collective struggle to improve the quality of life is cultivated. Students from all social backgrounds, cultural groups, and abilities must be allowed to find their own voices, reclaim and affirm their histories, develop a sense of individual and collective identity, and learn how to act upon their commitments to personal and social well-being (Darder 1991; Giroux 1981; Giroux and McLaren 1989; McLaren 1989). The urgency of these social needs and the kind and magnitude of the related political, moral, and ethical obligations they impose upon schooling are crucial features of the educational regimes envisioned in multicultural education and critical pedagogy.

Both refocus the role of schools as agents of socialization and cultural transmission from the perpetuation of the society that now exists to the creation of one that is desired. They situate the debate over the primary purpose of education in the broader contexts of critical citizenship, shared political power, and the dignity of human life, rather than restricting it to the narrow domain of preparation for the economic marketplace. Public education then becomes the site for cultivating a genuine sense of community among diverse groups in which the principles of social justice are extended to all spheres of their economic, political, and cultural lives for mobilizing moral visions of equality and for organizing struggle against oppressive practices that mediate against human solidarity (Giroux and McLaren 1989). The critical democracy to which these efforts are directed toward creating "presents both a vision of an ideal...society and a process by which this vision can be sought after" (Goodman 1989, p. 91). These approaches to education transform what some people see as the divisive potential of ethnic, racial, and cultural pluralism into opportunities and strengths for creating solidarity within a new social order (Banks 1991/92).

PRAXIS PROPOSALS

Multicultural education and critical pedagogy offer some alternative ways for redesigning the education enterprise to correct the flaws and for bringing it more in line with the true realities of U. S. history, society, and culture. Among the most significant conceptual principles which guide these action proposals are critical dialogue, representative voice, resistance to domination and oppression, emancipatory pedagogy, knowledge as power, social reconstruction and transformation, the democratization of the educational process, pluralism without hierarchy, counterhegemony, and the legitimacy of subjective realities. An explanation of the practical applications of each of these far exceeds the space constraints of this chapter. Only three are examined in detail to illustrate how theoretical principles translate into practical possibilities. They are voice, empowerment, and transformation.

VOICE AND VISIBILITY

A persistent theme in multicultural education is correcting the errors of commission and omission related to ethnic diversity and cultural pluralism that routinely occur in school curricula, instructional materials, and classroom teaching. It is analogous to the critical educational principles of employing "border pedagogy" to "give voice" (Aronowitz and Giroux 1990; Giroux 1991, 1992) to people and experiences that have been long silenced in society and schools. One method of achieving these goals is to include significant contributions of a wide variety of racial, ethnic, and cultural groups in curriculum content. This inclusion has two major dimensions. One is replacing the stereotypical portrayals of groups of color and other marginalized people, such as females, the poor, urban dwellers, and the elderly with more accurate information. Traditionally, these groups have been presented as victims, servants to society, passive participants, second-class citizens, and imperfect imitations of European, Anglo male models. They exist on the periphery or margins of society, and make few, if any, significant contributions to the history, life, and culture of humankind and the United States. They also were presented as being incapable of speaking for themselves and directing their own destinies. The only content about their life experiences considered acceptable was generated by so-called objective social science scholars who were not members of these marginalized groups. Conversely, Europeans, middle-class, Anglo males have been portrayed as active agents in shaping life, who monopolize the centers of culture and are paternalistic, benevolent protectors of everyone else.

The second dimension of changing school curricula has to do with including groups and experiences that traditionally have been excluded entirely from the cultural centers of U. S. education. The desire is to correct the impressions that U. S. culture is an outgrowth of only Western European origins and to counter the hegemonic message that "the only knowledge worth knowing and the only stories worth telling are associated with the heirs of Greece and Rome" (McCarthy 1990, p. 120). These erroneous depictions should be replaced with factual information which proves that U. S. cultural heritage is a composite of contributions from many different ethnic, racial, gender, social, and national origin groups from around the world. In this sense, it is a "global" or "world" rather than merely a "Western-based" culture. This globalistic character is evident in the pluralistic contributions made to every aspect of this country's developments in economics, politics, war, art, science, literature, music, language, cuisine, recreation, education, and mass media. Attention must be given to contributions of historical and scholarly significance instead of to ethnic individuals and events that are trivial, superficial, isolated, and exotic (Banks 1990; Crichlow et al, 1990; Hilliard 1991/92).

In the language of critical pedagogy, broadening the boundaries of knowledge to include contributions of marginalized groups is a key element of border pedagogy. It provides students with opportunities to reexamine and demystify presumptions of cultural dominance and to learn about cultural systems other than their own. Border pedagogy "decenters as it remaps" by contextualizing learning in different cultural references, perspectives, and experiences. It facilitates students becoming bordercrossers as they explore different cultural realms of meaning, social relations, and bodies of knowledge. Multiculturalists might call these border-crossers multicultural persons, cultural codeshifters, cultural brokers, or individuals who are bicultural because they have developed skills to function effectively in more than one cultural system (Banks and Banks 1993; Bennet 1990; Darder 1991).

Strategies for including accurate content about cultural diversity in school programs should reflect the results of revisionist scholarship as well as the "insiders viewpoint"—that is, the personal stories of people who lived the experiences and events being studied. For example, landmark events in the development of the United States, such as early explorations and migrations, the Great Depression of the 1930s, territorial expansion from the Atlantic to the Pacific Oceans, the world wars, and the industrial, social, and scientific revolutions, are analyzed from the perspectives of not only European males but also females, African Americans, Asian-Americans, Latinos, Native Americans, and various social class and age groups as well. The techniques and data sources used to conduct these analyses are varied, too. Rather than assume that there is a single, foregone conclusion to be reached which validates a Eurocentric prerogative and interpretation, multiple possibilities of meaning and a wide variety of conclusions are explored critically.

The data sources used to study multiple perspectives on issues and events should be equally as diverse. They must be interdisciplinary and might include social commentaries, historical accounts, personal memories, original documents and artifacts, literary treatises, biographies, and artistic impressions. All of these are combined to teach students that when any event is experienced by many different people, it generates multiple realities. In the quest for knowledge, truth, and human understanding these different realities are worthy of careful analysis. In so doing, ethnic groups and cultural experiences that have been long silenced are "given voice" and allowed to tell their own stories. These experiences, told from an inside perspective, are legitimate knowledge that is an essential part of the corpus of education for all children.

These emphases help to explain the reasons underlying arguments that multicultural education is for all students in all subjects at every grade level and in every school setting. They also further illuminate Sizemore's (1979) contentions that for the educative process in the United States to be adequate, it must, of necessity, be multicultural, multiethnic, multiracial, and multidimensional. In this context, the quest to multiculturalize school curricula by including the contributions of diverse groups is simply a question of scholarly validity and an effort to provide a more truthful and realistic rendition of the whole human experience. Instructional programs and practices thusly committed must be pluralistic, because "the simple fact is that human culture is a product of the struggles of all humanity, not the possession of a single racial or ethnic group" (Hilliard 1991/92, p. 13).

Although the identification, affirmation, and celebration of multiple cultural heritages and ethnic contributions are essential elements of the theoretical principle of "*giving voice*, " this principle involves much more than that. There is decidedly a strong political dimension to it as well. When students "come into voice," they also engage critically and analytically with all forms of cultural texts and confront ways in which historical legacies, power, and politics can be understood and used to expedite the struggle to democratize social, political, and economic life (Giroux 1988, 1991, 1992; Darder 1991). "Counter-memories" (Aronowitz and Giroux 1990) are evoked to make explicit the experiences of groups who are "not making it" and for whom the image of the United States as the "mecca of unlimited opportunities, the land of the free, and the home of the brave" is tarnished by devastating experiences of cultural, political, economic, and physical oppression and exploitation. These exposures help to locate and define aspects of society that violate principles of human dignity, social equality, justice, and personal freedom which need to be deconstructed and transformed. They create a foundation and focal point of struggle for reforming society so that it will be, as Langston Hughes (1971) challenges in "Let America Be America Again," the dream it promises to be but never has been for so many culturally different groups.

Aronowitz and Giroux (1990) describe "counter-memory" as the cultural heritages, sociopolitical experiences, alternative lifestyles, perceptual realities, and worldviews of people who traditionally have been relegated to the margins of U. S. history, life, and culture. For example, slave narratives on the ingenuous resistance efforts and creative cultural survival strategies they devised are counter-memories of enslavement to the general descriptions of large-scale compliance, subservience, docility, and cultural annihilation written by many mainstream historians. Navajo perspectives on the coming of White migrants to the Great Plains is a counter-memory to the Eurocentric notion of the "westward movement" as a manifest destiny for Europeans. The agricultural, hydroelectronic, and recreational activities that have resulted from rechanneling the natural resources of the Columbia River are "technological advancements" from the vantage point of European American culture but acts of cultural obstruction and destruction from the counter-memory viewpoints of many Pacific Northwest Native American groups.

Curricular and instructional practices are inadequate and incomplete when they do not thoroughly examine issues like the disproportionate representation of African Americans and Mexican-Americans in the penal systems; institutional racism embodied as slavery, the holocaust, the internment of Japanese-Americans, and the geo-cultural dislocation of Native Americans to reservations; the disparities in educational opportunities and outcomes, the gross inequities in health, housing, and employment by ethnicity, class and gender. Comparing power uses and abuses and protests against oppression between diverse groups and within many different sociopolitical and temporal contexts is another example of the counter-memory dimension of "giving voice to cultural diversity." The intent is to help students understand the origins, varied manifestations, and multifaceted effects of these practices and to develop the value commitments and political action skills needed to combat them. Thus, counter-memory as an element of giving voice to cultural pluralism lays a foundation for creating a moral vision and a strategic point of reference for transforming society to achieve greater cultural representation, justice, and egalitarianism.

The evocation of counter-memories in giving voice and visibility to cultural pluralism in educational programs is an attempt to acquire an accurate and authentic understanding of the full magnitude, complexity, and range of ethnic, racial, and cultural differences within particular historical contexts and social locations. It includes positive, negative, and yet unresolved dimensions of experiences. Crimes of human atrocities committed in various forms of economic exploitation and cultural appropriation are sounded as loudly and welcomed as warmly as shouts of praise in accomplishments and visions of potentials yet unrealized. They are needed to achieve an accurate understanding of what the United States currently is and how it came to be, as well as what it might become. Counter-memory breaks down the master narrative of Eurocentrism, attacks cultural hegemony, and penetrates the grand myth that U. S. society is a homogeneous, unitary cultural system. As a pedagogical strategy it recognizes that the democratic tradition is a worthy ideal but an imperfect experiment and an unfinished agenda that is characterized by struggle within and between multiple groups, values, and traditions. Future efforts to achieve democracy in this culturally pluralistic society must embrace composite, heterogeneous, and diverse understandings and actions (Aronowitz and Giroux 1990; Giroux 1992), operating in concert with each other. This does not mean harmonizing, anesthetizing, or obliterating differences. Instead, it means genuinely accepting diversity as the new normative standard for creating national unity and human solidarity. It is what Molefi Asante (1991/92) means by achieving "pluralism without hierarchy."

Recognizing and providing ownership to multiple voices in the educational process requires changing the nature and quality of pedagogy as well as changing curriculum content. Larry Cuban (1973) recognized this need over twenty years ago. He explained that "to graft ethnic content onto white instruction will shrivel and ultimately kill a hardy, vital effort to reform what happens in the classroom (p. 104). By "white instruction" he means traditional methods of teaching that emphasize telling, explaining, and clarifying; a view of learners as passive absorbers of factual information; the idea that acquisition of all the facts must precede analysis; the belief that highly controversial, moral, and ethical issues are inappropriate for classroom discussion; and the overreliance on curriculum content revisions as the primary conduit of reform. In other words, "white instruction" is the normative teaching style that has been repeatedly documented by research on classroom interactions, such as the findings reported in John Goodlad's (1984) seminal study *A Place Called School.* Pedagogical styles more appropriate for attending effectively to critical issues raised by ethnic diversity and cultural pluralism need to engage students as critical thinkers and participatory learners. They should focus on clarifying values and ethics related to human rights, power, and privileges; developing analytical skills; envisioning actions strategies to reform society; and using varied techniques to achieve learning mastery. While knowledge is important it is not preeminent; rather, it is instrumental to the mastery of skills (Banks 1991; Bennett 1990; Garcia 1982; Gay 1988; Hernandez 1989).

Cuban's position has been further refined and elaborated by multiculturalists and critical pedagogues. Their ideas are driven by the belief (which is substantiated by research findings) that the pedagogical process is the most significant determinant of the quality of the educational opportunities students actually receive in the classroom. Therefore, if culturally different students are to be given genuine and significant opportunities to "speak," to have voice, and to have equitable access to high status knowledge and learning experiences, the instructional process, like curriculum content, must be informed by cultural pluralism.

Interaction, presentation, performance, communication, and learning styles are elements of cultural voice, too. Consequently, a thorough understanding of how cultural conditioning shapes these dimensions of teaching and learning should form the basis for transforming pedagogical practices to make them more affirming of and congruent with different cultural learning styles. There is some research (Boggs, Watson-Gegeo, and McMillen 1985; Neisser 1986; Shade 1989; Spencer, Brookins, and Allen 1985; Spindler 1987; Trueba, Guthrie, and Au 1981) which suggests that many of the problems children of color have with achieving success in school are more procedural than substantive, more social than academic. When their cultural styles of talking, relating, and behaving are "out of sync" with those most teachers accept, they are penalized by being denied opportunities to participate in academic activities. Refusing to allow students to learn, interact, and communicate in styles commensurate with their cultural socialization is another very effective way to silence cultural diversity and practice pedagogical hegemony in the classroom.

Multicultural education provides some techniques for practicing border pedagogy and giving voice to cultural diversity vis-a-vis alterations in teaching styles. These are embodied in the concepts of cultural context teaching and matching teaching styles with the learning styles of students. The essence of these strategies is situating teaching and learning into the cultural frames of reference of different ethnic, social, and cultural groups. This is done by changing the classroom climate, how students are organized for learning, interactions between students and teachers, the substantive examples used to illustrate academic concepts, and by using performance assessment techniques to reflect the values orientations, background experiences, and cultural perspectives of a variety of ethnic, racial, social, and national origin groups. At issue here are two fundamental pedagogical principles: (1) differences in how students assign meaning to learning stimuli and how this is affected by the diverse social and cultural formations which give them voice, agency, and identity; and (2) the obligation of teachers to use the cultural frameworks of students to make knowledge more relevant and accessible (Giroux 1992).

African American, Latino, Native American, and poverty cultures tend to be highly communal, group-based, and action-oriented. Therefore, teaching and learning strategies that are participatory, cooperative, collaborative, and that use frequently varied formats are likely to be more culturally compatible and successful for students from these backgrounds than the more traditional uses of competitive, individualistic, passive, and monotonous routines. Using a variety of culturally pluralistic materials, experiences, and examples to illustrate, practice, and demonstrate

mastery of theoretical principles and intellectual skills has significant potential for improving the academic success of culturally
different students. Such techniques create a meaningful bridge
between academic abstractions and the lived experiences and
referent points of diverse students. The result is increased relevance, interest appeal, and applicability, all of which lead to
greater academic effort and improved achievement.

Two highly successful intervention programs provide graphic
illustrations of the praxis possibilities of cultural context teaching
at an even more specific level. One is the Kamehameha Early
Education Program (KEEP) for native Hawaiian students. By
matching the styles used to teach reading and language arts skills
with native Hawaiian cultural styles of learning, communicating,
and interacting, this program succeeded in radically reversing the
extremely low levels of academic achievement for the participating
students (Boggs, Watson-Gegeo, and McMillan 1985; Trueba,
Guthrie, and Au 1981). These results were accomplished by
making more changes in the processes of teaching than in the
substantive content of the curriculum. The other example is the
successful efforts of Jaime Escalante in teaching advanced placement calculus to Mexican-American students in the Los Angeles
schools who were failing general math. Profiled in the popular
movie *Stand and Deliver*, his techniques demonstrate how teacher
expectations for high performance combined with cultural
compatibility between instructional and learning styles can
produce phenomenal academic success.

Both KEEP and Escalante "gave voice," allowed cultural diversity "to speak," and caused previously "marginal or borderland
cultures" to become the new "centers" of their pedagogical
processes. By decentering the teaching process from Eurocentric
cultural, hegemonic control, they simultaneously remapped, multi-
culturalized, emancipated, empowered, and transformed learning
for their respective constituent groups. These examples demonstrate the multicultural education principles of matching teaching
and learning styles and implementing "pluralism without hierarchy, " as well as the critical theory ideas of border pedagogy—i.e.,
bringing the "multiple cultural texts" of marginal groups into the
center of the educational process and allowing diversity to "speak"
significantly in reconstructing and transforming schooling.

EMPOWERMENT AND TRANSFORMATION

"Giving voice" to cultural pluralism in the content and operations
of the educational process as discussed above serves multiple

purposes. Among the key ones are to dethrone European cultural, hegemonic dominance; to empower culturally different students through self-affirmation, greater academic success, and social consciousness; and to lay the groundwork for transforming society toward greater cultural inclusion, equality, freedom, and justice. Thus, personal empowerment and social transformation are, simultaneously, intended outcomes and instrumental methods of both multicultural education and critical pedagogy. These philosophies believe that education must liberate all students from the current ideological and privilege constraints which either advantage or disadvantage individuals and groups on the basis of their race, class, gender, ethnicity, national origin, and/or language. Personal liberation will have a corollary positive effect on transforming society since individuals and society are inextricably linked together.

Personal competence and social efficacy are dialectically related and necessary elements of empowerment. Each has psychological, sociological, and political dimensions and requires individual, institutional, and community change (Dewey 1916; Kreisberg 1992; Sleeter 1991). Kreisberg (1992) describes empowerment as "a personal transformation out of silence and submission that is characterized by the development of an authentic voice...[and] a social process of self-assertion into one's world" (pp. 18–19). It emphasizes the importance of a community of shared struggle and support in which individuals and groups come to develop mastery of their lives, control of valued resources, and skills to engage in collective sociopolitical action for mutual problem solving. Banks (1992) adds that "when students are empowered they have...knowledge of their social, political, and economic worlds, the skills to influence their environments, and humane values that will motivate them to participate in social change to help create a more just society and world" (p. 154). If students are to maximize their potential for personal power and autonomy, they need to believe that they are capable and valued, experience academic success, and understand how and why the conditions of society directly affect their personal opportunities and possibilities.

A careful reading of multicultural and critical pedagogy scholarship reveals a consensus that affirmation, knowledge, and action are essential ingredients of personal empowerment and social transformation. The acquisition and exercise of power begins with confidence in one's personal value and capability. In schools powerful messages are conveyed to students about the value and significance attached to them as members of different ethnic, cultural, and social groups through who is included in curriculum content and what kinds of images are portrayed. Students quickly learn that groups, events, experiences, and contributions habitually absent from the curriculum or relegated to the margins of society and the educational process, are insignificant and should likewise be demeaned, ignored, or patronized. Individuals from these invisible and devalued groups may personalize these messages, develop feelings of helplessness and worthlessness, and come to believe that their destiny is totally dependent upon the wishes and wills of others (Holliday 1985). Pai (1984) warns against the danger of demeaning diversity and its negative consequences for the empowerment process. He explains that "the culture to which one belongs...becomes the root of the individual's identity,....To reject or demean a person's cultural heritage is to do psychological and moral violence to the dignity and worth of that individual" (p. 7). People thusly affected become emotionally alienated and culturally dislocated from self, and have little if any belief in their own power potential.

The manipulation of information is a powerful weapon of domination. George Orwell (1948) provides a very disturbing but compelling portrayal of the consequences of this strategy in his fictional and satirical account of society in *1984*. Oppressive populations use propaganda, distortions, and misinformation to defame, stigmatize, stereotype, and distort the reality of dominated populations and thereby deny the total true human experience (Hilliard 1991/92). Within the context of schooling this practice occurs when textbooks and other instructional materials fail to include content about the range, significance, and complexity of the contributions different ethnic, racial, social, and cultural groups have made to the United States and humankind. A fundamental component of liberation struggles across time and place is information accuracy and the search for truth. As Hilliard (1991/92) suggests, "Curriculum change must proceed first and foremost from the assumption that there is truth in the whole of human experience," and help students to understand that "some racial and ethnic groups have endured hundreds of years of systematic defamation that has distorted, denied, and deformed the truth of their cultural and history reality" (p. 14).

Thus, the process of personal empowerment recommended by critical pedagogues and multiculturalists begins by modifying curriculum and instructional strategies to develop self-consciousness, respect, and confidence for diverse students through cultural validation. Seeing images of themselves and their cultural heritages in positions of importance and influence in school programs,—that is, being culturally vocal and actively engaged in the center of the significant narratives—grounds children, and validates their personal worth. It recenters those who previously have been culturally dislocated and creates a psycho-emotional continuity that has positive consequences in academic, social, and political actions (Asante, 1991/92). Individuals who have a strong sense of personal identity and worth are more confident and competent in all levels of intellectual, social, interpersonal, creative, and ethical task performance (Conger and Petersen 1984). This phenomenon explains the reasons behind multicultural education arguments that providing diverse role models, including accurate multicultural content, improving academic achievement, and developing positive self-concepts among ethnic, racial, and cultural minorities are conterminous imperatives of school reform.

Another crucial component of personal empowerment and a necessary condition for social transformation is knowledge acquisition. Critical pedagogues and multiculturalists agree that knowledge is a form of cultural capital, and the possession of it empowers. True acquisition of knowledge is contingent upon access, accuracy, analysis, and application.

One of the greatest resources for and sources of empowerment in schools is access to high status knowledge that has culturally pluralistic accuracy and instrumental value for use in multicultural settings. It embodies Holliday's (1985) notions of "situational competence" and Gardner's (1983) ideas of "multiple intelligences." This new knowledge requires that old records be completely purged from school programs (Hilliard 1991/92). Consequently, students will learn that there is no United States history and culture without the presence and contributions of a multitude of racial, ethnic, and national origin groups. Reading skills are mastered by using diverse samples of multicultural literature from many different genres and groups. Critical thinking is combined with learning math and science skills in examining the differential effects of developments in medicine, technology, and communications on different racial and social class groups. Multiple means of communicating are used to articulate ideas and values about issues paramount to improving the quality of life in pluralistic settings, such as human rights, the inequitable distribution of economic resources, and the ethical use of political power.

While necessary, access to accurate information about cultural diversity it is not sufficient for true empowerment. Students must also learn how to critically engage with the knowledge they encounter. They need to develop habits and skills for critiquing the presumed universality of any one canon of truth regardless of its source and for understanding how knowledge is a formidable leverage of power. These skills are underscored by ethical outrage and moral indignation at the way the democratic imperative is routinely distorted to justify Eurocentric cultural hegemony and political dominance.

Another way to empower students is by complementing the "cultural capital" derived from knowledge of how their own groups ascribe power, authority, voice, and identity with the study of other historical and cultural traditions within the larger national and global community. These studies must challenge the "forces within existing configurations of power that sustain themselves by a spurious appeal to objectivity, science, truth, universality, and the suppression of difference" (Giroux 1989, p. 147).

The comparative and critical study of diverse cultural systems provides students with the opportunity to acquire and practice a variety of intellectual, interpersonal, and social action skills. Among these are how to use multiple referents to examine social issues; how to analyze cultural texts to determine how they represent and express different ideological interests; how to demystify the traditional reverence and sanctity attached to knowledge and textual authority by viewing them as social productions that are always culturally contingent and therefore mutable; how to extrapolate political messages and influences from who and what are included and excluded from cultural dialogues and documents; and how to recognize opportunities and obstacles in sources of authority and power for transformation in the interest of creating more egalitarian educational, social, and political systems (Giroux 1992). For example, an education that empowers students to resist and transform racist practices uncovers the deeply ingrained ideological, historical, economic, cultural, and political factors in society which generate, embody, and perpetuate racism. It also teaches the differential effects of racist practices on dominant and subordinate groups, tests the effectiveness of various strategies used to combat racism, reveals points of dissension and convergence among different groups in liberation struggles, and provides practice in building cultural and political coalitions for exercising power.

Therefore, critical thinking and metacognitive skills are anchors of the personal empowerment processes proposed by multiculturalists and critical pedagogues. They are used in concert with and reinforced by several other specific pedagogical techniques. Among these are moral dilemma discussions, integrated curriculum and holistic learning, values clarification, concept attainment, cooperative learning, literary criticism, prejudice reduction, comparative analyses, self-reflection, conflict resolution, inquiry, and problem-solving. Individually and collectively these strategies engage students actively in the acquisition, production, and reconstruction of knowledge and the application of it in the creation of new social, cultural, and political possibilities. They create an esprit de corps of healthy skepticism, discontent with the existing order of things, personal agency, belief in virtually unlimited possibilities yet to be realized, and collaborative efforts that give rise to a particular vision of the kind of actions that empower individuals and transform society.

The capstone of the empowerment process is translating new knowledge, values, and skills into action strategies designed to reform society so that it models the ideals of pluralism, equality, and justice. Opportunities must exist for students to engage in anti-oppressive struggles, to link ethical values with political actions, and to apply skills of justice, autonomy, and reciprocity learned in the microculture of the classroom to the macroculture of society. Social and personal thoughts, beliefs, and behaviors are fueled perpetually by a commitment to actively resist all policies or programs, individuals, and institutions which practice domination and oppression. Students also aggressively create and pursue opportunities to establish coalitions among diverse constituencies for the common purpose of building a society and world that are more inclusive, caring, celebratory, and empowering of genuine cultural pluralism (Giroux 1992).

These expectations comprise the behavioral correlates of "the basics" for effective citizenship in a culturally pluralistic, democratic society. Their realization is contingent upon students having social consciousness, moral courage, and political competence. Students must truly believe that they can make a difference in shaping the worlds they inherit and inhabit. These processes of empowerment and transformation begin in the classroom with students practicing how to acquire, use, and share power. Central to developing these skills are such action-oriented instructional strategies as participating in cooperative, heterogeneous, and interracial learning groups; conducting case studies of actual events and experiences to discern contradictions between social ideals and realities; planning and implementing school and community action projects to combat different forms of oppression and inequalities; and organizing education campaigns to inform students, parents, and community groups about equity issues in schools and society and options at their disposal to bring about changes. Students should learn that to actively resist social and political inequities and to struggle for what one believes and values are a fundamental part of their birthright as citizens of a society which claims to be a democracy. To fully evoke these rights in the name of creating more freedom, equality, and justice for historically oppressed, dominated, and marginalized groups is merely practicing good, democratic citizenship.

The attention that multicultural education and critical pedagogy give to resisting oppression of all kinds, to individual autonomy, to communal commitment, and to political action guided by moral vision and critical knowledge, place them well within the purview of U. S. democratic ideals. One of these is the principle that when social contracts fail to serve the best interests of those for whom they are designed, it is the right of the discontented to declare the contracts null and void and to create new ones. Multiculturalists and critical pedagogues contend that the terms of the contract for public education in the United States have been violated for too long for too many individuals, especially for ethnic groups of color, females, and the poor. In the event that new negotiations fail to find a way to achieve greater equity and excellence for these groups, an entirely new contract should be created. While there is still hope in the possibility of reforming or reconstructing education, the needs may be so momentous that nothing less than radical transformation will suffice. Multicultural education and critical pedagogy concede the possibility of the former option but enthusiastically endorse the validity of the latter.

RETROSPECTIONS

Multicultural education and critical pedagogy are, as this discussion has demonstrated, complementary and parallel images of each other. They derive from and advocate essentially the same ethics, spirit, values, principles, and actions, which are shaped by an unwavering belief in the legitimacy, strength, and potentiality of multicultural perspectives and experiences, critical knowledge, and social responsibility for reconstructing and maximizing the development of individuals and societies. Although their lexicon and rhetorical styles are different, their intentions and messages are analogous. The ultimate purpose of both is to empower students and transform schools and society for greater freedom, equality, and justice within the contextual realities of cultural pluralism. Each is grounded in convictions that the democratic imperative is still valid and attainable. However, this imperative requires a radical transformation of the education process, with primary emphasis on dismantling all forms of cultural hegemony and sociopolitical dominance and replacing these with knowledge, symbols, values, ethos, and icons that are more culturally pluralistic and socially just.

As pedagogies of difference, resistance, hope, and possibility, multicultural education and critical pedagogy are inherently revolutionary and transformative. Their messages and methods are fundamentally different from the normative structures, programs, and practices which currently prevail in most curriculum and instruction. The commitment to creating communities of critically thinking, morally courageous, and politically engaged individuals, who work together and share power to reform society and who genuinely value diverse realities, voices, individuals, and cultures is a radical departure from conventional pedagogical emphases of individualistic competition, passive conformity, and cultural homogeneity.

Additional efforts to create an active coalition between the philosophy, theory, and practice of multicultural education and critical pedagogy should be pursued vigorously. An ideological foundation is already in place for this to occur if educational scholars and practitioners have the wisdom and the will to recognize the opportunity and act upon it. Both multicultural education and critical pedagogy make convincing arguments for including multiple referents in analyzing fundamental human and social issues and for fashioning a community of solidarity out of individual diversities. Multicultural education and critical pedagogy should apply the same principles and proposals they offer to others to themselves in establishing a mutually supportive relationship with each other. The commitment to pluralism that is so prominent in both means that they do not have to try to do the impossible by speaking in a single voice. The fact that the issues of significance to both are virtually identical creates enough kindredness and common affinity to generate a strong, feasible, and effective partnership. A confluence of their diverse viewpoints will sharpen the issues of analysis even further; it will enrich, enliven, and deepen the transformative dialogues and strengthen the power and potential of the reform efforts undertaken.

Multicultural education and critical pedagogy recognize that social and political coalitions are essential to genuine personal empowerment and social transformation and that neither individuals nor societies can fulfill all their potential without working and living in conjunction with each other. This same idea applies to these two schools of thought as well. Neither can be all that it might be by operating in isolation. Thus, the implied correspondence that exists between them needs to be made more explicit and formalized. This is both pedagogically sound and politically expedient. A union of the two increases the power-base of each, extends the boundaries and influence of their collective voice, and adds another dimension of comprehensiveness, inclusion, and representation to their advocacy and agency. It makes them an even more formidable force to contend with than when they operate separately. This coalition does not impose uniformity of methods; nor does it necessitate an amalgamated identity. There continues to be a vital place for a multitude of perspectives, narratives, and actions in designing and implementing operational strategies for transforming schools and society for greater quality, equality, freedom, and justice.

Maxine Greene (1993) captures eloquently the passions for pluralism, hope, and possibility that permeate multicultural education and critical pedagogy. These passions have untapped potentials as beacons of light to guide educators through the maze of challenges, problems, and opportunities which confront U. S. public education as it seeks more constructive directions for a future that is increasingly and unavoidably culturally pluralistic. Along with the corollary ethics, morality, and actions, these passions deserve serious reflection to ensure that educators continue to focus on what the real issues are in the struggle for social democracy, personal empowerment, and educational equity, and to not become unduly distracted by those that are insignificant. It is within this spirit that Greene's (1993) comments should be taken. She reminds us that:

> Of course, there will be difficulties in affirming differences and, at once, working to create community....But the community many of us hope for now is not to be identified with conformity...it is a community attentive to difference, open to the idea of plurality....
>
> No one can predict precisely the common world of possibility....Many of us, however...would reaffirm the value of principles like justice and equality and freedom and commitment to human rights; since without these, we cannot even argue for the decency of welcoming. Only if more and more persons incarnate such principles...and choose to live by them and engage in dialogue in accord with them, are we likely to bring about a

democratic pluralism....Unable to provide an objective ground for such hopes and claims, all we can do is speak with others as eloquently and passionately as we can about justice and caring and love and trust....But, as we do so, we have to remain aware of the distinctive members of the plurality, appearing before one another with their own perspectives on the common, their own stories entering the culture's story, altering it as it moves through time...as each one moves to a heightened sense of craft and wide-awakeness, to a renewed consciousness of worth and possibility (p. 194).

Multicultural education and critical pedagogy should continue to provide variations and multiple perspectives on the common concern of improving the quality of education and life for individuals from a wide variety of racial, ethnic, cultural, and social backgrounds. However, they should act in closer and deliberate concert with each other. Such a community of struggle makes hope for the future brighter, the voice of reform more commanding, and the possibility of being "heard" more likely.

REFERENCES

Aronowitz, S. and Giroux, H. A. 1985. *Education under seige: The conservative, liberal, and radical debate over schooling.* Hadley, MA: Bergin and Garvey.

———. 1990. *Postmodern education: Politics, culture, and social criticism.* Minneapolis: University of Minnesota Press.

Asante, M. K. 1991/92. Afrocentric curriculum. *Educational Leadership* 49: 28–31.

ASCD (Association for Supervision and Curriculum Development) Multicultural Education Commission. 1977. Encouraging multicultural education. *Multicultural education: Commitments, issue, and applications,* ed. C. A. Grant, pp 1–5. Washington, DC: Association for Supervision and Curriculum Development.

Banks, J. A. 1990. Citizenship education for a pluralistic democratic society. *The Social Studies* 81: 210–214.

———. 1992. A curriculum for empowerment, action, and change. In *Beyond multicultural education: International perspectives,* Edited by K. A. Moodley, pp. 154–170. Calgary, Alberta: Detseling Enterprises.

———. 1991/92. Multicultural education: For freedom's sake. *Educational Leadership* 49: 32–36.

———. 1991. *Teaching strategies for ethnic studies.* 5th ed. Boston: Allyn and Bacon.

Banks, J. A. and Banks, C. A. M., eds. 1993. *Multicultural education: Issues and perspectives.* 2d ed. Boston: Allyn and Bacon.

184

Bennett, C. I. 1990. *Comprehensive multicultural education: Theory and practice.* 2d ed. Boston: Allyn and Bacon.

Boggs, S. T., Watson-Gegeo, K., and McMillen, G. 1985. *Speaking, relating, and learning. A study of Hawaiian children at home and at school.* Norwood, NJ: Ablex.

Cazden, C. B., John V. P., and Hymes, D., eds. 1985. *Functions of language in the classroom.* Prospect Heights, IL: Waveland Press.

Conger, J. J. and Petersen, A. C. 1984. *Adolescence and youth: Psychological development in a changing world.* 3d ed. New York: Harper and Row.

Crichlow, W. et al. 1990. Multicultural ways of knowing: Implications for practice. *Journal of Education* 172: 101–117.

Cuban, L. 1973. Ethnic content and "white" instruction. In *Teaching ethnic studies: Concepts and strategies*, ed. J. A. Banks, pp. 102–113. Washington, DC: National Council for the Social Studies.

Darder, A. 1991. *Culture and power in the classroom: A critical foundation for bicultural education.* New York: Bergin and Garvey.

Dewey, J. 1916. *Democracy and education.* New York: Macmillan.

Garcia, R. I. 1982. *Teaching in a pluralistic society: Concepts, models, strategies.* Cambridge, MA: Harper and Row.

Gardner, H. 1983. *Frames of mind: The theory of multiple intelligences.* New York: Basic Books.

Gay, G. 1975. Organizing and planning culturally pluralistic curriculum. *Educational Leadership* 33: 176–183.

———. 1979. On behalf of children: A curriculum design for multicultural education in the elementary school. *Journal of Negro Education* 47:324–340.

———. 1988. Designing relevant curricula for diverse learners. *Education and Urban Society* 20: 327–341.

————. 1991. Culturally diverse students and social studies. In *Handbook of research on social studies teaching and learning*, ed. J. P. Shaver, pp. 145–156. New York: Macmillan.

————. 1993. Ethnic minorities and educational equality. In *Multicultural education: Issues and perspectives*, ed. J. A. Banks and C. A. M. Banks, pp. 171–194. 2d ed. Boston: Allyn and Bacon.

Giroux, H. A. 1981. *Ideology, culture and the process of schooling*. Philadelphia: Temple University Press.

————. 1983. *Theory and resistance in education: A pedagogy for the opposition*. South Hadley, MA: Bergin and Garvey.

————. 1988. *Teachers as intellectuals: Toward a critical pedagogy of learning*. South Hadley, MA: Bergin and Garvey.

————. 1991. Postmodernism as border pedagogy: Redefining the boundaries of race and ethnicity. In *Postmodernism, feminism, and cultural politics: Redrawing educational boundaries*, ed. H. A. Giroux, pp. 217–256. Albany: State University of New York Press.

————. 1992. *Border crossings: Cultural workers and the politics of education*. New York: Routledge.

Giroux, H. A. & McLaren, P. L. 1989. Introduction: Schooling, cultural politics, and struggle for democracy. In *Critical pedagogy, the state and cultural struggle*, ed. H. A. Giroux and P. L. McLaren, pp. xi–xxxv. Albany: State University of New York Press.

Giroux, H. A. & Simon, R. 1989. Popular culture and critical pedagogy: Everyday life as a basis for curriculum knowledge. In *Critical pedagogy, the state and cultural struggle*, ed. H. A. Giroux and P. L. McLaren, pp. 236–252. Albany: State University of New York Press.

Goodlad, J. I. 1984. *A place called school: Prospects for the future*. New York: McGraw-Hill.

Goodman, J. 1989. Education for critical democracy. *Journal of Education* 171: 88–115.

Grant, C. A. ed. 1977. *Multicultural education: Commitments, issues, and applications.* Washington, DC: Association for Supervision and Curriculum Development.

Greene, M. 1993. The passions of pluralism: Multiculturalism and the expanding community. In *Freedom's plow: Teaching in the multicultural classroom*, ed. T. Perry and J. W. Fraser, pp. 185–196. New York: Routledge.

Grossman, H. 1984. *Educating Hispanic students: Cultural implications for instruction, classroom management, counseling, and assessment.* Springfield, IL: Charles C. Thomas.

Hernandez, H. 1989. *Multicultural education: A teacher's guide to content and process.* Columbus: Merrill.

Hilliard III, A. G. 1991/92. Why we must pluralize the curriculum. *Educational Leadership* 49: 12–14.

Holliday, B. G. 1985. Towards a model of teacher-child transactional processes affecting Black children's academic achievement. In *Beginnings: The social and affective development of Black children*, ed. M. B. Spencer, G. K. Brookins, and W. R. Allen, pp. 117–130. Hillsdale, NJ: Lawrence Erlbaum.

Hollins, E. R. and Spencer, K. 1990. Restructuring schools for cultural inclusion: Changing the schooling process for African American youngsters. *Journal of Education* 172: 89–100.

Hughes, L. 1971. Let America be America again. In *The search*, ed. A. Murray and R. Thomas, pp. 29–32. New York: Scholastic Book Services.

Kreisterg, S. 1992. *Transforming power: Domination, empowerment, and education.* Albany: State University of New York Press.

McCarthy, C. 1990. Multicultural education, minority identities, textbooks, and the challenge of curriculum reform. *Journal of Education* 172: 118–129.

McLaren, P. L. 1988. Schooling the postmodern body: Critical pedagogy and the politics of enfleshment. *Journal of Education* 170: 58–83.

188   *Gay*

McLaren, P. L. 1989. *Life in schools: An introduction to critical pedagogy in the foundations of education.* New York: Longman.

Neisser, E., ed. 1986. *The school achievement of minority children: New perspectives.* Hillsdale, NJ: Lawrence Erlbaum.

Nieto, S. 1992. *Affirming diversity: The sociopolitical context of multicultural education.* New York: Longham.

Orwell, G. 1949. *1984.* New York: New American Library.

Pai, Y. 1984. Cultural diversity and multicultural education. *Lifelong learning* 7: 7–9, continued on 27.

Parekh, B. 1986. The concept of multicultural education. In *Multicultural education: The interminable debate*, ed. S. Modgil, et al., pp. 19–3 l. Philadelphia: Falmer.

Shade, B. J., ed. 1989. *Culture, style, and the educative process.* Springfield, IL: Charles C. Thomas.

Shade, B. J. and New, C. A. 1993. Cultural influences on learning: Teaching implications. In *Multicultural education: Issues and perspectives*, ed. J. A. Banks and C. A. M Banks, pp. 317–33. 2d ed. Boston: Allyn and Bacon.

Sizemore, B. 1979) The four M curriculum: A way to shape the future. *Journal of Negro Education* 47: 341–356.

Sleeter, C. E., ed. 1991. *Empowerment through multicultural education.* Albany: State University of New York Press.

Sleeter, C. E. and Grant. C. A. 1988. *Making choices for multicultural education: Five approaches to race, class, and gender.* Columbus: Merrill.

Spencer, J. T., ed. 1983. *Achievement and achievement motives: Psychological and sociological approaches.* San Francisco: W. H. Freeman.

Spencer, M. B., Brookins, G. K., and Allen, W. R., eds. 1985. *Beginnings: The social and affective development of black children.* Hillsdale, NJ: Lawrence Erlbaum.

Spindler, G. D., ed. 1987. *Education and cultural process: Anthropological approaches.* Prospect Heights, IL: Waveland Press.

Stanley, W. B. 1992. *Curriculum for utopia: Social reconstruction and critical pedagogy in the postmodern era.* Albany: State University of New York Press.

Trueba, H. T., Guthrie, G. P., & Au, K. H. P., eds. 1981. *Culture and the bilingual classroom: Studies in classroom ethnography.* Rowley, MA: Newbury House.

Williams, L. R. 1987. Teaching from a multicultural perspective: Some thoughts on uses of diversity. In *Teacher renewal: Professional issues, personal choices,* ed. F. S. Bolin and J. M. Falk, pp. 139–147. New York: Teachers College Press, Columbia University.

6

Sonia Nieto ——————————————————————————————

From Brown Heroes and Holidays to Assimilationist Agendas: Reconsidering the Critiques of Multicultural Education

Multicultural education is currently beset by criticism from all directions or, as a colleague has described it, by "backlash and frontlash."[1] From classrooms to state boards of education, from national newsrooms to the sanctuaries of intellectual discourse, the dilemmas and pitfalls of multicultural education are everywhere discussed. Cummins has framed this discussion in terms of criticism spanning the political spectrum from left to right. (Cummins, 1992) Generally, the multicultural education movement has been criticized by the Left for its hopelessly romantic optimism in the face of persistent structural inequalities that require nothing short of radical restructuring. Critics on the right, fearing the potential of multiculturalism to disturb or replace the venerated canon (what they have considered the "truth") with new, oppositional, and even dangerous knowledge, have charged proponents of multicultural education with everything from curriculum distortion to "ethnic cheerleading" (Bloom 1987; Hirsch 1987; Ravitch 1990; Schlesinger 1992; D'Souza 1991). These critics are quite rightly threatened because heretofore subordinated groups are moving from the margins to the center, in the process displacing those who have had unchallenged dominance (Kalantzis and Cope 1992). While this movement has meant challenging the curriculum in schools in particular, it also challenges formerly uncontested power in the general society.

The purpose of this chapter is to consider some of the criticisms of multicultural education from a number of ideological perspectives and to propose a reframing of critical and comprehensive multicultural education that can respond to and learn from these critiques. In the first part of the chapter, I will place multicultural education within the tradition of critical pedagogy and briefly explore linkages between the two. Next, I will address a

191

number of pitfalls endemic to multicultural education, from a variety of ideological perspectives. Finally, I will reframe the issues and propose critical and comprehensive multicultural education that reconsiders the major goals of education for liberation. This reframing leads to a reevaluation of some of the criticisms previously considered, as well as to a discussion of implications for developing a more critical multicultural education.

MULTICULTURAL EDUCATION AND CRITICAL PEDAGOGY

Beginning as it did as an outgrowth of the civil rights movement, multicultural education has always contained within it the seeds of critical pedagogy. In the 1960s and 1970s, some early conceptualizations of multicultural education alluded to its emancipatory potential. (Apple 1977; Gay 1977; Weinberg 1977; Suzuki 1979; Cheng, Brizendine, and Oakes 1981) Dickeman (1973) referred to teaching cultural pluralism, with its emphasis on rooting out racism from our schools, as "a subversive task" because it implied being truthful about our history and the great chasm between the promise of equality and the practice of unequal schooling. The connection between critical pedagogy and multicultural education has been developed in stronger theoretical terms since the 1980s by educators concerned that the growing trivialization of multicultural education makes it simply a bland celebratory program that overlooks its roots in political struggle and its challenge to racism and other forms of institutionalized oppression. (Banks 1991; Sleeter 1991; McLaren 1991; Darder 1991; Nieto, 1992)

The connection between multicultural education and critical pedagogy has become even clearer when advocates have considered the benefits they derive from each other, as Gay does in this volume, rather than calling for a one-way infusion. That is, not only has multicultural education become enriched through an incorporation of tenets of critical pedagogy, but critical pedagogy has become more grounded with an injection of considerations of race, class, gender, and difference. Such constructs as empowerment, problem-posing education, and the social construction of knowledge have been used to extend the boundaries of more conservative conceptions of multicultural education. Sleeter (1991), for example, has argued that "*empowerment* and *multicultural education* are interwoven, and together suggest powerful and far-reaching school reform" (p. 2). By linking power and empowerment with dimensions of difference in education, Sleeter's has been a key voice in articulating the social change and explicitly political mission of multicultural education.

Walsh (1991), in examining the underlying philosophical assumptions of critical pedagogy, has also implied the need to reevaluate multicultural education. In defining the major understandings that inform and shape the practice of critical pedagogy, including the nonneutrality of education and its potential for generating knowledge that can challenge social reality, she further solidified the potential connection between multicultural education and critical pedagogy. Darder also explores the value of critical pedagogy in working with students who she calls "bicultural" because of the two cultural systems they must contend with and the sociopolitical forces that set them apart from students from the dominant group. (Darder 1991) Finally, my own definition of multicultural education has incorporated critical pedagogy as one of its major characteristics. (Nieto 1992)

In spite of these meaningful connections, multicultural education has a long way to go in both theoretical and practical terms to become truly empowering. One of the major dilemmas confronting the field has been its inadequacy in responding to criticisms from varying ideological perspectives about both theoretical and practical problems. Many of these criticisms must be heeded and attended to if we are to move forward in our conceptualization of critical pedagogy and multicultural education. Although I am not suggesting that responding to these critiques will necessarily strengthen the connection between multicultural education and critical pedagogy, I do believe that such a response can help move us in the direction of reframing a critical and comprehensive multicultural education. It is for this reason that I now turn to an exploration of some of the major critiques of multicultural education.

REVISITING THE CRITICISMS OF MULTICULTURAL EDUCATION

I will review a range of criticisms, placed roughly in the political spectrum from left to right here. I do not mean to suggest, however, that these criticisms have equal status or merit equal attention, because they are coming from different positions of power in society. The Right, understanding that its power and prestige are being threatened, has used a variety of means, most of which are not available to the left, to counteract what it considers the excesses of multiculturalism. It is no accident, for example, that critics from the Right have generally had much greater and unchallenged access to the popular media. (Bloom 1987; Hirsch 1987; D'Souza 1991; Schlesinger 1992) In addition, as correctly pointed out by Sleeter, they have for the most part conveniently ignored the most representative writers in the field and have instead aimed their

severest attacks on the most controversial examples of multiculturalism, which are usually found at the university level and are
certain to incite fear and anger in the general public. (Sleeter 1995)
Thus, for instance, the right has been particularly enamored of the
Jeffries case at the City University of New York and has ignored the
more mundane manifestations of multicultural education in schools
and colleges.

Therefore, although both the left and the right may point out
some pitfalls and inadequacies of multicultural education, the criticisms from the right have clearly been the most far-reaching and
threatening to progressive conceptualizations of diversity. It is
important to note that these criticisms are derived from different
epistemological frameworks and are therefore manifested quite
differently. Because the right glorifies European Western philosophy, which is characterized by the negation of multiplicity and
difference, their conceptualization of truth is based on dichotomies
that create an either/or reality. As a result, they criticize multicultural education for considering the possibility of more than one
truth and for exploring it through other than what the right in
general considers the only acceptable way of approaching truth,
the positivist quantitative method.

Multicultural education, which has generally developed a
discourse of pluralism that makes meritocracy possible, has
tended to follow a liberal path that denies the politics of difference.
Thus, the left, although generally sympathetic to multicultural
education, nevertheless questions this superficiality and criticizes
it for not taking responsibility for exploring the political dimensions of education. That is, the left questions the traditional epistemology upon which meritocracy is based and instead attempts
to critique the norm (as defined by a male/White/middle-class/
heterosexual perspective) and present a new standpoint where
difference and more inclusionary categories become other truths
to be explored.

In spite of these differences, and while acknowledging that not
all criticisms are of equal power, it is nevertheless important to
understand all the charges leveled against multicultural education
in an attempt to strengthen its conceptual base.

Criticisms from the Left

Theorists and educators on the left have criticized multicultural
education for issues that can be grouped into four overlapping
tendencies: an avoidance of discussions of racism and other controversial issues; a decontextualization of multicultural perspectives;

its assimilationist agendas; and a sometimes simplistic acceptance of "a multiplicity of perspectives." Each of these will be briefly reviewed.

Although antiracism is an essential feature in most theoretical discussions of multicultural education, this has not been the case in many of its practical applications. It is not unusual for schools to address multicultural concerns through such strategies as international fairs, diversity dinners, and plays about "brotherhood." These are often well-intentioned but safe and incomplete ways of focusing on more significant issues of diversity as they manifest themselves in schools. Strategies such as these divert attention from other realities such as racist textbooks, low expectations based on race, ethnicity, and gender, and the interethnic violence and hostility faced in school every day by students.

Racism and other systems that privilege some groups over others are often considered too political for inclusion in the curriculum. Instead, many schools and colleges go in for a "soft" approach to racism awareness, indulging in such activities as sensitivity training rather than facing privilege and power directly. I would instead suggest engaging in *arrogance reduction*, that is, taking stock of our own arrogance, be it based on race, gender, class, or other categories that give advantage to some groups over others, and actively confronting it. Becoming "sensitive" to racism and other forms of discrimination is simply not enough.

Furthermore, racism is a taboo subject that not only contradicts other curricular content but is often perceived as unnecessarily divisive, particularly by those of the dominant culture. Tatum (1992), whose discussion of a college-level course on racism is a fine example of critical pedagogy in action, asserts that "An understanding of racism as a system of advantage presents a serious challenge to the notion of the United States as a just society where rewards are based solely on one's merits" (p. 6). Many educators are not prepared to explore or challenge simplistic beliefs about racism. Although they may indeed understand the necessity for confronting privilege, they may conclude that any form of multicultural education will automatically "take care" of racism. (Weinberg 1990). Multicultural education without an explicit focus on racism and other systems of exploitation is like a movie set made of cardboard: while it may appear authentic, it will take little to knock it down and reveal it as a sham.

A related criticism of multicultural education is that it has tended to decontextualize multicultural perspectives by trivializing bits and pieces of the lived experiences of dominated groups in the curriculum (a similar critique from the right will be considered further on). Rather than a focus on the traditional European or European-American "Holidays and Heroes" this decontextualization can lead to an equally uncritical "Brown Holidays and Heroes" approach. (Banks 1991). The tendency to separate people from their experience may result in, for example, a treatment of the Navajo culture through an art project or a representation of the independence struggle in Puerto Rico through a single poem. These may indeed be worthy projects, but, decontextualized as they are from any sense of connection with the larger history of a people, they can easily become mere artifacts that have no meaning in and of themselves. In the final analysis, a culture cannot be understood through one art project or a complex era of history through a poem.

Yet teachers and schools, in their enthusiasm to incorporate a multicultural perspective, often end up presenting cultures as artifacts. This practice is due in no small part to our own experiences as students, in which education has been presented as a monocultural and monolithic truth. We have few models for incorporating multicultural perspectives fully and fairly; therefore we often rely on projects that seem to include those groups and individuals usually excluded from the curriculum. The result is that the integrity of what Ward Churchill (1982) has called "White Studies" remains untouched, while bits and pieces of exotic content are added to its margins.

Multicultural education has come into its severest criticism from the left for its assimilationist agendas, including calls to create a so-called common culture. This criticism is often levelled against conservatives such as Ravitch, who support what she has termed "pluralist multicultural education" because it suggests that a common culture already exists and that we have only to honor it. (Ravitch 1990; Schlesinger 1991) This contention is hotly disputed by those from the left who maintain that creating a common culture by force or fiat negates the particularities, tensions, and dilemmas inherent in our society.

Proponents of pluralist multicultural education seem to want to skip the difficult step of facing racism and inequality, jumping ahead to a mythical common culture before tackling the process of acknowledging and affirming individual cultures. Yet, as Suzuki (1979) cautions, multicultural education must first start "where people are at" before it can hope to "decenter people" in order to depolarize interethnic hostility and conflict. Thus, it seems that "pluralist multicultural education" is nothing more than the "melting pot" in new clothes, a good example of how progressive ideas and labels are appropriated by the conservative right and turned around to suit their own agendas. As suggested by Kalantzis, Cope, and Slade in their book *Minority Languages:*, (1989) behind the trivialized view of culture, the implicit conservatism and unconscious racism, is a hidden agenda of assimilation.

The assimilationist agenda is further criticized by those who perceive it as a way for dominant groups to maintain the status quo in their favor. The burden is once again on those in the margins to conform to the mainstream, although the new mainstream is now identified as "multicultural." Skutnabb-Kangas (1990) addressed the issue as it is manifest not only in the United States but also in other highly technological societies: "This static and ethnocentric view, where the whole burden of integration is on the incomer alone, and where the dominant group's values are presented as somehow 'shared' and 'universal,' rather than particularistic and changing, like all values are, still prevails in many countries" (p. 87).

A fourth major critique of multicultural education from the left is the danger of a simplistic reliance on a *multiplicity of perspectives*. This concept, a central tenet of multicultural education, is based on the assumption that knowledge is not neutral or fixed but always contested, negotiated, and changing. A multiplicity of perspectives needs to be presented to students so that they can understand and appreciate why different groups feel, perceive, and behave as they do. Understanding the motives and particular conditions under which different groups operate, students can then "step into someone else's shoes," an often powerful and eye-opening experience.

A multiplicity of perspectives approach can indeed be an important strategy to use in multicultural education but, when used uncritically, it can result in accepting all perspectives as equally valid, no matter how outrageous. People and events can, in the process, lose their moral center. For example, some might call for "equal time" for the Nazi point of view during World War II or for the plight of White segregationists during the civil rights movement, claiming that all viewpoints have equal validity, including contentions that the Holocaust never happened or that the impact of slavery in U.S. history has been given too much play in newer curricula. Here, then, is another clear instance where the curriculum might be reduced to no more than a variety of contesting folklores.

An example related to the hotly contested "Curriculum of Inclusion" of the New York State Department of Education is a case in point (New York State Social Studies Review and Development Committee 1991). After receiving the report of the committee appointed by him to review the controversial curriculum, the Commissioner of Education, Thomas Sobol (1991), wrote a memorandum to the Board of Regents making the following statement concerning "multiple perspectives": "The syllabi should be so written as to help students perceive phenomena from multiple perspectives....Life and history are complex, and it is the mark of an educated person to see things in their multifaceted complexity. We must not permit those who want only simple answers to frustrate this educational purpose" (p. 6). This statement would no doubt be endorsed by most proponents of multicultural education, but it is followed by a more problematic one: "From the point of view of Europe, Columbus did indeed 'discover' America—and it was an event of profound importance not only for Europe but for the world" (Ibid.).

If this thinking were extended to its logical conclusion, it would make every perspective of equal validity, and we would be hard pressed to deny curriculum inclusion to those who claim that the Holocaust never happened, to those who insist that creationism is a science, and so forth. In fact, an uncritical multiplicity of perspectives might very well result in our students believing that there is neither truth nor ethics, except on a personal or purely relative level. If we accept the claim that Columbus "discovered" America, then we need to accept other such claims even if it means suspending disbelief.

Criticisms from the Right

Multicultural education has also, and primarily, been the target of criticisms from the right. Generally, these criticisms fall into three broad and interconnected categories: the potentially divisive nature of multicultural education; its uncritical glorification of nonmainstream cultures; and its propensity to focus on groups rather than individuals. Much has been said about the divisiveness of multicultural education, especially related to ethnic studies content. (Ravitch 1990; Schlesinger 1991). The argument, as usually framed, maintains that extremist proponents of multicultural education slide into a separatist monoculturalism that pits European and European-American history and culture against the histories and cultures of people of color, creating a divisive "us versus them" mentality, harking back to the days of separatism and segregation. Proponents of Afrocentrism have come under particular scrutiny here, and they are charged with perpetuating racist and shallow perspectives that see only victims and victimizers. Proponents of Afrocentrism, on the other hand, have suggested that it has a potentially liberatory and progressive role to play in education. (Hale-Benson 1986; Ladson-Billings and Henry 1990) More will be said about this later.

A related criticism is that multicultural education systematically glorifies and sentimentalizes the cultures of oppressed groups, similar to the critique from the left charging that it trivializes and marginalizes the cultures of dominated groups. Of particular concern from the right are two issues: that the scholarship being done in ethnic and women's studies is shoddy and unscientific and that the traditional canon, largely European and European-American, is being replaced by a new and threatening scholarship from the margins. (Bloom 1987; Hirsch 1987) Given the oppositional dichotomies of the right, this stance is understandable: it is difficult to accept that truth can come from other than their own historical experience because, according to them, such truth simply does not exist. Kalantzis and Cope (1992), although agreeing that ethnic studies courses "frequently are based on an epistomological relativism that privileges individual voice and experience over engagement with other intellectual frameworks, thus precluding a new synthesis," nevertheless maintain that it is premature to dismiss these efforts because such courses need to be viewed with a broader understanding of their stimulating intellectual role and impact on traditional scholarship. (p. B. 3) They conclude that such challenges to monoculturalism should be welcomed enthusiastically because of the debate and energy they bring.

A third and related criticism from the right poses one of the greatest challenges to multicultural education: its overreliance on "groups" rather than on individuals as the defining element of the curriculum. The issue is usually articulated thus: By focusing only on groups (ethnic, racial, gender, and so on), multicultural education risks overdetermining the role that social characteristics have on learning and on life in general. It is important to recognize that this insistence on individual differences rather than on group membership is a fundamental characteristic of U.S. mainstream culture, based on the liberal philosophy of meritocracy and individual achievement. Multicultural education, because it challenges this ideology and instead suggests that success often has more to do with privilege based on race, class, and gender, is criticized for overemphasizing the role of social groups.

Many of these criticisms from both the left and the right have either been attacked uncritically or have gone unheeded. Although some of the critiques are clearly reactions to a loss of privilege and hegemony (what I call "the last gasp of White supremacy," albeit a long, drawn-out gasp), I believe that simple knee-jerk reaction responses to them miss an important opportunity to think more deeply about the challenge to create a multicultural education truly grounded in critical pedagogy. In the next section, I will suggest how reframing the goals of multicultural education can be helpful in this regard.

Reframing a Critical and Comprehensive Multicultural Education

The criticisms thus far reviewed have made explicit some important issues that need to be considered in strengthening the connection between multicultural education and critical pedagogy. In this section, I would like to reframe multicultural education by suggesting two primary goals that need to be placed at the center of any discussion of educational reform movements: student learning and preparation for possible participation in democracy. Based on this reframing, I will advance implications for developing a more critical multicultural education.

In our enthusiasm to embrace multicultural education, I believe that we have sometimes lost sight of the major goals of education. At the same time, as critical educators, we have sometimes despaired of the promise of equality in the face of the brutal inequality so prevalent in schools. We need to bridge this gap by refocusing on what I believe should be the two central goals of education:

- Raising the achievement of all students and thus providing them with an equal and equitable education; and

- Giving students the opportunity to become critical and productive members of a democratic society

These goals are not meant to be simplistic or hopelessly idealistic but rather are proposed as a way to reclaim largely unfulfilled promises of equity. Instead of falling into despair that our educational institutions can never become places of equal educational opportunity, grounded as they are in structures of inequality based on race, class, and gender, these two goals push the inherent tensions between inequitable structures and democratic ideals. Each will be reviewed with an eye toward developing links to multicultural education and critical pedagogy.

Raising the Achievement of all Students and Providing them with an Equal and Equitable Education

Even proponents of multicultural education too frequently forget that student learning is a primary purpose of schools. Cummins (1992) has suggested that a major reason for the criticism of multicultural education from the left is that it has not been adequately grounded in a causal analysis of school failure among subordinated group students. Although learning in and of itself is an incomplete goal because it skirts the issues of what kind of learning, and learning as defined by whom and challenges us to remember Paulo Freire's fundamental question, "Education in whose interest?" (Freire 1970), we can nevertheless say that student learning is an essential although insufficient condition for an equitable education. If we refocus on the centrality of learning for all students, then political and pedagogical issues such as multicultural education can be viewed in a different light.

Ogbu (1992), in contrasting the relevance of conservative reform movements (what he calls the "core curriculum" movement) with that of multicultural education, points out that neither, as presently articulated, can have an appreciable impact on the learning achievement of students who have not traditionally done well in school because they are not based on either a solid understanding of cultural diversity or on the cultural differences of certain "involuntary minority" students. He thus offers what Sleeter has termed an "anthropological critique" of multicultural education that centers on its tendency to oversimplify "minority" student achievement and rely too heavily on changing teacher attitudes and instructional strategies (Sleeter, 1995). Ogbu's (1992) fundamental challenge to both movements needs to be taken seriously: "These movements," he goes on to say, "fail to recognize that the meaning and value students associate with school learning and achievement play a very significant role in determining their efforts toward learning and performance" (p. 7).

Ogbu suggests that reform movements such as multicultural education must be guided by an understanding of the nature of the learning difficulties of students from specific ethnic groups before they attempt to design interventions and strategies. Further, he proposes strategies that may help students from what he calls involuntary minority groups (including African American, Mexican American, Puerto Rican, and American Indian students) succeed in school, including helping them to learn to separate attitudes and behaviors enhancing school success from those that lead to either the extreme of "linear acculturation" (complete assimilation) or of "acting White." (Ibid.)

Ogbu's work has been instrumental in placing the achievement of students from culturally dominated groups in a sociopolitical context, but some of his recommendations need to be viewed critically. He suggests, for example, that students adopt the strategy of "accommodation without assimilation;" that is, that they learn to accommodate to the demands of the school culture without in the process losing their own ethnic cultures. While this is a helpful recommendation, it is incomplete because it places the burden for academic success only in the hands of students and their families and fails to focus on the responsibilities that schools must have in the adjustment process. The intent is to place students as prime actors in their own learning, but if used in isolation, the effect may not be very different from the deficit theories popularized in the 1960s that posited academic failure as a result of the social characteristics of certain ethnic and racial groups. I would argue instead that we ask the question "Who does the accommodating? and that, rather than always being the student (as is inevitably the case), schools too need to adopt the strategy of "accommodation without assimilation."

Ogbu's insistence on the central role of student learning can nevertheless help advance the connection between multicultural education and critical pedagogy. For example, his suggestion that there needs to be a focus on students' responsibility for their own academic performance is not only helpful but goes hand in hand with tenets of critical pedagogy that focus on active and critical learning on the part of students.

A review of four studies. There is a growing body of empirical research connecting critical pedagogy with multicultural education. These studies of successful interventions invariably focus on student learning as a primary goal. A brief review of four studies, each quite different in approach, will help illustrate some of the ways in which student learning is connected to multicultural content and process.

Peterson's study in fourth and fifth grade bilingual inner-city classrooms is an example of multicultural education with a critical perspective. (Peterson, 1991). Rather than stress the simple transfer of multicultural content to students, he suggests that a critical approach helps students challenge all kinds of knowledge. The author also provides numerous pedagogical examples that demonstrate how using the experiences of students, including their culture, language, and dialect, can lead to reflective dialogue. These include using generative themes and other activities that serve to organize classroom dialogue so that students learn, based on Freire's approach, how to "read the world and change it."

Moll (1992), in a review of recent trends that challenge a low-level emphasis on learning for language minority students, asserts that most schools fail to use the varied, rich family and community resources that students bring with them. This failure happens in part because both bilingual and nonbilingual programs make assumptions about the limited resources and, consequently, the perceived academic abilities of language minority students. Moll claims that, in most schools with large numbers of such students, there is an obsession with only teaching English. This is evident in the rote memorization, drill and practice, and intellectually limited learning experiences provided to them. In contrast, he presents an example from a study in a bilingual classroom that addressed broader social and academic issues than just learning English or "basic" skills. Here, the emphasis was not on which language they used (English, Spanish, or a combination) but rather on the fact that students were engaged in active learning and used the community as an important resource for that learning.

Furthermore, Moll (1992) reviewed research with thirty families of language minority students; the research that found they had enormous knowledge and skills, from agriculture to medicine, that could be useful in students' learning. He cites as an example how a sixth grade teacher used community knowledge in a unit on construction and building: "What is important is that the teacher invited parents and others in the community to contribute *intellectually* to the development of lessons; in our terms, she started developing a social network to access funds of knowledge for academic purposes" (p. 23, emphasis in original).

A study by Moses et al. (1989), in which students from a range of ability backgrounds took part in an algebra program at the middle school level, also centers on connecting student learning with multicultural content. In the study, the authors argue that lack of access to programs of high-level learning effectively bars students from acquiring the necessary knowledge and skills to participate effectively in our society. Specifically, they maintain that math and science instruction must be viewed more broadly than as simply "technical instruction," particularly for educators concerned with the life chances of traditionally unsuccessful students. Based on pedagogy derived from the civil rights movement, the program uses three aspects of the Mississippi organizing tradition: the centrality of families to the work of organizing; the empowerment of grassroots people and their recruitment for leadership; and the principles of "casting down your bucket where you are," a theme suggested by Booker T. Washington that one must organize in the context in which one lives and works, using the resources found in that context. As a result of this program, 39 percent of the first graduates were placed in honors geometry or honors algebra courses when they entered high school, an unprecedented achievement.

In a study focusing on culturally congruent pedagogical practices, Ladson-Billings and Henry (1990) studied the strategies employed by successful teachers of Black students in predominately Black schools in Canada and the United States. The researchers found that these teachers used approaches grounded in Afrocentricity, specifically, making pedagogical choices that link subject matter to the students' experiences and drawing on their cultural roots. Citing numerous examples of the ways in which they mediated the content of the curriculum through culturally empowering strategies, the authors point out the liberatory aspects of Afrocentricity.

Benefits of centering student learning in multicultural education. All four of these studies underscore the necessity of placing student learning at the very center of multicultural education. When this is done, criticisms that multicultural education is "ethnic cheerleading" or that it is simply a tool for assimilation can be challenged. In the studies reviewed above, high-level learning and thinking are at the core of educational innovations. In conjunction with this focus, the experiences and resources possessed by students, their families, and their communities are used in the service of learning. This focus is by its very nature multicultural because students arrive at school with a variety of experiences and resources. It is also consistent with critical pedagogy because it challenges students to take responsibility for their own learning while at the same time supporting and respecting their cultures, languages, and experiences.

It is important to note that student and community cultures were neither sentimentalized nor reified in the studies reviewed above. On the contrary, they were analyzed carefully, becoming examples of critical pedagogy in action. For example, Ladson-Billings and Henry (1990), while championing the use of an Afrocentric perspective, also caution that it can become "romantic, mythic, and monolithic," thus pointing out the kind of critique necessary in all areas of multiculturalism.

Placing student learning at the center of multicultural education also means that school policies and practices must be analyzed in terms of the impact they have on providing all students with an equal and high quality education. This goal is, however, not sufficient to ensure that learning moves beyond a ritualistic, irrelevant, and transmission model of education (Cummins 1994). For that to occur, we need to look to the potential for using education as an apprenticeship for critical civic participation.

Providing an Apprenticeship for Participation in a Democratic Society

Preparing students for active membership in a democratic society is often cited as a major goal of U.S. schooling (Dewey 1916), but the possibility for an apprenticeship in democracy in schools is rarely provided because policies and practices, such as rigid ability grouping, inequitable testing, differentiated curriculum, and unimaginative pedagogical strategies, mitigate against this noble aim. There are two often diametrically opposed priorities for school reform that expose the supposed tension between equity and excellence: support of the economic market system, with its inherently unequal outcomes; and support for social democracy, with universal enfranchisement. (Bastian et al. 1985)

The battle between these competing aims has resulted in democracy being perceived as a hollow and irrelevant issue in many schools. In a cogent analysis of dominant approaches to educational reform, Giroux (1992) argues that the current crisis of U.S. schooling is symptomatic of the broader crisis in the meaning and practice of democracy in general. He suggests that what he calls "the discourse of democracy" has been effectively appropriated and trivialized to mean such things as uncritical patriotism and mandatory pledges to the flag, and he makes a compelling case for reclaiming schools as democratic sites: "We need a language in our leadership programs that defends schools as democratic public spheres responsible for providing an indispensable public service to the nation; a language that is capable of awakening the moral, political, and civil responsibilities of our youth" (Ibid., p. 8).

Although multicultural education is often assumed to be grounded in democratic practice, this is not necessarily the case. The challenge that lies ahead is to link multiculturalism, democracy, and equal educational opportunity. Howe (1992) has attempted this synthesis by suggesting that equal educational opportunity needs to be redefined. He criticizes conservatives such as Hirsch for insisting that "caste-like" or "involuntary immigrant" students abandon their identities because "requiring people to sacrifice their identities in order to succeed is not a kind of opportunity *worth wanting*; nor is working hard and doing well pursuing the false promise that education is enabling." He comes to the conclusion that "The principle of equal educational opportunity can only be realized for cultural minorities by rendering educational opportunities worth wanting, and rendering educational opportunities worth wanting requires that minorities not be required to give up their identities in order to enjoy them" (Ibid. pp. 468, 469, emphasis added). Others have suggested that democracy in and of itself is an empty concept unless is it tied to "empowerment" and to "access to participate" in democracy. (Kreisberg 1992; Clark 1993) That is, when students are denied the very access to participate in democracy, when they are invisible and passive in the curriculum, then they are denied the possibility of an equitable and democratic education.

The attempt to link multiculturalism with democracy and equal educational opportunity remains an indispensable and crucial task if education is to serve the interests of all our students. As articulated by McLaren (1991): "If we are concerned about bringing a critical multiculturalism to the United States, then we need to see it in regard to the context of constructing democratic practices" (p. 133). Yet, in many schools, democratic practices are found only in textbooks, usually confined to discussions of the American Revolution. Most students are not given the opportunity to experience day-to-day democracy with all its messiness and conflicts, because strategies for democratic practice such as student councils often become popularity contests with little power over the quality of school life. (Shor 1987) Even the standard curriculum, while full of noble and idealistic words about democracy, is often at odds with the lived realities of most students. Because there are many definitions and manifestations of democracy (participatory, representational, elitist, will of the majority, communitarian, etc.), perhaps the greatest advantage of multicultural education is its potential to explore and expand what democracy means not only in theory but in practice as well.

Because schools mirror the unfamiliarity and discomfort most U.S. citizens have with democratic practices in our society in general, the lack of democracy in schools is not surprising. Although there are certainly numerous possibilities for democratic involvement in our society, they are becoming less visible and even less viable. For instance, governance by town meeting, the romantic preindustrial epitome of democracy, is increasingly unworkable both in large urban centers and in small towns, at least as they are currently organized. Jury duty is often viewed as a distasteful, time-consuming activity that ends up relying largely on senior citizens or middle-class stay-at-home housewives who hardly represent the "jury of their peers" called for in the Constitution.

Other institutions, whether private corporations, places of worship, or civic organizations, also suffer from a dearth of democracy, functioning more as authoritarian structures than as sites of democratic participation. Involvement on advisory boards, which can serve as a powerful opportunity for democratic decision making as well as for community development, is generally available only to highly educated and well-positioned members of the community, those who have the time, resources, and disposition to take advantage of this opportunity. Thus, voting once every four years becomes about the only way in which citizens practice their democratic responsibilities, and even this is becoming the function of a minority.

Schools, as socializing agents of society, are charged with teaching all students about their democratic rights and responsibilities as articulated through U.S. history and civics. In the process, little attention is paid to the undemocratic, exclusionary, and indeed ugly side of our history that is just as much a part of our collective heritage as is the democratic, inclusive, and noble side. Thus, not only is the *process* of democracy missing, so is the critical *content* of democracy that would expose all its contradictory dimensions. If schools are to provide students with an apprenticeship for the possibility of participation in democracy, both need to be included.

I am not suggesting, however, that making schools more democratic will solve broader social issues. As mentioned above, democracy is not only largely absent in schools but in society in general, with few people having the opportunity or the inclination to participate directly in democratic decision making. Schools cannot be expected to turn this situation around, but they can become sites of resistance by highlighting the serious contradictions to democracy inherent in our everyday lives. That is, when students leave democratic classrooms only to confront authoritarian and anti-democratic institutions organized to welcome the participation of the wealthy and well-heeled minority while excluding all others, they may begin to challenge practices that undermine the theory and practice they have been learning in school. Therefore, making schools democratic is not so that they reflect a democratic society, which they often do not, but rather so that they challenge a society with democratic ideals to put them into practice. In addition, democratic participation prepares students with the collective action skills that are the bedrock of democracy for those most excluded from decision making in the larger society. Learning social action skills is not an automatic process but a learned proposition, and just as students learn the skills of literacy by practicing them, so must they learn those of democracy.

In an important paper that explores the potentially powerful link between multicultural education and democratic education, Parker (1991) has suggested that both are weakened as a result of being disconnected. For example, he demonstrates how democratic education has often been explicitly monocultural and assimilationist, disengaged from the problems and issues of multicultural education. Calling them "symbiotic ideas," he carefully links them to benefit all students:

> Common ground and open, inclusive discussion, in short, are the critical attributes, the antecedents and the consequences, of democratic community. The centerpiece of education for democracy therefore is instruction on the discursive practices and principles that support open discussion of the public's problems (eg., racial inequality, drug-addiction, public debt, care for the elderly, the achievement crisis in our schools, AIDS).

Parker suggests that both multicultural and democratic educators need to pay more attention to curriculum sites, that is, to teaching and learning the subject matters of multicultural and democratic education.

Implications of Reconsidering the Aims of Education

The first major aim that was considered, that is, student learning, focuses primarily on the content of education. The second major aim, the preparation of young people for participation in democracy, focuses on the form of education. Given these two aims, many of the critiques of multicultural education can be addressed more comprehensively because power relations in schools and in the larger society are treated as central issues in schooling. I will now address three implications that emerge from this reconsideration of the goals of education. The first will be explored in greater depth and the remaining two will be briefly mentioned.

Challenging sacred cows in education. The first central implication of these aims is that there is no room for sacred cows in a critical, multicultural education. That is, all educational innovations, strategies, and ideologies must be assessed in terms of their ability to advance student learning and prepare students for their roles as citizens of a democracy. Anything that does not contribute to these aims needs to be reconsidered.

The charge from the conservative right that multicultural education is self-esteem boosting "ethnic cheerleading" needs to be evaluated in light of this implication. I would submit that our traditional Eurocentric curriculum has always been a prime example of self-esteem boosting "ethnic cheerleading," but the ethnic group, in this case, has been the dominant White, English-speaking, male, and middle-class culture.[2] Nobody who has studied traditional U.S. curricula can doubt this: the insistence on "Columbus discovered America," "Lincoln freed the slaves," "Washington never told a lie," and other uncritical myths; the silence with respect to racism, sexism, anti-immigrant hysterica, anti-Semitism, and other ills in our society; and the absence of most great leaders or movements from outside the mainstream are clear examples of this "ethnic cheerleading" to support the status quo.

I also suspect that the charge of ethnic cheerleading by the right is made more out of a sense of loss of control over the curriculum (*their* ethnic cheerleading is now being challenged) than out of a sincere desire to promote critical thinking in students. Nevertheless, as we have seen, the left has also criticized the tendency in multicultural education to both trivialize and romanticize the histories and lived realities of subordinated groups. The challenge to avoid romanticizing the curriculum must be faced head on because we do *all* our students a disservice if we simply follow the same tired model of ethnic cheerleading, changing only the actors (a good example of the saying in Spanish, *quítate tú pa'ponerme yo*," or "you get out so I can take your place.")

Replacing the Eurocentric curriculum with a replication of top-down, transmission models of education, even if the subjects are now primarily subordinated groups, hardly moves education to a higher level. Idealizing our ancestors, romanticizing their struggles, or presenting them as only heroes and saints is both dishonest and insulting to students. Just as they feel betrayed when they find out for the first time, for example, about the internment of the Japanese during World War II because it contradicts everything they have learned about social justice in our society, so too will they react when they learn the unvarnished truth about all people. No group has a monopoly on righteousness or fair play. This is a hard lesson to learn but an ultimately crucial one if we are serious about developing a more critical multicultural education.

The charge that multicultural education centers exclusively on groups rather than individuals likewise needs to be explored. This criticism is often made because it contradicts the "rugged individualism" so central to U.S. mainstream culture. Nevertheless, it is a criticism that needs to be assessed in terms of the major aims of education articulated earlier. For example, social characteristics, if not viewed critically, can lead to stereotypes and can even frame the academic expectations that teachers have of students based on their membership in a particular group. As a case in point, the predominant view that all Asians are successful in school is grossly overstated and limits pedagogical initiatives that might be helpful to those students not falling into this category. For example, one-quarter of all dropouts from the New York City public schools are Asian (Divoky 1988). Perceiving all Asians as "whiz kids" has a negative impact on them and on educational initiatives that might help those who do not fit this stereotype.

In a related vein, research in cognitive styles can become simplistic in suggesting only a cultural basis for learning, when in reality we know that an individual from a particular culture may differ more in style, character, temperament, and personality from another individual of the same culture than from an individual from a completely different culture. Without a consideration of individual differences, we are left with only group explanations that may limit our understanding of very complex processes. Consequently, even learning style research can sometimes be used as a rationale for poor or inequitable teaching. For example, in integrated classrooms in which Hispanic children were present, Ortiz (1988) found that they tended to receive a lower-quality education than others based on teachers' perceptions and subsequent pedagogical decisions about their supposed "learning styles."

Afrocentrism has been particularly vulnerable to charges of both separatism and intellectual dogmatism. Because much of the Afrocentric scholarship challenges the Western tradition and discourse, we need to remember that the critique is coming from those who have most to lose, namely, scholars firmly entrenched in the conventional canon who feel the threat from Afrocentric scholars will displace their hegemony. In this regard, Kalantzis and Cope (1992) offer a helpful observation when they maintain that, for example, feminist perspectives would never have developed quite as fully if they had not been separate from the mainstream for a time. They add: "Older paradigms are, by their very nature, hostile to any challenge to cherished assumptions; to change a model, one has to move outside it, at least for awhile" (p. B3).

Nevertheless, because it is sometimes accompanied by dogmatism and a lack of tolerance for differences other than race, Afrocentricism also needs to come under careful analysis: The dilemma is well articulated by Bender (1992) who says, "Both Eurocentric and Afrocentric ideologues, for example, are ethnocentric because they think of their cultures as tightly bounded, self-contained, pure, and fixed. None of these qualities, however, is realized in existence" (p. 12). Ironically, these are some of the very same charges that have been leveled against the traditional canon by proponents of multiculturalism. West (1993), in a critique of Afrocentricity, also maintains that it needs to be viewed more critically and in a broader sociopolitical context than has until now occurred. Defining Afrocentricity as "a gallant yet misguided attempt,'" he writes: "It is gallant because it puts black doings and sufferings, not white anxieties and fears, at the center of discussion. It is misguided because—out of fear of cultural hybridization, silence on the issue of class, retrograde views on black women, homosexuals and lesbians and a reluctance to link race to the common good—it reinforces the narrow discussions about race"(p. 4).

These criticisms help us move forward in developing stronger links between critical pedagogy and multicultural education because they suggest that all ideologies need to be evaluated on a number of dimensions. The issue becomes one of authentically and realistically incorporating the cultures, lifestyles, and histories of formerly excluded groups into the curriculum while at the same time maintaining a critical eye about how they are included.

The implication that there can be no sacred cows also means that all strategies, even those perceived as "progressive" or ideologically correct, need to be evaluated carefully. Delpit (1988), for instance, has suggested that students of color are often neglected in the debate concerning the "skills" versus "process" approaches to literacy. Her critique is an important one because it strikes at the heart of educators' propensity to jump on the bandwagon without thinking about the implications of their curricular and pedagogical decisions. Thus, although she supports the tenets of the whole language approach that help students acknowledge their own expertise, she also feels that it is absolutely essential that some students, particularly African American and other educationally disempowered youth, be explicitly taught the codes needed to be successful in the U.S. mainstream. While Delpit does not suggest that direct instruction ("the skills approach") is the answer, she makes a powerful case for not simply accepting educational practices because they may be considered empowering.

Similar critiques have been made about whole language and process writing for language minority and other students (Reyes

1992; Dyson 1992); cooperative learning (Grant 1990; Sapon-Shevin and Schniedewind 1991 ; McCaslin and Good 1992); transitional bilingual education and multicultural education when underlying structures are not challenged (Skutnabb-Kangas and Cummins 1988); using student knowledge as the sole content of the curriculum without bridging it with school knowledge (Sleeter and Grant 1991); and simple detracking without more profound changes in teaching (Goodlad and Oakes 1988; Wheelock 1992).

A related corollary of this implication is that we need to concentrate on ends rather than means. Many constructive and creative strategies can be used to reach our dual goals of student learning and preparation for participation in democracy, but it is crucial that we focus on the primary aims themselves. Because education as a field has been notorious for adopting and dropping particular means at the drop of a hat while not reflecting carefully on the ends they were meant to reach, this is a particularly difficult challenge. Choosing a reading approach, selecting a math program, developing an assembly program about AIDS, or deciding how to arrange a classroom: these are all means that must be considered within the objectives they were designed to reach.

Including student voices in the curriculum. A second implication of developing a critical, multicultural education is that we must attend to the voices of students in order to make substantive and meaningful changes in education. Although most educators pay lip service to "student needs and interests," students are rarely directly asked for opinions concerning their education or asked for suggestions about the curriculum or instructional practices. When they are asked, the results are often surprising and enlightening. For instance, students in California from a wide range of backgrounds in ethnicity and achievement were asked to identify factors that affect their engagement with schools and learning. (Phelan, Davidson, and Cao 1992). The researchers found that the students' views on teaching and learning were remarkably similar to those of contemporary theorists concerned with current learning theories. Major findings included the following: students like classrooms where they feel they know the teacher and other students; they want teachers to recognize who they are and listen to what they have to say; they like to feel emotionally safe; and, most importantly, they place tremendous value on having teachers who care for and about them.

Zanger's research (1993) with Latino youngsters from the Boston area is another example of the power of students' voices. In this study, even academically successful Latino students, who tend to feel relatively connected to school, talked movingly about their sense of exclusion, isolation, and cultural invisibility in school. In my own research with students from a variety of ethnic, linguistic, and social-class backgrounds, I discovered that they had very definite ideas about good teaching (which most defined as active, engaged, and respectful of their backgrounds and interests) and that the conflict and pain they felt about their native cultures and languages could be linked to the schools' lack of support for it (Nieto 1994). Because they had rarely been directly asked to comment on these issues, the interviews themselves were empowering strategies that allowed them to make sense of their world. Listening to students is important not because of any romantic notions of student knowledge but because doing so can help inform our curriculum and instructional strategies and even challenge us to change our unintentional biases.

Transforming teachers. Finally, and related to this last point, is the third implication in constructing a more critical multicultural education: teachers themselves must be involved in their own reeducation and transformation, including challenging their attitudes, knowledge, and practices. In the words of Aronowitz and Giroux (1985), teachers must become "transformative intellectuals." Not only do they need to demand to be treated and perceived as professionals rather than as technicians but also they must be involved in changing their role from transmitters of knowledge to creators and challengers of knowledge with their students. Cummins suggests a shift from "coercive relations of power" to "collaborative relations of power," based on the assumption that power is not a fixed quantity but rather one that can be shared. Collaborative relations of power are based on two interconnected premises: redefining teachers' roles and challenging policies and practices within schools that may limit student learning and their apprenticeship for democracy (Cummins 1994; Kreisberg 1992; Nieto 1992).

CONCLUSION

Addressing the problems of inequitable and disempowering education means looking carefully at our own practice as teachers and asking hard questions related to the curriculum and the social context for learning. Even teachers who are considered talented by their peers and supervisors sometimes unwittingly perpetuate low expectations of their students by giving them access to only low-level knowledge or providing educational environments that are disempowering.[3] Coming to terms with our own biases, including our unacknowledged racism, sexism, and classism and how they get played out in relations with students and their parents, is an especially necessary process.

A critical multicultural education can only be forged by those who are convinced that all our students deserve a better, more complete, and more challenging education. Maxine Greene (1986) has answered the question, "What might a critical pedagogy be for teachers now?" by stating:

> Perhaps we might begin by releasing our imagination and sum-moning up the traditions of freedom in which most of us were reared. We might try to make audible again the recurrent calls for justice and equality. We might try to reactivate the resistance to materialism and conformity. We might even try to inform with meaning the desire to educate 'all the children' in a legitimately common school" (p. 440).

Democracy and learning, in this conception, move beyond romantic notions of equality to tangible proof that all students can and should become active learners and citizens. In the final analysis, a critical multicultural education can only come about when educators accept the challenge that all our students deserve the right to dream.

NOTES

I am grateful to Christine Sleeter, Carmen Rolón, Jim Cummins, Patricia Ramsey, and Ira Shor for providing insightful and helpful critiques of an earlier version of this chapter.
1. Patricia Ramsey, a colleague at Mt. Holyoke College, first introduced me to this expression.
2. For a discussion of how this issue has been used to trivialize attempts at reforming education, see J. A. Beane (September, 1991), Sorting out the self-esteem controversy, *Educational Leadership*: 25–30. 3.
3. See, for example, K. Bennett, (1991), Doing school in an urban Appalachian first grade. In *Empowerment through multicultural education*, ed. C. E. Sleeter (Albany, N.Y.: SUNY Press); and J. Goodlad, (1984), *A place called school* (New York: McGraw-Hill).

REFERENCES

Apple, M. W. 1977. "Justice as a curricular concern." In *Multi-cultural education: Commitments, issues, and applications*, ed. C. A. Grant, Washington, D.C.: Association for Supervision and Curriculum Development.

Aronowitz, S. & Giroux, H. A. 1985. *Education under siege: The conservative, liberal, and radical debate over schooling*. South Hadley, MA.: Bergin and Garvey.

Banks, J. A. 1991. *Teaching strategies for ethnic studies*. 5th ed. Boston: Allyn and Bacon.

Bastian, A., et al. 1985. *Choosing equality: The case for democratic schooling*. New York: New World Foundation.

Beane, J. A. 1991. Sorting out the self-esteem controversy. *Educational Leadership*. (September): 25–30.

Bender, T. 1992. Negotiating public culture: Inclusion and synthesis in American history. *Liberal Education* (March/April) 78: 2, 10–15.

Bennett, K. 1991. Doing school in an urban Appalachian first grade. In *Empowerment through multicultural education*, ed. C. E. Sleeter. Albany: State University of New York Press.

Bloom, A. 1987. *The closing of the American mind: How higher education has failed democracy and impoverished the souls of today's students*. New York: Simon and Schuster.

Cheng, C. W., Brizendine, E., and Oakes, J. 1981. What is "an equal chance" for minority children? In *Education in the 80's: Multiethnic education*, ed. J. A. Banks. Washington, D.C.: National Education Association.

Churchill, W. 1982. White studies: The intellectual imperialism of contemporary U. S. education. *Integrated Education* 19(1, 2): 51–57.

Clark, C. 1993. *Multicultural education as a tool for disarming violence.* Unpublished doctoral dissertation, University of Massachusetts.

Cummins, J. 1992. Foreword in *Affirming diversity: The sociopolitical context of multicultural education*, by S. Nieto. White Plains. N.Y.: Longman Publishers.

————. 1994. From coercive to collaborative relations of power in the teaching of literacy. In *Literacy across languages and cultures*, ed. B. M. Ferdman, R. M. Weber, and A. Ramirez. Albany: State University of New York Press.

Darder, A. 1991. *Culture and power in the classroom.* New York: Bergin and Garvey.

Delpit, L. D. 1988. The silenced dialogue: Power and pedagogy in educating other people's children. *Harvard Educational Review* 58(3): 280–298.

Dewey, J. 1966; first edition 1916. *Democracy and education.* Reprint. New York: Free Press.

Divoky, D. 1988. The model minority goes to school. *Phi Delta Kappan* (November): 219–222.

Dickeman, M. 1973. Teaching cultural pluralism. In *Teaching ethnic studies: Concepts and strategies*, ed. J. A. Banks. Washington, D.C. 43d Yearbook of the National Council for the Social Studies.

D'Souza, D. 1991. *Illiberal education: The politics of race and sex on campus.* New York: Free Press.

Dyson, A. H. 1992. *Whistle for Willie, lost puppies, and cartoon dogs: The sociocultural dimensions of young children's composing or Toward unmelting pedagogical pots.* Technical Report #63, University of California, Berkeley: National Center for the Study of Writing and Literacy.

Freire, P. 1970. *Pedagogy of the oppressed.* New York: Seabury Press.

Gay, G. 1977. Curriculum design for multicultural education. In *Multicultural education: Commitments, issues, and applications*, ed. C. A. Grant. Washington, D.C.: Association for Supervision and Curriculum Development.

Giroux, H. A. May, 1992, Educational leadership and the crisis of democratic government. *Educational Researcher* 21(4): 4–11.

Goodlad, J. I. 1984. *A place called school.* New York: McGraw-Hill.

Goodlad, J. I. and Oakes, J. 1988. We must offer equal access to knowledge. *Educational Leadership* 45(5): 16–22.

Grant, C. A. 1990. Desegregation, racial attitudes, and intergroup contact: A discussion of change. *Phi Delta Kappan* (September): 25–32.

Greene, M. 1986. In search of a critical pedagogy. *Harvard Educational Review* 56(4): 427–441.

Hale-Benson, J. E. 1986. *Black children: Their roots, culture, and learning styles.* Baltimore, MD.: Johns Hopkins University Press.

Hirsch, E. D. 1987. *Cultural literacy: What every American needs to know.* Boston: Houghton Mifflin.

Howe, K. R. 1992. Liberal democracy, equal educational opportunity, and the challenge of multiculturalism. *American Educational Research Journal* 29(3): 455–470.

Kalantzis, M. and Cope, W. 1992. Multiculturalism may prove to be the key issue of our epoch. *Chronicle of Higher Education* (November): B3, BS.

Kalantzis, M., Cope, W. and Slade, C. 1989. *Minority languages.* London: Falmer Press.

Kreisberg, S. 1992. *Transforming power: Domination, empowerment, and education.* Albany: State University of New York Press.

Ladson-Billings, G. and Henry, A. 1990. Blurring the borders: Voices of African liberatory pedagogy in the United States and Canada. *Journal of Education* 172(2): 72–88.

McCaslin, M. and Good, T. L. 1992. Compliant cognition: The misalliance of management and instructional goals in current school reform. *Educational Researcher* 21(3): 4–17.

McLaren, P. 1991. Critical pedagogy, multiculturalism, and the politics of risk and resistance: A response to Kelly and Portelli. *Journal of Education* 173(3): 109–139.

Moll, L. C. 1992. Bilingual classroom studies and community analysis: Some recent trends. *Educational Researcher* 21(2): 20–24.

Moses, R. P., et al. 1989. The Algebra Project: Organizing in the spirit of Ella. *Harvard Educational Review* 59(4): 27–47.

New York State Social Studies Review and Development Committee. June, 1991. *One nation, many peoples: A declaration of cultural Interdependence.* Albany: New York State Department of Education.

Nieto, S. 1992. *Affirming diversity: The sociopolitical context of multicultural education.* White Plains, N.Y.: Longman Publishers.

Nieto, S. 1994. Lessons from students on creating a chance to dream. *Harvard Educational Review* 64 (4): 392–426.

Ogbu, J. U. 1992. Understanding cultural diversity and learning. *Educational Researcher* 21(8): 5–14.

Ortiz, F. I. 1988. Hispanic-American children's experiences in classrooms: A comparison between Hispanic and non-Hispanic children. In *Class, race and gender in American education,* ed. L. Weis. Albany: State University of New York Press.

Parker, W. C. 1991. Multicultural education in democratic societies: Searching for a curriculum site. Paper presented at the Annual Meeting of the American Educational Research Association, Chicago, Illinois.

Peterson, R. E. 1991. Teaching how to read the world and change it: Critical pedagogy in the intermediate grades. In *Literacy as praxis: Culture, language, and pedagogy*, ed. C. E. Walsh. Norwood, N.J.: Ablex Publishing.

Phelan, P., Davidson, A. L., and Cao, H. T. 1992. Speaking up: Students' perspectives on school. *Phi Delta Kappan* (May): 695–704.

Ravitch, D. 1990. Multiculturalism: E pluribus plures. *The Key Reporter* 56(1): 1–4.

Reyes, M. 1992. Challenging venerable assumptions: Literacy instruction for linguistically different students. *Harvard Educational Review* 62(4): 427–446.

Sapon-Shevin, M. and Schniedewind, N. 1991. Cooperative learning as empowering pedagogy. In *Empowerment through multicultural education*, ed. C. E. Sleeter. Albany, New York: State University of New York Press.

Schlesinger, A. M., Jr. 1992. *The disuniting of America.* New York: Norton.

Shor, I. 1987. *Critical teaching and everyday life.* Chicago, IL: University of Chicago Press.

Skutnabb-Kangas, T. 1990. Legitimating or delegitimating new forms of racism: The role of researchers. *Journal of Multilingual and Multicultural Development* 11(1 and 2): 77–100.

Skutnabb-Kangas, T. and Cummins, J. 1988. *Minority education: From shame to struggle.* Clevedon, England: Multilingual Matters.

Sleeter, C. E. 1991. *Empowerment through multicultural education.* Albany: State University of New York Press.

———. 1995. An analysis of the critiques of multicultural education. In *Handbook of research on multicultural education*, ed. J. A. Banks and C. A. M. Banks. New York: Macmillan.

Sleeter, C. E. and Grant, C. A. 1991. Mapping terrains of power: Student cultural knowledge vs. classroom knowledge. In -

Empowerment through multicultural education, ed. C. E. Sleeter. Albany: State University of New York Press.

Sobol, T. 1991. *Understanding diversity.* Memorandum to the Board of Regents, July 12.

Suzuki, B. 1979. Multicultural education: What's it all about? *Integrated Education* 17: 97–98, 43–50.

Tatum, B. D. 1992. Talking about race, learning about racism: The application of racial identity development theory in the classroom. *Harvard Educational Review* 62(1): 1–24.

Walsh, C. E., ed. 1991. *Literacy as praxis: Culture, language, and pedagogy.* Norwood, New Jersey: Ablex Publishing Corporation.

Weinberg, M. 1977. A historical framework for multicultural education. In *Teaching in a multicultural society: Perspectives and professional strategies*, ed. D. E. Gross, G. C. Baker, and L. J. Stiles. New York: The Free Press.

———. 1990. *Racism in the United States: A comprehensive classified bibliography.* Westport, CT.: Greenwood Press.

West, C. 1993. *Race matters.* Boston: Beacon Press.

Wheelock, A. 1992. *Crossing the tracks: How "untracking" can save America's schools.* New York: The New Press.

Zanger, V. V. 1993. Academic costs of social marginalization: An analysis of Latino students' perceptions at a Boston high school. In *The education of Latino students in Massachusetts: Issues, research and policy implications*, ed. R. Rivera and S. Nieto. Boston: Gaston Institute for Latino Community Development and Public Policy.

7

JOHN RIVERA AND MARY POPLIN

Multicultural, Critical, Feminine and Constructive Pedagogies Seen Through the Lives of Youth: A Call For the Revisioning Of These And Beyond: Toward A Pedagogy For the Next Century

Constructive, critical, feminine, and multicultural pedagogies have all been proposed as contemporary alternatives to the reductionistic pedagogy prominent in most education settings today. These four contemporary pedagogies share powerful assumptions about teaching and learning and yet also hold premises which can be contradictory to one another. This chapter will present voices of middle and high school students, drawn from participatory research, discussing their experiences in school and will relate their stories to the principles and practices of these four alternative pedagogies. We will also contrast their stories with traditional reductionistic pedagogy, which these students currently experience and critique. The students whose voices we have drawn here are currently enrolled in public schools where the dominant pedagogy remains reductionistic; that is, their school day is structured with traditional subject matter divisions and their teachers, more or less, see their role as the transmission of a set of skills, concepts, and facts drawn from the official curriculum.

This picture is in contrast to constructive, multicultural, feminine, and critical pedagogical theory and practice which all view learning as a process of constructing new meanings around the content of the curriculum versus acquiring the meanings of others. The premises of this chapter include (1) that schools still largely operate on reductionistic pedagogies that emphasize transmission (primarily one-way) of a particular set of skills, meanings, and concepts which are claimed to be value neutral, (2) that the wise and skillful application of many of the principles and practices of constructive, multicultural, critical, and feminine pedagogies would improve the situations in schools considerably, (3) that

221

each of these pedagogies, taken separately, is insufficient and would be more responsive in combination with one another were we to eliminate their incompatibilities in the light of student needs, and (4) that even in combination there are aspects of human growth that cry out for more than is offered by the four, even in combination. A complete pedagogy for the next century is needed which draws on the wisdom contained in each of these, eliminates contradictions and false assumptions, and adds to them principles not currently present.

We will look at each of the four issues above through the lens of an assumption common to the four alternative pedagogies, that learning involves the active construction of new meanings. We will show how this assumption is differently conceived in each of these pedagogies and how it differs from traditional, reductionistic pedagogies. We will do this primarily through excerpts of students talking about school.

CONSTRUCTIVE, MULTICULTURAL, FEMININE AND CRITICAL PEDAGOGIES

While is not the purpose of this paper to review multicultural, feminine, critical, and constructive pedagogies, we will briefly state how each approaches the definition of learning. Each of these theories holds to the assumption that in order to learn one must construct new meanings for oneself around the content of instruction. However, each pedagogy emphasizes a different aspect of the creation of meaning, and each stems from a body of research and practice that is largely independent of and not reflected in the others. All the alternative pedagogies assume that the construction of meaning is a good thing and should be encouraged. With the freedom to construct, these theories assume students will create meanings which are compatible with human progress. They also all believe that student voices as they construct meaning should interact with one another.

Constructivists focus primarily on the individual learner and on the construction or reconstruction of cognitive concepts and meanings with very little attention to the sociopolitical, cultural, or affective contexts as either influencing or influenced by meanings. An exception is the recent attention given to Vygotsky's work related to culture. (See Vygotsky, 1986; Moll, 1992). Constructivists are concerned primarily with change within individual cognitive meanings rather than with social or larger personal change. Largely through research with individual children from the dominant culture, constructivists have defined precisely the ways in which ideas and concepts (meanings) come to be formed through processes such as assimilation, accommodation, and scaffolding around the content of instruction and what is already known by the learner. This cognitive orientation, as was the research which spawned it, is highly individualistic in orientation. Constructivists are concerned with the meanings made between self and the content of instruction. They believe that all learning stems first from an individual's current meanings (determined by developmental levels, previous experience, and integrity of the brain) and that current meanings shape those that are being constructed just as new meanings shape current experience. Learning for constructivists involves the transformation of meanings within cognitive structures that results largely from student inquiry and action.

Critical pedagogues are concerned with bringing about social change toward a more just society and thus are interested in encouraging meanings from instruction which are constructed around and within larger sociopolitical realities. Their research and practice is largely derived from the observation of educational programs with adults living in oppressive situations, e.g., peasants in Brazil, union organizers, and civil rights activists in the United States. These programs have as their explicit goals the liberation of a group of people living in oppressive situations. The individual meanings of interest to critical educators have to do with how learners see their role in the process of social change; thus they are interested in the meanings that learners make in relation to self and society. Critical pedagogy seeks to draw out student voices and put these voices into dialogue with others in a never ending cycle of meaning making characterized by reflection/action/reflection/new action and so forth. Critical theorists directly relate learning and the transformation of a society toward justice, largely defined as economic and political power shifts between dominant and subordinate groups.

Unlike critical or constructivist educators, the feminine pedagogues are acutely aware of the role of personal relationships, aesthetics, and emotion in the construction of knowledge within the context of instruction and schooling. While their work also has sociopolitical overtones, it has in the past also been more oriented toward the individual and her or his natural personal relationships. We are using feminine pedagogy as expressed by those concerned with the value of what is traditionally called the feminine side of all of us, not the feminist pedagogy that emphasizes issues of equality and expectation, which is more similar to critical pedagogy or multicultural pedagogy. Feminine pedagogy is an outgrowth of research and practice largely, but not exclusively, with girls and women which revealed that connectedness between subject matter and self is mediated by connectedness in personal relationships. Like the critical pedagogists, feminine pedagogists are concerned with the body of research on moral development and reasoning. Gilligan (1982) makes a distinction between moral reasoning that is justice centered versus care and relational centered. The critical pedagogists are concerned with the justice side of moral reasoning while the feminine pedagogists are more concerned with the care voice of moral reasoning. The connection of meaning between self and other here emphasizes connections within a limited range of personal relationships rather than societal ones.

For multicultural pedagogues the construction of meaning is a social and cultural act—not merely individual, cognitive, affective or political ones. Their concern is with meanings that are developed between self and others who are different from themselves, within the context of communities. They raise issues largely left out of the other pedagogical theories such as the interplay of language and culture, the critical role of others' expectations, the importance of preserving and expanding students' bilingual and bicultural abilities, and the missing voices in the curriculum we bring to schools. Multicultural pedagogy addresses the way these experiences influence the creation of meaning around instruction for students inside school. The work and principles of multicultural pedagogies are derived more from the actual experiences of students, particularly students of color currently in public school and society, than are the principles of other pedagogies whose research is drawn more from private research settings and private education settings. Like the critical theorists, multicultural theorists study relations between dominant and oppressed groups. Multicultural pedagogy is deeply concerned with the effects of institutional racism, inherent in many of the unnamed assumptions of traditional and other pedagogies, on students' opportunities to learn from instruction. For example, the assumptions of implicit and common knowledge, often a part of constructivist and feminine pedagogy, and the logical rationality inherent in critical theory are all drawn from the dominant culture's views of the purposes of education.

Traditional, reductionistic pedagogy, which is still dominant in most schools today, emphasizes not the construction of meaning but the acquisition of meanings constructed by others. These meanings are expressed in the official curriculum and texts designated by those who have the power to designate such things as important pieces of common knowledge for all a nation's citizens. While certainly common knowledge is a necessary part of any vital community, the power to name these things can be seriously misused. Then traditional pedagogy uses practices which, by necessity, must control, instruct, monitor, reward, and punish students as they acquire the appropriate content. Meanings of interest to reductionistic pedagogues are almost exclusively content related because the process is tightly controlled by the instructor rather than engaged by the learner. The content in reductionistic pedagogies is not only predetermined but defined as objective and value neutral. Reductionistic pedagogies only deal with the seen; outcomes are defined as observable. Assessment systems are designed to judge the degree to which one has acquired the predesignated meanings and are used, themselves, as methods of reward and punishment. Reductionistic pedagogy is a derivative of logical positivism which spawned behaviorism. These pedagogies assume learning is rational, sequential, and logical and that students act (learn) in response to self-interest. Thus their pedagogy uses techniques of manipulation to convince students of the self-interest of learning predesignated content.

These are, of course, oversimplified descriptions of the similarities and differences between the pedagogies. In each pedagogy one can find representatives that express multiple perspectives and in practice rarely would one see a theory in isolation. Nevertheless, each theory's authors do have a primary focus for their work be it cognitive, affective, cultural, or political. The practices which exist bear these emphases as well. Thus, classrooms using these practices, even ostensibly the same practice, look very different, and different students respond very differently within them. For example, cooperative learning is a strategy advocated by all of the pedagogies but for different reasons. The reductionistic pedagogue must use cooperative learning to teach cooperative behaviors, while multicultural educators use the strategy because is it more compatible with cultures who value cooperation over competition. The constructivist advocates use of cooperative learning because social language among peers stimulates cognitive processes and meanings, and the critical pedagogists use cooperative learning to draw out students' voices and put those in critical dialogue with others' voices. Depending on the reason one implements cooperative learning, the strategy, the content, and the practice look very different. Unfortunately, in practice, teachers are often taught "methods of instruction" with no theoretical reasoning attached; thus teachers have no way to evaluate and modify (construct their own meanings around) the strategy or method. We must develop a pedagogy that allows for the understanding and use of multiple purposes at various times; thus the teacher could develop and use multiple strategies depending on the purposes.

THE PROBLEMS OF SCHOOLING AND PEDAGOGY ACCORDING TO STUDENTS

In an extensive participatory research project, participants in four typical schools in Southern California sought over eighteen months to name the problems of schooling in the United States from inside the classroom (Poplin & Weeres, 1992). During this process, teachers, students, custodians, secretaries, librarians, food service personnel, parents, and administrators at two elementary schools, a middle school and a high school sought to describe the problems of schooling from their own points of view. As the participatory research progressed, increasingly teachers and other adults and students began to agree on the nature of the problems of schooling.

Seven common themes emerged as the problems of schooling from insiders points of view. These seven issues suggested that previous reports on schooling had not identified the problems of schooling but rather the consequences of them. Still, the underlying causes of these problems have not been named. We will take up only the first four of these issues—relationships, racism, values, and the teaching process. At first glance, we could simply assign to each of the above list of issues a pedagogy for which it is a primary concern: for example, feminine pedagogists and relationships, multicultural educators and racism, critical educators and values, and constructivist and the teaching process. However, this approach denies the reality of the findings which suggest these are not separate but inextricable issues. And the fact that pedagogies have built up around one or the other suggests that this is the reason our pedagogies are individually inadequate and even contradictory. The naming of the problems as seven separate entities is more a result of the inadequacy of our qualitative research methods and of our language to accommodate the complex reality of human stories. In actuality, students never spoke of one and then the other. Their text was much richer, and one issue was always delicately woven with others.

We will take a few examples that will show the necessity of using multiple pedagogies and the urgency of solving their contradictions and of filling their inadequacies. For what generally happens with alternative proposals is that in the midst of their struggles with one another, the dominant traditional explanation takes precedence by virtue of the confusion and disorder among proponents of alternatives. Clearly constructivist and feminine pedagogies would be more adequate if they were inclusive of problems of racism, and critical pedagogists might make more rapid growth in social change if they incorporated the knowledge constructivist and feminine pedagogies have about how people change their meanings. Constructive, feminine, and multicultural pedagogies would be richer and more transformative if they involved the issues raised by the critical theorists. But to do this, some peace must be made with the diverse purposes of these pedagogies, and some effort made to find and fill the missing principles based on the lives of students and the reality of the world they and we live in.

RELATIONSHIPS

One student states: "Teachers should get to know their students a little better, not to where they bowl together but at least know if they have any brothers and sisters. I have found that if I know my teacher I feel more obliged to do the work so I don't disappoint them. Once my trust is gained I feel I should work for myself and also for the teacher." In just a few lines, this student has laid out the complexity of the relationship between motivation, learning, and caring. Caring involves a degree of knowing about each other, note that it is not simply the teaching getting to know the student but also the student knowing the teacher. This requires us to build an authentic relationship with students where we both reveal who we are and know the other. He goes well beyond the abstract and gives us some suggestions (know about brothers and sisters) which require a conversation. Yet, he is tempered by realism (not to where they bowl together), recognizing the limits of their relationship inside the system. We often argue theoretically about internal versus external motivation and getting students to do things for us versus for them. These conflicting theories/practices for motivating students have always been a strong point of contention between traditional and alternative pedagogies. However, for this student, these are not the dualities they appear to be in theory. He is clear; in a classroom with a good teacher, he does things for both reasons (work for myself and them). Note that this student refers to the fact that the relationship developed between teachers and students holds both good and bad potential (trust and disappointment). This is an issue not yet fully addressed in any of the pedagogies.

The authenticity of the relationship just described goes beyond the older notions of humanism where the "client" was to be known but not the therapist. This inequality of knowing results in a power differential between participants that is similar to the strict hierarchical authority used in behaviorism. Authenticity is easily spotted by students. Consider two quotes regarding the same act; shaking students' hands. A high school student writes: "My first period teacher seems so malevolent and shows no clemency toward us. We are supposed to have our hands shook every morning, this teacher does it with such an attitude like she doesn't want to." (In another section of the response this student remarks that she can tell the teacher does not like students like her, who are black). A second high school student writes: "When I walk into my second period class, my teacher is there to meet you with a handshake and a smile which makes you know it going to be a good day. He knows your name which makes you feel good." These texts emerged because the school had an in-service day on behavior management in which a nationally known speaker suggested the teachers shake students' hands. Such perceptive remarks by students highlight the danger of turning any pedagogical idea into a method. More importantly, the first student raises the issue of relationships within the context of racism. Students perceive what their teachers feel and the attitude with which they perform their daily routines. Although it is a goal of multicultural pedagogy, none of the methods have yet found a reliable and thorough way of effectively changing attitudes.

RACISM

Though many students raised issues of racism even in the initial survey, which only asked for what one liked and disliked about schooling, almost no adults inside the schools initially raised the issue. Most of the teachers in the schools were Euro-American. Identifying and seriously discussing issues concerning race, at first, was avoided even contested. At last, student voices brought all participants to a level of honesty not previously reached. Racism remains an issue that is addressed in a guarded manner particularly by Euro-American adults inside schools.

Primarily, students (and to a lesser extent their parents and some educators of color) identified aspects of racism which they felt impacted their schooling. Middle and especially high school students also raised issues of racism in the larger society. Racism was identified as all of the following: comments made by students to one another across ethnic group lines, racist teachers and other school staff, differential expectations, lack of explicit knowledge of how things work, and the racism inherent in the curriculum. Like the tenets of multicultural pedagogies, students called for someone to teach them about each other, to have more teachers of color, to rid the schools of racist teachers, to have ethnic studies courses, to have clubs based on themes like black studies, as well as clubs that would bring all races together and to hold high expectations for students of color. Again, their voices raise the issues in their complexity. They ask for both unity and diversity.

One high school student challenges the curriculum in this way: "One thing that should be done is to change the history books. Our history books show Hannibal, a man coming from Africa on elephants, as white. It shows Egyptians as tan, and we don't even teach about the Zulu Nation, but we teach about the Roman Empire—what's the difference?" Of course, both multicultural and critical educators, as well as this student know the difference and would agree—the difference has to do with who gets to designate the official curriculum, the canon. While multicultural educators encourage us to expand our curriculum, critical pedagogists urge us also to take the issue on as a political issue that shapes and forms classroom dialogues.

One high school student extends the discussion of institutional racism, he wants "...definitely someone to explain to Mexican parents (like mine) how the system works here. I think this is very critical and needed, because many Hispanic parents don't understand the pressure, stress, and responsibilities that are imposed on us. Their schooling was totally different. They don't know they have to encourage us like Americans do their children. This is very true and important. Don't ignore this; I'm speaking from experience." We can see that the school experience has helped this student define himself as not being American. His concern about what is not understood is larger than just concern with his own experience. He is concerned with the experience of "many Hispanic parents." What is his definition of encourage, his perception of the pressure, stress, and responsibility of schooling? Traditional pedagogy assumes pressure on students will be pressure on parents and that everyone understands the rules. The rules used here are those of behaviorism—shaping, rewarding, and punishing. How can we develop rules that everyone can know and will be, if not equitable, at least fair and productive?

Teachers in this school revisited these issues several times. First, there was an assumption that because Latino/Latina parents did not attend school functions, they did not care. However, when suggested and led by a Latina office assistant, a dinner was held for Latino parents where it was announced Spanish would be spoken, 250 people attended. (Only fifty Euro-American parents had attended a similar, previous function). Secondly, teachers in the research process began to dialogue about the differences in the way they felt when Euro-Americans took their children out of school for vacations and when Mexican-Americans took their children to Mexico for the Posada (Christmas celebrations) or funerals. Ultimately, the difference lay in the sophistication of parent initiated negotiations between those who knew and did not know "how the system works." This issue of institutionalized racism is difficult to avoid when raised through the critical dialogue and action created within participatory research. This is similar to the reflective dialogue and action critical pedagogists suggest be created inside classrooms.

Another student writes: "I have disliked many experiences in school. For example: One of my teachers was prejudiced last year. We had a student store and group of four girls were working. I was one of them. Then one of the girls stole over a hundred dollars and blamed it on me. They blamed me for taking the money and the teacher believed her just because I wasn't white." A student store, while appealing to the action involved in constructivism and other alternative pedagogies yet is not free of the racism emphasized by multicultural pedagogues who incorporate in their pedagogies an emphasis on the role that expectations play in student achievement. This student's whole experience of schooling has been obviously impacted by her acute awareness of this injustice; an injustice that critical educators encourage us to bring as open dialogues into our classrooms.

The issue of lowered and/or negative expectations and the destructive system which builds around them is readily apparent to many students of color. Another student complains, "I have been treated differently because of my race. When I first transferred here, I had a 3.00 GPA grade. And the counselor and teachers couldn't believe it. They asked me did I cheat or are those my real grades. Why do they ask that? It is because I'm BLACK!" Another student relates not only an observation of expectations but also a full analysis of the relationships between tracking and race: "...being and looking Mexican, I've been treated as if I were one of those who came to bum around and live off the government money which really upsets me. Because they put the LATINO race down and for those like myself who was born here, live here, raised here, would be tracked like them (other Latinos), and I am trying hard to make something out of my life, like my parents have." Both students express the relationship between racist expectations and common social perceptions in the larger world and the impingement of this racism on their trying to be the best they can be. Quite sophisticated understandings of the concepts presented by multicultural and critical educators emerge very early in the lives of students of color, such as distinctions between immigrant and nonimmigrant, physical features of darker or lighter, issues of the state welfare system, and the relationship of opportunities, grades, and expectations. Students want schools where they can be treated fairly, be expected to do their best, be respected and cared for, be taught about their cultures and learn to relate to one another across racial barriers, and where they can learn to challenge racism in a productive way.

Students are able to identify racist teachers: "Some students are prejudiced and so are some teachers. I have personally dealt with and been through racist teachers and students. I've heard teachers here call KIDS nigger or beaner but never honkie. This school has an all white staff with the exception of an Indian and a Black teacher. I have classes where some teachers will not pay attention to colored or Mexican kids. They call us trouble makers. A teacher may not tell a student in front of a class but they will when the teacher and student are alone and some threats are made. The school should expand their staff to more than just whites; it would make the kids a lot more comfortable knowing that." Here explicit and institutional racism is identified. The call for more teachers of color began to appear in our data, even in elementary schools. After the study, a group of students went to the principal with a list of names of racist teachers on campus and sent the same list to each person who had been indicted. This act alone (one which would be encouraged by critical and multicultural educators) quickly caused outward behaviors to change faster than through hundreds of hours of "training;" however, again, do we have a pedagogy that can permanently change the attitudes of the people involved?

Racism is evident and raised as an issue by students regardless of color: "Just about everyone displays racism here. They say racial things, they do racist acts, and they play racist music. The teachers are afraid of talking about some things because they might have racial over/undertones. A lot of Blacks and Mexicans look down on me because I am a white guy with long hair. We should learn more about each other. Then we wouldn't think "we" are better than the other guy." The desire to know more about each other leads to the list of student recommendations to reduce racism and to make classes more interesting and relevant. It is not an abstract knowledge these students want; they want to have serious conversations with one another. Students of color want the official texts to tell them their histories and represent their literatures just as predicted by the multicultural pedagogists.

Multicultural educators are the only pedagogues who emphasize race and cultural issues to the degree that students do. These issues clearly preoccupy most students in multiethnic environments, regardless of race. However, most teachers have little idea of the importance and dominance of these issues for students. Where is the pedagogy that teaches us to have productive conversations with one another? Students call for real conversations rather than for the classes or exercises, which often fill our multicultural curriculum, to teach them "about" each other. They have real issues in front of them every day and do not appear to need exercises brought in from outside. They long for a safe place where the issues of racism within their lives can be worked through to some hopeful solutions. Even the telling of different versions of history, which build up distinct identities, rarely embed these identities back within the larger sociocultural context. That is, we have not yet articulated a vision for the collective which is as unified as each singular culture story hopes for its own identity.

VALUES

During the study, the dominance of conversations about basic values was evident. All participants spoke of values as they answered questions and discussed data. They made clear differentiations between things they considered "good" or "bad." These discussions transcended comments about schooling and drew in the larger societal issues. Students, regardless of their academic status, reported that school was boring because it had nothing to do with the important things in life. Students begged to have teachers raise these important issues and values in the classroom. One student remarked: "If I talk [about important things] to my parents, sometimes they get mad at me because of what I say to them. Or maybe they're too busy. If I talk to teachers, I can't tell them if I said a bad word or something because they suspend me. So I guess the only people who understand are gangsters. They always understand and they always help me solve it too." Another student responds: "I belong to two groups. Both are gangs, and we are all proud of what we are. Teachers see you as a cholo, gangster, lowlife, drug dealer, etc. and that makes them treat you differently than everyone else because they stereotype us and don't give us a chance to show them what we can do. Not all of us are bad; some of us want to get a good education." Here concepts of badness and goodness, racism, relationships, the importance of education and expectations lie intertwined. These values occupy all students even those whom the system often labels as not having values (perhaps especially these students). In this dialogue, the students express values most of us hold. Indeed throughout the study we found strong indications that basic values do not differ across groups, by age, race, gender, or socioeconomic class; however, as this young man relates, the ability to act on values and to be credited with them does. What conversations are taking place inside gangs that are not taking place inside schools? These are conversations that multicultural and critical educators promote; however, do even these "help them solve it too?"

Constructivists would acknowledge that because students want to raise such issues, they should become part of the curriculum, but the methodology of constructivism also does not help us have really serious conversations with children. Conversations that matter often lie well outside the cognitive domains valued by constructivists and critical thinking advocates who stick closely to logical/rational models of thought. The feminine pedagogists recognize the importance of students feeling connected, but these students *are* connected. How do any of these pedagogies help the students connect to school *and* family? Critical and multicultural pedagogies allow for powerful conversations about economic, social, and political justice (usually defined as equality) but what of the other values of friendship, family, and goodness versus badness?

Student and adult data were replete with references to basic values of hard work, courage, family, friendship, loyalty, justice, fairness, virtue, care, responsibility, and the value of a good education. All participants value education and family. The manner in which these values are prioritized and applied may vary, but the basic human values do not. These are the meanings that students long to construct. Perhaps it is not so much that we need to teach values but that first we must recognize that people have values waiting to be drawn out. Constructivists would agree, for they emphasize that the purpose of education is to draw out of students what is already there.

There is no current pedagogical theory that speaks of "goodness" and "badness" as students do. Each theory has its major values which are assumed to be good; for example, justice and

equality to critical and multicultural pedagogists, care to the feminine pedagogue, and intellect to the constructivist. It would be
productive if in the combining of these pedagogies a conversation
were to develop to define inclusively these issues that children long
to understand. All of the alternative pedagogies, theoretically, have
given up the idea that any pedagogy is value-neutral, an idea
promoted by behaviorism and reductionistic pedagogies. However,
by not coming to clearer conclusions about values, we are left with
three choices: an uneasy relativism, a kind of unconscious submission to the dominant values promoted in reductionism, or
simply succumbing to always diametrically opposing these values.
From the voices of students, it appears things are not this simple;
for example, they want punishment and care, unity and diversity,
and they want to understand good and evil. Taking their wishes
into account will be a critical part of our going beyond the simple
combination of these pedagogies.

TEACHING

Related also to the issue of how teachers should teach and to the
despair often expressed inside school are many pleas by students
for teachers to help them understand the world in which they live.
They ask for curricular content to be connected to "real life." One
middle school student, upon reviewing a draft of the report,
remarked, "If they want us to make a better world, they have to
talk inside the school." Another said: "I think they are right about
kids in despair. I think parents should get a child psychologist and
let their kids let out all their feelings. Many parents have no time
because they had a busy day at work." Critical and multicultural
pedagogists would support students' desires to talk about a better
world, and feminine pedagogists would encourage their letting out
their emotions. Reductionistic pedagogists would shape the
conversation so that it conformed to dominant values. However,
each pedagogy would shape the conversation to its own values.

A high school student explained about current instruction:
"When teachers just go through the motions and say do this, this
and that [it makes it hard to learn]. They don't take the time to
discuss things. By allowing students to share their opinion about
the subject, by allowing us to exchange opinions with other
students and by discussing the problems that are going on in the
world TODAY, NOW!! [they would make classes more interesting and
meaningful]. I think you should offer classes that show you how to
deal with problems without violence and how to prevent it! The
only thing I can say is that human relations will be helpful to the

future." Here we see the notion of content coming more to the fore—content that is relevant to today. Constructivist theory clearly places learning within the context of what students think and care about. In the passages from the study, they tell us they care about the world they live in and about solving its problems. Critical and multicultural theories have ways to lead students into these discussions, and feminine educators do value what this child is calling "human relations." Meaningful activities in the class are defined for us in this quotation. They deal with subject matter, the present, opinions, discussions, problems, solutions, and being human. Inside this student's statement we have one of the strongest pleas for the unification of the pedagogies and beyond. How can we develop these pedagogies so that they can not only teach students to understand and think through world problems but also "deal with problems without violence and how to prevent it!?"

Students recognize the reasons teachers don't talk about important things as well. While some believe it is because teachers don't care, many students believe that teachers are afraid of having serious conversations. A teacher corroborates their sense: "It isn't that I don't want to talk about critical things with them, but no one has ever taught me how to have a really serious conversation with children." This is an indictment of teacher education programs which structure many activities around the content to be taught and also, more recently, around some constructivist and multicultural practices. Teachers may also be afraid to try any of the alternative pedagogies because teacher educators often fail to model the pedagogies we often say we teach. Thus, teachers have never experienced these newer pedagogies in their own lives. How have we worked to make sure teachers can hold serious conversations with children? Do any of our pedagogies really do this? Certainly each offers forms of conversations but even critical pedagogy uses a kind of political analysis that would keep some students from the table. These children want serious, authentic conversations with adults about important things.

Summary

Students, like the constructivists, want to work in school; they abhor wasting time and boring work. They want their work to be fun, full of discussions about life and values, and they want real work. One teacher summarizes the data: "This really hit me yesterday when we were looking at all the school's information upon the board. To me, the children and the parents, even the teachers, keep saying well, where did all the fun go? Where did the fun go?" Activities which capture the minds of students hold the characteristics identified by the constructivists. They engage the learner in rich content, generally involve social interactions with peers, call on students to construct new meanings from their own experiences, and seek to use error for instruction. Nevertheless, fun is not enough.

＊ As students and multicultural educators point out, the curriculum must be representative, the opportunities fair, and expectations high. Students must come know each other, and racism must be openly recognized and attended to pedagogically. These issues are particularly difficult because it is primarily people of color and children who recognize the importance of these issues, and yet it is primarily Euro-American adults who control and teach in schools. Thus, these issues are the ones most likely to be avoided. While constructivism has enjoyed popularity among educators through subject matter projects and many state curriculum reforms, multicultural education is often viewed as being imposed and often legislated. Clearly students, regardless of their race, resonate with the issues raised by multicultural educators.

Like the feminine educators, students believe they learn best from people who care about them and try to understand them. They define these relationships as being critical to their work in school. The relationships students long for are authentic ones, not one-way relationships reminiscent of humanistic education. One student stated that good teachers are those that "work with me through my problems in my studies and can tell when I'm having difficulties in my life and sometimes pull me aside for a pep talk." Relationships with one another are also of tremendous importance to students, and these involve the issues of race and values as well as those issues raised by feminine pedagogy. The feminine pedagogists also note the importance of aesthetics as did the students in our study who complained of the physical environments of their schools.

Like the critical educators, students are cognizant of the politics of society and want to talk about them. They long to understand what is going on in the world. They are acutely aware of the problems in the world and want adults to lead them to discuss the causes and solutions of these problems within the context of instruction. Students are attentive observers and markers of injustice; they are ripe for critical educators' methods; however, adults are often afraid of losing control or afraid that they themselves may lose the privileges associated with being Euro-American, thus making critical pedagogy a difficult one to implement in schools.

Students want to be part of the solution and want to have serious conversations and construct sociopolitical meanings as recommended by the critical theorists. Indeed they already construct these meanings.

While each of these pedagogies differs in orientation, they each believe that learning takes place as students construct new meanings around the content of instruction. When listening to students, it is clear they are constructing many meanings and longing for these meanings to become a part of their curriculum. Their critiques of school reveal that traditional pedagogy still reigns. They are still being asked to learn things that have not been related to their own meanings and lives, that are disconnected from their relationships with others, that have not been cleansed of the racism inherent in schools and society, and that still do not allow them, except in few circumstances to raise and discuss important issues of values, such as justice, mercy, and love within the context of the curriculum. So while these pedagogies each speak to the construction of meaning in one way or another, students' voices suggest we must attend to all of these different approaches. This will require schools whose teachers can exemplify all of these pedagogies in a way in which the incompatibilities have been worked out and missing principles added so that our new pedagogy can address real student needs. Students' voices suggest that all four pedagogies, properly combined, will be necessary for teachers to have at their disposal. When students describe good classes, they seem to be places where the construction of meaning happens within the contexts of previous experiences, cultural and linguistic reality, supportive relationships, and a critical analysis of the world that allows for the further development of solutions and preventions. But there is more needed pedagogically for students than has been thus far articulated by these four contemporary theories.

Two Essays on School

A continuation high school student, we will call him Juan, in the greater Los Angeles metropolitan area wrote: (real names and places have been omitted or changed to protect the student's identity)

> Well, about my background. My background is pretty sad. I grew up in California. I grew up in [city] here. My mom drop out of high school in the 9th grade. She had a baby when she was 17 teen years old when she had me. My real dad left my mom when he found out that she was having baby. All I know about him is

his name [name]. My mom got got married to another guy named [name] he is in the Marines. We move to [city] for a little while. My mom used to go out drinking meeting different guy's. Then step dad would catch at the house and then he would beat her up. Then if my mom was not there when we got home. Then he would take his anger out on me. It went on for 4 years at [another city]. But that was a while back. Now my mom and step dad are getting a divorce. I am living with my grandparther's. My mom was living there to but she got kickout of the house because she started to use drugs. We can't stop here [her] from using. She almost o.d. a couple of times. she told me. She been sleeping out on the streets. My little brother [name] is living with my step dad. He already try to kill himself. About 2 times. He is trying to hang on. Me I am just bearly hanging on. Sometimes I feel like I am going crazy. My grandparther's are old and they are trying hang on to. My Aunt [name] and Uncle [name] live there to and there are getting tired but they are trying to hang on. Me I want to help my mom but she doesn't want to get help. I already feel like my mom already lose her mind. I am trying to go school everyday. Plus I go to work so I won' t think about the promble's [problems] that I have. I don't know how to read. See I can read but I can't understand what I read. Everyone is starting to stop losing [hope?] about my mom but me I am not. Sometimes at night I think or I look out the window to see if my mom is coming home. Or sometimes I think did she O.d. will they find her in a trash can. Will she be oh right. All those things go through my mind. So that's everything the whole truth. That's why sometimes kids like me have a hard time making through school.

The same student wrote a second essay, which follows:

These are my reasons for not going to school!!! Well what got me here [the continuation school] first of all. It was the cutting school I hang around the wrong people. I would leave home and act like I was going to school. But then I would go to my friends house kick back listing [listening] to music drink some beer, call up some girls to come over. I did that my whole freshman year. I did the same thing again almost my 10th year in school. I got in alot of trouble with the cops and with the teachers at school. I even got in trouble with my parents. I ran away from home about three or four times because of family prombles. I didn't get along with my step dad. Then we move over here in [city]. Then I went back to school over her in [school]. Then I went for a little while then I drop out again because of the cholos the gangbangers kept of bothering me. Geiveing me hard looks looking me up and down. Following me home from school. Then I was so worry to even walk out of my house to go to the store because I thought I was going to to get jumped. Or I thought my house was going to get shot up. I ain't even a gangbanger. Sure I have cousins from gangs but they are not from around here.

I bet about 50% percent of the kids drop out because of the prombles at home. I bet 60% up to 70% percent don't want to go to school because these so called gangbangers. And they are nothing. But that's just "my opoin [opinion]." That's just what I think. Those are the reasons why I didn't go to school.

Because of hate, pain, hurt, mad, fear, scare of getting jump by the gangbangers. About 20% don't go to school because they have to drop out so they can support there family because there families is poor.

Beyond Current Alternative Pedagogies

Pedagogically speaking, Juan's essays could be used to prove each theory's assumptions about education. All of these pedagogies would have drawn out Juan's story, his construction of meaning about school. What happens once the story is out? What are the dangers of this kind of "confession" without a solution oriented follow-up? What is the effect of his essay on us and how do we respond to our own feelings of impotence, anger, and/or frustration so that Juan is helped? How will we act differently when he misses school the next time? How will whatever we do in class have any significant impact on Juan's life at this moment, in this place?

Though Juan has written two essays about school, Juan has not indicted the school for anything, not even for the traditional pedagogy he receives. Traditional pedagogy has tracked him into a continuation school, he is marked deficient. The system has announced its low expectations for him by his placement. Not only has he not critiqued the school, but also he has automatically accepted that school is something that should be good for him; but is it?

In fact, though both essays are supposed to be about school, it is not until the second essay that Juan even mentions school. Instead, he talks about his parents and family, and states his identity, which is tied to his life in the family and neighborhood, not to school. How can we develop a pedagogy that is truly responsive to Juan's family and community? For if it is not, it is unlikely we will reach Juan in any significant way. What is it that Juan's family needs that the school could offer? How could we develop a parent program that would truly be accessible? How accessible are those we have? How can we apply the notions of learning spelled out by constructivists, critical, multicultural, and feminine pedagogies and other principles to educate Juan's mother and grandparents. How can we create a pedagogy that makes them a learning community, not just a family that is trying to hang on? How can educators who largely drive in and out of his community to work be the instruments of a responsive education? How can we educate such educators?

The constructivists might note in his essay that Juan is defined by the school and, at first, by himself as a nonreader but that he writes eloquently when engaged in making meaning for (and about) himself. Clearly, his reading problems are not really with reading but with understanding (which he also understands). Juan actually makes three cognitive distinctions between reading. Why would someone who can write and think as clearly as Juan not understand what he reads? Typical reductionistic school explanations would center on deficits—his inability to concentrate. Were Juan white and middle-class he would probably be diagnosed as having attention deficit disorder. However, Juan is Latino, so school (reductionist) explanations are more likely to indict his family conditions, his primary language, and his so-called lack of intelligence, or his inexperience with school or academic tasks.

While the constructivists might call on Juan to make his meanings and teach him to read through writing, how will constructivist teachers respond to the meanings Juan makes? Even constructivism does not teach us how to respond to a person in despair. Multicultural education would have available curriculum relevant to his life; thus, he might come to better understand (to care more about) what he reads. Multicultural pedagogy would be able to help him with the implicit details of the English language and have him reading and writing in Spanish. Still, how will an educator, learned in multicultural pedagogies respond to the desperation in his essay? None of our pedagogies have yet developed an adequate way of responding to many of the meanings learners construct. So, we have to ask ourselves, what value is the drawing out of a student's meanings if we cannot take those meanings and use them for his instruction and education?

In Juan's case, his teacher responded by giving him bonus points for his writing and writing the following comments. On the first paper the teacher wrote: "Good 2 $3/4$, 1 bonus = 3 $3/5$" on the top of the first page. Next to the section that describes his stepfather's beating of him, the teacher wrote, "sounds bad!" and next to the comment that this was why some kids have trouble in school was written: "Good!" On the second essay, the teacher wrote next to the comment that this was just his (the teacher's) opinion, "Shows you think for yourself." At the end of the paper he added again a series of points: "2 + 1 $^1/_2$ = 3 $^1/_2$." The points at this school are used to accumulate credit demanded by the "real" high school to determine where in the system an adolescent might reenter and/or are used for graduation requirements, should they not reenter.

Read through the eyes of Juan's story, the comments we make as teachers, the pedagogical discussions of assessment, and the grading systems we devise seem, at best, lame and, at worst, damaging. Certainly, Juan's teacher, who shared his work with one of the authors because of his concern, has the best intentions; indeed, he wants to help him, but he is also overwhelmed by the demands of the school and the inability to know what to do to help. In fact, none of the pedagogies we have just discussed has developed a true alternative assessment, one that would be adequate to respond to the real content of Juan's essay, not just the concepts or the mechanics. Even our alternative pedagogies offer little to Juan's teacher.

Critical pedagogy also recommends that we draw out Juan's story, look at that story in the context of the stories of others, with texts, and help him place his story in the context of the larger sociopolitical world. Clearly, the critical and multicultural add a great deal to our understanding of Juan's situation, which is created and sustained by a complex interaction between an unjust society, which has participated in the oppression of his people, and Juan's family. Of course, we are responsible for teaching Juan to use critical social analysis. However, will raising these sociopolitical issues at this moment inspire Juan to fight his own drinking, help him come to school safe, help him reach his mother or little brother? Will these kinds of analyses currently help him hang on or will they encourage him to let go of life?

Juan is in physical danger as well. He is being forced to choose a side—to be a "cholo" or not. It is a situation he feels he cannot get out of, one he does not control, and one that confronts him most inside school, not out. Yet, his teachers do not know that Juan is not a gang member; they do not have the ability to discern these things. They do not see the things their students see. Their students complain, like those in our study, of safety issues unperceived by the adults on campus. How do our pedagogies help here?

While critical pedagogists often use the word hope, where is the hope in their pedagogy? Is not their hope more an abstract hope for the world and not a specific hope for Juan? Does hope come from the encouragement of his anger? We think not. Juan tells us his hope still lies within his family and friends, all of whom are also struggling for hope. These are the same family and friends that we indict as part of his problem (to constructivists concerned with developmental issues) or as the victims of a hegemonic society's problem (to the critical pedagogists). These students' hope is embedded in mothers, grandparents, uncles, aunts, brothers; the so-called wrong crowd. All of them struggle to find hope for themselves and for others for whom they feel considerable love and responsibility.

We are not talking about the caring community inside the classroom of the feminine pedagogists, either. It is not enough to care as a partner inside the context of the classroom. This care too often leads to a patronizing liberalism that frequently calls on us to deliver these students *from* their homes and communities rather than *to* their homes and communities in a way that strengthens the health of the entire family and community.

Like students in our study, Juan talks a great deal about right and wrong. None of our pedagogies really addresses right and wrong, except for reductionistic ones in which right and wrong are defined from a particular privileged and materialistic vantage point. Our other pedagogies can reveal a great deal about the sociological issues surrounding what Juan calls right and wrong, but would they encourage Juan to continue to develop his moral sensibilities and act on them? Because the alternative pedagogies have been good at social analysis, our pedagogies may currently offer Juan more a set of excuses for his actions than real hope or specific help. Might these kinds of analyses merely create more conflict for him?

What of "hanging on?" How do these pedagogies encourage Juan not just to hang on but to thrive? While critical and multi-cultural pedagogies can analyze and suggest causes and while feminine pedagogy can respect the emotion, how will any of them really address this concern? Juan's job is actually the only thing helping him hang on, not because of what vocational educators discuss about vocations but because it provides him with a mental break from his worries that school does not provide. Do any of these pedagogies have answers to worry? Most of them would prefer that Juan did not work so that he could concentrate more on his education. Still, what would classroom education, even it if were multicultural, critical, feminine, and constructivist, do for Juan in his real life?

What is necessary is a pedagogy that guides us as teachers to help students. Such a pedagogy must not only express, analyze, or empathize with "the hate, pain, hurt, mad, fear, scare" of Juan and other students but also inspire healing action (not just cognitive, social, or emotional) on the part of educators and students. We need a pedagogy that helps teachers "have a conversation with students about important things" within the context of important, relevant content. We need a pedagogy that helps us discern the important from the unimportant and one that gives us the strength and courage to act on the real issues of life. We need a life-giving pedagogy, not only for the oppressed and the bicultural but also for the privileged and monocultural who also must be transformed if we are to have a better world. We need to envision a classroom that uses all the pedagogies and goes beyond, that admits and addresses the impotence we feel when teaching students like Juan and reading their essays. We need to envision schools for Juan and for those who oppress him. As J. Rivera (1992) noted in his article, the Simi Valley jurors, and the police were all educated in the same system.

REFERENCES

Moll, L. (Ed.). (1992). *Vygotsky and education: Instructional implications and applications of socio-historical psychology.*
Cambridge: Cambridge University Press.

Poplin, M. & Weeres, J. (1992). *Voices from the Inside: A report on
schooling from inside the classroom.* Claremont, Ca: The
Institute for Education in Transformation at The Claremont
Graduate School.

Rivera, J. (1992). *Aftermath: The police, Rodney King, Martin Luther
King and education: How does it all add up?* ACE Abstract.
Claremont, Ca: The Institute for Education in Transformation
at The Claremont Graduate School.

Vygotsky, L. (1986) (Rev. Ed.). *Thought and language.* Cambridge,
Ma: MIT Press.

8

CAMERON McCARTHY ————————————————————————

The Problem with Origins:
Race and the Contrapuntal Nature
of the Educational Experience

Epic discourse is a discourse handed down by tradition. By its very
nature the epic of the absolute past is inaccessible to personal
experience and does not permit an individual, personal point of
view or evaluation. One cannot glimpse it, grope for it, touch it; one
cannot look at it from just any point of view; it is impossible to
experience it, analyze it, take it apart, penetrate into its core. It is
given solely as tradition, sacred and sacrosanct, evaluated in the
same way by all and demanding a pious attitude to itself.

Bakhtin

INTRODUCTION

The publication in the late eighties and early nineties of culturally
narrow-minded texts such as Allan Bloom's *The Closing of the
American Mind* (1987) and Dinesh D'Souza's *Illiberal Education*
(1991), and the neonationalist response of Afrocentric writers such
as Molefi Asante, ushered in a new phase of eruptive particularism
in educational discourses on culture and race. This new phase in
educational and social life is marked by a revivified investment in
ethnic symbolism and an almost epic revalorization of the ethnic
histories and origins of some embattled dominant and subordi-
nant groups. We are living in a time in which racial hysteria and
racial anxiety ride the undersides of the public discourse on
schooling and society as rapid demographic changes alter the
racial and ethnic configuration of America. These developments
have spawned what I wish to call the new essentialisms that have
infected both popular and academic theories of race. An increasingly rigid and constricted language has overtaken the discussion
of racial inequality and racial antagonism in education. This is
powerfully reflected in contemporary discourses of cultural exceptionalism, the declaration of privileged epistemologies, and the

245

balkanizing identity politics that now inform ethnic prioritization and race-based agenda setting practices of embattled social groups in education.

In this essay, I offer a critique of essentialist theories of race. I suggest that such theories have limited explanatory and predictive capacity with respect to the operation of race in education and in daily life. Further, I argue that one cannot understand race, paradoxically, by looking at race alone. One must look at the dynamics of class, ethnicity, and gender. These dynamic variables operate in contradictory and discontinuous ways in the institutional setting. Dynamics of gender and class often cut at right angles to race. For example, working-class black women and men have radically different experiences of race relations than their middle-class counterparts because of the ever-widening economic divide that separates different groups of black people in the United States. In addition to critiquing contemporary theories of race, I will look at a number of ethnographic examples of contradiction in the experience of racial inequality that underscore the heterogeneity associated with the operation of racial dynamics in schooling. Finally, I will draw some conclusions about curriculum and educational reform that take the complexity and the heterogeneity of race into account.

THE PROBLEM OF RACE, THE PROBLEM OF ORIGINS

In a recent *New York Times Book Review* article Henry Louis Gates (1991) relates a story that has made its rounds in the jazz world. The story takes the form of an answer to what Gates calls "The perennial question: Can you really tell?" The question is about racial authenticity, racial origins and their predictive capacity with respect to cultural behavior and meaning of style. Can you really tell who is the black one, who is the white one? Can you really tell? According to Gates:

> The great black jazz trumpeter Roy Elridge once made a wager with the critic Leonard Feather that he could distinguish white musicians from black ones—blindfolded. Mr. Feather duly dropped the needle onto a variety of record albums whose titles and soloists were concealed from the trumpeter. More than half the time, Elridge guessed wrong (*New York Times Book Review* November 24, 1991, p. 1).

What Gates fails to mention is the fact that the blindfold test is an institution of *Down Beat* jazz magazine for well over a quarter century now and that white jazz musicians presented with the blindfold test regularly confuse black musicians with white ones and vice versa. The problem of racial origins and racial authenticity is a problem all around. The elusiveness of racial identity not only affects blacks; it affects whites. Racial identities can never be gathered up in one place as a final cultural property. As we approach the end of the twentieth century, what seemed like stable white ethnicities and heritages in an earlier era are now entering a zone of recoding and redefinition. Michael Omi and Howard Winant (1991) put the problematic of waning white ethnicity in this post–civil rights era in the following terms:

> Most whites do not experience their ethnicity as a definitive aspect of their social identity. They perceive it dimly and irregularly, picking and choosing among its varied strands to exercise, as Mary Waters (1990) suggests, an "ethnic option." The specifically ethnic components of white identity are fast receding with each generation's additional remove from the old country. Unable to speak the language of their immigrant forbears, uncommitted to ethnic endogamy, and unaware of their ancestor's traditions (if in fact they can still identify their ancestors as, say, Polish or Scots, rather than a combination of four or five European—and non-European!—groups) whites undergo a racializing panethnicity as "Euro-Americans." (Omi and Winant 1991, p. 17)

Nowhere is this sense of the "twilight of white ethnicity" felt more deeply than on American college campuses. In these deeply, racially balkanized and polarized sites of the American education system, we are entering the "brave new world" of the post–civil rights era—a new world registered in the popular culture by films like *Falling Down* (1993), *White Palace* (1990), and *Dances with Wolves* (1990)—a world in which the proliferation of ethnic diversity has led to a heightened state of race-consciousness on the part of minorities and whites. The post–civil rights era is the era of the displaced and decentered white subject. White students on college campuses find themselves positioned as the antagonists in an unpredictable racial drama in which middle class subjects speak in the voice of the new oppressed—a progeny spawned in an era of the discourse of racial resentment and reverse discrimination. For instance, white students interviewed in a recent study on racial diversity (Institute for the Study of Social Change 1991) conducted at Berkeley emphasized a reuse of racial encirclement, ethnic instability, and the new conflictual nature of identity. A few examples of comments made by white students and recorded in the report underscore these new dilemmas over racial/ethnic identity:

Student Comment I: Many whites don't feel like they have an ethnic identity at all and I pretty much feel that way too. It's not something that bothers me tremendously but I think that maybe I could be missing something that other people have, that I am not experiencing.

Student Comment II: Being white means that you're less likely to get financial aid...It means that there are all sorts of tutoring groups and special programs that you can't get into, because you're not a minority.

Student Comment III: If you want to go with the stereotypes, Asians are the smart people, the Blacks are great athletes, what is white? We're just here. We're the oppressors of the nation. (p. 37)

These stories of racial/ethnic instability come at a critical juncture in debates over racial inequality, racial identity, and curriculum reform in the educational field in the United States. They also point to the crisis in the theorization of race and racial logics in education. However, it is also, paradoxically, a time in which there is a peculiar language of racial and ethnic certainty, of panethnic camps drawn tightly around specular origins. The world is a vast Lacanian mirror in which theorists of racial purity and racial essence see themselves standing in front of their ancestors. It is the perfect image, the snapshot of history collected in the nuclear family photo album. It is the story of the singular origin, the singular essence, the one, true primary cause. The old Marxist and neo-Marxist orthodoxies of class and economic primacy in education debates are rapidly being replaced by the new panethnic cultural assertions of racial origins. The proponents of Western civilization and Eurocentrism and their critics, the proponents of Afrocentrism, now argue for the heart and soul of the educational enterprise (this is not of course to suggest that there is an equivalence in the deployment of material and political resources here, for, in some ways, the playing out of this conflict involves a certain encirclement of black intellectual thinking). Conservative educators like Diane Ravitch join conservative ideologues such as George Will (1989) in insisting, for instance, that: "Our country [the United States] is a branch of European civilization... Eurocentricity' is right, in American curricula and consciousness, because it accords with the facts of our history, and we and Europe are fortunate for that" (p. 3). Europe, through this legerdemain, is collapsed into the United States without any difficulty.

History and tradition in this country are seen as interchangeable with those of Europe's.

On the other hand, Afrocentric theorists, such as Molefi Asante (1987), argue for the panethnic unity of all black people of the diaspora, pointing to the origins of African people in the "spatial reality of Africa." We are in the historical moment of what Stanley Aronowitz and Henry Giroux (1991) call the "politics of clarity." Of course, it is important to emphasize here that Afrocentrism is a liberatory discourse. When one reads the work of Asante, Jawanza Kunjufu, and others, one recognizes immediately a sustained effort to connect to an intellectual and political history of struggle waged by racially subordinated groups in the U.S. Nevertheless, Afrocentrism also contains within its discourse a language that masks issues of contradiction and discontinuity within the diaspora, between the diaspora and Africa, between different economically and socially situated African Americans and other minority groups, and between differently situated men and women.

Beyond these concerns is the issue of the intellectual and cultural worker and his or her problematic relationship to anything that begins to sound like a singular cultural heritage or cultural stream. It is a necessary condition of dynamic intellectual and cultural work that the intellectual worker has the flexibility to draw on the well-spring of history, to draw on the variety of cultural resources that fan out across the myriad groups that make up this society and the world. "Culture," writers such as Coco Fusco, Cornel West, and Stuart Hall suggest, is a hybrid. For that matter, race is a hybridizing process as well—it is the product of encounters between and among differently located human groups. By hybridity here, I am not referring to a Joseph's coat trope of difference—the proverbial social quilt that happily embraces a cornucopia of differences, laying down these agreeable differences, one after the other, side by side. Instead, I am drawing attention to the contradictory nature of identity formation and the fact that, to use the language of Hall (1933), "dominant ethnicities are always underpinned by a particular figured masculinity, a particular class identity," and so forth (p. 31). In any one group or individual there are always competing identities, competing interests, needs, and desires wrestling to the surface. In saying this, I am not denying that there are certain stabilities associated with race. I am not here denying that there is the persistence of what Hall (1989) calls "continuities" between, say, the peoples of Africa and the peoples of the Afro-New World diaspora. Neither I am trying to contest the fact that there are brutal realities associated with the patterns of racial exclusion that affect minorities in the United States. What I am saying is that racial difference is the product of human interests, needs, desires, strategy, capacities, and forms of organization and mobilization. Furthermore, these dynamic variables which articulate themselves in the form of grounded social constructs, such as identity, inequality, and so forth, are subject to change, contradiction, variability, and revision within historically specific and determinate contexts. Race is a deeply unstable and decentered complex of social meanings constantly being transformed by cultural and political conflict (Omi and Winant 1991). Racial identities are therefore profoundly social, historical, and variable categories.

Against the grain of this historical and social variability, Afrocentrics and Eurocentrics now argue for school reform based on the narrow limits of ethnic affiliation. For the Afrocentric the intolerable level of minority failure in schooling has to do with the fact that minority, particularly African American, cultural heritage is suppressed in the curriculum. Black students fail because schools assault their identities and destabilize their sense of self and agency (a good example of this thesis is to be found in *Countering the Conspiracy to Destroy Black Boys* by Jawanza Kunjufu [1990]). For the proponents of Western Civilization, Western cultural emphasis in the curriculum is color-blind. Black students fail because of the cultural deprivation that exists in their homes and in their communities. To become literate in Western civilization would be the best antidote for failure among the black poor. As E.D. Hirsch (1987) suggests, broad cultural literacy would help disadvantaged black youth enter the mainstream.

This essay is written in response to this moment of race/ethnic based diagnosis of inequality in education and prescription for change. It is a diagnosis that is driven by a peculiarly recalcitrant concept of race that is discursively based in nineteenth-century biology and naturalization of human distinctions.

A nineteenth-century concept of race now inhabits much mainstream and radical thinking about inequality in education. Race theory is particularly unreflexive about the category of *race* itself. Educational theories of racial inequality are at bottom still informed by notions of *essences*, notions of near-indelible characteristics in culture, linguistic style, cognitive capacity, family structures, and the like. I set myself up against these *essentialist* approaches to the theorization of racial inequality and racial identity in education. By essentialist I am referring to the tendency in current mainstream and radical writing on race to treat social groups as stable or homogeneous entities. Racial groups such as Asians or Latinos or Blacks are therefore discussed as though members of these groups possessed some innate and invariant set of characteristics that sets them apart from each other and from whites. Feminist theorists such as Michele Wallace (1990) and Teresa de Lauretis (1987) have critiqued dominant tendencies in mainstream research to define differences in terms of transcendental essences. Wallace (1990), for example, maintains that differences in the political and cultural behavior of minority women and men are determined by social and historical contingencies and not some essentialist checklist of innate, biological, or cultural characteristics.

Following Wallace, I argue that current tendencies towards essentialism in the analysis of race relations significantly inhibit a dynamic understanding of race relations and raced-based politics in education and society. I argue further that essentialist thinking about race contributes to the ever-increasing balkanization of cultural and public spaces in education and society. Common to these approaches to race and education as well as some of the more recent formulations around multiculturalism is a tendency to undertheorize race (Ogbu 1992; Tiedt and Tiedt 1986). Within these paradigms of educational and social theory, racial antagonism is conceptualized as a kind of deposit or disease that is triggered into existence by some deeper flaw of character or society. I inflect the discussion of race away from the language of deprivation and cultural and economic essentialism that now dominates the research literature on racial inequality. The fact is that racial differences are produced. These differences, as Edward Said (1985) points out, are "the product of human work." Racial relations of domination and subordination are arranged and organized in cultural forms and in the ideological practices of identity formation and representation inside and outside social institutions such as schools—what Louis Althusser (1971) calls the "mise-en-scene of interpellation." I am therefore interested in the ways in which moral leadership and social power are exercised "in the concrete" and the ways in which regimes of racial domination and subordination are constructed and resisted in education.

The theoretical and methodological issues concerning race are complex and therefore require a comparative and relational approach to analysis of and intervention in unequal relations in schools. Such analysis and intervention must pay special attention to contradiction, discontinuity, and nuance within and between embattled social groups, what I have called elsewhere the process of "nonsynchrony" (McCarthy 1990). Rather than treating minority groups as homogeneous entities, I point to the contradictory interests, needs, and desires that inform minority educational, cultural, and political behavior and define minority encounters with majority whites in educational settings and in society. By invoking the concepts of contradiction and nonsynchrony, I wish to advance the position that individuals or groups, in their relation to economic, political, and cultural institutions such as schools, do not share identical consciousness and express the same interests, needs, or desires "at the same point in time" (Hicks 1981, p. 221). These discontinuities in the needs and interests of minority and majority groups are, for example, expressed in the long history of tension and hostility that has existed between the black and white working class in this country. Also of crucial importance within this framework are the issues of the "contradictory location" (Wright 1978) of the "new" black middle-class within the racial problematic and the role of neoconservative black and white intellectuals in redefining the terrain of contemporary discourse on racial inequality toward the ideal of a "color-blind" society (McCarthy 1990). Just as important for a relational and nonessentialist approach to race and curriculum is the fact that minority women and girls have radically different experiences of racial inequality than those of their male counterparts, because of the issue of gender (it is these dynamics that Wallace, in her book *Invisibility Blues* [1990] calls "negative variations"). A relational and nonessentialist approach to the discussion of racial identities allows for a more complex understanding of the educational and political behavior of minority and majority groups. I argue for such a complex understanding of racial inequality that focuses on the contradictory and highly non-synchronous formulation of racial subjectivity and identity and the dynamic intersection of race with variables of class, gender, and nation. Examples of the contradictory character of race relations drawn from contemporary developments in the political arena and from my own ethnographic work and that of others will be discussed in what follows. I believe that any strategy for educational reform in the area of race relations must take this complexity into account.

CONTRADICTIONS IN THE EXPERIENCE OF RACIAL INEQUALITY

As Michael Burawoy (1981) and Mokubong Nkomo (1984) make clear with respect to South Africa, economic divides that exist between the black underclass from the Bantustan and their more middle-class counterparts working for the South African State (the police, nurses, Bantustan bureaucrats, etc.) often serve to undermine black unity in the struggle against racial oppression. Similar examples exist in the United States where some middle class minority intellectuals such as Shelby Steele and Thomas Sowell have spoken out against affirmative action and minority scholarship programs in higher education, suggesting that such ameliorative policies discriminate against white males. A case in point is the 1990 ruling by the U.S. Department of Education's former Assistant Secretary for Civil Rights, Michael Williams, that maintained that it was illegal for a college or university to offer a scholarship only to minority students (Jaschik 1990). The irony of this situation is underlined by the fact that the former Assistant Secretary for Civil Rights is a black man. The fact is that without these scholarships a number of very talented minorities would not be able to pursue higher education. Here again, the "point man" on a reactionary Republican policy that effectively undermined the material interests of African Americans and other minority groups was a neoconservative member of the emergent minority middle class.

One should not, however, draw the conclusion that contradictions associated with race and specific social policies such as affirmative action only affect blacks. These dynamics are also reflected in the politics of identity formation among Asian Americans. Let us look at two examples of the contradictory effects of inclusionary and exclusionary ethnic practices among Asian Americans and Pacific Islanders. In order to consolidate and extend their political clout and benefits from land trust arrangements, native Hawaiians voted four-to-one in January 1990 for a highly inclusionary definition of their ethnic identity—one that expanded the definition of their people to anyone with a drop of Hawaiian "blood." According to Omi and Winant (1991), "Previously only those with at least 50 percent Hawaiian 'blood' were eligible for certain benefits" (p. 9). They also point to a second example, this time of the exclusionary effects of intraethnic contradictions in the politics of Asian-American identity formation and affirmative action policy:

> By contrast, in June 1991 in San Francisco, Chinese American architects and engineers protested the inclusion of Asian Indians under the city's minority business enterprise law. Citing a Supreme Court ruling which requires cities to narrowly define which groups had suffered discrimination to justify specific affirmative action programs, Chinese Americans contended that Asian Indians should not be considered "Asian." At stake were obvious economic benefits accruing to designated "minority" businesses. (Ibid.)

The contradictory phenomenon of racial identity formation in this post–civil rights era also manifests itself inside schools. Linda Grant (1984) calls attention to these discontinuities in terms of the operation of gender at the classroom level. Based on the findings from a study of "face-to-face interactions" in six desegregated elementary school classrooms in a Midwestern industrial city, Linda Grant concludes that "Black females' experiences in desegregated schools....differ from those of other race-gender groups and cannot be fully be understood by extrapolating from the research on females or research on blacks." Among other things, Grant contends that the teachers (all women, three blacks and three whites) she observed did not relate to their black students and white students in any consistent or monolithic way. Grant places particular emphasis on the way in which black girls were positioned in the language of the classroom and in the informal exchanges between teachers and students. She notes the following:

> Although generally compliant with teachers' rules, black females were less tied to teachers than white girls were and approached them only when they had a specific need to do so. White girls spent more time with teachers, prolonging questions into chats about personal issues. Black girls' contacts were briefer, more task related, and often on behalf of a peer rather than self. (Ibid., p. 107)

Although these teachers tended to avoid contact with black male students, they were still inclined to identify at least one black male student in their individual classroom as a "superstar." In none of the six desegregated classrooms were any of the black girls identified as a high academic achiever. Instead, Grant maintains, black girls were typified as "average achievers" and assigned to average or below average track placements and ability groups. Gender differences powerfully influenced and modified the racially inflected ways in which teachers evaluated, diagnosed, labeled, and tracked their students. Grant therefore points to a hidden cost of desegregation for black girls:

> Although they are usually the top students in all-black classes, they lose this stature to white children in desegregated rooms. Their development seems to become less balanced, with emphasis on social skills...Black girls' everyday schooling experiences seem more likely to nudge them toward stereotypical roles of black women than toward [academic] alternatives. These include serving others and maintaining peaceable ties among diverse persons rather than developing one's own skills. (Ibid.)

While black girls have a differential experience of schooling, one in which their talents are marginalized and delegitimated, black boys often experience a profound alienation from an academic core curriculum. Teachers in the urban setting, even black middle-class teachers, often tend to distance themselves from black boys as Grant (1985) points out. The following excerpt taken from my ethnographic work in an inner-city high school in a large Western city is yet another illustration of what I am calling nonsynchrony. This research was conducted in the summer of 1990 and involved an evaluation of Teach For America's Summer Institute.[1] In what follows, I will give an extended account of the operation of nonsynchrony in a classroom that I observed; this extended account is drawn from my fieldnotes. It is intended to get at some of the dynamism of racial identity formation in the inner-city classroom in which, often, the conflictual loyalties, needs, desires, and interests of black, adolescent male youth collide with the needs and desires of teachers and other adult staff operating in the school setting. The school under study is St. Paul's High School.

IDENTITIES IN FORMATION: NOTES FROM AN INNER CITY CLASSROOM

I report on a class that was taught by a Teach For America intern, Christopher Morrison. Christopher is a white male. He was about twenty-two years old at the time of the study. He hails from the South and has had some military training. His assignment to do a four week teaching stint in Golden Arches High School was his first exposure to an inner-city school. Christopher's cooperating teacher was a black female, Ms. Marshall. She was in her early sixties, close to retirement. She exuded an air of having seen it all. The students in Christopher's classroom were predominantly African American. This classroom, which I am about to describe, was taken over by accounts of police violence. Christopher had introduced the topic of police harassment based on some queries made by one of his students the previous day. However, in the torrent of accounts offered by the students, Christopher lost control of the class. So too did Ms. Marshall.

What was fascinating about this development was the sharp, unpredictable collision of interests, needs, and desires that fragmented the classroom as a learning community. Even more important within this framework were the lines of division that cut through racial affiliation, pure and simple. The black cooperating teacher, Ms. Marshall, seemed (because of dynamics of age, class, and gender) remarkably alienating to her students, even though she clearly empathized with their stories about harassment and humiliation. Black male students did affect a difficult but clearly emergent bonding with Christopher. This relationship was not unproblematic, however, as we will see in moment.

Before the class started, Christopher had indicated that his lesson would deal with "Imperialism in South Africa and India." This was to be part of a unit on "The Building of Empires." There were seventeen students in Christopher's class; one Hispanic and sixteen African Americans, nine males and eight females. Students trickled into the class one-by-one and sometimes in twos. It was 10:27 A.M. It was seven minutes after the period was suppose to begin before the lesson got started. Students were hurriedly writing down the assignment that was on the chalkboard for the period. Christopher had written up this assignment in bold letters. Here, he was emulating his cooperating teacher, Ms. Marshall, who was inclined to write an enormous amount of work on the board. It seemed as though the objective was to keep the students occupied. Nevertheless, Christopher wrote the assignment in this manner on one of the three large chalkboards in the classroom:

Period 2, 31 July 1990   Ms. Marshall
                                          WORLD HISTORY
I. READ CH. 28, PP. 518–538
II. SECTION REVIEWS I–4, IV–13
                         II–1, 3, 4, V–ALL
                         III–3, 4, VI–ALL

As Christopher was about to begin to address the class, a black student came sauntering in dressed in blue overalls. He wore a red, gold, and green belt around his waist—the colors of black solidarity associated with the Rastafarians of Jamaica and radical black groups like the Nation of Islam. Morgan, one of the students whom Christopher had previously identified to me as a gang member, shouted: "Hey Morrison, don't you notice the beautiful colors that our brother is wearing. That's powerful! That's powerful!" "Yes," said Christopher, "They are beautiful." Christopher then shifted the topic adroitly. "Before we begin the lesson today, I just wanted to let you know that I did some research on the question that Ramon asked yesterday. Tell them the question you asked, Ramon!" Ramon obliged: "Can the police arrest you for what he thought?" There was an instant change in the temperature in the classroom; some students were already itching to jump in and say their piece. Christopher responded, "Well I talked to a police officer of the LA Unified System and he said that chances are, if the police picked you up, it may be because somebody called in."

Morgan, who had established himself as a spokesperson for his peers inside and outside the school, was quick to note, "They have to have probable reason." As would become clear later, Morgan had a history of run-ins with the police. He started up again: "For instance, let me tell you something [addressing Christopher]. For instance, one day I was cruising up the road to Marsha, one of my friends, who tell me she was having some trouble with this dude. He was pushing her around. And I, I had my Wankar and my forty-five in my pocket. And they [the cops] stop me man. They stop me. Now they had no probable reason, no probable reason. And they knew it, man. They knew it." Christopher asked politely, "And what did you do?" Morgan replied indicating his sense of incredulity at Christopher's question: "What do you mean? I told them they had no probable reason." "Probable cause," Christopher corrected. "If you had a gun on you, then you gave them probable cause." Morgan shouted, "What do you mean by that Mr. Morrison. I did not do anything. I was only carrying my Wankar." [students laughed]

By now the flood gates were opened on this topic of police harassment. There was no going back. Elvis, another black student, asked the cooperating teacher, "And how do you feel about the police, Ms. Marshall?" Ms. Marshall was a little upset with the defiant language of her students. She felt that this kind of defiance endangered them in their encounters with the police:

> I say if you walk like a duck and you hang out with ducks, then you are a duck. I believe that some of the things they do are not right. But you guys sometimes walk around without any books like the rest of the guys on the street. If you do that, they [the cops] will pull you over. [Here, Ms. Marshall was speaking out of a sense of concern, even a sense of fear, about her students' confrontation with the cops. Maybe, as a black woman, she felt specially responsible for telling these students how to survive]....One day I saw them [some police officers]. They had this guy spread eagle against this car. And they were really harassing him. You should not hang out with those guys [here, guys seemed to be an euphemism for "gang bangers"]...don't hang out with the Bloods, or the Cribs, or the Tigers.

This got Rasheed (who seemed to identify with a gang called the "Tigers") really upset: "What do you have against the Tigers? The Tigers don't do anybody anything." Again, Christopher tried to subtly change the topic to diffuse the tension that was building in the room:

> Let me tell you a story about myself. Maybe this will help. Once
> I had some friends. They were hanging out on the college
> campus. But they did not look like college students. They were
> white, but they had long hair.

A number of students interjected, "You mean like a hippie." "Like
a hippie," Christopher said. Then he continued with his story,
"They arrested these guys. You have to understand that the police
go on images. They rely on images. They need categories to put
people in so that they can do their work. And sometimes these
categories are right. And if you, Morgan, had a gun then you gave
them probable cause. You fitted into one of their categories."
Morgan seemed dismayed. But he was emphatic: "It wasn't the
gun. They were just riding through the 'hood. If I had given them
any trouble they would have sweated me." Christopher disagreed
with this assessment of danger: "I don't think they would do that
to you. You can complain if you feel that your rights have been
abused. Look, people are being blown away at a faster rate than
ever in this country. Just don't give them cause. If you got something [a gun] on you, then that is giving them cause."

Ms. Marshall, the cooperating teacher, supported Christopher:
"When a group of you guys are hanging out together that gives
them cause for concern. You don't even carry books. You need to
be nonthreatening." Rasheed, contended: "You mean to say that if
I am going around with my friends at night I need to haul along a
big old bunch of books over my shoulder." Misha, a black female,
joined in: "There are cops who walk around killing people at
random. I have friends of mine whose houses have been bust into.
That is why if any of them [police] comes to my house, I will take
out a knife and go [motion indicating stabbing a fictional police
officer] 'Oops sorry, I didn't know you was a cop.'"

Elvis contended: "I will kill a cop." There was an uncomfortable
silence in the room: "If you kill a cop, you will be dead!" said Ms.
Marshall. "Well," said Morgan, "Cops is a gang. They been going
around with colors. They got cars that say that they are from the
LA Police Department." By now, Christopher felt that his lesson
plan was overtaken by events. It was already thirty minutes into
the period. "I want to wrap this up because I have got to move on.
Now, has anybody here ever been frisked? The way to stop yourself from being harassed by the police is to be as nonthreatening
as possible. If you say 'yes sir' and 'no sir,' it will help. You can't
turn this into a thing about power. The minute they start to feel
threatened, they are going to search you."

It was quite amazing how these classroom actors in this emerging little drama kept searching for some kind of understanding of each other and yet kept missing each other like ships in the night. First, there was Christopher, the Teach For America student-teacher on his first beat in the classroom, trying to understand these inner-city kids' backgrounds but being ultimately as white and middle-class in his values and understandings as could be. Second, there was the cooperating teacher, Ms. Marshall, black and middle-class, about to retire, having seen a lot of the world and having grown up in a different age; kids might have been less assertive with adults in that age, particularly black kids. She seemed to be fearing the worst, wanting to save these kids from the danger and the law and the cops. And then, there were the kids, young, black, and male—teenagers in search of identity and self-assertion. Being black and male and from the inner city, made them particularly vulnerable to police harassment. They were trying to understand these two adults who were telling them to be "nonthreatening" in the face of harassment from the police. They were particularly dismayed by Ms. Marshall, who was preaching compromise. Ms. Marshall persisted:

> You guys [referring to her male students] start this stuff at school. You get angry at the teacher because that person is an adult...If you do that with the police you will get into trouble.... You need to keep your mouth shut. You must remember that he [the police officer] has the advantage. He has a billy club, he has a gun...

Morgan interrupted: "And what about free speech!...You talk funny. You're funny that way. The last time I talked with you, you said, 'Go with the flow.'" "The question is not one of right and wrong. It is a question of who has the power," Ms. Marshall replied. Morgan was by now frustrated with Ms. Marshall, and it was showing: "I don't understand you. Your position is lame, lame, lame." Another male student, Raymond, seem to side with Ms. Marshall: "If you don't give them [the police] no head, they won't beat you." There were a few sharp exchanges between Morgan, Raymond, and Ms. Marshall. Christopher felt that the students were being disrespectful to Ms. Marshall: "Morgan and Raymond, show some courtesy here!"

Raymond was struggling with what was being proposed about their relationship to the police: "The conflict is: what is the right thing to do?" There was no answer to this question. It was clear that Ms. Marshall and Christopher wanted to wrap up the discussion about police harassment and get back to the formal curriculum. Ms. Marshall attempted to bring about closure: "I would just like to say to those of you who had these experiences [encounters with the police] that I wish to thank you for sharing them with us because all of us haven't had those experiences?" However, Morgan would not let her get away with this: "So what is the conclusion? What is the conclusion?"

Christopher tried to be direct and honest: "There is no conclusion. What I am saying is this. I once had a billy club on my neck too, but I am here. I have a degree, and I am teaching. And this is because I was not hostile back to the police....And isn't that the goal? Isn't the goal to be left alone? If you don't give them reason to be hostile to you, maybe they won't beat you [Christopher's voice trembled a little when he said this. He seemed to be experiencing an internal conflict too. He seemed to be losing faith in what he was telling the students]. Anyway, you need to get to your test."

In this way, Christopher made an awkward transition to the review exercises that the students had to complete in the period. Somewhat ironically, these review exercises were on "The Building of Empires" unit in Welbak's *History and Life* textbook. Student participation in the proceedings in the classroom changed from the vigorous but inconclusive discussion about what to do about police harassment to overt and covert forms of resistance to the routinized curriculum assignment. A notable feature of the latter part of this eventful double period was the fact that many of the girls, for the most part silent throughout the informal discussion of police harassment, came into their own and dominated the formal curriculum—the question and answer session associated with the review exercises.

This example of the classroom culture of an inner-city school in Los Angeles foregrounds in quite a striking manner the specificity of inner-city, black male youth experiences of schooling—a context in which the repressive arm of the state seemed ever near (for instance, the Los Angeles school system has its own police force). It is a context in which their academic experiences were deeply informed by social deprivation and inequality. The intensity of this deprivation and inequality and social violence contributed to their alienation from the formal school curriculum. Their teachers were at a lost as to how to bridge this huge gulf between lived experience outside the school and the formal requirement of participation and achievement in the classroom. They opted instead for a form of defensive teaching and a routinized curriculum as a sort of holding strategy—a strategy that was constantly subverted by nonsynchronous dynamics of race, gender, class, and age. While reports of police harassment were not everyday classroom events, it was clear that the lives of these adolescent students were under stress and overdetermined by dynamics of class, gender, race, and age that intensified misunderstandings between themselves and the two teachers in their classroom, one black and one white. Christopher Morrison and Ms. Marshall positioned themselves differently in relation to the dilemma of police harassment versus adolescent rights and self-assertion. Christopher, white, hip, but with a military background and a conservative upbringing in the South, tried to cross the enormous racial gulf and to reach out and touch his black students. His basis of affiliation drew on the raw material of a relatively privileged background. As a middle-class white person, he felt "the system" worked. All one had to do was to obey the law and "complain" when the policing institutions of the state treated you unfairly. On the other hand, Ms. Marshall tried to empathize. She reached back across the years of her life as a black woman in this country and drew on encounters in which the system worked against black people. The police were gratuitously violent towards black men. In her opinion, black youth were vulnerable to an inequality that reflected itself in the unregulated power of the police. Since power was unequal, Ms. Marshall suggested to her students that they avoid confrontations with the police, even in cases when the students were "in the right." Both teachers in their different ways suppressed the students' questions about representation and identity—difficult questions about self-assertion before the law. Again, the issues of racial solidarity or racial response to inequality and racism seemed to be subverted, marginalized, or just simply displaced by dynamics of ethnicity, class, gender, and age.

CONCLUSION

The point that I want to make here, then, is that you cannot read off the educational, cultural, or political behavior of minority and majority youth or adults based on assumptions about race pure and simple. Different gender and class interests and experiences within minority and majority groups often cut at right angles to efforts at racial coordination and affiliation. In each of the examples of nonsynchrony discussed earlier—the case of black middle-class bureaucrats versus Bantustan peasants and workers and the struggle against racial domination in South Africa, or black girls' differential academic experiences in a desegregated classroom, or inner-city black male youth, police harassment, and the dilemmas of affiliation for their black and white teachers, or in the cases of intraethnic conflict and instability among Asian Americans and among white youth—dynamic variables of gender, class, and race/ethnicity seem to confound one another. These realities were reflected in highly complex and deeply unstable sets of racial effects that imperiled race-based predictions, solutions, or modifications. It is in this sense that I want to argue that to predicate race relations reform in education on the basis of static definitions of what white people are like and what minorities are like can lead to costly miscalculations that can undermine the goal of race relations reform in education itself.

My principal theoretical and methodological concern is therefore to stress the importance of social context, nuance, and language in understanding the dynamics of race relations. I also want to emphasize the need to pay attention to the differential patterns of historical and contemporary incorporation of minority and majority groups into the social and cultural relations that exist in the school setting. Of course, in affirming the positive moment in history and culture, we should not fall back on the idea of race as some essentialist or primordial expression of language and cultural solidarity. Neither should we rush head long into the politics of cultural exceptionalism or the celebration of cultural diversity for its own sake. For as Abdul JanMohamed and David Lloyd (1987) argue, "Such pluralism tolerates the existence of salsa, it even enjoys Mexican restaurants, but it bans Spanish as a medium of instruction in American schools" (p. 10). Rather than taking the easy path to exceptionalism, I maintain that critical and subaltern educational activists must begin to see racial difference as *one*, not the *only*, of the starting points for the drawing out of the various solidarities among subordinated minority youth and adults and working-class women and men over our separate but related forms of oppression. Indeed, it is the failure of progressive groups to see the limitations of a calcified position around racial identity that contributed to the paralysis around the recent nomination of the ultraconservative black judge, Clarence Thomas, to the Supreme Court. One cannot read off racial interests or diagnose racial politics by looking at racial experience alone—even if this experience places you in Pin Point, Georgia (the ominous location of Thomas's origins). Such intensely complex problematics help to underline the fact, as Toni Morrison (1992) has forcefully put it, "that the time for undiscriminating racial unity has past...[We are] in a new arena, and the contestants defy the mold" (p. xxx).

The challenge before us is to move beyond tendencies to treat race as a stable, measurable desposit or category. Racial difference is therefore to be understood as a subject-position that can only be defined in what Homi Bhabha (1992) calls "performative terms"— that is, in terms of the effects of political struggles over social and economic exploitation, political disenfranchisement, and cultural and ideological repression. In this respect, discourses over racial inequality in education cannot be meaningfully separated from issues such as police brutality in African American and Latino neighborhoods (as we saw in the Los Angeles inner-city classroom discussed above) or the sexual and mental harassment of minority women on the shop floor. Nor can oppression and inequality be meaningfully confronted by simply adding more "sensitive" curriculum materials to or including "new voices" in the school syllabus (Carby 1990, 1992). We must come to recognize that examining race relations is critical, not simply for an understanding of social life as it is expressed in the margins of American society, but ultimately for an understanding of life as it is expressed in its very dynamic center. For as Stuart Hall (1981) reminds us:

> If you try to stop the story about racial politics, racial divisions, racist ideologies short of confronting some of these difficult issues; if you present an idealized picture of a "multicultural" or "ethnically varied" society which doesn't look at the way racism has acted back inside the working class itself, the way in which racism has combined with, for example, sexism working back within the black population itself; if you try to tell the story as if somewhere around the corner some whole constituted class is waiting for a green light to advance and displace the racist enemy...you will have done absolutely nothing whatsoever for the political understanding of your students. (p. 68)

The complex dynamics of the operation of race identified by Hall serve as a caution against dogmatism and totalizing solutions to the problem of racial inequality and racial antagonism in education and society. It is these same contradictions that behoove us to guard against quietism and cynicism. As a further corollary to this, we should by now be disabused of the idea that the contradictory politics and practices associated with racial and identity formation only address the experiences of minority individuals and groups. In this essay, I have sought to draw attention to the fact that these discontinuities and contradictions also apply to whites. Much work needs to be done to understand and intervene in the ways in which whites are positioned as "white," in the language, symbolic, and material structures that dominate culture in the West and the

U.S. There is a need to move beyond static definitions of whites and blacks as they currently pervade existing research in education (Fusco 1988; Roman 1993). This means, for example, that we should not continue to position all whites as the other of multicultural curriculum reform and other transformative projects in education. It means that in every local setting, particularly in the urban setting, we must find the moral, ethical, material, and political resources for generalized affective investment in schools. Such an investment must be grounded in a critical reading of the differential needs of embattled urban communities and the particular needs of inner-city school youth. Such a "differential consciousness" (Sandoval 1991) must constantly challenge individual constituencies to think within but, at the same time, to think beyond the particularity of their experiences and interests. Schools cannot continue to function as armies of occupation in the inner-city setting but must become arenas in which diversifying urban communities can participate in building new solidarities for educational access, mobility, and affirmation for minority youth. Ultimately, then, a vigorous attempt to read the dynamism and complexity of schools as social institutions that are deeply infiltrated by society, stratified by difference and by unstable alliances, needs, desires, and interests is a vital first requirement in thinking through the parameters of race relations reform in education.

NOTES

1. Teach For America is the much talked about voluntaristic youth organization that has sought to make a "difference" in the educational experiences of disadvantaged American youth. The organization, patterned on the can-do humanism of the Peace Corps, recruits graduates from elite universities and colleges around the country to serve a two-year stint in inner-city and rural public school districts in need. At its annual Summer Institute held at the University of Southern California, corps members or teacher recruits are exposed to an eight-week crash course in teaching methods and classroom management. Four of these weeks are spent in the form of an internship in Los Angeles inner-city schools.

REFERENCES

Althusser, A. 1971. Ideology and ideological state apparatuses. Notes towards an investigation. In *Lenin and philosophy and other essays*, ed. L. Althusser, pp. 121–173. New York: Monthly Review.

Aronowitz, S. and Giroux, H. October 1991. The politics of clarity. *Afterimage* 19 (3): 5, 17.

Asante, M. 1987. *The Afrocentric idea*. Philadelphia: Temple University Press.

Bakhtin, M. M. 1981. *The dialogic imagination*. Edited by M. Holquist and translated by C. Emerson and M. Holquist. Austin: University of Texas Press.

Bhabha, H. 1992. Postcolonial authority and post modern guilt. In *Cultural studies*, ed. L. Grossberg. C. Nelson, and P. Treichler. pp. 56–68. New York: Routledge.

Bloom, A. 1987. *The closing of the American mind*. New York: Simon and Schuster.

Burawoy, M. 1981. The capitalist state in South Africa: Marxist and sociological perspectives on race and class. In *Political power and social theory*, ed. M. Zeitlin, Vol. 2, pp. 279–335. Greenwich, CT: JAI Press.

Carby, H. 1990. The politics of difference. *Ms.*, September/October, pp. 84–85.

Carby, H. 1992. The multicultural wars. *Radical History Review* 54 (Fall): 7–20.

de Lauretis, T. 1984. *Alice doesn't: Feminism, semiotics, and cinema.* Bloomington; Indiana University Press.

D'Souza, D. 1991. *Illiberal education: The Politics of race and sex on campus.* New York: Free Press.

Fusco, C. 1988. Fantasies of oppositionality. *Screen* 29(4): 80–95.

Gates, H. 1991. "Authenticity," or the lesson of little tree. *The New York Times Book Review,* November 24, 1991, p. 1.

Giroux, H. 1992. *Border crossings: Cultural workers and the politics of education.* New York: Routledge.

Grant, L. 1984. Black females' "place" in desegregated classrooms. *Sociology of Education* 57: 98–111.

———. 1985. *Uneasy alliances: Black males, teachers, and peers in desegregated classrooms.* Unpublished Manuscript, Department of Sociology, Southern Illinois, Carbondale.

Hall, S. 1981. Teaching race. In *The school in the multicultural society,* ed. A. James and R. Jeffcoate, pp. 58–69. London: Harper and Row.

———. 1986. Gramsci's relevance to the analysis of race. *Communication Inquiry* 10: 5–27.

———. 1989. Cultural identity and cinematic representation. *Framework* 36: 66–81.

———. 1993. What is this "black" in black popular culture. In *Black popular culture,* ed. G. Dent, pp. 21–33. Seattle: Bay Press.

Hicks, E. 1981. Cultural Marxism: Nonsynchrony and feminist practice. In *Women and revolution,* ed. L. Sargeant, pp. 219–38. Boston: South End Press.

Hirsch, E. D. 1987. *Cultural literacy.* Boston: Houghton Mifflin.

Institute for the Study of Social Change. 1991. *The diversity Project: Final report to the Chancellor.* University of California, Berkeley.

JanMohamed, A. and Lloyd, D. 1987. Introduction: Minority discourse—What is to be done? *Cultural Critique* 7: 5–17.

Jaschik, S. 1990. Scholarships set up for minority students are called illegal. *The Chronicle of Higher Education* 37 (15): A 1.

Kunjufu, J. 1990. *Countering the conspiracy to destroy black boys.* Chicago: African American Images.

McCarthy, C. 1990. *Race and curriculum.* London: Falmer Press.

Morrison, T. 1992. Introduction: Friday on the Potomac. In *Racing justice, engendering power: Essays on Anita Hill, Clarence Thomas and the construction of social reality*, ed. T. Morrison, pp. vii–xxx. New York: Pantheon Books.

Nkomo, M. 1984. *Student culture and activism in black South African universities.* Westport, Connecticut: Greenwood Press.

Ogbu, J. 1992. Understanding cultural diversity and learning. *Educational Researcher* 21 (8): 5–14.

Omi, M. and Winant, H. 1991. *Contesting the meaning of race in the post–civil rights period.* Paper presented at the Annual Meeting of the American Sociological Association, August 23–27.

Roman, L. 1993. White is a color! White defensiveness, postmodernism, and anti-racist pedagogy. In *Race, identity and representation*, ed. C. McCarthy and W. Crichlow, pp. 71–88. New York: Routledge.

Said, E. 1985. Orientalism reconsidered. *Race and Class* 26 (1): 1–15.

———. 1992. Identity, authority, and freedom: The Potentate and the traveler. *Transition* 54: 4–18.

Sandoval, C. 1991. U.S. third world feminism: The theory and method of oppositional consciousness in the postmodern world. *Genders* 10: 1–24.

Tiedt, I. and Tiedt, P. 1986. *Multicultural teaching: A Handbook of activities, information, and resources.* Boston: Allyn and Bacon.

Wallace, 1990. *Invisibility blues.* New York: Verso.

Waters, M. 1990. *Ethnic options: Choosing identities in America.* Berkeley: University of California Press.

Will, G. 1989. Eurocentricity and the school curriculum. *Baton Rouge Morning Advocate*, December 18, p. 3.

Wright, E. O. 1978. *Class, crisis and the state.* London: New Left Review.

9

CARL ALLSUP

Postmodernism, the "Politically Correct," and Liberatory Pedagogy

The concept and actuality of "difference" has rarely, until recently, compelled such attention in the intellectual and political focus of Western society. This focus today primarily concerns the issues of race, gender, and class as analytical and concrete explanations of individual and collective status and participation in human communities. While past interpretations of human development have certainly included such factors, those efforts have not clarified or even "named" the actors in the examined play. Rather, a dominant center formed by unstated but understood race, gender, and class characteristics presented, for acclaim, a "universal" explanation of human endeavor whose narrators were white, Eurocentric (eventually), elite males.[1] The public discourse implied and at times explicitly articulated, [a world of] biological determinism, which included intellectual and moral superiority and therefore a "natural" order ruled by the "natural" masters. While others (i.e., white women, people of color) participated and even assured the survival and positive evolvement of all human groups, the dominant discourse and its concrete manifestation perpetuated the myth of the ascribed hierarchy. This created and continuously restated history achieved and continues to hold mythological status.

The most recent conceptual challenge to this omnipresent ideology is by those previously marginalized and excluded by this context and content. Calling this challenge multicultural education, feminist theory, or critical pedagogy, its advocates pose their inquiry unambiguously. Oppression and oppressive social relations, racism, sexism, and classism constitute the core dimensions of a paradigm that denies the universal opprobrium of classic Western tradition, most specifically the dominant discourse of that tradition's educational postulates.

As multicultural analysis (also known as ethnic studies), feminist theory, and critical pedagogy possess their own historical origins from their specific experiential reference, their more recent

269

evolution is also significantly informed by postmodernism. The postmodern critique asserts that apolitical contemplation without cultural bias or social agenda cannot actually exist. This critique adds a most valuable conceptual instrument by which we may more accurately reconceptualize our understanding of the past and therefore, our own contemporary condition.

This essay will examine the relationship of postmodernism and liberatory pedagogy (feminist and multicultural theory). It will develop the most necessary and, I believe, poignant theme that we must never cease to critique the acquisition of "knowledge" and its various formats. It will conclude with comment on the most severe attack toward that critique organized under the rubric of the "anti-politically correct." This essay is informed by the author's "position"/location of a Mexican-American, Chicano historian who is also a male feminist.

PERSPECTIVES FROM THE MARGINS

Liberatory pedagogy finds its conceptual center in an inclusive view of human experience. It is most influenced by the experience of those who have been historically denied an equal or perhaps, more importantly, equitable participation in the formation of human society. While they might include any group at some moment in human history, a more discrete purvey would indicate that, at least in what we now designate as Western civilization, very consistent issues have been utilized as monitors of human participation. The development of patriarchy (Lerner 1986), the establishment of its controlling parameters, and its subsequent discourse clearly depict a gendered construct of male domination. This statement would not seem to be so revelationary, but the explicit narrative of that history is quite contrary to the central organizing principle of popularized Western tradition. Indeed it is the decentering of male discourse and the repositioning of the marginalized, in this case, female, that compels reconceptualization of human knowledge. Female voice has never been absent in the formulation of human society. Nevertheless, the experience of women, their comprehensive participation, and their opposition to such marginalization was removed from contemporary significance and historic narrative (Anderson and Zissner 1988) Its reestablishment or discovery derives from the site of resistance that ceased to be bounded by the universal or traditional construction of knowledge as defined by the dominant center.

The very process of this emergence mandated that the factors of oppression, power, and privilege be understood and therefore explicitly explained and detailed. As feminist theory (in the late twentieth century) has decentered male discourse, it has formed a feminist discourse which has more comprehensively described those elements of human society in its structure and value system that do not easily exist with previous and certainly still insistent overtures of transcendent (read male) harmony. From the feminist perspective, the telos of human history becomes more of a male gendered triumph than a fruition of progressive human nature.

A different location of entry to the knowing of human society has been called multicultural theory or education. This euphemism, multicultural, is presented in this essay as racial theory and identifies the construction of race and its impact as a fundamental component of the human community. Unlike traditional, dominant center explanations of pigmentation as the basis for race which procede from the given of white superiority and describe the triumph of Western society over darker people, multicultural theory attempts a comprehensive and inclusive history. This viewpoint perceives and analyzes social constructs about race as a fundamental influence and seeks to incorporate a more real narrative and understanding of the completeness of racially defined societies (Omi and Winant 1986). As with gender dominance, so has racial (white) power produced its own discourse and marginalized the "other" (people of color) from a racially oriented position. The fact that structural evidence of racism, such as slavery, has been perhaps more concretely obvious than sexism, has not prevented the dominant center from reconfiguration and denial of the fundamental nature of white racism. Western tradition perpetuates a constructed explanation by the conqueror that embraces its own rationalizations. Multiculturalism, particularly in the university and academy, seeks to deconstruct those rationalizations (Williams 1991); as with feminist theory, so also does this conceptual and historical analysis name names. The term "white" and the values, actions, and characteristics of the group so designated is considered apart from the norms of the dominant discourse. The universal or assumed protagonist is revealed and the assumed but unnamed standards by which all others have been rendered problematic in the sense of human equity and value are reconceptualized. The result is a decentering of an accepted conceptual base that may have been comforting and reaffirming to those included in that base but simply false for those who were excluded.

It should be noted that both feminist and multicultural theories are not singular or monolithic in their respective analyses of human society. While feminist pedagogy centers its conceptual base and analytic tract on the experiences of women and multicultural on the experience of people of color, there is much variance. Some scholars label these distinctions as conservative, liberal, and/or radical employing the traditional perspectives of the individual, collective, and systemic structure as key indices. For example, one of the more astute feminist analyses of feminist theory sets out four major theoretical areas in feminist theory and pedagogy; liberal, socialist, Marxist socialist, and radical (Jaggar 1983). Liberal feminism seeks female equity in the liberal meritocracy and opts for the "same" rights and opportunities as males and finds minor fault with basic precepts of liberal individualism. Socialist feminism seeks more systemic change in the state, particularly in economic/social relations. Socialist-Marxist feminism attempts to "fit" or reconfigure Marxist theory to incorporate feminist analyses which traditional Marxism, at best, considers a secondary issue. Radical feminism finds no reasonable means by which patriarchy can reform itself and proposes separation as the final resolution. All four areas (and their own subsidiaries) grapple with the social construction of gender vis-a-vis the essentialism of sexual nature. (However, as explained later in this essay, the issue of race is not included as central or even secondary to these approaches.)

Multicultural theory finds similarity at the core of the historical and contemporary experience of people of color confronted by white racism. Beyond that cohesive and, at times, unifying point, each major group (African American, Latino(a), Native American, and Asian-American) presents its history and cultural production as a somewhat exclusive experience with very different locations in the history of the United States. More recent examination by university scholars of multicultural experience utilize marketplace perspective, materialist determinism, and/or cultural hegemony as prominent forces working against people of color. (Barrera 1979; Montijano 1987; West 1987; Wilson 1987) While some conservative historians have suggested the mitigation of race in recent U.S. history, I contend that this is a convenient, if not intentional, misinterpretation by dominant center (Eurocentric, conservative) scholars (Wilson 1980, 1987). It does appear that the intersection of race and class now compose the most commonly developed foci for the understanding of communities of color. There is a noted point of departure with the Native American perspective which considers worldview in culture as more fundamental to the Native American experience than other peoples of color (Allen 1986). This is not to obviate the role of white racism, imperialist expansion, and materialist consideration but to suggest that the Native American perspective finds "difference" more located in spiritual and cultural distinctions than in the historical-cultural relations of Latino(a), African American and Asian-Americans with European groups.

Race and gender, multiculturalism and feminism proceed from a primary, cohesive vision relevant to sex and gender or race and color. However, each analysis must develop in a tendentious environment already created by those that would, and historically did, deny access. The language, symbols, and overall communicative structures by which we convey thought, meaning, direction, and order is and has been a particular obstacle for liberatory theory and pedagogy, not to mention active opposition to oppression. How do we interpret or, more basic, even describe the world of oppression, privilege, and power in a syntax not altered by those who would and have created that world? This conundrum is at the roots of the mythology of a universal society that assumes the natural order, presents it as "the way it is and always has been," and creates the language to rationalize and operationalize this order. A recent contribution to that dilemma, which ironically is Eurocentric in its origin, is postmodern philosophy.

THE CRITIQUE OF POSTMODERNISM AND ITS OWN PROBLEMATIC

While there are many themes within the conceptual umbrella of postmodernism, the challenge and question posed by this philosophical inquiry that is most valuable and even critical for liberatory, feminist, and multicultural theory is the authenticity of discourse. I do not include the more reified debate revolving around deconstructionism as a literary critique (although I also do not intend to trivialize or demean its validity). Authenticity of discourse is very compelling for liberatory inquiry into the authenticity of human enterprise, specifically its created narrative and the self-proclaimed priority of its discourse. From this vantage the postmodernist philosophy of Michel Foucault is paramount.

Foucault emphasized the centrality of discourse as a representation of power. All different discourses are in competition with each other, and the discourse of those in power seeks as one of its primary functions the prevention of any challenge to its authority. Therefore, every human creation (for example, culture) is a result or product of our (human beings') insistence that theological origin establishes authority. According to Foucault (1972), we then seek the moment of greatest perfection from which we fall and then attempt to seek recovery or redemption to the universal. That universal is expressed by the discourse of power or the dominant center. In reality, all relations are governed and meaningful as relations of power, not only as ideas. Rather than one eternal truth, each society has its regime of truth and the individual or group is most affected by the forces of history, not a mythically free struggle for the transcendent or permanent truth (Ibid 1972). The discourse of power conveys the rules and regulations and does not reveal independent truth but controls the human subject. Change must be understood by its historicist character and with the clear understanding that power is not eternal in terms of possession but capable of radical trans-formation in its instrumental manifestation, whether that manifes-tation be called reason, prisons, or sexuality (Foucault 1977, 1978) or even objectivity. Foucault's work and his blunt, uncompromising view of the human subject in relation to knowledge and power alerts us to the seemingly intransigent resistance of Western cultural hegemony. Race, gender, and class are "points of emer-gence" to control and dominate where the discourse of that authority or power "masks these actions as a higher morality and, in exchange, regains its strength." According to Foucault (1984):

> If interpretation were the slow exposure of the meaning hidden in an origin [Truth] then only metaphysics could interpret the development of humanity. But if interpretation is the violent or surreptitious appropriation of a system of rules, which in itself has no essential meaning, in order to impose a direction, to bend it to a new will, to force its participation in a different game, and to subject it to secondary rules, then the development of humanity is a series of interpretations. (Rabinow 1984, p. 86)

> An entire historical tradition (theological or rationalistic) aims at dissolving the singular event into an ideal continuity as a theo-logical movement or a natural process. Effective history, however, deals with events in terms of their most unique char-acteristics, their most acute manifestations. An event, conse-quently is not a decision, a treaty, a reign, or a battle, but the reversal of a relationship of forces, the usurpation of power, the appropriation of a vocabulary turned against those who had once used it. (Robinow 1984, p. 88)

While many feminists scholars agree that Foucault is valuable in his assessment of "authoritarian effects," there is also the femi-nist critique that Foucault's own analysis is a "representation of masculine power." His ban on "continuous history would make it impossible for women even to speak of the historically universal mysogyny from which they have suffered and against which they have struggled and would appear to reflect the blindness of a man who so takes for granted the persistence of patriarchy that he is unable to see it" (Balbus 1987, p. 120). That is, Foucault identifies a Nietzschean will-to-power as gender-neutral and consequently subverts his own demand for historicist identification.

Certainly, as Foucault also mandates that all theory (power) must be subject to forthright and continuous critique, so must his gender-neutral language be challenged, but Foucault provides that very methodology. As a recent critic of Foucault suggests, the unrelenting pessimism of Foucault's work indicates his belief that the corruption of human society (as easily revealed by historical and historicist interpretation) is overwhelming (Nehamas 1993). So-called or understood relationships of power reappear and reassert themselves. However, Foucault also revealed a deep sympathy (and empathy) in his writings with the disenfranchised. His later work, without dismissing his earlier pessimism, also emphasized that critique

> will be genealogical in the sense that it will not deduce from the form of what we are, what is impossible for us to do and to know; but it will separate out, from the contingency that has made us what we are, the possibility of no longer being, doing, or thinking what we are, do or think—It is seeking to give new impetus, as far and wide as possible, to the *undefined work of freedom*. (Nehamas 1993, p. 22, emphasis mine)

That freedom does not permit the acceptance of universal interpretation; misogyny can be identified without the insistence of its universal application or transhistoric nature. Furthermore, as Nehamas (1993) points out, "every form of power, in Foucault's new view, contains the possibility of its own undoing, since every prohibition creates 'the space of a possible transgression.' Since power is productive, the subjects that it produces, being themselves a form of power, can be productive in turn" (Nehamas 1993, p. 34). Foucault does not, therefore, aim at a "true self" or a metaphysic truth but emphasizes that "creativity, too, is always historically situated" and we do not understand the world without rearranging the discourse(s) by which we examine it (Ibid.). Lois McNoy (1993), in her very recent analysis of Foucault and feminism, concurs that the historic self and the dynamic potential of reshaping is similar to feminist reconceptualization and also valuable in the problematics of essentialism.

Whether Foucault is gender neutral or gender blind does not negate the value of his inquiry to understand and interpret misogyny, patriarchy, or any oppression. However, there are other critical caveats to be confronted as we attempt to intersect postmodernism with liberatory theory and pedagogy. They apply to Foucault and to postmodernism scholars in general.

Postmodern critiques rarely visit the conceptual location of people of color. The large majority of postmodern commentators are white, Eurocentric, male and the next largest group are white female, Eurocentric, and/or feminists. Even as their critique offers insight into the experiential history of people of color, in postmodernism's emphasis on the mythology of the universal narrative, the centralizing utilization of power, and the oppressive nature of dominant discourse, these postmodernism scholars tend to be exclusionary in their credentialed inquiry. The contributions of feminist theory to postmodern critique are too often ignored or minimized as if the student (feminism) is simply replicating the teacher (postmodern theory); or the typical (white, Eurocentric, male) authority posits an elitist pose in which the Other is a passive receptacle unable to participate or even discern a dialog of equity. As bell hooks (1990) comments:

> I find myself on the outside of the discourse looking in. As a discursive practice it [postmodernism] is dominated primarily by the voices of white, male intellectuals and/or academic elites who speak to and about one another with coded familiarity. Reading and studying their writing to understand postmodernism in its multiple manifestations, I appreciate it but feel little inclination to ally myself with the academic hierarchy and exclusivity pervasive in its movement today. (p. 24)

Postmodernism is also often noted for its dismissal of the human subject and the smug repudiation of human agency in resisting oppression. The linguistic focus of much, if not most, postmodern writing may display "a tone of mockery a callousness toward the domestic struggles of everyday life" (Caraway 1992, p. 67). This theoretical distancing from the concrete reality of oppressed lives is at most discomforting, if not alienating, for those whose historical and philosophical centers or locations are significantly formulated and derived from a value system and worldview at least potentially imposed by those who are so resolute about its irrelevance. I am speaking here of the white (male and female) postmodernists who only speak to each other and thereby maintain their own possible complicity and racist posture by their oblivion to the marginalization of communities (historic and contemporary) of color (Takaki 1993). As much postmodernist analysis positions its own discourse in, at times, smothering deconstructionist and theoretical "wanderings," so does it reduce and undermine its value in perceiving the dynamic oppression of the world it observes (Ibid.). Racism is not an imagined or misperceived experience; postmodern writing too often renders it invisible. Again, as bell hooks informs us, (1990) "It is sadly ironic that the contemporary discourse which talks the most about heterogeneity, the decentered subject, declaring breakthroughs that allow recognition of otherness, still directs its critical voice primarily to a specialized audience that shares a common language rooted in the very master narratives it claims to challenge" (p. 25).

The relationship of postmodernism and feminist theory is much less problematic; indeed, feminist theory is often included as postmodernism, at least in its critique of the patriarchal society and its paradigmatic construction. As Jane Flax comments, feminist theory, postmodern philosophy, (and psychoanalysis) investigates "how to understand and (re)constitute the self, gender, knowledge, social relations, and culture without resorting to linear, teleological, and hierarchal, holistic, or binary ways of thinking and being" (Caraway 1991, p. 55). Feminist theory certainly and acutely challenges the authority of dominant discourse in social custom, social relations, the construction of knowledge, and the formation of the dominant center discourse. Feminist theory (and multicultural analysis), however, provides an often much needed balance to a particular and sometimes dissonant characteristic of postmodernism, its seeming despair at the possibility and potential of human liberation (Takaki 1993). Both feminist theory and multicultural analysis are liberatory and emancipating in that their conceptual inquiries opt for a constructive resolution to and for human endeavor.

Still, postmodernism offers the resources to deconstruct, decenter and (as with Foucault) recognize the role of power and discourse while feminist theory and multicultural analysis also refocus and reconceptualize cooperative human agency. In describing this potential symbiosis between at least the fundamental core of postmodernism and liberatory theory, we must also examine the opportunity that postmodern critique presents for a self-critical review of feminist and multicultural thought by its own practitioners/presenters. First, I will suggest the parameters of that area viewed by multicultural analysis and then by feminist theory and the relationship between the two.

MARGINALIZING BY THE MARGINALIZED

Obviously the center and primary focus of multicultural analysis is the role, the influence, and the effect of race in the historical experience of people of color in the comprehensive society and their own community. Racial identity relates to individual and collective location and therefore determines structural participation. As it also reflects self-knowledge and worth, so does the *construct* of race become formed and utilized in a multiracial society. White racism is one dynamic of the dominant, white, Eurocentric center in its control of others, in this instance, people of color. The dominant discourse reconfigures the actuality of white racism to relegate its survivors as passive and marginalized and depicts the resolution of this peculiar moral obligation as a triumph of Western justice. Multicultural discourse demonstrates the ongoing ubiquity of racism, the continual struggle of people of color, and the "triumph" of Western tradition as a resistance to the initiatives and work of people of color; motives and incorporated values are more complex and structural than the transcendent interpretation of the dominant discourse would suggest (Omi and Winant 1986). We would also incorporate Foucault's challenge to the notions of liberty, democracy and community.

As this very brief narrative outlines the broad configurations of the multicultural critique and analysis of its subject, it now offers a "postmodern" question: Does not the centering of racism and power (in terms of competing groups) embrace a universal construct of the dominant center that it would interrogate? Does multicultural analysis understand or present, for example, gender as a prominent theoretical and concrete aspect of its thought and narrative? Does class and its parameters affect the emphasis of the centering of race and racism? As stated earlier in the essay, other perspectives, especially class, have begun to share with race a more complex or broad analysis of the experience of people of color. Unfortunately, except for a very significant exception, gender analysis, particularly as presented by feminist theory has not.

The reasons for such omission are volatile and relate to the relationship of feminist theory to white racism as substantive to understanding the experience of women, and I will more thoroughly address this later in the essay. What is apparent or should be more specifically scrutinized is the warning of postmodernism which is that no discourse, explanation, cultural assumption, or transcendent belief is above critique. While people of color, including scholars of color, should be very cautious in interrogating by tenets of postmodernism the experiences initially defined by race, we should not refrain from questioning our potential and problematic embracing of our uniqueness by creating our own (male of color) universal inquiry. Until very recently, multicultural inquiry has not positioned the experiences of women of color as a substantial or even marginal factor in that analysis. Those experiences, as they are explained by a racial and gendered analysis, have been subsumed by the male of color viewpoint. That male of color viewpoint certainly provides a very "different" explanation of the human community, as it separates the particular white male discourse from its universal anchor. Nonetheless, the relative exclusion of gender, by males of color prevents multiculturalist analysis from representing a more inclusive and complex quality in communities of color. Ironically, that exclusion also establishes a commonality with the white Eurocentric center. White males struggle against males of color.

If we so accurately assess the dominant Center discourse of its oppressive nature, then we must also interrogate our own discourse. However, we do not, nor should we, look only to white feminist theory to educate us (males of color) in our self-critique. Fortunately, we may listen to those who have already provided that necessary voice—feminists of color. In discussing their contribution, I would suggest a dichotomy between white women's feminist theory and that of feminists of color. I will then examine the most fundamental flaw of white feminist theory: its own universal postulate and self-proclaimed, although unstated, privilege.

White Women's Feminism

The core of feminist theory has posited gender as the basic formulation of human relations and declared male dominance or patriarchy as the root of gender oppression. While this is problematic in terms of assuming its own mythological worldview, it is also indicative of Foucault's explanation of power, discourse, and human history. While not contradicting the accuracy in feminist theory's analysis of the role of patriarchy, one must emphatically point to the unstated and implicit flaw in this contention: the privileging of race. For the most part, feminist theory has been conceptually grounded in and from the experience of white women (Spelman 1989). The analysis of sex and gender has been through the prism of white middle to upper-class women. While incorporating the language of solidarity within a discursive context of universality, white or race consciousness has been implicit by the very omission of the experiences of women of color (except as a secondary variable). While effectively interrogating patriarchal discourse from its own standpoint of the omission of female thought and action, the overwhelming content of feminist theory excludes racial designation as important or necessary and thereby portrays women as white women.

Even more harshly, one may suggest an assumption by white women feminists of representation by race: that white feminist theory is sufficient and all-embracing of women (Spelman 1988; Caraway 1991). Even as feminist theory has sought more critical understanding of variation among female groups, the greatest variance is attributed to class and its own subtext (Jaggar 1983). Except for a very few writers, feminist theorists maintain a "center" of unstated racial consciousness and thereby exclude and marginalize feminists of color.

A troubling but necessary analysis of this perhaps perplexing and vexing quandary is what has separated feminism from multicultural analysis in their intellectual histories. The initial critique of second phase feminism by *women of color* included emphasis on the neglect of feminism's own culturally innate racism. Except for a very brief history of inter-racial solidarity between feminist females, white women have profited from their racial alliance with white men. White women depended on the racism of the white male patriarchy to consolidate and protect their own position. White male constructs privileged white females over females of color, and white women complied in that result (hooks 1989; Spelman 1988; Davis 1983). Most white feminists of the late nineteenth and well into the twentieth-century repudiated racial sisterhood with vehement racist language or (later) "simple" omission. Meanwhile, white women hired women of color without any conspicuous guilt or notions of sisterhood, and this historical relationship became the historical metaphor for the relationship between white, middle-class women and women of color (Davis 1983). That complicity with Eurocentric racism continued and continues in the great bulk of feminist theory and writing (Lorde 1992); if feminists of color object, they are indicted as privileging race over gender and of false consciousness. Even where feminists of color are "included" in the analysis of patriarchy, it is problematic or, as Caraway (1991) who is a white, female feminist, informs us, "If Black feminists genre play does not replicate in style and tone that of official feminist discourse, it is often ignored, exoticized as a funky or gutsy backdrop to the real project of theorizing" (p. 39).

This tendency of white feminists to privilege their theoretical constructs to the empirical additions of feminists of color or to the writings of women of color suggests, again, the warnings of postmodernism on discourse and power. Again, as Nancy Caraway (1991) asks, "Why do so many Black feminist writers and critics feel driven out of the realms of academic acceptance while their rich literature is flourishing among students and the reading public? This reflects a condescending attitude on the part of those white academic feminist guardians who, it seems, are doing the work of the patriarchal establishment by their hierarchial ranks of the work of feminists of color" (p. 40). Even more distressing, this privileging perpetuates the divisive effect of a racism that forms at least part of the feminist analysis that is so valuable and insightful in its interrogation of the patriarchal society but so oblivious to its own cooptation by a white, racist patriarchal society.

RESOLUTION?

Where does this conflicting connundrum leave us? I will now suggest that liberatory analysis and pedagogy must be just that. We must seek to know our society by recognizing it not as a hierarchy and privileging of oppression (which ultimately is a singular and limiting view) but as a matrix in which race and gender and class intersect as defining factors or elements in the individual, group, collective, and/or societal moment. I will briefly illustrate that intersection, its link to the philosophy of postmodernism, and some problems in pursuing that matrix.

As Audre Lorde (1992) has described, we are "walking coalitions." Each individual is a combination of obvious biological "facts" with social constructions (race and class and gender) devised to influence that singular and collective endeavor known as human activity. While our institutional or formal educational narratives have selectively labeled those factors, we now more lucidly or, at least with greater candor, "name the game." Women of color are the most obvious group to teach us about coalitions or intersections and even this designation must be more specific when appropriate to both the theoretical and concrete explication. An African American, middle-class woman's coalition is similar and dissimilar to a working-class, Mexican-American, female. This last statement illustrates the primary contentions of what and how to formulate and interrogate the intersection: the historical given and nonsychrony.

The standpoint of each individual and her or his group identity is historically rooted (in Foucault's sense of the word). No one aspect (race, gender, or class) can be the sole expression or even the primary source of the contemporary location of individual group standpoint (although each will have different historic prominence). Until recently liberatory theory and pedagogy has emphasized or promoted the singular ontological view. As stated, most feminist theory virtually replaces or dismisses race and class influence, and most multicultural analysis does the same with gender (class is much more pervasive in multicultural analysis). Why is there this conflict, especially with the availability of such astute and specific theoretical and historical narrative and interpretation?

Postmodern theory points to a logical but volatile conclusion (even as such theory is conspicuous for its own Eurocentric flaw). Feminist and multicultural discourse are oppositional to the dominant discourse of the dominant center of white, elitist, Eurocentric male society; while their inquiry is centered in historical fact, its position has often implied a more transcendent nature and acquired an ahistorical posture even (and most significantly) as they critique that flow and manipulation in dominant discourse. Women and men are passed almost as abstractions through an ahistorical novel or play without the complications of race, gender, and class or any such combination. The oppositional voice and subsequent discourse accepts, indeed depends on, its representational power and quickly presumes its own ascription or origin and historical omnipresence. What is most fascinating is the precise location of this privileging; white females speak for all females, or males of color represent all people of color. Class analysis is most often that of white male authority. The oppositional standpoint reconceptualizes the knowledge of the inclusive society by, in part, reconfiguration of its own complicity in the enactment of power and the reification of its discourse. At this recognition one, indeed, might share the pessimistic (and for some nearly cynical) postmodern critique.

At this juncture one needs to most critically assess those attempts to overcome divisiveness or, as is most often expressed, to seek similarity and commonality. This desire and/or goal appears most often as a mandate of those who already control or have the most influence on the issue being debated. That is to say, it is white women who would embrace the similarity or sameness in the search for *sisterhood*; or it is the white teacher who would express the sameness of all as the "salvation" of the isms in society. Rarely do women of color postulate sisterhood as a solution but more as a denial of white female racism; rarely do radical, multicultural analysts embrace sameness but identify the white teacher as part of racist society, not as someone removed from it. The pursuit of similarity is a facade if (as it usually does) it includes the dismissal of, or, at best, minimalist attention to responsibility—that is, to accountability. The intellectual and social recognition of this fallacy derives from the acceptance of the "historical" as the basis for establishing the cohesiveness of difference within the purveyance of liberatory theory as it seeks emancipatory results; nonsynchrony is the historical and, for the moment, its most valuable manifestation. The contemporary imperative is the reality of human society in the utilization of the authority of power with its signifiers of race and gender (and class). Cameron McCarthy (1988) and Iris Young (1990) offer incisive critiques on this process and the (postmodern) mandate to remove the totalizing paradigm from liberatory theory.

In his examination of education, McCarthy (1988) argues that "ideology, culture, and politics are important determinants in shaping race relations in schooling as is the economy" (p. 266). He chides neo-Marxian dissembling of the causes for racial inequity and decries the totaling effect of class theory. McCarthy is also blunt in his critique of the monocausal approach to racial inequality by American multiculturalists. His analysis of "liberal" multiculturalism and neo-Marxian approaches to American education illustrates the application of at least a quasi-matrix approach which begins with historical reality and seeks to thoroughly analyze nonsimilarity or what he calls nonsynchrony. "I emphasize the materiality of ideology and argue for the codetermination of culture and politics, along with the economy, in radical accounts of the elaboration of the racial character of schooling" (Ibid., p. 266). McCarthy addresses the danger of oppositional discourse producing its own fallacious/self-serving agenda as he underlines a powerful tract in multicultual programs *in American schools* to avoid the historical framework of its own deliberation—white racism.

Iris Young (1990) presents the strongest caveat about the creation of coalition through notions of mutuality, subjectivity, and community. According to Young, if we truly listen to the voice of others and if the dominant group within the marginalized evolution can overcome the need for reciprocity, it may discover a jarring and disconcerting fact: empathy is neither expected nor desired by the marginalized within the marginalized. Consciousness, self-esteem, self-validation, and reconciliation may be appropriate goals and criteria in a homogenous grouping, but political action is not dependent on a reciprocal subjectivity, at least not in the context of sisterhood or a multiracial coalition (Young 1990). Nancie Caraway (1991), in her superlative book *Segregated Sisterhood=Racism and the Politics of American Feminism* warns against the "vision of politics as a sphere of love (because) as Hannah Arendt warned us that vision contains the seeds of totalitarianism" (p. 200).

The creation of the matrix of race, gender, and class is not grounded in the bonding of sisterhood, multiracial community, or projected (and very problematic) empathy. It must proceed from the political act and from the activity of solidarity. This nontranscendent coming to knowledge must enjoin the historical moments; that is, the intersection and interplay of race, gender, and class. That historical expression, derived from the experience and theoretical analysis of the other, must also address the understanding and caution explicit in postmodern perspective about discourse of power.

If the privileged within the marginalized can overcome the imperative of dominant standpoint and "surrender" their "authority," then that solidarity may be achieved. "The other option is to decide to actively hold to one's own greater power. That involves believing that one's own perceptions and understanding of the world are more important and correct than the 'others' with whom one is interacting" (Zierath 1991, p. 2). The continued denial of access betrays a "lack of trust of the other and lack of trust in oneself to respond without fear to a situation when one's power has been reduced" (Ibid., p. 3).

As a Chicano male, as a multiculturist and as a feminist, I am confident that this recall of memory and historical recognition is proceeding, albeit or perhaps unavoidably, with a cacophonous, volatile evolution. This discourse is an endeavor of struggle by those who do not accept unearned privilege nor the inevitability of the "what has been." My last comments will focus on the external comments and posture of those who are quite determined to defend that privilege.

THE "POLITICALLY CORRECT"

The term *politically correct* (p.c.) is now a fascinating example of the reification employed by all cultural communication but most significantly by dominant discourse. The attempts by liberatory theory and pedagogy to understand and to provide inclusive education beyond the confines of oppressive agendas have been ridiculed by the popular media as silly, absurd, or even a duplicitous distortion of minor human pecadillos. It is considered nonsensical to attempt gender-free and racially sensitive language. The attempt to consider racial and gender sensitivity in written/media presentation is somehow a threat to freedom of speech. The label politically correct, as used by more Right Wing critics, becomes an abridged reference to "feminazis" or "radical militants." To be described as politically correct by the dominant center becomes an assured judgment by those "in the know" about the Other—those without appreciation of Western and particularly American pluralism and principles of justice. According to the guardians of this sanctified tradition, the most egregious of the "thought police" are in that academy of knowledge and apolitical inquiry—the University. (While I am obviously resorting to a lot of sarcasm, it is astonishing how serious the above statement is presented by the anti-politically correct).

Much of this "debate" would not deserve more than minimal attention except that the usual suspects for the anti-politically correct are affirmative action, quotas, lowered academic standards, hiring of minorities and women, and the attack on freedom of speech. ("It is horrible but needed for persons to have the right to express detested ideas—such as racial slurs and sexual insults"). All of these issues compel rational dialogue but as demonstrated ad nauseum, ad infinitum by liberatory and postmodern analysis, the standpoint of most anti-politically correcters proceeds from the unstated but clear assumption that the existing standards or the determinants of the university demographic profile are just and right. These standards are without political context or bias, and these created norms of white, Eurocentric, elite males at best need only some modification, not some radical challenge by "totalitarian" militants. Theodore Hammerow, a leading member of the National Association of Scholars, commented on a faculty hiring plan at the University of Wisconsin-Madison in 1989. He "was disturbed by the suggestion that the plan proposes faculty hiring with an emphasis on ethnic origin and a *lesser regard* (emphasis mine) than in the past for merit" (*Newsweek* December 24, 1990 p. 52). Should one even point out that "lesser regard for merit" may have been (is) a codification of "more than just white males," or that his disapproval of the "emphasis on ethnic origin" is another way of questioning the ability of non-European, nonwhite scholars? Professor Hammerow, in expressing his nonopposition to ethnic studies emphasized, "I do feel that students should know the history and culture of their own country first...I feel that an American student should know American history before he or she turns to Afro-American history or Asian-American history" (Ibid., p. 53).

This shallow but demogogic orthodoxy and banal, insipid media narrative is cause for concern as it represents the power of dominant discourse to dissemble substantive challenge and disarm those in liberatory theory and pedagogy who seek reconceptualization. As Michael Kinsley (1993) states [p.c. (or anti-p.c.)] has degenerated into an all-purpose term of political abuse that means little more than a view I disagree with. But it is meant to suggest a stifling orthodoxy, an intolerance of opposing views that verges on censorship, victimization chic and stagy oversensitivity to robust remarks" (*Time*, August 9, 1993 p. 66). A most pernicious assault representing this orthodoxy comes from those academicians whose past work challenged more narrow perspectives but who now illuminate (and affirm) the embeddedness of dominant cultural discourse.

The principal alarm sounded by these eminent academicians is the political focus of the politically correct. As Hammerow implied, and Vann Woodward and Schlesinger denounced, an agenda, indeed the central "threat" of the politically correct coalition, is political organization for what should be and has been apolitical intellectual inquiry (Vann Woodward 1991; Schlesinger 1991.) The point of liberatory/postmodern contention, that intellectual inquiry and its most prevalent university manifestation, curriculum, has been and still is of a particular Eurocentric paradigm and worldview, is oblivious to these guardians of academe who reduce the serious and comprehensive analysis of liberatory theory to political indoctrination (D'Souza 1991; Vann Woodward 1991; Schlesinger 1991).

The final anti-p.c. theme to be depicted in this very brief survey is perhaps the most perplexing question and/or puzzlement for the anti-p.c. coalition, including the defensive academicians: How can the feminists, and most clearly, the multiculturalists degrade the concept and fact of the one, common, binding culture and value system which has provided the "unique source of those liberating ideas of individual liberty, political democracy, the rule of law, human rights, and cultural freedom that constitute our most precious legacy and to which most of the world today aspires" (Schlesinger 1991, p. 32)?

Again, if such a value system and tradition does indeed exist, then it must be comprehended in its totality which includes accountability. One cannot establish the paradigm of Western philosophy and then explain its crimes while mitigating the causes within that uncritical acceptance. To be critical, however, does not mean reconfigurating "the things that cannot be taught" once they reach a consciousness through the inquiry of such as liberatory theory. Slavery, genocide, and misogyny are not by-products of the tradition but fundamental to it; reduction or alteration may occur but not by some inherent self-correcting, ahistorical process. If a society chooses to fulfill an ideal, then it had best seek an accountability for its failures. When the subjects of those failures become more than abstract objects of transcendent largesse, they acquire a voice and materialist power; they compel critique beyond aberrant euphemisms. At that point the dominant center and its discourse denounce critical inquiry and call it irrational. Indeed, how can one reject a tradition that is so inclusive in its exclusion? The high priests of the temple of the one culture tremble when the supplicants demand that the sacrifices be ended.

CONCLUSION

Liberatory theory, as represented by feminism and multiculturalist analysis, has challenged the dominant discourse as comprehensively flawed in its very representation of the language of control and power. To escape the quandary and self-defeating nature of Western inquiry by the one group paradigm, postmodern philosophy, particularly that of Michel Foucault, offers the conceptual opportunity to understand the oppressive aspects of this discourse as it reflects the historical and historicist condition. The coalition of these inquiries about human society permits the reconceptualization that may avoid the trap of privilege and power between and within the oppressed and marginalized. However, it is only by the surrender of the dominant standpoint and the refusal to be affirmed by unearned privilege that we may proceed. The "one culture, the one tradition" may be attainable. It first must be understood that such is *not* our present reality and it must be understood with the harsh and relentless history of that reality. We may conclude with William Carlos Williams (as he addressed the accountability of white America to Native American history in 1925):

> However hopeless it may seem, we have no other choice.
> We must go back to the beginning.
> It must be done all over. (Drinnon 1990, p. XIX)

NOTES

1. A particular component that has energized this analytical trio, while also grounded in its normative condition, is capitalism; hence the adjective "elite" and its economic connotation.
2. While the cultural-spiritual traditions of all communities of color is significant, it is important to understand the more traditional cultural-spiritual aspects of the Native American (i.e., the indigenous experience of Native Americans is more impactive on their interaction with Europeans than it is for other groups because they had more resources to retain their traditional culture). Again one should not infer that this retention has not been without tremendous struggle against the desire of white, Eurocentric supremacists to eliminate the traditional Native American culture.

REFERENCES

Allen, Paula Gunn. 1986. *The sacred hoop: Recovering the feminine in American Indian traditions*. Boston: Beacon Press.

Anderson, Bonnie and Zinsser, Judith. 1988. *A history of their own*. New York: Harper and Row.

Balbus, Isaac. 1987. Disciplining women: Michel Foucault and the power of feminist discourse. In *Feminism as critique*, ed. Seyla Benhabib and Drucill Cornell. Minneapolis: University of Minnesota Press.

Barrera, Mario. 1979. *Race and class in the southwest: A theory of racial inequality*. Notre Dame: University of Notre Dame Press.

Caraway, Nancie. 1991. *Segregated sisterhood: Racism and the politics of American feminism*. Knoxville: University of Tennessee Press.

Davis, Angela. 1983. *Women, race, and class*. New York: Random House, Vintage Books.

Drinnon, Richard. 1990. *Facing west: The metaphysics of Indian hating and empire building*. New York: Schocken Books.

D'Souza, D. 1991. *Illiberal education: The politics of race and sex on campus*. New York: The Free Press.

Foucault. Michel. 1972. *The archaeology of knowledge*. New York, Harper and Row, Harper Torchbooks.

———. 1977. *Discipline and punish: The birth of the prison*. New York: Pantheon

———. 1978. *The history of sexuality.* Vol. 1. An Introduction. New York: Pantheon.

hooks, bell. 1974. *Feminist theory, from margin to center.* Boston: South End Press.

———. 1981. *Arn't I a woman: Black women and feminism.* Boston: South End Press.

———. 1989. *Talking back: Thinking feminist, thinking black.* Boston: South End Press.

———. 1990. *Learning race, gender, and cultural politics.* Boston: South End Press.

He wants to pull the plug on the pc. *Newsweek.* December 24, 1990, p. 52–53.

Jaggar, Alison. 1983. *Feminist politics and human nature.* Totowa N.J.: Rowan and Allanheld.

Kinsley, Michael. *Time,* Aug. 9, 1993.

Lorde, Audre. 1992. Age, race, class, and sex: Women redefining difference. In *Race, class, and gender, an anthology* ed. Margarat Anderson and Patricia Hill Collins. Belmont, CA: Wadsworth.

Lerner, Gerda. 1986. *The creation of patriarchy.* New York: Oxford University Press.

McCarthy, Cameron. 1988. Rethinking liberal and radical perspectives on racial inequality in schooling: Making the case for nonsynchrony. *Harvard Educational Review* 58: 265–279.

McNoy, Lois. 1993. *Foucault and feminism: Power, gender, and the self.* Boston: Northeastern University Press.

Montejano, David. 1987. *Anglos and Mexicans in the making of Texas, 1836–1886.* Austin: University of Texas Press.

Nehamas. March 10, 1993. Review of *The passion of Michel Foucault* and *Michel Foucault. The New Republic,* p. 20–26.

Omi, M. and Winant, H. 1986. *Racial formation in the United States.* New York: Routledge and Kegan Paul.

Rabinow, Paul ed. 1984. Nietzsche, geneology, and history. *Foucault Reader.* New York: Panthen, p. 76–100.

Schlesinger, Arthur. 1991. The disuniting of America, what we stand to lose if multicultural education takes the wrong approach. *American Educator* (Winter): 14–33.

Spelman, Elizabeth. 1988. *Inessential woman: Problems of exclusion in feminist thought.* Boston: Beacon Press

Takaki, Ronald. June 1993. Interview with Jean Ferocqua, Wisconsin Public Radio.

Vann Woodward, C. 1991. Freedom and the universities. *The New York Review of Books*, July 18, p. 32–37.

West, Cornel. 1987. Race and social theory: Towards a genealogical materialist analysis. In *The Year Left 2.* ed. M. Davis et al. Versa. Chicago.

Williams, Patricia. 1991. *The alchemy of race and rights.* Cambridge: Harvard University Press.

Wilson, Julius. 1981. *The declining significance of race.* Chicago: University of Chicago Press

———. 1987. *The truly disadvantaged. The inner city, the underclass, and public policy.* Chicago: University of Chicago Press.

Young, Iris. 1990. The ideal of community and the politics of difference. *Feminism/Postmodernism.* New York: Routledge.

Zierath, David. 1991. Comments on power, white male professors, and the politics of tenure. Unpublished.

10

CARMEN MONTECINOS

Culture as an Ongoing Dialog: Implications for Multicultural Teacher Education

Recently, an acquaintance of mine told me about her trip to Chile, my native land. She went there for a few days to participate in a university-sponsored conference, as the keynote speaker. Knowing that for Latin Americans punctuality is not a necessity, she left the States prepared to make the necessary cultural adaptation, that is, to deal with delays. In fact, she reported, she was looking forward to the trip because it would give her a break from the pressures of her time-driven life. Things, however, did not turn out the way she had expected. Once she got there, the break never came: the conference program, which included several tours of the area, was run on a very tight schedule. She came back from Chile, she told me, feeling exhausted.

So where could my acquaintance's knowledge of Latinos' views on time and punctuality have misled her? I suggest two places. First, she could have failed to realize that as much as she could use her knowledge to adapt to the Cultural Other[1], the Cultural Other could do the same thing and adapt to her. For example, wanting to make her feel at home, the Chileans might have adopted what they thought was the conceptualization of time among people from the United States. They rushed, therefore, to make sure that things happened exactly on time and not within a few minutes of the scheduled time. Second, her knowledge of Latinos' meaning of time was stripped of context. It seems she assumed that what she knew to be true for the Latino group was also true for the Chilean subgroup. Similarly, she seemed to assume that among Latinos *time* is a fixed concept. However, in Chile the social desirability of punctuality depends upon the social context and its actors: showing up late for a party is okay; showing up late for work is not.

More generally, I believe she was misled by the conceptualization of culture (i.e., the belief that culture is a self-contained whole made up of coherent patterns) and the multicultural knowledge (i.e., it

291

involves knowing those patterns) that underpinned her approach. In this chapter I will argue that a multicultural teacher education curriculum that is based on these conceptualizations of culture and multicultural knowledge is inadequate for the task of developing a knowledge base for teaching in multicultural classrooms. To develop this argument I will first note why these conceptualizations are untenable and the shortcomings that a self-contained view of culture entails. I will then propose an alternative conceptualization of culture and multicultural knowledge, one which emphasizes the permeable, relational dimension of cultural life in multicultural societies. In the remainder of the chapter I will explore types of knowledge and pedagogy that an open-ended, dialogical view of culture suggests for multicultural teacher education.

ASSUMPTIONS ABOUT CULTURE AND REPRESENTATION

Sleeter and Grant (1988) noted that some proponents of multicultural education expect teachers to represent in the curriculum each ethnic group as "the group would depict itself and show the group as active and dynamic" (p. 153). In multicultural teacher education these goals are often translated into course content that represents various ethnic groups through patterned depictions. McDiarmid's (1992) quote from a presenter at a Los Angeles Unified School District's multicultural training program can illustrate this approach to depicting a cultural group: "Oh, another thing that you need to know is that Mexican family life is basically very, very conservative. It's strong. You know it's patriarchal" (p. 86). For teachers, as for my acquaintance, the usefulness of acquiring this type of information about a cultural group rests on two untenable assumptions. First, culture is assumed to be a "self-contained whole made up of coherent patterns" (Rosaldo, 1989, p. 20) (e.g., the Mexican family structure is assumed to be fixed and impermeable to influences from other cultural/social practices with which different families come into contact). Second, it is assumed that an ethnic group's social life can be reduced to, in the words of Kellner (cited in Giroux 1988, p. 16), 'master narratives' that attempt to subsume every particular, every specific viewpoint" (e.g.. there is a Mexican-American family structure that encompasses any differences due to social class, whether the family is headed by a male or a female, and so on). My acquaintance experienced the futility of cultural knowledge based on these assumptions. As I will show later on, this conceptualization of culture and cultural life and the assumptions they engender among teachers are untenable and are, therefore, destined to provide an inadequate account of a group's cultural life in multicultural societies.

Although the term multicultural education has come to signify different things to different scholars, there is some consensus that it includes the principles I enumerate next (e.g., Banks 1993; Sleeter and Grant 1988). A multicultural curriculum is one that allows all students, not just those who nicely fit ethnically-based descriptions, to see themselves represented in it. A multicultural curriculum is one which seeks to challenge hierarchical and oppressive relations among people who belong to different social groups, not just to gain greater insights of the Cultural Others. A multicultural curriculum seeks to maintain the polyphony that characterizes a pluralistic, democratic society not just give the illusion of plurality. Developing teacher education curricula and pedagogy that is multicultural involves the application of these principles. Still, can a self-contained, monovocal view of culture support these principles?

A self-contained view of culture diverts attention away from the ways in which cross-cultural encounters that occur in the school context account for the disparities in the educational attainment of various ethnic groups. For instance, this conceptualization of culture can lead teachers to believe that most, if not all, children from an ethnic minority group will behave in the school in patterned ways learned at home and not in ways learned in school through interactions with teachers and schooling (e.g., the academic failure of a child can be traced to what he or she learned at home and not to what and how he or she is being taught in school). Representations that portray groups as self-contained have been criticized because they obscure a significant dimension of cultural life in multicultural societies, that is, power/knowledge differentials among various social groups (McCarthy and Crichlow 1993). By portraying groups as self-contained, we neglect to attend to an important dimension of cultural life, that is, the need for groups to negotiate common cultural life as they attempt to adapt to the demands they place on each other. In the classroom, student alienation results from unsuccessful negotiations among all those who create that social space and inequity results from the imposition of one form of social organization.

The use of a master narrative to represent a group is bound to provide an a very narrow depiction of what it means to be Mexican-American, African American, white, and so on. McCarthy and Crichlow (1993), Simon (1992), and others have aptly noted that a master narrative essentializes and wipes out the complexities and richness of a group's cultural life. This type of representation ignores the cultural life of students who belong to multiple, overlapping cultural groups. A monovocal account will engender not only stereotyping but also curricular choices that result in representations in which fellow members of a group represented cannot recognize themselves.

Having noted the limitations that a self-contained, univocal view of culture entails, we can now examine an alternative conceptualization of culture and cultural life found in critical and poststructuralist theories. Briefly, anthropologist Renato Rosaldo (1989) has proposed a conceptualization of culture that is open-ended, permeable, and continuously produced in the midst of cross-cultural encounters. The work of critical and poststructuralist theorists brings attention to the multiple, overlapping, and disjunctive nature of the narratives that can be produced to represent a group's culture and to the politics of representation involved in any one of them (Habermas 1972; Giroux and McLaren 1991; O'Connor 1989; Weedon, 1987). This conceptualization of culture suggests that the curriculum must focus on the permeable, relational dimension of cultural life, where dialogue, interaction, conflict, and change are more significant than fixed characteristics. The multicultural curriculum must reject the possibility that a master narrative can be used to represent a group's cultural life. In the remainder of this chapter I elaborate on this conceptualization as it relates to the development of multicultural teacher education curricula and pedagogy.

Cultural Life in Multicultural Societies

As noted by anthropologist Renato Rosaldo (1989) a large part of social life in the United States is deployed in the "cultural borderlands". In multicultural societies an individual's life is constantly crisscrossing with the lives of people from various racial, age, ethnic, social class, and gender backgrounds. Cultural life in the borderlands, Rosaldo argued, makes cultural purity an impossibility because ethnic groups are interconnected with each other. In the borderlands, groups' cultural programs evolve historically as groups adapt to changes in the social environment (Bullivant 1989). Schools and classrooms typify the borderlands as people from diverse age, social class, gender, and ethnic backgrounds come together and influence each other in this setting. For instance, in the classroom elements of a child's home culture must often be forsaken if they are in conflict with the behaviors and values that are required to gain social acceptance as well as success in school.

Culture in multicultural societies cannot, therefore, be understood as a self-contained whole. Instead, it must be understood as a "porous array of intersections where distinct processes criss-cross from within and beyond its borders" (Rosaldo 1989, p. 20). This definition of culture shifts the focus of multicultural knowledge away from knowing about within-group patterns towards knowing about the patterns of social relations between groups.

Attending to this open-ended, relational dimension of culture makes the task of curricular representation quite problematic for teachers. If a group's cultural life cannot be fixed because its demarcations are constantly shifting and if there are multiple narratives, then what kinds of knowledge can help teachers develop a curriculum that would represent a group as the group would depict itself? Can teachers represent the multiplicity of ways in which one can be a Chicana, white, African American, and so on? These questions are explored next.

Social Identity in the Multicultural Societies

One key to developing a curriculum that gives all students an opportunity to see themselves reflected in their schooling rests in teachers' abilities to grasp how students' social identities are formed. Social identity involves those aspects of the individual's self-image that derive from the various social categories that he or she uses as self-descriptions (Ferdman 1990). As members of one or more ethnic group(s), students' ethnicity can be a significant marker of who they are. The degree of significance associated with ethnicity as well as the primacy given to that social identifier over other identifiers will vary from student to student (Ibid.)

I can recall how my seven-year-old daughter started to develop a sense of "Hispanic" identity after a teacher told her in school that she was Hispanic. She came home that day and asked me, "Mommy, did you know that we are Hispanics?" Until then nobody had given her that name, and I had to explain to her what that meant. This little girl's experience clearly illustrates the significant role that Cultural Others, in this case her teacher, play in developing one's ethnic identity. Teachers and schooling provide for many children the first opportunity to internalize ethnicity as a category for self-description. This category, as Weedon (1987) reminds us, will be constantly redefined.

Weedon (1987) described subjectivity—one's sense of oneself and our way of understanding our relation to the world—as "precarious, contradictory, and in process, constantly being reconstituted in discourse each time we think or speak" (p. 33). Consequently, subjectivity is not fixed, and experience has no inherent essential meaning. Our subjectivity evolves within the

society and culture within which we live and, as such, it changes
as our social environment changes. The self, fundamentally dialogical in nature, represents the internalization of dialogues we have
had with ourselves and significant others (Taylor 1992).

To illustrate this conceptualization of subjectivity and identity,
I turn to my own experience as an immigrant. Until recently,
nobody had ever asked me if I was an Indian: it was obvious I was
not; neither was I asked if I was a "minority" or a "Hispanic." I
never had to talk about myself in those terms. It was only after I
came to the United States that I had to learn the many ways in
which those terms were socially constructed by diverse groups in
this country. As I searched for my identity in this new society, I
learned a different system of meanings and values. As I heard
people call me "Hispanic", I changed the way I made sense out of
my social relations, and I learned to call myself a "minority", a
"Hispanic", a "Latina", and a "foreigner." I learned that these
different identifiers were not interchangeable because each
denoted a different version of reality, served conflicting interests,
and involved different alliances. For example, by calling myself a
minority as opposed to a Latina, I was defining myself as part of a
much larger social group. A search for identity

> is more than a problem of individual psychology. Without
> agreeing on who we are, we cannot agree on who are our allies
> and who our enemies. The issue of our identity as a people is
> inseparable from that of political, cultural or economic union
> among kindred people. (Rojas 1991, p. 29)

This conception of identity and subjectivity suggests that
multicultural teacher education needs to help teachers learn how
to listen carefully to what self-descriptors a child uses and why the
child chooses that descriptor. Teachers also need to be aware of
the meanings that different forms of self-description and Other-
descriptions entail as well as the politics involved in each one.

Describing the Cultural Other, Describing Oneself

In the cultural borderlands teachers' and students' social identities are jointly shaped as they participate in a "plurality of
partially disjunctive, partially overlapping communities that criss-
cross" (Rosaldo 1989, p. 182). This interdependence among groups
implies that the Cultural Other that teachers must learn about
and represent in the curriculum does not live in a world completely
separated from the one the teacher lives in. Learning about the
Cultural Other is learning about oneself as one's own life is, in a

sense, shaped by the life of the Cultural Other. For example, native English-speaking teachers' depictions of the school failure of a language minority student cannot be separated from these teachers' understanding of their own academic success as native speakers of English. The same institutional factors that serve to support their success operate in ways that promote the failure of children who are from language minority backgrounds. Therefore, when depicting others as they would depict themselves, teachers are also depicting a part of their own lives.

Teachers who understand the formation of students' identities are teachers who also understand the formation of their own identities. I do not mean this exclusively in the sense of developing a multicultural teacher education curriculum that helps white students understand that prevailing social practices are the product of Eurocentric cultures. I also mean it in the sense that teachers, including ethnic minority teachers, must learn to examine the consequences that those prevailing social practices have jointly had in the creation of their own lives and the lives of their students. Multicultural teacher education curriculum, thus, needs to help teachers uncover how their lives and the lives of their students intertwine.

Situated Knower, Situated Knowledge

When teacher education curriculum uses a master narrative to describe a cultural group, it erases within-group differences that stem from the particular social intersections from which various individuals participate in and create cultural life. Constructivism tells us that all knowledge must be understood as partial to the social position of the knower—the knower's race, gender, class, and so on will determine what is paid attention to and how things are interpreted (Weedon 1987). Ethnic groups need to be understood as multivoiced and must be described in terms of a wide range of social orientations that compete for legitimacy (Giroux 1988; O'Connor 1989). Learning to depict a group, therefore, involves learning to recognize the multiple ways in which any one group can be described.

Individuals, as well as groups, can recognize and articulate a range of voices because they simultaneously belong to multiple social groups whose boundaries are constantly shifting. For example, within the United States' Latino community a common ethnicity does not negate a plurality of voices that stem from differences in social orientations due to class, gender, level of insertion into mainstream society, national origin, and so on.

Similarly, within the African American community, contrary to common portrayals in the schools which privilege the voice of Martin Luther King, Jr., a wider range of voices articulate the aspirations of that community.

Rejecting the possibility of a master narrative does not necessarily imply that any description of an ethnic group is in fact just someone's idiosyncratic way of representing cultural life. An individual's understanding must be further understood in terms of the particular set of wider social, political, and cultural practices that have shaped that understanding (Giroux 1988). When a knowledge claim is disassociated from the particular social practices that generated it, then it is universalized. A universal claim, in turn, serves to perpetuate the hegemonic tendencies that multicultural education seeks to challenge.

To the extent that a group's cultural life cannot be subsumed into a master narrative, the use of such a narrative only gives the illusion of plurality. That narrative represents a monovocal discourse that negates diversity if majority and minority voices within an ethnic group are not heard. Representing groups as dynamic involves representing the conflicts, contradictions, and consensus that exist within, and between, ethnic groups. To represent the plurality of voices that compete for legitimacy, any description of a group's social life needs to be interrogated to uncover the politics of representation implicated in that description: Who holds the power to speak for the group? Who defines whom, who interprets, how in what ways, and towards what end? (Crichlow et al. 1990)

Recognizing both the collective and partial nature of knowledge claims does not negate the need for teachers to learn about such things as the structure of the Mexican family, the costumes of Puerto Ricans, the religious beliefs of the Hopi, etc. It does suggest, however, that any description must make explicit how that account has been configured at a particular intersection of ethnicity, class, gender, and so on. From this perspective, when teachers listen to a description of the Mexican family structure, such as the one quoted earlier in this chapter, they must interrogate that representation to uncover those who are acknowledged and neglected by that account. For instance, the teacher can ask those who present the information questions such as: Who are the Mexican people represented in this account? Who are the Mexican people who cannot see themselves in those descriptions? Are Mexican families headed by women represented in that description? Are families who have lived in the United States in relative isolation from other Mexican families represented in that description?

NEGOTIATING CULTURAL LIFE IN THE CLASSROOM

In the preceding paragraphs I have provided a rationale for conceptualizing culture as dialogical and multivocal. The implications of this conceptualization for the task of the multicultural educator (i.e., creating a classroom that is a democratic, pluralistic, and empowers students) are explored next. When one turns away from a focus on within-group patterns towards patterns of social relations between groups, the studies of culture and social criticism become intertwined (Rosaldo 1989). Following Walzer (1989), Rosaldo stated that "social criticism involves making complex ethical judgments about existing social arrangements" (p. 182). The task of the social critic is to improve the lives of social groups that have been subordinated. Several proponents of multicultural education stress the importance of providing teacher education curricula that explicitly address issues of racism, sexism, and classism (e.g., Banks 1991, 1993; Sleeter and Grant 1988; Suzuki 1984). All of these are social behaviors that do not emerge from differences nor do they emerge within a homogeneous group. McDermott and Gospodinoff (1981) noted that these behaviors are all derived in social spaces marked by heterogeneity and governed by a politics of social relationships that define different kinds of people as antagonists (cited in O'Connor 1989). From this perspective, multicultural teacher education curriculum needs to focus on helping teachers uncover and challenge practices and policies that translate differences into inequalities. Below I describe two approaches to this task. First, I attend to the possibilities offered when teachers engage in a public dialog with students. Next, I attend to the importance of making explicit the values that shape teachers' educational choices.

Knowledge and Public Dialog

Several of the authors referenced in this chapter have written extensively on the dialogical nature of a pedagogy that fosters social criticism, that is, critical pedagogy (e.g., Freire 1985; Giroux and McLaren 1991; McLaren 1991; O'Connor 1989; Simon, 1992). It is beyond the scope of this paper to provide a detailed discussion of critical pedagogy. I will, however, illustrate the value and necessity of engaging teacher education students in dialogical teaching practices that make possible the deconstruction and reconstruction of cultural life in the classrooms and elsewhere.

Listening to the Cultural Other

A process for understanding, as Gadamer (1975) noted, involves openness to questions posed by others and to the responses others give to the questions we pose to them. From this perspective, a critical component of multicultural approaches to teaching involves constantly risking teachers' preconceptions or, using Gadamer's term, prejudices in a dialog with Cultural Others. If all knowledge is assumed to be partial to an individual's social location, it is through conversation that people can learn to see things from someone else's perspective. Through our efforts at finding points of connection with the Other, we can enlarge our horizons, and, eventually, as suggested by Gadamer, fuse our horizon with that of the Cultural Other. As people share their personal experiences with others, they can begin to recognize that what they have experienced as personal failures are socially produced conflicts and contradictions shared by some but not by others (Weedon 1987). This process of discovery can lead to questioning the existing social arrangements that translate differences into antagonisms.

Michelle Fine (1987) has described the process by which institutionalized policies and practices produce silence in the schools in an attempt to bury the contradictions of what is and what should be. The possibilities for a more open dialog in the classroom are constrained by power/knowledge differentials and institutional policies that tend to privilege certain perspectives and silence others (e.g., teachers over students, Western-European perspectives over non-Western, etc.). Multicultural education as a form of social criticism must develop pedagogical practices that circumvent these problems. These practices must allow for the possibility of each person speaking from any one of his or her many identities and from others listening to the plurality of voices a person can articulate. Multicultural knowledge will not emerge when we listen to only part of what the Cultural Others have to say. Students need to be heard when they answer a teacher's question as well as when they pose questions to teachers.

The conceptualization of social identity advanced in this essay confers centrality to its permeable dimension, recognizing that it is being continuously recreated. This conceptualization of identity further emphasizes the necessity of dialog among teachers and students. Paying attention to students' identities involves teachers who know how to listen to students' accounts of what is. Students' stories are telling the "history of our becoming, our own unfinished, partial, and contingent story of the self" (McLaren 1991, p. 137). As significant forces in shaping a child's social environment, teachers are in a unique position to help students develop identities of empowerment as opposed to identities of subordination.

Disrupting the Teacher-Student Dualism

A pedagogy that listens to what Others have to say to us rejects a transmission model of teaching in favor of a reciprocal interaction model. This reciprocity involves flexibility on the part of teachers as they focus not only on the intentions of their practices but also on the consequences as perceived by students (Cummins 1986). This reciprocity involves teachers who can bridge the distance that separates them from their students such that they (the teachers) can identify with them; they can recognize the "'we' that is in an 'I' and an 'I' that is a 'we'" (Hegel, cited in Taylor 1992, p. 50). As noted earlier, when depicting the Cultural Other, teachers need to recognize that they are also depicting themselves. Reciprocity involves teachers who examine how the varied ways of interpreting students' behaviors can serve the purpose of social transformation versus maintenance of the status quo. Another element of reciprocity in teaching is that teachers and students articulate and strive toward a common goal (Taylor 1992). Reciprocity involves teachers who explicitly acknowledge to students what teachers have learned from interacting with students.

Multiculturalism recognizes the potential worth of the stories people from diverse cultural backgrounds, diverse sexual orientations, diverse religious beliefs, diverse abilities, and diverse social classes have to tell about what it means to be a human being (Ibid.). The construction of multicultural knowledge requires altering social relations of knowledge production that have fixed social actors in a traditional teacher/student dichotomy. The construction of multicultural knowledge in the classroom does not involve teachers giving knowledge to students; instead, it involves people sharing and challenging each other's views.

A pedagogy that fosters social criticism recognizes the centrality of students' experiences as teachers work to help students develop a greater understanding of how their realities are historically and socially constructed (Sleeter 1991). I would add that students' knowledge is also central for developing in teachers an awareness of how teachers' realities are historically and socially constructed. By listening to the stories Cultural Others tell them, teachers can learn to examine how their own pedagogical practices and perspectives perpetuate inequalities or improve the lives of students who come from socially subordinated groups.

To illustrate the impact of teachers' public dialog on students, I will quote two minority teacher education majors I interviewed for a study on multicultural teacher education:

> [Teresa, Mexican-American junior]: I remember it was a math teacher and I don't remember what he was talking about anyway. I was sitting there looking through the book and he was talking about something totally off the subject of math. Someone said, "Oh, don't you do" something, some kind of work, and he goes "That? No, that is for Mexicans, that is labor work, that's for Mexicans." Everyone just looked at me, and I didn't even catch it and this one guy said "Oh my God! did you hear what he said?" I said, "What?" I was not paying attention. Then they told me, then the bell rang. I went and talked to another teacher...Then I went up to talk to him about it and he said, "Oh, I don't look at you that way. You are just another cute girl with a nice touch." He said that! Can you believe a teacher! I just walked out of the class. (Montecinos in press)

Teresa's experience evidenced her teacher's blatant prejudice and the students' ability to name it and address it. From my perspective, what makes this teacher especially damaging to students is not that he makes racist statements. What makes him harmful is his inability to acknowledge his own prejudices when confronted by Teresa. Teachers, and students, bring into the classroom a vision of teaching and act through their cultural lenses, prejudices, and stereotypes. Successful multicultural teachers are the ones who are open to learning from their students by critically and publicly examining and changing those views that preclude them from relating positively to the Cultural Other.

In contrast to Teresa's story, Cheryl had a teacher who was willing to admit to the difficulties of the task, to acknowledge his own limitations, and to offer students a multicultural education:

> [Cheryl, African American sophomore]: My junior year I took a black history course....In South Africa they use blacks as cops and they had to report on their own people. We divided into groups, half the time whether you were black or white, half were the natives and the other half the cops. If you saw somebody do something you had to report it....You are lucky to have a job but then if you do your job which is to keep your own people down, then what is going to happen to you...We did things like that all the time...the White people in there realized that, you know, that it is a tough thing...He was the best teacher I ever had black or white. He realized it was hard being a white person teaching black history because people would say "What do you know?" What made him good was because he showed both sides of the coin.

The Values that Shape Practice

Freire (1985) has argued that learning how to ask critical questions regarding existing social arrangements must start from learning how to analyze one's immediate reality. Teacher education courses represent an aspect of the immediate reality of the teacher education student. In what follows I suggest that one place to begin engaging students in a public dialog of their desires, hopes, and values is to problematize teacher educators' choices for multicultural education.

As it has been described at length in the literature, multicultural education means different things to different people (Sleeter and Grant 1988). These alternative meanings cannot be understood as value-free—they are assumed to represent alternative social interests. Habermas (1972, cited in Gordon, Miller, and Rollock 1990) described three types of knowledge interests and their corresponding methodological traditions that are reflected in the five approaches to multicultural education described by Sleeter and Grant (1988; prediction and control, understanding, and emancipation. These are delineated below.

To the extent that advocates of the *Teaching the Culturally Different* approach stress that minority students must develop appropriate learning skills to cope with taken-for-granted school demands, their primary interest is in creating knowledge that allows for the prediction and control of these students' learning. To the extent that proponents of the *Human Relations* approach emphasize tolerance and acceptance within existing social structures, they are primarily interested in creating knowledge that allows for cross-cultural understanding. To the extent that proponents of the *Education that is Multicultural and Social Reconstructionist*, the *Single-group Studies*, and the *Multicultural Education* approaches are interested in promoting social change, their primary interest is in emancipatory knowledge.

With the demise of objectivism, and its corresponding foundationalist view of knowledge, it is not possible to talk about an epistemologically 'right' approach to multicultural education. In other words, none of these approaches has a priori claim to truth; therefore, teachers' choices cannot be based on a morally neutral set of facts. The truth value ascribed by a teacher to any one of these approaches depends upon the teacher's values and beliefs. One task of teacher education, then, is to help students make explicit the values and belief systems that shape their choices for multicultural education.

When one reads empirical studies on multicultural teacher education, however, little attention is given to ways in which the curriculum helps teachers make choices for multicultural education. Typically, what seems to happen is that the teacher educator, or the textbook author, has made the choice for teachers through the selection of particular content and pedagogy. Understanding knowledge as socially constructed suggests that the multicultural teacher educator is not a neutral scientist/expert but rather that his or her practices are embedded in biography, commitments, and values. By making explicit how these factors have impacted his or her choice for multicultural education, the teacher educator can model the processes of examining how values shape practice. For example, teacher educators could make explicit their own views on the goals of multicultural education. They could publicly examine how they came to believe in those goals and not others, and they could publicly examine why and how they have chosen to ask students to complete certain tasks, and so on. An open discussion of the teacher educator's practices is crucial to opening spaces for legitimizing alternative discourses because as Simon (1992) reminds us, teaching practices that attempt to authorize particular forms of social organization threaten to disorganize others. Similarly, critical pedagogy is deeply concerned with exposing the teacher/student relationship not only in terms of its effectiveness but also in terms of power/knowledge differentials that are constructed through voice and silence. If critical teacher educators expect teachers to alter this differential in the K–12 classrooms, then they must model it in their own classroom.

Following and elaborating on the teacher educator's modeling, students can begin to ask themselves: What kind of person am I if I take this approach? What kind of society will I help construct if I take this approach? Why do I feel comfortable choosing this approach and not that one? and so on. Instead of spending time reading or listening to generalized descriptions of Cultural Others, students can compare and contrast choices made by different people in the class and outside of it. Working in groups students can examine questions such as: What can explain the fact that most people in the class choose approach X? What commonalities can be seen among those who choose X? Among those who choose Y? How are the people who choose X different from those who choose Y? An examination of these types of questions can better illuminate the social construction of cultural life than listening to generalizations about an ethnic group's cultural life.

SUMMARY

In this chapter I have argued for a conceptualization of multicultural knowledge that emphasizes knowing: (a) how to uncover the multiplicity of ways in which members of an ethnic group talk about social life; (b) how to interrogate these alternative perspectives to uncover what Crichlow et al. (1990) have called "the politics of representation" implicated in each account; and (c) how to interrogate and challenge social behaviors that emerge in places where diverse groups come together and that translate differences into inequalities. These types of knowledge, rather than knowledge of a group's cultural patterns, can help teachers steer away from stereotypical thinking, nurture the diversity found in multicultural classrooms, and foster educational equity.

Knowing patterned descriptions of the Cultural Other and acting on that knowledge risks forming social relations that subdue the Cultural Other. In the situation described at the beginning of this chapter my acquaintance and her hosts seemed to have imposed a meaning of time on the Cultural Other, thus, compelling them to act in certain ways. Alternatively, my acquaintance and her hosts could have engaged in a conversation to negotiate a common meaning of time to govern their cross-cultural encounter. This need for dialog and negotiation can also be seen in the classrooms. If teachers are told that children from a particular ethnic group have a particular learning style, but they do not know how to uncover the specifics of a child's social identity, then teachers risk creating a child that has that learning style. Thus, rather than knowing the Cultural Other, what teachers end up doing is creating the Cultural Other according to predetermined specifications learned in their multicultural teacher education courses.

NOTES

I am grateful to Christine E. Sleeter and Robert Boody for their comments on an earlier draft of this manuscript.

1. In this paper I use the term "Cultural Other" to refer to people or groups with whom we interact that we perceive as different from ourselves.

REFERENCES

Banks, J. A. 1991. A curriculum for empowerment, action, and change. In *Empowerment through multicultural education*, ed. C. E. Sleeter, pp. 125–142. Albany: State University of New York Press.

———. 1993. The canon debate, knowledge construction, and multicultural education. *Educational Researcher* 22: 4–14.

Bullivant, B. M. 1989. Culture: Its nature and meaning for educators. In *Multicultural education: Issues and perspectives*, ed. J. Banks and C. A. McGee Banks, pp. 27–45. Boston, MA: Allyn and Bacon.

Crichlow, W. et al. 1990. Multicultural ways of knowing: Implications for practice. *Journal of Education* 172: 101–117.

Cummins, J. 1986. Empowering minority students: A framework for intervention. *Harvard Educational Review* 56: 18–36.

Ferdman, B. M. 1990. Literacy and cultural identity. *Harvard Educational Review* 60: 181–204.

Fine, M. 1987. Silencing in public schools. *Language Arts* 64: 157–174.

Freire, P. 1985. *The politics of education: Culture, power, and liberation*. South Hadley, MA: Bergin and Garvey.

Gadamer, H. G. 1975. *Truth and method*. edited and translated by G. Barden and J. Cumming. New York: Seabury Press.

Giroux, H. A. and McLaren, P. 1991. Radical pedagogy as cultural politics: Beyond the discourse of critique and anti-utopianism. In *Theory/pedagogy/politics: Texts for change*. ed. D. Morton and M. Zavarzadeh, pp. 154–186. Champaign, IL: University of Illinois Press.

Giroux, H. A. 1988. Postmodernism and the discourse of educational criticism. *Journal of Education* 170: 5–30.

Gordon, E. W., Miller, F., and Rollock, D. 1990. Coping with communicentric bias in knowledge production in the social sciences. *Educational Researcher* 19: 14–19.

Habermas, J. 1972. *Knowledge and human interest*. Boston: Beacon Press.

Kellner, D. 1988. Postmodernism as social theory: Some challenges and problems. *Theory, Culture, and Society* 5: 239–269.

McCarthy, C. and Crichlow, W. 1993. Introduction: Theories of representation, theories of race. In *Race, identity, and representation in education*. ed. C. McCarthy and W. Crichlow, pp. vii–xxix. New York: Routledge.

McDermott, R. P. and Gospodinoff, K. 1981. Social contexts for ethnic borders and school failure. In *Culture and the bilingual classroom*. ed. H. T. Trueba, G. P. Guthrie and K. H. Au. Rowley, MA: Newbury House.

McDiarmid, G. W. 1992. What to do about differences? A study of multicultural education for teacher trainees in the Los Angeles Unified School District. *Journal of Teacher Education* 43: 83–93.

McLaren, P. 1991. Decentering culture: Postmodernism, resistance, and critical pedagogy. In *Current perspectives on the culture of schools*. ed. N. B. Wyner, pp. 231–257. Boston: Brookline Books.

Montecinos, C. In press. Remembering high schools: Students of color make the case for an education that is multicultural. *The High School Journal*.

O'Connor, T. 1989. Cultural voice and strategies for multicultural education. *Journal of Education* 171: 57–74.

Rojas, M. 1991. Reinventing identity. *Report on the Americas* 24: 29–33.

Rosaldo, R. 1989. *Culture and truth: The remaking of social analysis.* Boston: Beacon Press.

Simon, R. I. 1992. *Teaching against the grain.* New York: Bergin and Harvey.

Sleeter, C. E. 1991. Introduction: Multicultural education and empowerment. In *Empowerment through multicultural education.* ed. C. E. Sleeter, pp. 1–23. Albany: State University of New York Press.

Sleeter, C. E. and Grant, C. A. 1988. *Making choices for multicultural education.* Columbus, OH: Merrill Publishing.

Suzuki, B. H. 1984. Curriculum transformation for multicultural education. *Education and Urban Society* 16: 294–322.

Taylor, C. 1992. *Multiculturalism and "the politics of recognition".* Princeton: Princeton University Press.

Walzer, M. 1987. *Interpretation and social racism.* Cambridge, MA: Harvard University Press.

Weedon, C. 1987. *Feminist practice and poststructuralist theory.* London: Basil Blackwell.

11

Mary Ritchie

Whose Voice Is It Anyway?: Vocalizing Multicultural Analysis

Over the span of the history of multicultural education there have emerged a number of struggles concerning position, hegemony, epistemology, turf, efficacy, politics, and ideology; the list continues to grow. At the heart of the issue, however, is who is articulating what multicultural education really means. In others words, whose words are those? Whose voice, or which voices, contribute to the song of diverse education?

In the past several decades there have emerged "two somewhat different multicultural education traditions," says Christine Sleeter (1993). Educators of color, influenced by the struggle for civil justice, have pressed for input into curriculum. As this idea gained impetus, liberal whites from both the academic and the public education systems entered the mix. The movement toward multicultural identity became clouded by disputes over meaning, some of the fallout being backlash over "political correctness." These debates have been focused in the academic community as arguments over what constitutes a foundation of knowledge. They have often been tendered in language which nonacademics do not use but which sets up barriers to real cross-cultural communication. I hope to address some issues regarding how to bridge that jargon barrier in this chapter.

Multiculturalism may become a "problematic"[1] for people of color. In the process of creating a multicultural discourse, people of color have come to be the ingredients of the multicultural mix, which the dominant culture is determining for us to be accurate or authentic. There exists the potential for us to become the products of a meat grinder multicultural process. Our ideas and voices risk becoming blurred and buried by constant attempts at understanding people of color from a point of view which reifies a Eurocentric system and academic process of domination under the guise of expanding the current knowledge base. This is not acceptable to me, nor, I would guess, to other persons of color. We want a say in the outcome; we can speak for ourselves. What needs to happen is that our voices not be usurped or interpreted by our "benefactors."

The idea for this paper grew out of a conversation that I had with one of the editors of this book. She and I were discussing a recent interchange which I had with a friend over a paper that we had written together and which we presented for publication in a feminist teaching journal. My friend, a member of a nondominant group and also a university professor, did the final rewrite for the paper; when I read it I noticed that my words had disappeared in favor of an academic voice, but I agreed with what she had written and decided it would probably have a better chance of getting published. We have different styles in our approach to language and living which we work out in conversation. That difference was missing from the paper, and the editors of the journal did not publish it. We had succeeded in undoing a multivoiced piece and reshaping it into something monolithic. I say "we" because I kept my opinion to myself in favor of wanting to see what would happen.

Reflecting on this incident, I began to ask myself some questions. What happens to the words of nondominant "others" when we are asked to participate in a setting which has been built on the demise of ourselves? Who benefits, and why? Do academics of the dominant group, female as well as male, realize there may be a disparity in process and power between themselves and oppressed persons? If not, why not? Is there a difference between what academics write and what academics believe about language and oppression?

My place in this debate is a paradox, I think. Currently I am an undergraduate, age forty-eight, at a very small Midwest university. As a member of a nondominant group, a woman in midlife, and as a student I experience a kind of powerful powerlessness; I can have some influence on academia and oppression, and I can do it in the name of expanding my education. At the same time, I am plunging into academia head first. I hope to be one of those persons who will exert influence over how students think about the global process of living. My plan, however, is to do it without succumbing to what I call the lure of the jargon god. I want to avoid assuming the position of academic elitism.

This paper is a personal account, an act of resistance in a forum which demands attention to the power structure of nonpersonal, perhaps even antipersonal, academic writing. I believe that academic discourse is contained by certain precepts, often not articulated, which create boundaries and provide a gatekeeping function of exclusion that benefits those who seek to keep academic endeavor in the realm of "the canon." For example, rather than being simply a matter of style, academic speaking and writing is bound to a format that is recognizable among academics themselves as "serious." Often jargon-ridden, stilted, and personally distanced from both the reader and the writer, this writing serves notice that the boundaries of higher education have not been breached and that the writer has paid her dues and passed muster for proper attention to the sensibilities of fellow members of the academic community. After all, without this identifier, how would elite intellectuals know one another? What would happen to a "higher" education which was understandable by "the masses"?

Having been one of those "masses," I now find that I have difficulty, myself, with avoiding jargon. As an undergraduate, I am reading reams of academese. When I am writing, I write to standards set by the university which demand academic style and format. As a result, I have learned to talk and write like a member of the community that I am invested in changing. This process is sure to change me as a knower who knows from a "different" point of view. Often, I have to try harder to talk like a "normal" person when I am with people who do not live within the academy. As I write this paper, I am overwhelmed with the urge to succumb to convention and just write arcane, academic jargon. It is just so much easier than figuring out what to say, what I think, in plain and personal language. Personal politics and "objectivity" do not enter the picture here. This is hard work. If I say what I mean, plainly, and from my own point of view, however, I relieve the risk of being general and vague, and I take up the risk of giving offense and information that is rooted in my own point of view.

However, in the process of taking a stand, I leave no room for others to subsume my interpretation within their own. This, I believe, is the heart of the issue of multicultural process. We must develop ways to hear and hold multiple points of view within a dynamic process of knowing and understanding; we must resist the urge to reify our own position at the expense of someone different from us. We must not subsume the position. What does that mean, exactly? Perhaps some examples right about now would be useful.

The language of persons of color gets subsumed by the dominant culture in a variety of ways. The greatest instance occurs when dominant persons frame what nondominant persons believe or say in words which more readily describe their own existence in terms that they understand. Currently, there is debate regarding whether or not Native American religion should be taught by non-Native people. Some contention has been made that precepts of religion are universal and that the process of describing Indian spirituality is no different from describing other religious beliefs and practices. The notion that religion has universal precepts comes from the philosophical underpinnings of Western culture. Those very ideas imbue those teachings of Western universalism with power. According to Vine Deloria, Jr. (1993), unless this political disparity of power is recognized and attended to, the academy will "continue to perpetuate misconceptions and misperceptions" about Native spirituality. Deloria suggests that "unless and until religious studies, as well as every other social science, adopts new language and a new orientation," Western civilization will continue to "orient itself toward the proposition that...[it] is necessarily the highest expression of human striving" (Ibid.). Without an understanding of what it means to live a spiritual life very opposed to Eurocentric individuality, non-Natives attempting to teach Indian religion are merely talking to themselves. Their talk, however, has lasting implications for Native Americans as we are overcoming issues of identity imposed by centuries of outside definition.

However, misdefinition happens cross-culturally between persons of color as well. It is not caused by misunderstanding. It is a struggle for power. Eurocentric definitions of power give rise to struggle within non-European communities regarding what action is best concerning how to "fit" with Eurocentrism. As a Neshnabek[2] woman I have no idea what it means to be African American, or Asian-American, except in the broadest sense of racial difference. The information most available to me regarding identity/reality in these communities has been permutated by the Euro-American dream.

The distancing qualities of dominant *culture-talk* recently became very real for me at a meeting I attended with women from around my state who are working on a project for incorporating Women's Studies into the non-academic community. Part of the meeting was devoted to exploring ways to interact with various community projects. As I began my portion of the presentations, I was acutely aware of the fact that I was speaking from my life as an urban Indian woman while the others were speaking about programs and plans with which they were involved. I ended up feeling embarrassed and silly; the dominant culture gives little space for reality based in experience. Someone who is speaking experientially is suspected of "coming to consciousness" about an obvious issue. My guess is that the women in that room had no clue that there was a difference in the way we were operating. While I struggled to fit real life into a "program" agenda the others in the room listened with pained expressions on their faces. They attempted to be empathic, but, without a language for it, there seemed to be no way to bridge the cultural gap. Instead, I did the old standby; I, because it is in my best interest to know the dominant culture, helped them over the moment of unpleasantness by turning the discussion around to focus on them and their issues. This was not a "bad" move, but it was expedient. While I listened to their concerns and fears, I also did not put responsibility on them for examining those issues personally. Their voice became my voice in an effort to smooth out the encounter. Instead of a variety of ideas, we arrived at a "consensus" built on me finding ways to make them feel more comfortable. How useful is that? Who ends up speaking?

One way to think about issues of voice, power, and discursive meaning is to take a look at a book currently "hot" in multicultural circles, *I, Rigoberta Menchu.* The teller of the story, Nobel Peace Prize winner and Quiche' Mayan woman, Rigoberta Menchu, talks openly about her personal feelings and thoughts regarding her change from a silent peasant worker to a speaker against oppression internationally. What she keeps private are the cultural "secrets" which make up the context of her life and her understanding of the world. By standards of privacy held in the United States, she has it backwards. We expect that the context and practices of a culture will be common knowledge but that individual understanding and interpretation of context and practice are to be private. In a classroom discussion of the book, several women reported thinking that Menchu was contradicting herself because she held beliefs which did not mesh with each other. They were confused as to how she could be at once a Christian and a pantheist, a revolutionary and a conservative, a traditionalist and a leader taking her people out of the past and into the uncertain future. Menchu, in a word, is a paradox by notions of Western, capitalist identity. To hold more than one point of view is to embrace cognitive dissonance; the world must be interpreted one way or another. This ability to see a wider view is probably unsettling to Western minds. However, it seems necessary to a multicultural process.

Paying attention to many voices is not new to people of color; what is new is us paying attention to us. Our languages provide us with affirmation that what we see and hear is real. We must remember that people from the dominant culture rarely have to think about the world in ways that are "different" for them. While we struggle to maintain a sense of ourselves, we must also be aware of the need for outsiders to explore and challenge their own belief system. The work of social change requires all people to be heard, even people whose comments make us question our own authority to be part of the process.

Menchu, for example, recounts that she made a decision to learn Spanish, the language of her people's oppressor. Learning the language of the oppressor is a dangerous move for nondominant persons. Language shapes reality, forces us to use it as a technology of hegemony. When we speak in the language of our oppressor, we must be aware of how we are being swallowed up by concepts we did not create.

This is the problem of multiculturalism for people of color. Who is determining the concept? Who is creating the language? The academic community abides by rules of tradition and custom. Tradition and custom are powerful means of maintaining solidarity and power, and for disseminating knowledge. Academia assumes authority for the process in order to control the outcome. All arguments about the political correctness of the problem aside, where are the voices of people of color in all this debate?

Do we wait for the mainstream players to determine what our role will be and how we will speak from that role? Or do we stand aside as the steam roller of multiculturalism passes? Do we want to be involved in this debate? If so, in what capacity?

Personally, I think it is time to call academia on the collective carpet for not practicing good science. Appeals to tradition and authority are labeled "weak" and are discouraged for critical thinkers. However, evidence gathered from experience and tested by scientists lacks the point of view of the person of color, who often uses the appeal to authority and tradition as reason for doing something. Indeed, the point of view of anyone not entrenched in Western, empirical scientific custom is often considered uninformed and parochial. Anyone practicing good Western science appeals not to authority and custom, but to reasoned examination and replication. The question becomes what constitutes reason? Non-Western rationales exist. Academic science need only hear their voices to incorporate them into western academia. Some academics are investigating indigenous knowledge systems and learning that empirical science is not only the province of "advanced" cultures coming out of an Enlightenment tradition. The difference is in the way that science gets postulated and to what use it is put.

In societies which utilize tradition and custom as a way to know, empiricism is put to use to understand one's relationship within a "natural" order, not to overcome the limits of nature in an attempt to take one's place in manifest destiny.

This is not just my idea. For example, Evelyn Fox-Keller (1992) writes:

> Until we find an adequate way of integrating the impact of multiple social and political forces, psychological predisposi-tions, experimental constraints, and cognitive demands on the growth of science, working scientists will continue to find their more traditional mind-sets...far more adequate. And they will continue to view a mind-set that sometimes seems to grant force to beliefs and interests but not to "nature" as fundamentally incompatible, unintegrable, and laughable. (p. 36)

Western capitalism is built on notions of scientific method, hence the tendency in academia to pursue notions of universality and generalizabilty. Multiculturalism should be built on the concept that "[t]he 'limits to what we are able to utter and conceive' are cultural in nature. The lived experiences of people in a culture are different from those people occupying a distinctly different culture, and the more distant the cultures, the more different the limits," say Yvonne Dion-Buffalo and John Mohawk (1992, p. 17). They go on to say that the world contains fewer than a dozen civilizations, including the "west," but that there are 3000 to 5000 "distinct indigenous societies" which greatly offers the possibility of experi-encing "other voices" (Ibid.).

Native America has asserted its voice in the debate over what sort of influence the Haudenosaunee had on the Constitution of the United States. Bruce Johansen and Donald Grinde (1993) assert that the "reason the debate over influence has been so heated may be that it involves a new intellectual paradigm in which those people previously thought of only as subjects or informants now seek a role in shaping the agenda of debate and discussion" (p. 31). Johansen and Grinde also believe that "this debate may be less about multiculturalism than about the de-Europeanization of North America's history" (Ibid.). If this is not a decentering of power as it stands in Western culture, I do not know what is. The logic of linearity is reaching the end of its rope.

The strange issue here is that people of color are using the tools of oppression, language, and education to undo the power structure of the dominant culture. My belief is that the principles of patriarchal oppression have come back to bite white men in their collective derrieres. However, unless we wish to bite ourselves, we, members of the nondominant community must exercise caution and restraint in our attempts to "develop" our communities and to enter the multicultural arena. We need to give ourselves permission to be ourselves and to adhere to our sense of the collective self over the individual self, to speak our own thoughts and invite European influenced outsiders to take part in understanding our ideas. We must make room for mistakes and insults; we must lead by example those who wish to construe our realities for us.

Western culture is poised on the edge of a great social revolution. If it is a revolution of polarities, then the "others" will be swallowed up in the swing of the pendulum back to the centrist position. If it is a revolution from above, then there will be little opportunity for people of lesser status to affect the future of society. It will be hierarchy as usual. If, however, the revolution comes from the circle, from the so-called margin, then the future will be different indeed. People of the circle, who speak in turn and listen to all with respect and dignity, who include the ideas of others as worthwhile and useful by consensus, and who know that one single voice is no more important than the collective voice, will provide the model for a global village and a true new world order.

NOTES

1. A problematic is "a particular organization of categories which at any given historical moment constitutes the limits of what we are able to utter and conceive." Terry Eagleton, *Ideology: An Introduction* (New York: Verso), 1991, pp. 5–6.
2. This is the word that Potawatomi people use to identify ourselves. Potawatomi is a word from another tribe which they use to describe us; while this is perfectly acceptable, it is not the word we use for ourselves. In other words, we are "ourselves" and we are also "others." It matters to keep that in mind as we think about who we are and how we fit in the order of the world.

REFERENCES

Burgo-Debray, Elizabeth, ed. 1992. *I, Rigoberta Menchu: An Indian Woman in Guatemala*. London: Verso.

Deloria, Vine, Jr. 1993. Electronic communication, June 7.

Dion-Buffalo, Dionne, and Mohawk, John. Winter 1992. Thoughts from an autochthonous center: Postmodernism and cultural studies. *Akwe:kon Journal* 9(4): 16–21.

Fox-Keller, Elizabeth,. 1992. *Secrets of life, secrets of death: Essays on Language, gender and science*. New York: Routledge.

Johansen, Bruce and Donald Grinde, Jr. Summer, 1993. Native voices and diffusion of an idea. *Akwe:kon: A Journal of Indigenous Issues* 10(2): 30–39.

Sleeter, Christine. In a letter to the author. August 1993.

12

Buscando America: The Contribution of Critical Latino Educators to the Academic Development and Empowerment of Latino Students in the U.S.

Estoy buscando America
y temo no encontrarte,
tus hijos se han perdido
entre esta oscuridad,

I'm looking for you, America
and I fear not finding you
your children are now lost
within this great darkness,

Te estoy llamando America
pero no me repondes.
es que te han desaparecido
los que temen la verdad,

I'm calling you America
but you do not respond,
for you've been kidnapped
by those who fear the truth,

Sigo pensando America,
que vamos a encontrarte,
ese es nuestro destino,
nuestra necesidad,

I keep thinking America
that we will surely find you,
this is our destiny
and our necessity,

Si el sueño de uno,
es el sueño de todos
romper las cadenas
y echarnos andar

If the dream of one,
can be the dream of many
to break the chains
and begin the work,

Entonces tengamos confianza
que America es nuestra casa,

Then we shall have confidence
that America is our home,

Te estoy buscando America,
nuestro futuro espera
y ante que se nos muera
te vamos a encontrar.

I'm looking for you America
our future awaits us
and before you pass away
we shall find you again.

Ruben Blades

The words from the song "Buscando America" by Ruben Blades strongly echo for me what constitutes the heart of our struggle as

319

critical educators. We are in search of America but not the America that for so long has been defined by Euro-Americans. We are in search of the true America—an America of multiple cultures, multiple histories, multiple regions, multiple realities, multiple identities, multiple ways of living, surviving, and being human. No where is this struggle for the true America more profoundly being waged than in the classrooms of public schools in the United States.

DIFFICULTIES FACED BY LATINO STUDENTS

Despite thirty years of educational reforms and compensatory programs, Latino students in the United States continue to experience much difficulty in adjusting to the traditional expectations of the public schools. For many of these students, there exist cultural, class, and linguistic barriers that prevent their active participation and successful movement through the educational system. These barriers persist in students' lives in a variety of ways. Whether overtly or covertly, intentionally or unintentionally, the cultural standards and norms of the English-speaking culture of the mainstream shape, mold, and influence greatly teacher-student interactions, parent-teacher communication, teacher demands and expectations, the curriculum, instructional approaches, achievement testing, and the system of meritocracy utilized to evaluate and track students through the system.

As a consequence, it is not surprising to discover that in a variety of studies (Cardenas and First 1985; Cummins 1986; Fernandez and Velez 1989; Darder and Upshur 1991) that focus on the academic development of Latino students in public schools, there are a variety of barriers and environmental conditions which are consistently identified as contributing dramatically to their under achievement. These include:

- cultural conflicts between the school and home;

- language differences;

- stereotypical attitudes which persist despite all the talk about diversity and multicultural education;

- teachers who are ignorant about the realities faced by their students;

- insufficient role models for students of color;

- lack of knowledge by teachers regarding the pedagogical needs of bilingual/bicultural students;

- inconsistent and too infrequent communication between the school and parents;

- curriculum that is not connected to the student's lives nor reflective of their cultural values, beliefs, and practices;

- lack of adequate curriculum materials and technological equipment to enhance the student's learning opportunities;

- texts and educational materials that reflect inaccuracies and distortions or completely ignore the historical contributions of Latinos to U.S. and world history;

- bilingual programs that fail to support the development of genuine bilingualism;

- incompetent teachers teaching in bilingual programs;

- testing that reflects cultural and class biases;

- homework policies that are inconsistent with the realities of students' lives;

- overcrowded classrooms and uncomfortable conditions;

- toleration of racist attitudes and hate crimes against Latino students;

- questionable use of expulsion and other disciplinary actions;

- and utilization of educational funds to support honors/gifted students at the expense of those students who have greater needs.

The impact of these persistent conditions are quite evident in the grade retention and drop-out rates of Latino students across the country. In large urban school districts such as Los Angeles,

San Francisco, New York, Chicago, and Miami, attrition and drop-out rates for Latino students can range anywhere from 40 to 70 percent. In addition, the retention rates for many Latino students far surpass those of their white counterparts. This is particularly troubling since studies indicate that Latino students who have been delayed in their schooling as a result of retention are far more likely to drop-out of high school (Velez 1989). Even when Latino students manage to graduate from high school, this does not guarantee that they will readily have access to a college education or that they will be successful in their pursuit of a degree.

WHAT LATINO STUDENTS NEED

Unfortunately, it is not unusual to hear educators smirk at studies that focus on Latino students and insist that what Latino students need is what all students need—namely competent teachers who care; adequate textbooks, materials and equipment; clean and safe environments; parents who are involved in their education; and opportunities for the future. While on one hand I wholeheartedly agree, on the other hand I adamantly challenge the hidden assimilationist intent to obscure the cultural conflicts and subordination faced by Latino students in the United States and the particular educational needs derived from this subject position—educational needs that must be addressed by public schools if we are to move toward a culturally democratic society.

Historical Identity and Collective Consciousness

Recently, while in my office one of my white colleagues was examining a poster with a collage of Chicano/Mexicano historical figures. He was trying to identify their photographs based on a recent Mexican history class he had taken in Mexico. As he moved through this task, he commented that despite the fact that he had been a history major in college and a real history buff all his life, he knew very little about Mexican history. As he said this, I thought about what it had been like to grow up as a Latina child in U.S. public schools, never hearing anything substantial about my own history or the contributions of Latinos to this country or the world.

Such an educational reality subjects and conditions Latino students to a realm of historical amnesia and to a perpetual foreign identity of otherness in our own country. It means growing up without a firm grasp of our collective historical identity; without a sense of how Latinos as a group have survived; without a sense of our collective historical movement as a people; and without the knowledge that would help us to better understand accurately our struggles on this land that we call America. More specifically, what I am suggesting is that Latino children cannot undergo a process of genuine empowerment without the opportunity to come to know who they are as historical beings, not only as individuals but also as social beings.

For Latinos, as for other subordinate cultures in the United States, the development and cultivation of a collective conscious-ness is an essential component to the formation of bicultural iden-tity and the development of voice in Latino students who attend public schools. As has been defined by a variety of sociologists, psychologists, and educators in the field (Valentine 1971; Ramirez and Castañeda 1974; Red Horse et al. 1981; Solis 1980; Rashid 1981; de Anda 1984; and Darder 1991), "biculturalism" is a term that is used to describe a phenomenon experienced by people of color who must survive in the midst of societal institutions which, more often than not, are defined by a system of both affective and behavioral standards that are in conflict with those of subordinate groups.

To understand ourselves as cultural beings requires that we understand the manner in which social power and control function to structure the world in which we exist and to define our place within that world. Hence, to speak of biculturalism in the United States solely from the standpoint of an individual psychological phenomenon without addressing the impact of social, political, and economic contexts that have historically sustained the cultural subordination of people of color would constitute a fraudulent act. It is impossible to ignore that every group in this country perceived outside of the English-speaking (anglocentric) mainstream shares a history of what Iris Marion Young (1990) terms "the five faces of oppression": marginalization, exploitation, cultural invasion, powerlessness, and violence. It is also significant to note that this has been the case even when a large majority of the members of a particular subordinate cultural group have become predominantly English speakers (i.e., Chicanos, Japanese-Americans, African Americans, etc.).

The overt struggles by Chicanos and Latinos to resist subordi-nation and retain a cultural identity over assimilation to a national (homogeneous) identity have long been viewed as divisive and un-American acts by the U.S. mainstream. To counter such ethnic and cultural "divisions" in the population, the conservative "melting pot" ideology was combined with the liberal doctrine of individualism to fuel the "Americanization" movements of this century—movements that were driven as much by politically naive and well-meaning intellectuals as by politically astute intellectuals concerned primarily with preserving the dominant interests of the status quo.

One of the most pervasive impacts of these movements was the systematic erosion of the collective identity of non–English-speaking cultural and ethnic communities, including the Latino community. In its place was substituted a national or "American" identity reinforced by the institutionalization of the cultural standards and norms of the English-speaking (anglocentric). This institutionalization of an English-speaking worldview in the United States insured that those already in power would not only perpetuate but maximize their control over the country's political system and economic wealth. Camouflaged by a rhetoric of national unity and prosperity, "American democracy" flourished. This meant that an English-speaking wealthy elite flourished, while all other cultural and ethnic groups were systematically repressed and relegated to a subordinate status.

The systemic subordination of those groups perceived as threatening to the core values of "American democracy" has been carried out (even today) by implicit (or hegemonic) rather than explicit mechanisms of social control. Hence the country's institutions have championed conformity to "democratic" values, in the face of rampant capitalism, an obsession with an ever-changing "modernity", and a doctrine of rugged individualism.

This hegemonic rhetoric has been nowhere more alive and well than in the discourse of public schooling. To be good U.S. citizens, Latinos have been expected to assimilate to "American" standards and values and in so doing, discard the values of their primary culture, breaking free of all bonds to a cultural or ethnic identity. Just as schooling has been deemed apolitical and neutral by the mainstream, so too embracing values of "American democracy" has principally been deemed and portrayed as a matter of individual choice and personal freedom rather than of political exigency. In both cases, the great rhetoric of "American democracy" was flawed, for it in fact functioned to veil the social processes of power and deny the existence of an institutionalized system of subordination at work—a system that rigorously perpetuated the anglocentric values inherent in the predominant, colonizing culture of the United States.

Bicultural Identity

It is in the midst of institutional practices driven by such hegemonic rhetoric that subordinate cultural groups have struggled to retain their cultural identity and find a voice in this country. Thus, it is no wonder that there would exist diverse and contradictory patterns of responses among people of color with respect to questions of cultural identity.

In *Culture and Power in the Classroom* (1991), I present a framework to describe generalized patterns of response prevalent among bicultural students. In an effort to shed light on our understanding of bicultural development, four primary patterns are examined. These include alienated, dualistic, separatist, and negotiated cultural responses. Within this bicultural framework, there also are responses which might best be described within the scope of bicultural affirmation. These responses are less fixed than those which fall into the previous four categories mentioned. Instead, they allow a greater flexibility in responding to the social environment, without the necessity to abandon the reality of one's experience as a bicultural human being. In considering bicultural identity, these five positions can also reflect predominant categories for determining the strength of cultural identity experienced by students of color.

In addition to a students' consistent participation (or nonparticipation) in their cultural community of origin, it is also important to understand that their cultural identity and predominant bicultural responses, are also influenced by their efforts to contend with the social tensions that are inherent in conditions of cultural subordination. As a consequence, students from subordinate groups must interact within societal structures that consistently produce varying levels of cultural conflict and dissonance. Their responses to the power differential and to their consequent inferior social status play an important role in the development of bicultural identity. For example, does a Latino student primarily respond to the social tensions of cultural subordination by accommodating to domination or does the student respond with resistance? In accommodating, the student may attempt to completely move away from identification with the Latino culture or, instead, function with two faces without engaging the conflict or contradiction in values which exist between the two worldviews. On the other hand, when Latino students respond with resistance, they may choose to separate from the dominant culture and segregate themselves within their own primary cultural community, or they may struggle to negotiate between the dominant and subordinate structure of values in an effort to actualize some degree of social change.

When Latino students are functioning from a greater sense of affirmation with respect to their bicultural existence, their responses reflect greater flexibility and movement. This is clearly evidenced when a student's particular interaction at any given moment is more likely than not to emanate from a critical assessment of the actual power relations at work and, based upon their assessment, to respond accordingly. Needless to say, this type of cognitive, physical, emotional, and spiritual flexibility requires a greater sense of consciousness related to one's identity as both an individual and a social being—a consciousness that supports and nurtures both personal and collective empowerment.

The Bicultural Voice

In his writings on the nature of voice, Henry Giroux (1988) describes voice in the following terms.

> Voice refers to the principles of dialogue as they are enunciated and enacted within particular social settings. The concept of voice represents the unique instances of self expression through which students affirm their own class, culture, racial, and gender identities...The category of voice, then refers to the means at our disposal—the discourses available to use—to make ourselves understood and listened to, and to define ourselves as active participants in the world. (p. 199)

In more specific terms, the bicultural voice points to a discourse that incorporates the world views, histories, and lived experiences of subordinate cultural groups in the United States. From this standpoint, Latino students have at their disposal the consciousness to (1) critically reflect upon collective and individual interactions with mainstream institutions; (2) affirm the knowledge they possess given their particular subject position in U.S. society; (3) resist domination through explicitly challenging the implicit mechanisms of cultural subordination that dehumanize, disempower, and obstruct their democratic rights; and (4) enter into relationships of solidarity as equal participants.

From my observations of Latino students, it is quite apparent that there exists a strong relationship between bicultural identity, critical social consciousness, and the development of the bicultural voice. For example, Latino students who principally exhibit responses of cultural alienation are least likely to possess a strong critical consciousness and hence, also least likely to reflect a bicultural voice. Most of these students resist adamantly any differentiation between themselves and the dominant culture with a greater tendency to identify with and conform to the "American" culture or to hold conflicting, dualistic perceptions of themselves. On the other hand, Latino students who possess a strong bicultural identity tend to display a greater critical understanding of social contexts and a greater proficiency for giving voice to their experience as bicultural human beings in the United States.

Classroom Conditions that Support the Development of Bicultural Identity and Voice

Culture is an enacted phenomenon. This is to say that it results from the consistent dynamic human responses and interactions among cultural groups that function to preserve, reproduce, negotiate, reconstruct, or transform collectively sustained social values and belief systems. Therefore, Latino students, in order to fully develop their understanding of and participation in their culture, require consistent opportunities to engage actively with members of their cultural group. Gloria Johnson Powell's (1970) work suggests that there is a significant correlation between positive self-concept and a student's opportunity to learn and develop academically within a school setting that respects, reinforces, and enacts their cultural worldview. This supports the notion that Latino students require people in their environment who can serve as active cultural agents, translators of the bicultural experience, and as examples of critically conscious adults with whom students can directly identify and consistently interact. Further, it has been observed that many bilingual Latino students are more likely to give voice to the bicultural discourse when there are bilingual Latino adults in their classroom environments who legitimate their perceptions, insights, and concerns than when these adults are not present. (Darder and Upshur 1991).

In structuring classroom life to affirm and encourage the development of student voices, teachers must

> organize classroom relationships so that students can draw on and confirm those dimensions of their histories and experiences that are deeply rooted in the surrounding community,...assume pedagogical responsibility for attempting to understand the relationships and forces that influence students outside the immediate context of the classroom,...develop curricula and pedagogical practices around those community traditions, histories, and forms of knowledge that are often ignored within the dominant school culture,...create the conditions where students come together to speak, to engage in dialogue, to share their stories, and to struggle together within social relations that strengthen rather than weaken possibilities for active citizenship. (Giroux 1988, p. 199–201)

Herein lies the foundation for creating the conditions for a critical and culturally democratic educational environment where

Latino students may come to know themselves and the world in relation to their own conditions, rather than based upon contrived notions of life that are often completely foreign to their own existence. The bicultural voice is awakened through a critical process of dialogue and reflection in which Latino students have the opportunity to reflect together on their common lived experiences, their personal perceptions of the bicultural process, and their common responses to issues of cultural resistance, alienation, negotiation, affirmation, and domination (Darder 1991).

In summary, Latino students require teachers in their environments who understand the dynamic of cultural subordination and the impact that this has upon students, their families, and their cultural communities. Latino students also need critically conscious teachers who come from their own cultural communities, can speak and instruct them in their native language, can serve as translators of the bicultural experience, and can reinforce an identity grounded in the cultural integrity of their own people. Latino students also require classroom relationships that make explicit social injustice and that reinforce their inalienable rights to participate and have a voice within and outside of the classroom environment. Further, they require dialogical approaches and curricular materials that will assist them in knowing themselves as historical beings and empowered subjects in the world.

CRITICAL PEDAGOGY AND THE EDUCATION OF LATINO STUDENTS

To attempt a brief discussion of critical pedagogy is in itself a difficult task, for there is always the danger of oversimplification and reductionism—both of which are completely contrary to its very foundations. So what is necessary to emphasize here is that critical pedagogy is not a technique, model, framework, or recipe for educational practice. Instead, it posits a set of principles for the enactment of an emancipatory classroom culture—principles that are intimately linked to a paradigm or way of thinking about human beings, culture, knowledge, social power, and the world. To understand education in this way means to deinstrumentalize the practice of teaching and infuse it with the possibilities of passion and creativity which are informed by the vibrant critical presence of both teachers and students. To support an educational environment that can sustain the complexity and diversity of such a reality requires educators who are theoretically well-grounded in principles of democratic schooling.

The following descriptions represent an effort to provide a very general introduction to the major principles that constitute the theoretical foundation of critical pedagogy.

Cultural Politics

The fundamental commitment of critical educators is to empower the powerless and transform those conditions which perpetuate human injustice and inequity (McLaren 1988). This purpose is inextricably linked to the fulfillment of what Paulo Freire (1970) defines as our "vocation"—to be truly humanized social agents in the world. Hence, a major function of critical pedagogy is to critique, expose, and challenge the manner in which schools impact upon the political and cultural life of students. Teachers must recognize how schools unite knowledge and power and how through this function they can work to influence or thwart the formation of critically thinking and socially active individuals.

Unlike traditional perspectives of education that claim to be neutral and apolitical, critical pedagogy views all education theory as intimately linked to ideologies shaped by power, politics, history, and culture. Given this view, schooling functions as a terrain of ongoing struggle over what will be accepted as legitimate knowledge and culture. "In accordance with this notion, a critical pedagogy must seriously address the concept of cultural politics by both legitimizing and challenging cultural experiences that comprise the histories and social realities that in turn comprise the forms and boundaries that give meaning to student lives. (Darder 1991, p. 77)

Economics

Critical education theory contends that, contrary to the traditional view, schools actually work against the interest of those students who are most needy in society. The role of competing economic interests of the market place in the production of knowledge and in the structural relationships and policies which shape public schools are recognized as significant factors, particularly in the education of disenfranchised students. From the standpoint of economics, public schools serve to position select groups within asymmetrical power relations which serve to replicate the existing values and privileges of the dominant culture. It is this uncontested relationship between school and society that critical pedagogy seeks to challenge, unmasking traditional claims that education provides equal opportunity and access to all in this country.

Historicity of Knowledge

Critical pedagogy embraces the view that all knowledge is created within a historical context and it is this historical context which gives it life and meaning. This notion of the historicity of knowledge requires that schools be understood within not only the boundaries of their social practice but within the boundaries of their historical realities. Along the same lines, students and the knowledge they bring into the classroom must be understood as historical. As such, opportunities must be created that permit students to discover "That there is no historical reality which is not human. There is no history without men [and women]...there is only history of men [and women]. It is when the majorities are denied their right to participate in history as subjects that they become dominated and alienated" (Freire 1970, p. 125).

This historical view of knowledge also challenges traditional emphasis on historical continuities and historical development. Instead, there is a mode of analysis that stresses the breaks, discontinuities, conflicts, differences, and tensions in history, all which serve in bringing to light the centrality of human agency as it presently exists, as well as the possibilities for change (Giroux 1983).

Dialectical Theory

In opposition to traditional theories of education that serve to reinforce certainty, conformity, and technical control of knowledge and power, critical pedagogy embraces a dialectical view of knowledge that functions to unmask the connections between objective knowledge and the cultural norms, values, and standards of the society at large. Within the dialectical perspective, all analysis begins first and foremost with human existence and the contradictions and disjunctions that both shape and make problematic its meaning. Peter McLaren (1988) explains critical pedagogy as beginning

> with the premise that men and women are essentially unfree and inhabit a world rife with contradictions and asymmetries of power and privilege. The critical educator endorses theories that are, first and foremost, dialectical: that is, theories which recognize the problems of society as more then simply isolated events of individuals or deficiencies in the social structure. Rather, these problems are part of the interactive context between the individual and society (p. 166).

The purpose here is to assist students to engage the world within its complexity and fullness in order to reveal the possibilities of new ways of constructing thought and action beyond the original state. It seeks to nourish the dynamic interactive elements, rather than to support the formation of dichotomies and polarizations. Hence, this supports a view of humans and nature that is relational, objectivity and subjectivity that is interconnected, and theory and practice that is coexistent.

Dialectical thought brings to the surface the power of human activity and human knowledge as both a product and a force in the shaping of our world in the interest of domination or liberation. Hence, the process of dialectical critique is informed by an emancipatory interest in social change. In this way, critical pedagogy addressed two primary concerns: (1) the linking of social experiences and the development of modes to criticism that can interrogate such experiences and reveal both their strengths and weaknesses; and (2) the presentation of a mode of practice fashioned in new critical thought and aimed at reclaiming the conditions of self-determined existence (Darder 1991, p. 82).

Ideology

Ideology can best be understood as the framework of thought which is used in society to give order and meaning to the social and political world in which we live (Hall 1981). As important is the notion that ideology must be understood as existing at the deep, embedded psychological structures of the personality. Ideology more often than not manifests itself in the inner histories and experiences which give rise to questions of subjectivity as they are constructed by individual needs, drives, and passions, as well as the changing conditions and social foundations of society. In addition, ideology also provides the means for critique.

As a pedagogical tool, ideology can be use to interrogate and unmask the contradictions which exist between the dominant culture of the school and the lived experiences and knowledge that students use to mediate the reality of school life. Ideology can also provide teachers with the necessary context "to examine how their own views about knowledge, human nature, values, and society are mediated through the commonsense assumptions they use to structure classroom experiences (Darder 1991, p. 86). In this way it can serve as a starting point for asking questions that will help them to evaluate critically their practice and to better recognize how the dominant culture becomes embedded in the hidden curriculum—curriculum that is informed by ideological views that silence students and structurally reproduce the dominant society's assumptions and practices.

Hegemony

Hegemony refers to a process of social control that is carried out through the moral and intellectual leadership of a dominant society over subordinate groups (Gramsci 1971). Critical pedagogy incorporates this notion of hegemony in order to demystify the asymmetrical power relations and social arrangement that sustain the dominant culture. Further, hegemony points to the powerful connection that exists between politics, cultural ideology, and pedagogy. As such, teachers are challenged to recognize their responsibility to critique and attempt to transform those classroom conditions tied to hegemonic practices which perpetuate the oppression of subordinate groups. This process must be ongoing for hegemony must be fought for constantly in order to maintain the status quo. Each time a radical form threatens the integrity of the status quo, generally this element is appropriated, stripped of his transformative intent, and reified into a palatable form. This maintains the existing power relations. Understanding how hegemony functions in society provides educators with the basis for understanding not only how the seeds of domination are produced, but also how they can be overcome through resistance, critique, and social action.

Resistance

Critical pedagogy incorporates a theory of resistance in order to better understand the complex reasons why many students from subordinate groups consistently fail in the educational system. It accepts the notion that all people have the capacity and ability to produce knowledge and to resist domination. How they resist is clearly influenced and limited by the conditions in which they have been forced to survive.

A theory of resistance functions to uncover the degree to which student oppositional behavior is associated to their need to struggle against elements of dehumanization or is simply perpetuating their own oppression. As in other areas, the notion of emancipatory interests serves as the central point to determining when oppositional behavior reflects a moment of resistance.

Praxis: The Union of Theory and Practice

From a dialectical view of knowledge emerges the notion that theory and practice are inextricably linked. In keeping with this view, all theory is considered with respect to the practical intent of transforming inequity. Unlike the external determinism, pragmatism, and instrumental /technical application of theory so prevalent in traditional educational discourses, praxis is conceived as a self-creating and self-generating free human activity. All human activity is perceived as consisting of action and reflection, or praxis; and as praxis, all human activity requires theory to illuminate it and provide a better understanding of our world as we find it and as it might be. Hence, within critical pedagogy, all theorizing and truth claims are subject to critique, a process which constitutes analysis and questions mediated through dialogue and democratic relations of power (Giroux 1983).

Freire (1985) strongly supports this relationship between theory and practice within the educational process. He argues that a true praxis is impossible in the undialectical vacuum driven by a subject/object dichotomy. For within the context of such a dichotomy, both theory and practice lose their power to transform reality. Cut off from practice, theory becomes "simple verbalism". Separated from theory, practice is nothing but "blind activism".

Dialogue and Conscientization (Conscientizacao)

The principle of dialogue as defined by Freire is one of the most significant aspects of critical pedagogy. It speaks to an emancipatory educational process that is above all committed to the empowerment of students through challenging the dominant educational discourse and illuminating the right and freedom of students to become subjects of their world. Dialogue constitutes an educational strategy that centers upon the development of critical social consciousness or what Freire (1970) terms "conscientizacao".

Within the process of a critical pedagogical approach, dialogue and analysis serve as the foundation for reflection and action. It is this educational strategy that supports a problem-posing approach to education: an approach in which the relationship of students to teacher is, without question, dialogical—students learn from the teacher; teachers learn from the students. Hence, the actual lived experiences cannot be ignored nor relegated to the periphery. They must be incorporated as part of the exploration of existing conditions and knowledge in order to understand how these came to be and to consider how they might be different.

Conscientizacao is defined as the process by which students, as empowered subjects, achieve a deepening awareness of the social realities which shape their lives and discover their own capacities to recreate them. This constitutes a recurrent, regenerating process of human interaction that is utilized for constant clarification of the hidden dimensions, as students continue to move into the world and enter into dialogue anew.

Questions Informed by Critical Educational Principles

There are a variety of questions that are informed by the principles of critical pedagogy which can be asked in order to assess existing educational conditions and practices and their potential impact on Latino students. A few of these include the following:

- Does the curriculum reflect the cognitive, motivational, and relational styles of Latino student?

- Who is involved in the development of curriculum and the selection of materials?

- Are the everyday lives and community realities of Latino students integrated into the daily life of the classroom? If so how is this done?

- Are there consistent and ongoing opportunities for Latino students to engage together in dialogue that centers upon their own experiences and daily lives? If so, what are some examples of this practice?

- Are there adults in the classroom environment who are able to consistently engage Latino students in their native tongue and who address students' issues related to both their primary cultural and bicultural experiences?

- Are there sufficient opportunities for Latino students to engage with their personal cultural histories and to develop their consciousness with respect to their subject position in the United States? If so, what are some examples?

- Are Latino parents and community members involved in the students' educational process and school governance? If so, in what ways does this take place and what roles do they play?

- Are classroom relations and curricular activities designed to stimulate and nurture the ongoing development of cultural identity, voice, participation, solidarity, and individual and collective empowerment? If so, give some examples.

- Does the teacher make explicit relations of power at work in the classroom, school, community, and society with respect to the students' lives? If so, give examples of how this is done.

- Does the teacher struggle with Latino students to overcome limiting and debilitating forms of resistance, while at the same time supporting resistance to cultural subordination and human injustice? If so, how is this undertaken?

- Does the teacher understand the relationship between theory and practice? If so, how is this apparent in the manner in which the teacher perceives her (his) role, relates to Latino students, their parents, and community, defines student expectations, creates and establishes new curriculum, acknowledges personal limitations, and perceives the production of knowledge and the development of literacy and bilingual proficiency?

Unfortunately many of these questions are not asked within traditional educational environments where knowledge is perceived as neutral and education resembles what Freire (1970) describes as a "banking system"—namely, a system where students are massive objects who come to school in order to be filled with the knowledge of the teacher. Even more frustrating is the persistent failure to recognize the importance of cultural identity and the phenomenon of biculturalism experienced by students of color who live in disenfranchised conditions of social, political, and economic subordination. Instead of making explicit the power relations and elitist interests which shape institutional life (including schools) in the United States, these remain forever veiled in the hidden curriculum of conformity to idealized "American democratic values" which perpetuate class, race, gender, and cultural oppression and language domination—a subordination of identity, consciousness, and voice carried out, in part, by the best intentioned and well-meaning teachers and educational leaders of our time.

LATINO CRITICAL EDUCATORS

Despite the fact that much has been written about students of color during the last thirty years, few researchers have been willing to venture into the danger zone of controversy that is generated when one proposes to examine how the culture of the teacher influences their practice in the classroom. In fact, I would venture to say that this publicly uncontested arena constitutes one of the most profoundly oppressive, particularly in the manner in which the traditional discourse conceals its assimilationist expectations. Generally, when the question of the teacher's culture is raised, it immediately sparks concerns about essentialism along with a myriad of horror stories about teachers of color who treated their students of color even worst than the white teachers. What is hidden underneath this discourse reflects (1) the unacknowledged fear of displacement by white teachers and (2) the unexamined contextual issues which shape the conditions of assimilation under which teachers of color are educated and expected to survive professionally. As a consequence, important pedagogical questions are neglected in order to quell the possible conflicts and tensions which these questions might generate. It was an effort to introduce this factor into the dialogue that motivated me to conduct a study that points to some specific ways in which the culture of the teacher influences classroom practice. For the purposes of this paper, I will focus on what I have learned about Latino critical educators and their relationships to Latino students.

The Cultural Perspective of the Teacher

The cultural perspective held by Latino educators clearly impacts upon the manner in which they teach. Some of the ways in which this is evident is through their direct interactions with students. For example, Latino teachers often have a greater grasp of the reality from which their students come and, as a consequence, can relate to them on concrete terms which enhances their ability to establish trusting relationships with their students. These teachers often draw upon their own experiences to help their students engage with issues related to the language and cultural differences that the students must face daily.

Latino teachers exhibit an enhanced capacity to recognize and empathize with the academic and social needs of their students. These teachers strongly believe that Latino students require a greater level of encouragement, affirmation, and recognition of their worth by their teachers. By the same token, they are able to understand the expressed concerns of their students, particularly with respect to dealing with problems they encounter in society (i.e., racism, resistance, etc.). One teacher writes

> I distinguish between the realities of White children and children of color, in general, and between the various realities of different cultural groups...I consciously and overtly support Chicano, Latino, African American and other students of color.

Immigrant Latino teachers are able to work with newly arrived students in ways which validate and affirm the struggle these students face in acclimating to a new cultural and linguistic environment. In this way they are able to offer concrete support and encouragement utilizing anecdotes which are familiar or at least seem plausible given the conditions immigrant Latino students are currently facing. Immigrant Latino teachers are effective in moving their students through a transitional program that is based upon concrete knowledge of the immigrant experience. As a result, they are able to set goals for their students that are more realistic and which enhance and promote their success, rather than hinder the difficult process of transition into a new linguistic, academic, and social setting.

Latino educators strongly support the development of language and literacy skills in the primary language. Often these teachers promote bilingualism among their students and encourage parents to maintain the primary language in the home, unlike the traditional mandate given to parents which generally discourages them from perpetuating the use of their primary language.

Latino educators are acutely aware that all students can learn but many Latino students may not learn as well by traditional means. Hence, they acknowledge responsibility for carefully reflecting upon their own cultural learning experiences, observing the student's struggles to learn, and together with their students developing alternative strategies for approaching the learning process. It is interesting to note that these teachers believe that this requires a greater sense of openness and creativity on their part, as well as extra time with their students. They identify this process as ultimately setting the groundwork for greater participation by students in their learning and in their production of knowledge.

Latino educators express a strong commitment to making explicit the students' cultural worldview and histories not just from books but in the living experience of the classroom environment. The colloquial expressions they use with their students, the way in which they construct humor, the style of classroom management they employ, how they plan and prepare for the day, and how they interact with parents all are driven by the forces of an enacted culture which defies explicit articulation and goes beyond that which can be specifically reduced to definition. Instead, they speak of the heart and soul of the cultural experience which is comprised of the shared collective history and common knowing that extends itself across generational spaces within particular cultural communities. One teacher writes "I am constantly looking for ways to incorporate the culture into the lessons: through music art, language, literature and by connecting with them through discussion of everyday occurrences."

Latino teachers also function as translators of the culture of power. They believe that it is part of their responsibility to make explicit the power relations at work in the lives of their students. Through dialogue, journals, and classroom projects, they create the conditions that give Latino students an opportunity to understand their current conditions and to consider ways in which they might recreate them.

Latino Educators as Role Models and Advocates

One of the most significant contributions that Latino educators make to Latino students is to provide them with positive role models—people with whom their students can relate and with whom they feel comfortable expressing their views. One teacher who participated in this study describes his thoughts about this issue in the following way:

> I am constantly conscious of the significance of being a positive role model for all Latino youth. I have a strong identification with their struggle in the acculturation process as recent immigrants to this country. Helping them to understand themselves, helping them to express their voice, to appreciate their rich cultural heritage and to never forsake it, and their language are very important goals I communicate to them. I frequently speak to my Latino students on campus in Spanish both in the classroom and informally during lunch and class breaks.

Through the teacher's modeling, Latino students obtain greater confidence in their own ability and see the teacher as a person who has gone through the system and yet maintained his or her cultural integrity. In this way, Latino teachers affirm their students' linguistic and cultural experiences, share their own life struggles, and encourage their students with clear messages that they too are capable of learning and achieving academically. In addition, these teachers not only take the time to listen to their students' problems, frustrations, and their struggles but also assist them to identify possible solutions.

When Latino educators express pride and identification with their culture, this reinforces the legitimacy of the Latino cultural experience and helps to generate a sense of rapport and connection with their students. As a person in a position of authority, the teacher's respect for the culture and language communicates a strong message of acceptance, respect, honor, and dignity; hence, Latino students experience a greater opportunity to develop their voices and participation in classroom life. One teacher writes:

> I have found that as I give culture a place in the classroom, the students begin to "light up" in a variety of ways. They begin to talk about themselves more often, they bring things from home, they speak [Spanish]...It adds a very rich dimension to the environment for everyone. It provides the children with more opportunities to learn about themselves—in their own way.

In addition to affirming the worldview and realities which Latino students face, these teachers see themselves in a good position to challenge their students in ways that will cause them to reconsider many of the unexamined notions and ideas that they may hold about themselves and their own cultural community, as well as about the dominant culture, particularly those views which can lead to actions of injustice against others and the perpetuation of their own oppression.

Many Latino educators openly admit to feeling a greater affinity with Latino students. This affinity functions to enhance their ability to communicate not only with their students but also with Latino parents—a factor which has been shown to improve the academic achievement of students (Cummins 1968; Rivera 1990). In addition, many also express a greater sense of urgency to be an advocate for Latino students to succeed. One teacher described it as experiencing a "vested interest" in the educational success of children in our community.

The Pedagogical Approach

One of the major similarities in the pedagogical approach of Latino teachers is their strong emphasis on a variety of alternative methods which stress student involvement and participation in the process of their learning. These include the use of cooperative learning strategies and collaborative group work that provide many opportunities for student dialogue and the development of students' voices. These teachers also identify the development of critical thought, personal responsibility, discipline, and positive self-concept as important goals in the education of Latino students.

Latino educators strongly share the view that everyone in the classroom is both teacher and student. One teacher explains her perspective in the following way:

> My relationship with my students is based on authenticity and sincerity. I view everyone in the room as both teacher and student, including myself. All experiences are learning ones, however silly, fun, spontaneous, profound, or painful they may be. I want to instill a love of learning in a very dynamic, critical

and personal way within the social/cultural experience of the children.

Latino educators encourage student participation in the development of curriculum activities and decisions about reading, writing, and other classroom assignments. This participation is significant to the process of student empowerment. As students become involved in making group decisions about their learning, they also develop both critical thinking and social skills. Self-selected reading programs, writing workshops and journals, songs and performance activities are all utilized by the teachers to enhance language skills and the development of bilingualism and biliteracy.

The creation of a positive and accepting environment is another significant factor in the education of Latino students. Latino educators consistently voice their desire for students to learn and express a real faith in their students' capabilities. They stress that it is important that Latino students feel enthusiastic and enjoy coming to school. As a consequence, Latino educators make efforts to create an educational setting where disciplines are integrated as much as possible and where the culture of their students can serve as the bases for their learning. In this way Latino students, gain a better sense of their own place in the world and experience themselves as effective and competent.

A most significant factor related to pedagogy is that of addressing questions of bias in the classroom and the society at large. Latino educators stress the need for Latino students to understand the existence of bias and the manner in which it affects their life and the world. These teachers actively engage with issues related to bias, prejudice, and discrimination, particularly when these arise within the course of school life. In their handling of such issues, Latino teachers attempt to deconstruct with their students their current understanding of biases and prejudices and to examine the consequences of attitudes and behaviors which reflect injustice. Through such dialogues, the teacher and students reconstruct a deeper understanding of their world and their own participation with respect to differences among people.

Classroom Management Style

Although Latino teachers express a warmth and openness in describing their classroom management style, they clearly believe that it is important to maintain a sense of their authority as the teacher and to behave in a firm and direct manner when disciplining their students. They stress that Latino students need to know what is expected from them and that this must be communicated clearly and unambiguously. This knowledge then serves to define the boundaries which determine the criteria for respect between students and teachers. This is particularly important since the student offense cited as most serious by Latino educators was that of disrespect—disrespect for the teacher, fellow students, or self.

The disciplinary action taken by Latino teachers varies depending the degree of the problem. Generally, most teachers begin with calling attention to the behavior immediately. If it continues, the next step is an individual conversation with the student in an effort to explore together what is happening with the student and to determine the consequences if the behavior persists. If the behavior persists, many of the teachers will invite the parent to assist them in handling the situation. This is generally a last resort. It is interesting to note that the majority of the Latino teachers in the study appear to experience a real sense of efficacy with their classroom management and report few problems with Latino students.

Although Latino educators seem to exhibit little difference in how they approach classroom management problems with Latino students or white students, what seems a bit different is their understanding of the motivations which often drive Latino students to act up in the classroom. Most of the teachers are quite conscious of the manner in which resistance often works among students of color who have had difficulties achieving in public school. They are also aware that often Latino students collide head-on with dominant cultural values which are contrary to their own. As a consequence, they are more likely to engage students' frustrations within the classroom concretely and to consider with their Latino students the possible consequences of their behavior in their future. In this way, Latino educators are able to relate in a more connected manner to their Latino students and to assist them in developing more constructive approaches to dealing with their frustrations and more effective strategies for resisting what they experience as oppression in their daily lives.

Teacher Expectations

Latino educators hold a steadfast expectation that Latino students can and will succeed in their classrooms. They begin with a faith in the Latino student's ability to master the material and to be able to apply what is learned in the world. Also associated with this perception of their students is a clear sense that all their students possess knowledge which they bring with them into the classroom.

Therefore, an expectation exists that the students will build upon the knowledge they already possess.

Many of the expectations held by Latino educators for their students are centered not only upon successful academic achievement but also upon the student's development as a human being. In light of this, Latino teacher expectations often focus strongly on the notions of respect, personal discipline, social responsibility, and an understanding of the manner in which the students' bicultural reality impacts upon their view of themselves and their world.

These teachers challenge their students to grow and to struggle within the classroom environment, while providing them with the support and encouragement that is necessary for students to succeed with their academic tasks. Although many Latino educators express their expectations in a humorous and personable manner, there is no question that they also express a very serious desire to see Latino students succeed. Hence, these teachers not only cultivate and stress the development of language and math skills, group communication, critical problem-solving abilities, and a knowledge of history and culture but also nurture in Latino students a willingness to challenge and be challenged, the expression of creativity, their active classroom participation, a deep respect for differences, and a love for justice and freedom.

Parent Involvement

Latino educators express a strong belief in the importance of parent participation in the education of their children. They support Latino parents and engage them directly regarding their concerns over their children's education. Although more time consuming, most of these teachers utilize a very personal and direct approach in their communication with parents. In addition to notes that are written in the parents' primary language, they also frequently converse with parents over the telephone and personally invite them to make room visits, to assist in particular classroom activities, or to attend school meetings. This personal approach communicates to Latino parents that they are welcome and valuable.

Forming a sense of partnership or coalition with parents is also another strategy utilized by Latino teachers. Here teachers seek to consistently involve Latino parents in the education of their children through receiving their input, while addressing the concerns they share regarding the children. Teachers who establish such partnership with parents find that they are able to teach more effectively because they experience greater cooperation from both their students and the parents. Another benefit here is that Latino teachers are able to develop a variety of ways for parents to get involved, since they become more knowledgeable of parents' strengths and abilities and thus, of what they can concretely bring to the educational setting.

Another issue concerning parent involvement that is emphasized by many Latino educators is related to the nature of the interaction. These teachers stress that they make efforts to communicate consistently with parents about the positive progress their children are making in school, rather than to contact a parent only when there is a problem with their child. They have found that this practice enhances the sense of community between the parents and the school and leads to more conducive interaction when problems do arise.

IMPLICATIONS FOR TEACHER EDUCATION

When Latino educators are asked about the quality of teacher education programs, they overwhelmingly agree that these programs are not adequately preparing teachers to contend with the realities they will find in public schools. For the most part they point to the failure of these programs to engage critically and substantially with issues related to race, class, and gender. Instead, what is found is a smattering of superficial and simplistic presentations related to these issues. In addition, the faculty of these programs are predominantly white and very inexperienced with respect to differences in cultural worldviews and in cognitive, learning, and motivational styles as well as with an understanding of second language acquisition skills and critical principles of education. In addition, Latino educators express much distress over the deficient manner in which students of color continue to be portrayed within many teacher education programs. As one teacher describes this:

> The programs focus on children of color as appendages to "normal" white children. The education of children of color is seen as no different, just slightly exotic. The political and social implications of biculturalism are rarely addressed.

What these concerns obviously point to is the necessity to drastically recreate teacher education programs in this country, particularly those which are preparing their students to enter public schools in areas where there exist large Latino communities. Some of the ways in which these programs must change are implicitly echoed in the frustrations and concerns of educators who find themselves ill-prepared to contend with the needs of

Latino students. Some of these changes include courses and practical experiences that will, as one teacher stated, "normalize the experience of biculturalism...and place the issues of bicultural development at the center of the educational agenda." More specifically, this means the establishment of a curriculum that will assist all educators in understanding the developmental process by which Latino students become bicultural, bilingual, bicognitive, and biliterate. In addition, these programs must establish culturally democratic educational environments where issues related to culture, race, class, gender, and other social differences are engaged critically with respect not only to the development of curriculum and instructional approaches but also to the development of student teachers' abilities to position themselves contextually as cultural beings.

And lastly, teacher education programs must move beyond diversity in the abstract and recognize that in order to live diversity in the concrete there must exist diversity in the population to enact such an environment. Hence, this requires that teacher education programs value, nurture and support the recruitment and development of Latino faculty and student teachers. This is particularly significant given the current decline in the number of teachers of color entering the field. A report entitled *Education that Works: An Action Plan for the Education of Minorities* (1990), prepared by the Quality Education for Minorities Project at the Massachusetts Institute of Technology, describes the current situation:

> Over the next decade, when minority student [national] population in schools will exceed the present 30 percent and will approach 50 percent in most urban areas, minority teachers are expected to decline from the current 10 percent of the overall teacher workforce to just 5 percent. Fewer than 8 percent of the students in teacher preparation programs are minority, and this pool is likely to be cut in half by the candidate's subsequent failure to pass teacher competency tests required for licensing in most states. To achieve parity between the teaching force and the student population would require the licensing and certification of 450,000 minority teachers among the 1.5 million teachers needed for our schools during the next five years. Of the 700,000 new teachers who are expected to be trained in this period, only about 35,000 are estimated to be minority. (p. 41)

CONCLUSION

The intent of this paper has been to (1) discuss some generally neglected issues which play a significant role in the development of self-concept and, subsequently, the academic development and empowerment of Latino students; (2) provide a brief overview of critical pedagogy; (3) consider the contributions of Latino critical educators in order to highlight some of the ways in which the culture works to shape and mold the manner in which they interact with Latino students; and (4) consider the implications of these issues to the future re-creation and transformation of teacher education programs.

In conclusion, it is important to stress that the most significant knowledge obtained from this study is that it strongly reinforces the notion that Latino teachers who possess an implicit understanding of the cultural and linguistic community of their students and who also embrace the pedagogical principles of critical pedagogy are better able to create an educational environment that stimulates greater creativity, voice, and participation for Latino students. Although I believe that to a greater or lesser extent all critical educators and all Latino educators can contribute positively to the education of Latino students, it is the powerful combination of an emancipatory educational approach with the ability to enact and participate actively in the familiar cultural milieu of the student that can fundamentally potentiate the academic development and empowerment of Latino students in the United States.

REFERENCES

Cardenas, J. and First, J. M. 1985. Children at risk. *Educational Leadership*; September.

Cummins, J. 1986. Empowering minority students: A framework for intervention. *Harvard Educational Review* 56:18–36.

Darder, A. 1991. *Culture and power in the classroom.* New York: Bergin and Garvey.

Darder, A. and Upshur, C. 1991. *What do Latino children need to succeed in school?: A study of four Boston public schools.* Boston: Mauricio Gaston Institute for Latino Community Development and Public Policy.

de Anda, D. 1984. Bicultural socialization: Factors affecting the minority experience. *Social Work* 2: 101–107.

Fernandez, R. and Velez, W. 1989. *Who stays? Who leaves? Findings from the Aspira five cities high school study.* Washington, D.C: Aspiration Association.

Freire, P. 1970. *Pedagogy of the oppressed.* New York: Seabury Press.

————. 1985. *The politics of education.* South Hadley, MA: Bergin and Garvey.

Giroux, H. 1983. *Theory and resistance in education: A pedagogy for the opposition.* South Hadley, MA: Bergin and Garvey.

————. 1988. *Teachers as intellectual.* New York: Bergin and Garvey.

Gramsci, A. 1971. *Selections from prison notebooks.* New York: International Publications.

Hall, D. 1981. Cultural studies: Two paradigms. In *Culture, ideology and social process*. ed. T. Bennett et al. London: Batsford Academic and Educational.

McLaren, P. 1988. *Life in schools: An introduction to critical pedagogy in the foundations of education.* New York: Longman.

Powell. G. J. 1970. *Black monday's children.* New York: Appleton, Century, Crofts.

Ramirez, M. and Castañeda, A. 1974. *Cultural democracy: Bicognitive development and education.* New York: Academic Press.

Rashid, H. 1981. Early childhood education as a cultural transition for African American children. *Educational Research Quarterly* 6: 55–63.

Red Horse, J. et al. 1981. Family behavior of urban American Indians. In *Human services for cultural minorities.* ed. R. Dana. Baltimore: University Park Press.

Rivera, R. 1988. Latino parental involvement in the Boston public schools: Preliminary notes from the field. Boston, MA: University of Massachusetts, William Monroe Trotter Institute.

Solis, A. 1980. Theory of biculturality. *Calmecac de Aztlan en Los* 2:36–41.

Valentine, C. 1971. Deficit, difference, and bicultural models of Afro-American behavior. *Harvard Educational Review* 41: 137–157.

Velez, W. (1989) High school attrition among Hispanics and Non-Hispanic white youth *Sociology of Education* 62: 119–133.

Wheelock. A. 1990. *The status of Latino students in Massachusetts public schools: Directions for policy research in the 1990's.* Boston: University of Massachusetts, Mauricio Gaston Institute for Latino Community Development and Public Policy.

Young, I. M. 1990. *Justice and the politics of difference.* Princeton: Princeton University Press.

13

KHAULA MURTADHA

An African-centered Pedagogy in Dialog with Liberatory Multiculturalism

INTRODUCTION

Despite thirty-eight years of desegregation, restructuring efforts, reform movements, new and alternative curriculum strategies, public schools have yet to adequately educate large numbers of African American children and other children of color living in urban school districts. Across the country these children are either disproportionately labeled as behavior problems or in need of special education classes. Once labeled, it is as if the entire learning process is thwarted and the child who started school with enthusiasm and a desire to learn becomes a "left out" (usually called a drop out). Because of the obvious failure of the educational system serving these youth, educators have sought to find alternative strategies to educate African American children. African-centered, often called Afrocentric, education seeks to facilitate the internalization of a value system of use in the transformation of African Americans from a state of psychological, social, political, and spiritual disempowerment to one of awareness, knowledge, and empowerment for change. The first part of this chapter is a broad discussion of African-centered ideology and its implementation in school curriculum infusion strategies. While it can not be a cure-all remedy, its possibilities for affecting youth are being documented in movements emerging from a number of urban centers—from Portland, Oregon to Washington, D.C., from Detroit to Atlanta—introducing curriculum focusing on African and African American history and culture, creating all black, male academies and other optional school sites.

The second part of this chapter discusses the necessity of "dialog" with Others as African-centered communities examine the broad cultural, political context of the oppression of women nationally and globally, the suffering of other ethnic groups both nationally and globally as well as concerns of people with differing abilities. Since the term multiculturalism is frequently reduced to the addition of a few more pictures of women in nontraditional roles in textbooks or the inclusion of units on ethnic groups or panel discussions on human relations, the importance of work examining others' ways of knowing and being is critical. However, after years of distortion and general neglect of the sources of knowledge, creativities, and experiences of not only African American people but also all people of color—marginalized people with disabilities, people who are old, and people who are poor— there is a need to throw into question ideologies and educational reforms which lay claim to being empowering, liberating, and authentic. Liberating multiculturalism is a means of directing attention to the democratic principles of justice and liberation as well as to questions of agency and power relations.

ROOTS OF AFROCENTRICITY

The preface to a 1972 study guide and curriculum outline published by the United Federation of Teachers read in part: "Ours is a time of ethnic consciousness—even conflict. During periods such as this in our nation's history it is even more pressing that we have a sense of each other. Black Americans are demanding now—and with considerable justification—that their presence in our history be acknowledged and respected. It is a history which all of us—black and white—must comprehend if our social divisions are to be mended and their resulting injustices remedied." These words reflect the spirit of the 60s and 70s when Black studies had struggled to get a rightful place in academia. Between 1964 and 1975 approximately three hundred to five hundred African American studies departments, research centers, and programs challenged dominant myths, stereotypes, and misrepresentation which prevailed within the Eurocentric curriculum at predominantly white institutions.

The coinage of the term "Afrocentricity" has been attributed to Molefi Asante who has argued that the African studies scholar must begin analysis from the primacy of the classical African civilizations, Kemet (Egypt), Nubia, Axum, and Meroe. Diop's approach to the theory of African civilization is analogous to the way in which European scholars have structured the career of European civilization: modern European civilization is assumed to have its technical and intellectual roots in ancient Greek civilization; modern African civilization (and some would argue all civilization) should trace an intellectual and cultural legacy to the civilization of ancient Egypt. Diop (1967) sought to respond to European ideology by arguing that civilization began in Africa (ancient Egypt) and that ancient Egyptians were of African racial stock. From this point, Diop then goes on to argue that the classical foundations of modern African civilization should be located in ancient Egypt, not in Greece, France, or Britain.

In the late 1970s Asante attempted to conceptually unify the varied African-centered approaches to Black studies by labeling them Afrocentric. Explaining the importance of "speaking" from an Afrocentric perspective Asante's' point is,

> I recognize the transitional nature of all cultural manifestations of a social, economic or political dimension. I also know that in the United States and other parts of the African world, culturally speaking there is movement toward new, more cosmocultural forms of understanding. Nevertheless, meaning in the contemporary context must be derived from the most centered aspects of the African's being. When this is not the case, psychological dislocation creates automatons who are unable to fully capture the historical moment because they are living on someone else's terms. We are either existing on our own terms or the terms of others. Where will the African person find emotional and cultural satisfaction, if not on their own terms? By "term" I mean position, place or space.

It is important to note that significant works in African intellectual history have long stressed the the need for African-centered thought and practice, most notably those of Carter G. Woodson and W. E. B. DuBois. However since the introduction of the category, the discourse around it has been extensive and varied. The Nile valley, Kemetic/Egyptian sources of knowledge, the Muslim scholarly contributions (although this is disputed by some Afrocentrists), the spiritual /traditional ontological views and urban heritage of West African societies are stressed by these scholars. Karenga (1992) describes Afrocentricity as being rooted in the cultural image of African people, anchored in the views and values of African people as well as in the practices which, in a generative dialectic, emanate from and give rise to these views and values. This notion is supported by C. Tsehloane Keto, author of the historiography, *The Africa Centered Perspective of History*: "different regions of the world that have evolved distinct cultures are entitled to develop paradigms based on the perspectives of the region's qualitatively significant human cultures, histories and experiences." For Keto, studies about the rest of the world are overly influenced by the theories from a minority of the world's diverse families, a minority of the world's women, social structures, and cultures. He believes that a perspective called "pluriversal" can occur by examining global rather than regional trends.

There is a significant message that Afrocentricity brings to the historical/cultural perspective. Diop's (1967) *The African Origin of Civilization* points out that sedentary culture is a product of the Nile Valley civilizations of Africa and that migrants from the Nile Valley civilizations seeded cultures in other parts of the world. The concepts of matriarchy, of monotheism, of family and tribal organization, of astrological and mythic orientation of southern Asian, Mediterranean, Far Eastern and other cultures are deemed to be the offspring of an ancient African cultural parent. The central culture thesis distinguishes Afrocentric thought from other approaches to cultural history and is at the core of the definition that would inform an Afrocentric curriculum. It suggests that there is a fundamental human unity, equality of the sexes, and a spiritual dynamic in all human relationships.

Complex and multidisciplinary, Afrocentricity is a concept which embodies humanistic philosophy, scholarly methodology, and models of practical application. The main objective of its creators, according to Abarry, (1990) is to "liberate the research and study of African peoples from the hegemony of Eurocentric scholarship, whose concepts, history, and traditions, have been absolute yardsticks against which all other cultures are evaluated." Afrocentrism assails the canons of Western thought (philosophy, religion, and the sciences) not because they are viewed as the adversary but because they are falsely attributed to European cultural imperatives while denying their origins to people of color. Eurocentrism is the systematic projection of an image, a belief, that Europeans, particularly Greek and Roman civilizations, gave the world the current forms of higher branches of learning that we still find useful today. Afrocentric scholarship demonstrates that most of these, in the present form, were copied literally, from the Nile valley by the very same people—Pythagoras, Socrates, Thucydides—who are called the fathers of these disciplines today.

The African-centered worldview begins with a holistic conception of the human condition. There is no mind-body, affective-cognitive dualism. People are conceived as a totality, made up of interconnecting systems. This total being is at once a sensing, knowing, feeling, and experiencing human, living in a dynamic world where everything is interrelated and endowed with the supreme life force. Emotions, compassion, love, joy, and sensuality, are shared. The community is the basic human unit, not the individual, and as such the concern is for collective survival. Cooperation is valued above competition. Alienation is at cross-purposes with the cooperative ideal, so people work interdependently. The idea of interrelatedness includes the entire universe—gods, humans, animals, plants, and inanimate objects.

Asante's (1987) view of an Afrocentric rhetoric, committed to the propagation of a more humanistic vision of the world, would oppose the negation in Western culture. Substantially different from Western rhetoric, this rhetoric allows other cultures to coexist; it is neither imperialistic nor oppressive. It does not force the same separations as Eurocentric lines of argument. More significantly, Asante points out that most theory (literary and rhetorical) is essentially European, and that the rest of the world should not "abandon the theoretical and critical task to European writers who stand on literary 'peaks' as beacons for theory." Almost all theories are from a male, Eurocentric angle, which, having negated or ignored other perspectives, often is thought of as "universal." It has been suggested that both separately and collectively, spirituality, affect, and rhythm play a significant role in shaping the world view of African Americans. A summary of an Afrocentric discourse drawn from the works of Schiele (1990) and Abarry (1990) would include the following characteristics:

1. Human beings are conceived collectively.
2. Human beings are spiritual.
3. Human beings are good.
4. The affective approach to knowledge is epistemologically sound.
5. Much of human behavior is subjective.
6. The axiology or highest value lies in interpersonal relations.

SPEAKING FOR OURSELVES—DISRUPTION AND CENTERING

When people from the margins of this society raise their multiple, contradictory voices, they not only threaten to unsettle and destabilize the canonized collections of knowledges, but also disrupt notions of white supremacy, patriarchy-normalized notions of ableness, and the oppression of a capitalist economic system. The idea of "centering," which may be called placing, orienting, and locating, flies in the face of the current trend in academia on decentering and deconstructionism.

Prerequisites for normal human functioning based on a culturally centered identity as outlined by Nobles (1990) include:

1. A sense of self that is collective or extended.
2. An attitude wherein one understands and respects the sameness in oneself and others.
3. A clear sense of one's spiritual connection to the universe.
4. A sense of mutual responsibility (for other African people).

5. A conscious understanding that human abnormality or deviancy is any act that is in opposition to oneself.

Linda Myers's (1988) position supports the idea that reality is at once spiritual and material. If one adheres to this ontology, one loses the sense of the individualized ego/mind and experiences the harmony of the collective identity of being one with the source of all good. The idea of consubstantiation, the whole being in each of its parts with the self including all ancestors, the yet unborn, all of nature, and the entire community, is the optimal goal. According to Meyers, individualism, competition, and materialism provide the criteria for self-definition in the suboptimal conceptual system that dominates the Western culture.

CURRENT TRENDS IN CURRICULUM

Taken from the Proceedings of the First National Conference on the Infusion of African and African American Content in the School Curriculum, six points highlight curriculum deficiencies:

1. There is no significant history of Africans in most academic disciplines before the slave trade. In the total school experience of most Americans, virtually no attention is paid to the major part of history of African people, even though that history is integrally tied to the history of humanity. For example, the history of early man [sic], the history of the role that Africa played in the rise of early civilization, the history of Africa's part in world leadership in ancient times, and the history of the powerful influence of Africa on European culture is completely ignored.

2. There is virtually no "People" history. The history of African people is presented, if at all, in episodes and fragments of post slavery. Nowhere during the course of school curricula can students gain a sense of holism about the descendants of Africans and place Africans in their evolution with continuity and thematic treatment. African people, generally, are decontextualized. Person history is sprinkled almost as an affirmative action in some textbooks. People history is virtually absent.

3. There is virtually no history of Africans in the African Diaspora. Student do not get a sense that the descendants of African people are scattered all over the globe. As a result, many are shocked to find African populations in Brazil, Fiji, in the interior of the Philippines, and in Dravidian India, as well as many other places on the globe. They have no sense of where Africans are nor when or how they arrived at these locations.

4. There is no presentation of the cultural unity among Africans and the descendants of Africans in the African diaspora.

Treatments of African people almost universally tend to emphasize physical and cultural differences among Africans. While there are differences, just as Europeans differ, many are quite superficial. What is overlooked is the deep structural, cultural unity that can be found among many African populations all over the world.

5. There is generally little to no history of the resistance of African people to the domination of Africans through slavery, colonization, and segregation apartheid.

6. The history of African people that is presented fails to explain the common origin and elements in systems of oppression that African people have experienced, especially during the last 400 years.

For many Afrocentrists the goal of education is embodied in the teachings of ancient Kemet/Egypt. For Asante (1990) "The foundation of all African speculation in religion, art, ethics, moral customs, and aesthetics are derived from systems of knowledge found in ancient Egypt" (p. 47). The ancient method of teaching character, developing competence, confidence, and consciousness is through the training of a person's sense and mind by applying the "Laws of Ma'at," truth, justice, righteousness, harmony, balance, propriety, and order (Nobles 1990). The educational process was not only seen as acquiring knowledge but it was also seen as a process of transformation of the learner or initiate, progressing through successive stages of rebirth to become excellent (i.e., godlike). Ma'at is an ethical, social, and rhetorical term. The Egyptians understood it as the divine order of creation, nature, and society. The ancient Egyptians believed that humans reflected the deities and that the best moral position was to be in tune with the cosmos as overseen by the deities. Asante further points out that although the classical priests recognized certain unique capabilities of humans, they saw humans as having a special relationship with other animals under the power of the deities and that humans are expected to be in harmony with the forces of the universe. Therefore, evil and good are "not oppositional in human nature but appositional, a reflection of the internal harmony of the universe itself" (1990, p. 169). There was no debate as to whether humans were essentially good or evil; humans possessed both good and evil.

According to Karenga (1992) another contribution of the Afrocentric concept of education is the centrality of the ethical dimension. Attention is drawn to freedom as an attribute of the responsible person-in-community. The person-in-community acts with responsibility to conceive and create a social context for human flourishing and the pursuit of a good and just society, "a society marked and moved by civility, reciprocity and equality in all areas of human life and practice" (p. 20). This emphasis encourages students to frame questions and generate problematics around the purpose, quality, and direction of human life. The issues of life and death are taken up in ethical terms rather than in egoistic and "vulgarly pragmatic" ones.

Karenga further states that the Afrocentric stress on ethics becomes a way to integrate the disciplines because it raises questions about the relevance of knowledge and its use to humanity and the human community. No longer are ethical questions about the world, about life and death, assigned to religion but rather each discipline raises ethical questions and participates in discourse concerning ethical issues. This integration includes the "hard" sciences as they have produced products and processes which have had the greatest threat to humanity and the environment.

The reasons for looking at the ancient Kemetic system of education are summarized by Hilliard (1985):

Kemetic education is the best window on ancient African education continent-wide.

Kemetic education is the parent of "western" education and therefore it must be understood if ancient and modern western education is to be understood.

Kemetic education is a system that can provide guidance for the organization of African American people today.

For other Afrocentrists the multifaceted and complex system which describes the human, according to ancient Kemetic tradition, represents a series of allegories which define the workings of nature and the implied potentialities of human kind. The implications for education suggest that there is a universal knowledge from the "Akashic records." "One can reach into the recesses of one's consciousness and retrieve the world's most valuable knowledge" (Akbar 1985). This, according to Akbar, eliminates the apparent inequity in knowledge when it is assumed to emanate from outside. He further states that intelligence is multiple in its dimensions and that the intelligent person works in conjunction with a moral and spiritual obligation to the rest of the community. Knowledge of the soul/self is comprised of (1) *Ka*, (2) *Ba*, (3) *Khaba*, (4) *Akhu*, (5) *Seb*, (6) *Putah*, and (7) *Atmu*. These seven souls constitute the form of the human's being/psychology as well as of their evolution. Conclusions about human nature as implied by the description of the *Ba* and the *Atmu*, as well as the divine *Ka*, are that the human is essentially connected to the divine and with everything else in nature. The *Akhu* and *Putah* give a conception of intelligence which requires self-mastery and service to ones higher being in order to be considered intelligent.

Other Afrocentrists examine the Muslim scholarly contributions to education and discuss the importance of the nineteenth-century Muslim reformers in West Africa—Usuman dan Fodio in Northern Nigeria and Al Hajj Umar and Ma Ba Diakhou in the Senegambia. They believe that Islam can make a major contribution to development by strengthening the morals of the nation and providing a sense of community in sister and brotherhood as exemplified in the multicultural community at the university system of Timbuktu.

African-Centered Curriculum in Practice

For most Afrocentrists the educational project is one which not only addresses the historical distortions in terms of curriculum changes for inclusion but also examines other approaches to ways of presenting knowledge, classroom structure, and discipline. Perhaps if the theoretical components of Afrocentrism were examined closely and compared to recent reform efforts that are being incorporated in numerous districts across the country, they would be criticized less. For example, Afrocentric classroom practices emphasize the importance of students working cooperatively. Yet, R. Slavin's (1989) and Johnson and Johnson's (1987) work on cooperative learning is being lauded while African-centered schools are being lambasted. Another popular curriculum approach is interdisciplinary studies. Afrocentricists would refer to this as a "holistic approach" to knowledge in which thematic learning is encourages to support the understanding that knowledge is relational and contextual.

Afrocentric studies according to Karenga (1992) offers multicultural education a stress on critique and a corrective of the "established order." It operates within the framework of developing a new language and logic which can pose "different points of departure for understanding social and human reality." The communitarian African worldview contains within it the social and ethical value of social well-being, solidarity, interdependence, cooperation, and reciprocal obligations—all of which can contribute to equitable distribution of resources and benefits to society.

Beyond the above theoretical discussion, what does this African-centered curriculum look like in the classroom? There are numerous pictures because of the differing interpretations of

Afrocentricity, from the private, totally African-centered, school to the public African-centered content infusion corrective of a traditional five-discipline public school. An example of one strategy developed in an African-centered school in Detroit used a writing and research approach outlined below.

African Centered Curriculum Initiatives in Writing, Research, and Empowerment: A Sixth and Seventh Grade Skill and Activity Program

Overview

An African-centered perspective to writing and research may begin with the African proverb "I am because we are." For the sixth and seventh grade child this would mean the student would be introduced to the concept of researching data and writing as tools for the benefit of not only oneself but also one's community. To this end children in this African centered program will develop decision-making, problem-solving, writing and research skills in three broad strands: To better know one's community history by relating it to the present, to maintain one's health in order to contribute to that community, and to improve the community in which one lives.

The first strand of this research and writing project would begin with the students' examination of various geopolitical situations relating to Africa (including those of the diaspora) and their historical roots. After choosing a particular site, students will locate journals in the Reader's Guide to Periodical Literature, read articles describing events there, and write to politically active associations for further information. After discussions students may decide to be supportive or opposed to the work of such organizations.

The second strand would examine concerns for personal health. Issues surrounding AIDS, teen pregnancy, or drug abuse could be researched. An example would be collecting data from the Center for Disease Control and informing the community through published documents, i.e., a fact sheet or newsletter.

The third strand would work toward the improvement of ones community. Collecting data (who is responsible for maintenance, how long has a particular situation existed, and has there been a formal attempt at resolving the problem), then writing a letter of complaint to the Department of Recreation and Parks about a neighborhood recreational facility and its programs would be an example of this strand.

The classes described here briefly are writing, researching, problem-solving, advocacy, and empowerment for individual African

American children and their community. The need to be able to write for the advocacy of one's position and beliefs has all too often been ignored in many writing programs. Children are often taught the worthwhile skills of recognizing bias and persuasion as they read but too often are not given the tools to develop writing that is convincing and persuasive enough to solve problems. This form of writing, however, must be informed by factual information; therefore, students must be taught the skills of research and evaluation of data. For the empowerment of the community, students will have to learn the importance of recording and publishing data.

Methodology/Strategies for Implementation

Sixth and seventh grade students will meet with the instructor in small groups four days a week for thirty minutes. Once a week the entire class will meet to either discuss the projects as they develop, visit a university research facility, or listen to a guest, a researcher, or a lecture.

Objectives

1. Students will be able to distinguish the uses of the dictionary, the encyclopedia, the Reader's Guide to Periodical Literature, Books in Print, indexes for newspapers, as well as other reference and research aids.
2. Students will be able to gather data, statistical and qualitative, pertinent to understanding a specific African historical question, personal health or neighborhood related concerns or problems.
3. Students will be able to name the steps for problem solving.
4. Students will be able to identify those individuals who are key public officials responsible for the maintenance and development of neighborhood facilities, i.e., school grounds, recreation centers, street repair, and trash removal.
5. Students will be able to write letters and necessary follow-up correspondence related to acquiring information and resolving problems.
6. Students will be able to evaluate information and critique its usefulness as applied to specific problems.

Activities

There will be trips to city administrative offices, universities, and other research sites.

Assessment

Two forms of assessment will be used. One will be in the form of evaluating the methods of organizing information and its publication in the form of a newsletter to the school and letters to the editors of local newspapers and for national magazines. Second, a portfolio will be maintained containing copies of all correspondence developed by the students.

Because of space limitations, a list of African-centered classroom practices would not be feasible. A few examples would be the use of storytelling to convey ethical values; using the art of maskmaking to encourage creativity and to further an understanding of spirituality: and using the ancient Egyptian form of writing, MDW NTR (hieroglyphics), to help children learn to spell.

The critics of African-centered education, and even some of its adherents, incorrectly assume that the only purpose of Afrocentricity is an attempt to make African Americans feel good about themselves, building self-esteem and taking pride in historic accomplishments. These critics fail to recognize the significance of examining the historical record as a means for evaluating social, political, and economic events as well as their consequences and ramifications for the impact on people's lives. To the question of why it is imperative to bring historicity, an excellent response is made by Grace (1985):

> Our critical understanding of...contemporary developments will be enhanced if we locate our analysis...historically. One of the most promising developments in contemporary sociology of education has been the re-discovery of the heuristic power of historically located inquiry...It guards against...an unfortunate tendency towards a disembodied structuralism on the one hand or an unrelated world of consciousness on the other. More positively it has the advantage of sensitizing us to the principles and procedures which have been dominant in the past so that we are alert to the mode of their reproduction, reconstitution or change. It has the advantage also of concretely exemplifying and making visible the relations between educational structures of power, economy and control in particular periods of social change. Such exemplification and such making visible can provide us with *suggestive hypotheses and useful models in our attempts to clarify the present form of those relations.* (1985, p. 4, emphasis mine)

However the idea of centering should not be limited to a particular understanding of historical forms of knowledge nor should it be limited to engaging the unique language of a social group— expressing shared values, norms, ideology, and perspectives—a social dialect. The connection of centering with spirituality, not self-actualization or mental health, should be made clear. Centering becomes a referent for spiritual understanding and a search to find the inner being, but, beyond this, the process of centering takes place within the culture of the individual, and the struggles to make sense of a group's existence. The insight of James Macdonald (1988) is useful here as it applies to curriculum. "Centering as the aim of education calls for the completion of the person or the creation of meaning that utilizes all the potential given to each person. It in no way conflicts with the accumulated knowledge of a culture; it merely places this knowledge in the base or ground from which it grows. As such, centering is the fundamental process of human being that makes sense out of our perceptions and cognitions of reality" (p. 188).

Further theorizing of the African-centered project in dialog with a liberatory multicultralism will have to move beyond the binarisms set up in a strictly race discourse, Afrocentricity versus Eurocentricity. Cultural workers who are women of color have challenged and disrupted notions of a homogeneous black community by uncovering historically rooted gender antagonisms. African-centered theorists are then challenged to confront women's oppression as well. Though faced with several challenges, an affinity exists between the project of African-centered pedagogy and social reconstruction in the form of a liberatory multiculturalism.

A LIBERATING MULTICULTURAL DISCOURSE

> If we lived in a democratic state our language would have to hurtle, fly, curse, and sing, in all the common American names, all the undeniable and representative and participating voices of everybody here. We would not tolerate the language of the powerful and, thereby, lose all respect for words, per se. We would make our language conform to the truth of our many selves and we would make our language lead us into the equality of power that a democratic state must represent.
>
> June Jordan, *On Call Political Essays*

The discourse surrounding multiculturalism is vast. As pointed out by Sleeter and Grant (1988), when some people/institutions use the term multicultural education, they speak about racial or cultural diversity, while others conceptualize gender, social class, and additional forms of diversity. At the same time, many people who discuss gender equity and sexual orientation, share concerns similar to those of some multicultural education advocates but ignore race or give it only passing attention. The same can be said of those who address social class and disability. The conception of a liberatory multiculturalism in school curricula, however, requires the mapping of the differing advantaging systems named above with the referencing coordinates of three terms: democracy, culture, and pedagogy. McLaren rightly argues that "Multiculturalism without a transformative political agenda can just be another form of accommodation to the larger social order" (McLaren, Chapter 2 of this volume).

When considering the purpose of schooling, an argument can be made that education is to develop a politicized citizenry capable of fighting for various forms of public life. Students should be able to experience the accomplishment of social change, of transformation of existing social situations. Schooling in this sense is there to develop the cooperative/social intelligence necessary for democracy and freedom. Dewey (1916) expressed this idea: "a democracy is more than a form of government; it is primarily a mode of associated living, of conjoint communicated experience. The extension in space of the number of individuals who participate in an interest so that each has to refer to his own action to that of others, and to consider the action of others to give point and direction to his own, is equivalent to the breaking down of those barriers of class, race, and national territory which kept men from perceiving the full import of their activity." With the knowledge of self and political activism, students coming from this type of school environment should feel not only linked to their community but also compelled to recognize their interrelatedness with others.

Democracy and cultural studies are linked in this view of education. The liberal educational project would involve the continuous examining of a people's activity as they interact with others. Does one group value the others' values? Do they recognize ways that they could be mutually beneficial to each other with possibilities of forming coalitions to improve the lives of members differing groups? Do they recognize their own limitations to understand and cross borders into others' ways of being and recognize that there are times when borders may not and should not be crossed? The education of children to be critical in their perspectives goes further. While the student should be able to analyze, evaluate, and interpret information coming from and about different ethnic groups, form groups with diverse socioeconomic backgrounds, gender, and abilities, the liberatory, multicultural project, however, examines identity formation, social structures, notions of justice, and power relations, locating the ideological and material practices that are actively produced within day-to-day school life as originating in the wider society.

To examine pedagogy and a liberatory multiculturalism is to problematize the interaction between teacher, learner, and knowledge in the complexity of societal and culture gap relationships. In this sense it is not enough to raise questions about what and why specific subject matter is taught, or when someone has learned it. The importance of examining the aforementioned as well as other classroom practices and curriculum is crucial, but it is incomplete for an analysis of pedagogy because of the identity construction of the students. How does the student make sense of the world? What impact has the mass media, various print, visual, and audio technologies, had not only on meaning and values but also on desires? Pang (1991) has suggested that the comprehensive study of broad thematic units is beneficial to developing schools in a multicultural and democratic society. For example, using the concepts of equality, freedom, justice, democracy, power, pluralism, dignity, or honesty permits the intersection of objectives from language arts, geography, history, and citizenship. Most schools fail to interrogate the nation's social injustices in the form of inadequate hiring, poor-paying jobs, and health carelessness, endured by this country's people of color and the poor. Numerous examples of these types of thematic lessons exist but are all too often overlooked as teachers are required to cover specific discipline-based objectives. Democracy and pedagogy are linked in the examination of these economic, social, and political issues.

Curriculum can be defined as the organized environment for learning in a classroom and school; as such, it is never neutral but represents what is thought to be important and necessary knowledge by those who are dominant in a society. Given the diversity of cultures and, by extension, knowledge available, only a small fraction of it finds its way into the textbooks so widely used in the nation's classrooms. Decisions about what is important for students to learn are usually made by those furthest from the lives of the students. These decisions let students know whether the knowledge they or their communities value is accorded worth or prestige within the formal curriculum. Curriculum in this way serves as a means of social control, positioning the student as object. Additionally, decisions in schools tend to be rule and power-bound rather than negotiated. The assumption is that the administrator accepts school policy as handed down from the board, the teacher accepts school policy as handed down from the administrator, and the student accepts school policies and procedures and does what the teacher says. Schools in their assimilation, accul-turation, and socialization functions put stress on obedience and deference to those in authority. Purpel (1989) makes the point that the need for control produces control mechanisms and posits ethical questions about our supposed devotion to democracy: "Our political preference, indeed our passion for control, makes our traditional commitment to democracy highly problematic..." The current American preoccupation with individual advancement is mirrored in schools which promote competitiveness and singular academic achievement. The evaluative system in most districts uses numbers to demonstrate that schools have attained prede-termined objectives and have met their minimal requirements. Children's test scores are constantly being held up as a means of demonstrating what is happening with them academically and what is to be done with them.

The questions that beg to be asked are not merely around reading performance and graduation numbers; they are centered around *objectness* and choosing a way of being. For too many years the educational system has been used as a tool for assimi-lation and integration into a national agenda of American values which falsely purports to give equal opportunity to all, while insti-tutional racism guarantees the marginalization of Others. Minorities, people of color, appear to be the objects to be sorted and their places in society charted (though this positioning is contested and resisted). Under the guise of opportunity, the lived experiences of immigrants and other groups were devalued in educational settings as they were taught that the American values would lift them up from their "lower class" positions. African American and Hispanic-American children today have found these promises to be a lie, and the educational system which was to lift them has been abandoned for an economic means (the drug market) which, though it threatens their very lives, offers them a chance to exist beyond poverty. The children do not identify with school; they do not believe that what is presented nor what is done within the schools, under the guise of the teaching/learning process is worth the struggle.

Students as subjects see a future value to knowledge and can recognize subject matter as having a bearing upon their future. Education moves from object positioning to the student as subject when it considers the interest of the child, when it develops the capacity for growth, and when it takes place through the exami-nation, reconstruction, and reorganization of the historical and present social environment of the child.

The prelearning dissonance that occurs when students interrogate a text, inquire as to meanings, and are curious about taken-for-granted assumptions, becomes obscured in too many traditional classrooms. With little or no voice as to subject matter to be studied and no control over the length of instructional sessions and the rigid control over their physical movement, students develop minimal decision-making ability. Their daily lives, past experiences, and community histories are seldom the focus of curriculum objectives. Nevertheless, those in official authority—lawmakers, administrators, and frequently teachers—persist in refusing to change the alienating courses of study, pushing on toward a standardized, testable nationwide curriculum.

CONCLUSIONS

After examining this political hierarchy of knowledge, we can easily recognize that the current emphasis in most schools is global, economic competitiveness and that what becomes persistently devalued are the students' thoughts, languages, and lives. When students in urban neighborhoods are given the theorem to be learned and the data to be stored, couched in a language of fixture marketability, they compare the hoped for returns with the immediate cash availability in the drug market, and the future takes a shadowed retreat. Coupled with this is the devaluing of the students' life currency and the insistence that they are to know a prearranged, state-approved curriculum which is devoid of any relevancy. Students continue to resist the dominant curriculum along with its promise of future rewards of high test scores and good jobs. What becomes most alarming is that the student is blamed for not caring, the parent is blamed for not being involved, teachers for incompetency, and principals for a lack of visionary leadership.

Schools, and by extension the broader society, preparing for the twenty-first century will have to listen to the distress cries and painful utterances of the multiple groups who call this country home while their stories are treated marginally. These different groups are centering, saying who they are, how they historically came to be, what they believe, and what they desire; in so doing they come into conflict with other centering communities. The members of this multicultural society will have to be educated in ways that speak to justice and impartiality in ethical and democratic frameworks, learning to strike accords and resolve antagonisms which arise—that is, if the multiple sources of degradation, violence, domination and oppression that permeates our society are to be challenged and overcome.

When teachers work to develop curricula and classroom relations that eliminate oppressive social practices that are racist, sexist, and classist, they are working for a liberatory multiculturalism, are supporting a pedagogy aimed at restructuring the relations of power, and are engaging in a fight for freedom and justice. Centering students not only in their historical knowledges but also in the cultural struggles of diverse groups prepares them for the global diversity to which they are intimately linked.

REFERENCES

Abbary, A. S. 1990. Afrocentricity. *Journal of Black Studies* 2.

Akbar, N. 1984. Africentric social sciences for human liberation. *Journal of Black Studies* 14(4): 395–414.

———. 1985. *The community of self.* Tallahassee, Fla.: Mind Productions and Assoc.

Asante, M. K. 1987. *The Afrocentric idea.* Philadelphia: Temple University.

———. 1988. *Afrocentricity.* Trenton, N.J.: Africa World Press.

———. 1990. *Kemet, afrocentricity and knowledge.* Trenton, N.J.: Africa World Press.

Dewey, J. 1916. *Democracy and education.* New York: Macmillan Company.

Diop, C. A. 1967. *The African origin of civilization: Myth or reality.* Westport: Lawrence Hill.

Grace, Gerald. 1985. Judging teachers: The social and political contexts of teacher evaluation. *British Journal of Sociology of Education* 6(1): 4.

Hilliard, A. 1985. Kemetic concepts in education in *Nile Valley civilizations,* ed. I. Van Sertima. *Journal of African Civilizations* 6(2).

Hilliard, A., and Payton-Stewart, L. 1990. *Infusion of African and African American content in the school curriculum: Proceedings of the first national conference.* Morristown, N.J.: Aaron Press.

Johnson, D. and Johnson, R. 1987. Cooperative peer interaction versus individual competition and individualistic efforts: Efforts on the acquisition of cognitive reasoning strategies. *Journal of Educational Psychology* (73).

Karenga, M. 1992. Afrocentricity and multicultural education: Concept, challenge and contribution. Unpublished paper.

Keto, C. Tsehloane. 1991. *The Africa centered perspective of history and social sciences in the twenty-first century.* Blackwood, N.J.: K.A. Publications.

McLaren, P. 1986. *Schooling as a ritual performance: Towards a political economy of educational symbols and gestures.* London: Routledge and Kegan Paul.

Macdonald, J. 1988. A Transcendental developmental ideology of education. In *Curriculum,* ed. J. R. Gress and D. E. Purpel. Berkeley, CA.: McCutchan Publishing.

Myers, L. J. 1988. *Understanding the Afrocentric worldview: Introduction to and optimal psychology.* Dubuque, Iowa: Kendall-Hunt.

Nobles, W. 1980. African philosophy: Foundations for black psychology. In *Black Psychology.* ed. R. Jones. New York: Harper and Row.

————. 1990. The infusion of African and African American content: A question of content and intent. In *Infusion of African and African American content in the school curriculum.* ed. A. Hilliard. Morristown, N.J.: Aaron Press.

Pang, V. O. 1991. Teaching children about social issues: Kidpower. In *Empowerment through multicultural education.* ed. C. E. Sleeter, pp. 179–198. Albany, N.Y.: State University of New York Press.

Purpel, D. 1989. *The moral and spiritual crisis in education.* New York: Bergin and Garvey.

Schiele, J. 1990. Organizational theory from an Afrocentric perspective. *Journal of Black Studies* 21(2).

Slavin, R. 1989. Research on cooperative learning: Consensus and controversy. *Educational Leadership.*

Sleeter, C., ed. 1991. *Empowerment through multicultural education.* Albany, N.Y.: State University of New York Press.

Sleeter, C. E., and Grant, C. A. 1988. *Making choices for multicultural education.* Columbus, OH: Merrill Publishing.

Turner, J. E. 1984. Foreword: African studies and epistemology: A discourse in the sociology of knowledge. In *The next decade: Theoretical and research issues in African studies.* ed. J. E. Turner, pp. v–xxv. Ithaca, N.Y.: Cornell University Press.

14

Evelyn Newman Phillips ————————————————————

Multicultural Education Beyond the Classroom

Multicultural education has seldom been framed in the context of community-based education. Often, it is defined as a populist movement in schools that is designed to address systemic inequalities and cultural hegemony of dominant groups in pluralistic societies (Banks 1983). If multicultural education is a recognition and appreciation of pluralistic epistemologies in a society, does its practice have to be tied exclusively to the school environment? If multicultural education is an argument for "indigenization" of knowledge that represents cultural and political interests of the particular children and their communities (St. Lawrence and Singleton 1976, p. 22), can schools adequately fulfill that role?

As long as schools are complex bureaucracies that serve the needs of the state and African Americans and other minorities are in subordinated positions in the society, this institution most likely will not meet the challenge demanded by the multicultural movement. Support of this assertion is found in understanding the roles of schools. These institutions are designed to mobilize and prepare a workforce stratified by class, race, and gender in order to maintain the existing power structure (Bennett and LeCompte, 1990, p. 96). This societal role of school has been shown often in the existing practice of multicultural education within the school.

Multicultural education as ordinarily practiced tends to "insert" minorities into the dominant cultural frame of reference and leave intact existing cultural hierarchies and criteria of stratifications. Christine Sleeter (1992, p. 1) in *Keepers of the American Dream* writes that many school administrators operationally define multicultural education as another "program" to add on. Therefore, the current trend of multicultural education as most schools interpret it focuses on music, dance, folklore, and heroes of diverse cultural groups (Olneck 1990, p. 163). However, these cultural and ethnic traits are divorced from the political economy which shapes them. The discourse of multicultural education in schools generally does not reflect the indigenous voices of ethnic

371

and cultural minorities nor seek to transform existing social inequalities (St. Lawrence and Singleton 1976, p. 22; Olneck 1990, p. 163; Aronowitz and Giroux 1991, p. 161). "It is rather the voice of...educational professionals speaking about the 'problem' groups" (Olneck 1990, p. 163).

Multicultural education is an aspect of the African American struggle for power over cultural, economic, and political domination. This process is facilitated by their awareness of their ethnicity. Ethnic awareness is a recognition that American life is naturally multicultural but politically and economically structured by race, gender, and class (Sleeter and Grant 1988; Goodenough 1976). This complex and dynamic phenomenon provides ethnic groups with a consistent picture of their growth and development which arise out of their unique historical experience (Green 1981, p. 77).

African American ethnicity differentiates African Americans from other cultural groups and anchors them in the collective consciousness of their community to enable them to achieve instrumental and expressive goals within in the context of a pluralist society. African American youths who are aware of their ethnicity have the ability to interact effectively on their own terms in their own culture and with members of other cultural groups (Goodenough 1976, p. 5). In addition, this knowledge empowers African Americans against racial ascriptions and asserts the salience of their ontological perspectives relative to other worldviews. Hence, enculcating African American children in the worldview of their community is a form of multicultural education as it confirms their model of life.

These assumptions concerning multicultural education motivated the expansion of its praxis to the African American community in St. Petersburg. A multicultural education project that focused on the social history of African Americans in this city was designed for adolescent youths. The project sought to achieve three goals. One was to help African American youths to understand the social contexts that shape them and the life of their communities. The second was to give students opportunities to critically assess the history of their community from 1920 to the present. The third was to motivate students to transcend the barriers of race and to take a proactive role in their futures.

This chapter provides an overview of the development and implementation of this community-based program. It initially frames the project in the context of social change and conditions that are indigenous to African Americans in St. Petersburg. It particularly emphasizes the crisis of desegregated schools because their transformation has created an educational void in the African American community. This discussion also outlines how the oral life histories of the older residents were reconstituted for the education of the children and describes the process by which students examined their social heritages. Finally, it assesses the implications of the findings in this project.

EMPOWERMENT OR LYNCHING?

> The so-called modern education, with all it defects,
> however, does others so much more good than it does the
> Negro because it has been worked out in conformity to
> the needs of those who have enslaved and oppressed...
>
> Carter G. Woodson

The responsibility of a community for teaching its youths in its indigenous ways rests with each ethnic group. The desegregation experience of African Americans in St. Petersburg has shown that without common goals and experiences another group cannot socialize African American children into the native perspective of their ancestry. Asymmetrical power relationships existing between the African American community and the school system make this issue critical to the success and achievement of African American students.

Olneck (1990) proposes that if multicultural education is to have meaning it must achieve three goals: (1) It must enhance the communal or collective lives of groups that constitute a society. (2) There must be serious recognition of the claims of disfranchised groups as legitimate. (3) It has to support the salience of group membership as a basis for participation in the society. (p. 148) Aronowitz and Giroux (1991) suggest that this pedagogical practice allows students to recover their own voices so they can retell their own histories and in doing so "check and criticize the history they are told against the one they have lived" (p. 101).

The destruction of three African American neighborhoods, the community's loss of influence in desegregated schools, and the displacement of nearly two thousand people in St. Petersburg figure prominently in the social change of the African American community and the social disruption among its youth. Within the past ten years, an interstate highway physically split and blocked main arteries that lead from the community. During this time, African American communities also experienced a high incidence of school suspensions, violence, and drug abuse among their youth. These conditions signaled a disreputable reality for African Americans.

Although many families have been displaced by urban redevelopment since the late 1970s, African Americans link the primary problems of their youths to desegregation. Some school administrators, parents, and retired teachers suggest that African American children do not feel a part of the school system, and therefore they are suspended at a higher rate than other children (DeLoache 1981, p. 17). (The 1971 desegregation court order limits the African American population in Pinellas County schools to 30 percent or less. In some schools African Americans comprise 1 percent of the population.) The following statistics represent the entire county of Pinellas. However, St. Petersburg is the largest city in the school district. During the 1971–72 school year, African American students represented 22.5 percent of the 11,555 students suspended in Pinellas County (DeLoache 1980, p. 17). By 1979–80, 40 percent of the suspensions were of African American students (DeLoache 1981, p. 17). In the 1991–92 school year, African American students consisted of 17 percent of the entire student body in Pinellas schools, but they represented 39 percent of the students suspended in middle schools (Thomas 1993, p. 1). African American students in elementary school accounted for 44 percent of school suspensions and 55 percent of in-school suspensions (Thomas 1993, p. 6). During 1985–86 African American students represented 20 percent of the elementary school population, but they comprised 57 percent of the suspensions (Gibson 1987). The state board of education reported that the dropout rate among African American students in Florida is growing faster than their representation in the overall school population (Martin 1992). The Juvenile Welfare Board of Pinellas County (1988) concluded that black males in the ninth grade had a higher dropout rate than all other groups in the county. Twenty-eight percent of Florida's high school dropouts during the 1989–90 school year were African Americans. The African American community also found that their students were underrepresented in gifted classes and that they were overrepresented in classes for emotionally handicapped and other exceptional students (Serwatka, Deering, and Stoddard 1989, p. 520–522). In Florida, African Americans are 22 percent of the school population but they only comprise 4 percent of the gifted students (Ibid., p. 520). Hence, the predicament of many African American students presents a dismal picture.

Consistently, African Americans in St. Petersburg have linked the high rate of suspension and the low-achievement among African American children to issues of cultural sensitivity and to too few African American teachers and administrators in the school system. In a 1981 poll conducted by the *St. Petersburg Times* in St. Petersburg, 73 percent of the African Americans polled believed that their children did not disrupt classes any more than children of European descent but were suspended more often. Seventy-four percent suggested that the school system needed to hire more African American teachers and administrators. In 1992, the local African American weekly newspaper in St. Petersburg ran a series of editorials that suggested that a major consequence the retirement during the 1991–92 school year of 23 African American teachers would be an increase in the suspension rate among African American children and that there would be fewer opportunities for African American students to become knowledgeable of their African American heritage.

The school system disagreed with the African American community. It claimed that race was not directly related to the suspension of African American children. The system reported that children who were suspended were more likely to come from low-income families with poorly motivated parents. School officials suggested that race was an indirect factor when it was viewed as a variable strongly correlated with socioeconomic status (Thomas 1993, p. 6).

The African American community nevertheless perceived that race and income contributed to the displacement of African American children in the school system. Therefore, a committee requested that court-ordered busing be rescinded. The group also recommended that the formerly all-black Gibbs High School should again become the focal point of the African American community (Reed 1992, p. 1a). The committee suggested that Gibbs become a magnet school with a curriculum that focuses on African American culture and heritage. African Americans who proposed the change implied that desegregation disrupted the traditional role of African American teachers and schools—that of instilling pride and a sense of place in the community to African American children.

The status of African American children within the school system has been rather disappointing. The National Association for the Advancement of Colored People with the support of most of the African American community pushed for the desegregation of the schools during the 1950s. These leaders concluded that the only long-range hope for African American "social uplift" lay in education (Cruse 1987, p. 192). However, that goal seems thwarted when analyzing the status of the majority of African American youths.

Is the Past a Model for the Present?

Intellectuals ought to study the past not for the pleasure
they find in so doing, but to derive lessons from it.

Cheikh Anta Diop

African American teachers have had the unambiguous role of translating their community's worldview and the cultural ideas of European Americans to the youths. Michelle Foster (1991) who conducted oral histories of African American teachers throughout the United States found that these professionals had diverse roles. They perceived that effective teaching of African American students involved more than merely imparting subject matter. Foster documented that teachers were expected to teach students about "personal value, collective power and political consequences of choosing academic achievement." She argued that "integration" weakened the solidarity between African American students and teachers and limited these teachers' ability to engage in critical dialogue, a process crucial to the teaching of African American children (Ibid., p. 15). Discussing culturally specific messages to African American students in a "racially-mixed" audience would have been perceived as unprofessional and inappropriate. The new setting redefined the boundaries for African American teachers and children.

Historically, the "Negro" school was a major focal point in the enculturation of African American children. In St. Petersburg, club meetings and community activities were held at the school (White 1980, p. 19). It was the center of community. However, the 1954 Supreme Court ruling "integrated " the Negro school out of existence and denied the legitimacy of the community public school (Cruse 1987, p. 197).

African American folk theories of how to *get ahead* in American society differ significantly from theories presented in the predominantly European-American schools (Ogbu 1990, p. 48). Ogbu argues that "African Americans stress collective efforts as the best means of achieving upward mobility." This value system stands in stark contrast to the dominant American culture that emphasizes individuality as leading to success. African American perceptions and cultural experiences are different from the middle-class folk theories of European-Americans that significantly influence schooling in this country (Ibid., p. 49).

Increasing numbers of African Americans agree that a major aspect of saving African American children requires that they are taught their cultural heritage (Asante 1989; Kunjufu 1984; Nobles and Goddard 1989). Nai'm Akbar (1982) argues that African Americans must study their culture and their history as human beings (p. 7). Such knowledge will allow them to discover the patterns which dignify and make them who they are (p. 6). More than sixty years ago, Carter G. Woodson (1969) posited, "To educate the Negro we, must find out exactly what his background is, what he is today, what his possibilities are, and how to begin with him as he is and make him a better individual of the kind that he is...We should develop his latent powers that he may perform in society a part of which others are not capable" (pp. 150–151). Finally, in the *State of Black America* 1990, published by the Urban League, Bell and Jenkins (1990) added, "There is some evidence that strong ethnic identity may decrease involvement in self-destructive behaviors" (p. 151).

Research has shown that orienting youths in the ways of their ethnic heritage is beneficial. An American Folklife survey of 6,000 ethnic heritage schools revealed that the self-esteem of the youths was raised through classes that focused on the indigenous knowledge of their cultural group (Sacks 1985, p. 263). Eliot Wigginton (1986), a public school teacher in Rabun, Georgia, created the Foxfire project. He found that Appalachian students in the program who researched their backgrounds gained confidence and appreciation of their ancestral past. The Commission for Racial Justice of the United Church of Christ implemented a national rites of passage program for adolescents to prevent of African American teenage pregnancy (Warfield-Coppock and Harvey 1989). Warfield-Coppock and Harvey documented fifty-two community-based rites of passage programs in the United States. In Derry, Northern Ireland at a boys' secondary school, a curriculum was tied to the diverse cultures within the community (Nixon 1985). Students focused on the problems and issues that directly influenced their lives and discussed community controversies. Nixon proposed that this program helped students to examine their lives in a cultural context and integrate information intellectually (p. 9). Research implies that communities can reclaim their youths by enculturating them in their cultural heritage.

The idea of communities reclaiming their youth motivated the development of this project in the St. Petersburg community. The development of this project and its implementation are outlined in the next section.

FIELD SETTING

This project was located in a predominately African American community center. The Enoch Davis Center is located less than a mile from the city's urban redevelopment district, where an empty $138 million sport stadium stands. This center is a major gathering place for African American activities. It houses the James Weldon Johnson Branch Library and provides space for agencies and community groups. This facility serves as a site for senior citizen lunches during the weekdays. Tutoring, leadership training, and counseling are among the services offered at the center. The center filled the void for a meeting place that was created when the schools were desegregated.

The African American community has a special sense of ownership in this center, although it is managed by the city. For three years, St. Petersburg Module 16 Advisory Committee fought city hall to get $1.6 million to build a high quality cultural, performing arts, and social service office center in the center of the city's African American community (White 1981, p. 1). The committee was appointed to advise city officials on land use plans and improvement projects in the African American community. The city perceived the group's role as rather benign. Instead, the members became activists. They sought grants and fought against the city to fund the building. The city council resisted funding the project and suggested that the group hàd overstepped its boundaries. These community activists persisted and eventually won.

This community center is surrounded by African American neighborhoods. African Americans comprise between 86 and 99 percent of population in this area according to the 1990 Census. There is a total of 238,629 people who reside in St. Petersburg. The majority of the 46,726 African Americans in the city live near the center (Adair, 1991, p. 18). A significant number of African Americans settled near their downtown jobs during the early development of St. Petersburg during the late 1880s and the early part of this century. They came to St. Petersburg to work in the tourist industry and the development of the city. They were employed as maids, construction workers and hotel servants.

Prior to the 1950s tourism boomed in St. Petersburg. During the last half of this century the city became identified as a retirement center. However, by late 1970s leaders in this Florida Gulf coastal city were not pleased with the city's image as a place for people over sixty-five (Arsenault 1988, p. 313). Therefore, the city removed its green benches, once a symbol of its retired population. They also designated three of the oldest African American communities contiguous to downtown as blighted slums and embarked on a multimillion dollar downtown redevelopment plan. The city decided to woo, exclusively, "young progressive citizens" and tourists (Vesperi 1985, p. 45). Ten years after the plan was initiated, the Gas Plant neighborhood, once a viable African American community, became the site of an empty $138 million Florida Suncoast Dome and a parking lot.

The City pursued opportunities to acquire a baseball franchise after building the stadium. However, its efforts failed. The latest unsuccessful bid was the San Francisco Giants. On November 13, 1992, the baseball commission rejected the offer.[1]

Seventeen churches, twenty-seven businesses, 353 households, and 800 community residents were displaced and scattered. The land, a baseball team, and an upscale image of St. Petersburg seemed more valuable than the people who lived on the land. Adding irony to injury, these efforts have been laughably unsuccessful. These conditions provide the setting for this project.

"PROJECT LA CHURASANO"

> Thou art even as a finely tempered sword concealed in
> the darkness of it's sheath and it's value hidden....
> Baha'u'llah

Local African American students were presented opportunities to critically assess the social history of African American life in St. Petersburg from the 1920s to the present. Oral history interviews, archival documents, newspaper clippings, video tapes, and consultations with local historians form the foundation of this project. Included are interviews with thirty-two African American residents who lived in St. Petersburg for more than twenty years. The majority were older than fifty-five. Those interviewed were teachers, folk artists, maids, clerks, laborers, nurses, and sanitation workers. Additional information was drawn from street directories, newspaper articles on "Negro News", maps, city council files, census data, and books to supplement this ethnohistory. This information was summarized and presented in two four-week sessions. The project was called Project La Churasano: Remembering the Past to Control the Future. La Churasano means culture in the Mandinka language. Mandinka is a West African tongue spoken in The Gambia, Senegal, Mali, Guinea, Guinea Bissau, and Sierra Leone. The program addressed such issues as historical origins of African Americans, their migration, the power of their words in rap, blues, and preaching, and the changing spatial development of the African American community. Also, included in these discussions were changing styles of dress and the historical and political significance of the 1968 Garbage Strike in St. Petersburg.

The sessions were offered to middle and high school students. The first series were directed toward early adolescents between the ages of eleven and fourteen years. The second four-week sessions were geared to fifteen to eighteen-year-old students. Students were recruited through local black culture clubs, teachers, newspaper articles, and community service agencies. The sessions were free, but students had to register with their parents' permission. Group attendance was open and voluntary. An average of six students attended each group.

Classes were held three times a week. Students met on Thursdays and Saturdays. Thursday classes lasted for two hours while on Saturdays the group met for three hours, because they often took field trips. Therefore, students met for five hours each week for a total exposure of twenty hours.

Revelations of Critical Dialogues

> Shattered dreams are a hallmark of our mortal life.
> Martin Luther King, Jr.

Distinct characteristics emerged between the two groups of students. The initial group consisted of six students who routinely came to the library and community center after school, primarily because their parents were working. They ranged from ages eleven to twelve. Two of the students were enrolled in a class for the "emotionally handicapped." They were from working-class and lower-middle-class families. Two of the students' parents were college educated. Most of these students were encouraged to attend by their parents.

The second group of students was also from working and middle-class families. However, they lived outside of the immediate environs of the center. The majority of these students' parents had either high school diplomas or college training. The average student in this group was fifteen years old with a part-time job. All of the students except three were members of a black culture club. One student's family had migrated from Jamaica. Families of the other students had relocated from other parts of Florida and Georgia decades earlier.

Many of the high school students were involved in other activities. One was the president of her student body and the black culture club. She and three other group members also sang in a school choir. This particular student even had a part-time job. Another senior was a writer for her school newspaper and participated in an annual citywide black history month pageant. Three males attended. Each of them played school sports and had part-time jobs. One of the male students also attended a leadership training for high school students at one of the local colleges. Their participation in the classes was motivated by their interest but sometimes hampered by their other responsibilities.

The age differences between the groups helped to differentiate their attitudes towards the project. The younger students frequently saw African Americans in pejorative terms while the older students sought to know more about their ancestry.

The project began with the younger students. They seriously challenged the project format and resisted any attempts that linked their identities to Africa. The task of encouraging these African American students seemed quite formidable. They were poorly informed about the history of African Americans but well inculcated with the stereotypical images by which they are portrayed. Disregarding their blackness and Africanness, the students made negative comments about Blacks and Africans.[2]

The students perceived an African heritage to be absurd. During a session concerning the historical origins of African Americans, there was a consensus that their families did not come from Africa. James,[3] a rather outspoken young man, indignantly said, "I didn't come from no Africa. Africans ain't got no sense. They don't even have sense enough to put on clothes!" I used maps, drums, baskets, and other cultural artifacts from Africa to show their connections with African Americans.

Their body language suggested that they did not believe any of the information. The children nervously giggled at such ideas. Their disbelief was confirmed when James, who seemed to be speaking for the others, said, "Next she is going to tell us that Jesus was black!" It seemed impossible for them to consider that such "primitive people" as Africans were a part of their ancestry.

The students were questioned concerning the source of their beliefs and attitudes about Africans. They said that these things were shown on television. I asked if they believed everything they saw on television. In unison they replied, "Yes!" They offered the violence in their neighborhoods as an example. They rationalized that what they saw on television news was not too different from what they saw in their neighborhoods. They argued that blacks were always robbing, killing each other, and doing drugs in their neighborhoods just like on television. I countered their examples with models of people in the community who were not engaged in violence. Nevertheless, the students reasoned that if the information was not true, it would not have been shown on television.

Later during the session, I pursued James' comment about the color of Jesus. I anticipated that such an examination would help the students understand that race was socially constructed. The students were instructed to locate on the map the place Jesus was born. I asked them if they thought Jesus was "black" or "white." Each of the four students attending that day said, "white!" I suggested that people from that region of the world most often referred to themselves as Jewish or Arabic. Again, I pursued the question and asked them if they considered color to mean the same thing in the area where Jesus was born as it did in the United States? No answers were given.

I was curious to know what motivated the students to see Jesus as "white." I inquired how they reached such a conclusion. The students acted as if they could not believe that I was asking this question. James said, "All you have to do is look at his picture over the pulpit in the churches." Their observations were true. In the majority of the African American churches in St. Petersburg, Jesus was drawn with long blond hair and with Aryan features. For them, the church was the final word of truth.

My analyses confronted their realities. I perceived that I was defying not only their beliefs but also in their minds the teachings of the church. Therefore, I was treading in dangerous waters. The students regard the church as above reproach along with the television. This problem could not be resolved in one class session, I concluded.

It was difficult to discuss the history of African Americans in St. Petersburg without providing background information concerning the larger African American struggles. For example, students knew Martin Luther King, but their knowledge of him and his role in the Civil Rights movement was largely unknown. Therefore, I included the "Eyes on the Prize" series and other documentaries to provide context and content.

Toward the end of the four-week session a shift in James' attitude was observed. Before class one day, he told me that he hoped to be an engineer. He wondered if I had any books about black scientists that he could read. The following session I gave him a list of black inventors and a copy of Van Sertima's (1990) *Blacks in Science*. This author traces African scientific innovation from 2,000 B.C. to African Americans who are present-day nuclear scientists. Although Van Sertima's work is somewhat advanced, James read some excerpts. While discussing the book, he wondered how it was possible for early Africans to know about astronomy and build pyramids. His question seemed more of wonderment than of implying the denial of such feats existing among Africans.

During another session on the sixties, the younger students raised serious questions. The class included a video presentation about the student rebellion at Howard University, Mohammed Ali's fight against the draft board, and a guest speaker. The speaker discussed his experience as a student protestor at Florida A & M University during that period. The relationship between the striking students and the police was a concern of the students. They wanted to know how Ali was able to resolve his troubles with the draft. The sixties, however, seemed like ancient history to those youths. "How was it back in those days?" they would ask. They seemingly realized that these struggles were a part of their parents' realities but not of theirs.

The second series of classes with the older adolescents was strikingly different from the first group. These students were willing to analyze the African American community and its relationship with the larger community. They also perceived that structural barriers affected their lives. Naturally, they were more mature than the younger group.

The perceptiveness of the older students was shown during the first session. These youths were given the responsibility of videotaping interviews with each other. The goal of the session was to help the students become acquainted with each other. They were instructed to question their cohorts and some aspect of their culture and their families. The students chose to explore family backgrounds and rules about dating, sex, education, and career goals.

Inquiry into the Jamaican student's family's attitude about pregnancy generated a cross-cultural perspective concerning the rearing of young women. Melody was asked if her mother consistently warned her not to get pregnant and stay in school. She informed her cohorts that in her culture it was not automatically assumed that a teenage girl would get pregnant. She reported that her mother emphasized education. She reasoned that her mother never doubted that she and her sister would attend college. The experiences of the four girls who had grown up in St. Petersburg were contrasted. These girls unanimously stated that their mothers continually warned them against getting pregnant. Their mothers feared that they would have children before finishing school. Thus the admonishment not to get pregnant was stronger than the advice to get an education. I asked the students to consider which factor may have shaped these different cultural responses. Students from both cultures agreed that economics plays a key role in these approaches. The Jamaican student and the local students suggested that women were expected to be able to take care of themselves. Their analyses implied that these different African cultures were motivated by the same goal even if their methods varied.

A class on the African Diaspora and the origins of African Americans gave students a greater understanding of the relationship between Afro-Caribbean people and African Americans. Although these African American students understood and accepted that African Americans came from Africa, none of them considered Jamaicans and people from the Caribbean to be of African descent. They concluded that the slave experience was unique to Blacks in the United States. They thought that Afro-Caribbeans were indigenous to that area. African Americans students born in the United States wondered, Why, if Caribbean Blacks came from Africa originally, did people from the Islands act as if they were better than African Americans? The local students seemed to assume that if people from the Caribbean had histories similar to those of African Americans, then their status was the same as Blacks in the United States.

Such comparison of African Americans with Afro-Caribbeans was framed in the context of race and competition between "Island

Blacks" and "Blacks in the United States." Students were asked to consider how these groups were pitted against each other and stereotyped in this country. They offered the Haitian and Cuban refugees as examples. The group suggested that race was the predominant factor that prevented Haitians from being accepted in the United States. Tanya, the student body president, reminded the group that the Haitians were further stereotyped as having AIDS. Tanya, speaking of Afro-Caribbean people, said, "They ain't no better than us." She implied that race was also a burden for Afro-Caribbean people in this country.

A salient issue during these discussions was: "Why no one told us about these things before?" This question led to a discourse about the roles of schools in their education. Students disappointedly expressed that their schools never addressed the origins of African Americans. "They only talk about slavery," Jamal, a high school junior, mocked.

This student argued that when he sought to introduce an African American perspective in the class, he encountered difficulties. Jamal described a teacher's response to a paper he wrote on Malcolm X. He contended that the teacher criticized him for writing about Malcolm X. The teacher allegedly told Jamal that Malcolm X was a racist and a radical who hated white people. Also, he argued that many people feared Malcolm X. The student revealed that he tried to explain to the teacher that the image was a misconception that had been promoted by the media. The teacher prevailed nevertheless. Jamal commented that he would continue to read but keep his ideas to himself. This African American student perceived the school environment to be restrictive rather than nurturing.

He further pointed out that the African American students at his school did not embrace the idea of a black culture club. Black culture clubs have been used by African American students since desegregation to counter alienation, assert their collective presence, and provide a sense of belonging. Jamal's school, located in an ethnically-mixed, upper-middle-class neighborhood, has been unable thus far to organize a black culture club, although several attempts had been made. He reasoned that the Black students were too busy "being white" and assimilating into the dominant middle-class culture of the school. Jamal felt that students were too embarrassed to join a black culture club. Agreement with his observations concerning the club was later expressed by one of the counselors at the school.

By contrast, the other students in the group attended the once historically all-black Gibbs High school, of which African Americans now comprise 25 percent of the student body, and they were members of a black culture club. The Gibbs students expressed the feeling that the black culture club gave them opportunities to discuss issues concerning their history and community which otherwise may not be discussed in the classroom. They felt that this venue provided a safe haven for their thoughts. The Gibbs students indicated that their history teacher was instrumental in helping them to organize and sustain the club.

The students recognized that this teacher, who had spent his entire professional career at Gibbs, was their advocate in the system. They bragged to the other students that he had developed and taught a course on African American history after Reconstruction for the winter term of 1991. They compared him with other teachers and suggested that he actually understood them. This teacher also encouraged these students to attend my program. The community-based program and Mr. Solomon's guidance were mutually supportive. My program allowed students to localize the information they had learned in their classes and clubs.

The students were given opportunities to investigate the consequences of the displacement of the Laurel Park community by urban redevelopment. A field trip was taken to the site of the Florida Suncoast Dome. The students were charged to videotape the area and to interview residents and the remaining business owners to determine how these persons felt about the removal of the community.

Before interviewing the community members, the students had the chance to discuss the politics of hazardous materials and poor communities. Our arrival at the site was welcomed by a red ribbon that warned: Danger Asbestos. The cordoned off plot of land was the site of a future parking lot for the Suncoast Dome. The students had many questions. They wondered if the workers had been sufficiently protected while removing the asbestos. If the St. Petersburg Housing Authority knew that the Laurel Park complex, which it owned, had asbestos, why did the agency allow people to live there? they asked. Were the remaining residents and businesses informed that Laurel Park had asbestos when the demolition occurred? Not all of the students' questions were answered. However, a business owner told us that he had not been informed prior to the demolition that harmful substances were at the complex.

Adjacent to the area where the housing complex once stood, remained six homes, one five-unit apartment building, and two businesses. One store was owned by a Vietnamese family and the other by an African American man.

Interviews with the remaining residents and store owners showed that urban policies can disrupt peoples' lives even if they are not required to move. The residents and the storekeepers expressed a sense of loss over the dismantling of their community. The residents of Laurel Park had been a source of income to the store owners. They were hardly able to break even without this revenue. The African American owner told the students that he now supplemented his income by selling parking spaces on his property when events were held at the Dome. He acknowledged that such activities did not occur often. Two of the remaining residents revealed that the neighborhood had little choice in determining the course of events. One gentleman, who appeared to be in his late thirties, suggested that the city views the area as a crime-ridden eyesore. Another homeowner in her mid-sixties informed the students that she had lived in her home for over twenty years. However, she said that the current chaos had led her to decide to return to Georgia.

These direct encounters increased students' awareness concerning the ethics of urban redevelopment and political policies. As the group was leaving the neighborhood, Sam, a junior who had been videotaping the scene, excitedly turned to the rest of us while pointing at the huge columns that supported the interstate exchange above. "Look," he said, "This is not the first time this community has been torn up. Look at how this place has been cut up by the interstate." Other students surmised that the city had targeted this community a decade earlier and the latest removal was another aspect of its plan to remove African Americans from the area. Sam concluded that it was not possible for the city to build a stadium across from this community and allow the people to stay there. They argued that the presence of Laurel Park would have discouraged whites from coming to the area. Hence, the students realized that not all of the goals of urban policies are explicitly expressed.

"How could the black community let this happen?" asked Tanya, president of the black culture club. There was an overwhelming consensus among the students that poverty and image were directly linked to the dislocation of the Laurel Park residents. Sean, a junior, suggested that if the residents had not been poor, they would not have been removed. Tomeka, a senior, perceived that the black community did not support the Laurel Park residents because of its image as a housing project. It was home to "welfare mothers and their children." The students inferred that the "black leaders" also felt that Laurel Park was a blot on the black community's self-portrait. Therefore, they did not fight the removal of the Laurel Park residents. This discussion helped students to understand that, in this case, the divided views of the community concerning Laurel Park contributed to their removal.

Kari reminded the students that the director of the St. Petersburg Housing Authority was a "black man" and that he had played an instrumental role in removing the residents by selling the building to the city. This statement led the students to question the director's allegiance to the black community. The students believed that the director should have done more to prevent the removal of the residents rather than contribute to their dislocation. The director's behavior was not so unusual suggested the students. "Blacks in high positions often forget where they came from." Through the students' eyes, the director's role seemed straightforward. They felt he should have supported the residents of Laurel Park rather than sell their home to the city.

The ethnic history of African Americans in St. Petersburg has played a cogent role in informing students about their culture and the cultural assumptions of others. Group interactions with these youths have been supported by the assumption that their lives naturally intersect with diverse cultural views. Many times those cultural views conflict and threaten the existence of African Americans because of race, power, class, and finances. An examination of the complex structures of exclusion and racism permits the students to understand that the pressure to assume the cultural values of others may be subtly perpetuated through television, religious images, a dialogue with a teacher, or the absence of information. Students were also provided an opportunity to see and hear how a city's political agenda for development and modernization destroyed the cultural integrity of African American neighborhoods and affected the financial and emotional security of those who remained. The reconstruction of their community's history has taught students about the realities which shape their lives and the salience of their ethnicity when interacting with other groups. People who understand who they are able to become fully actualized (Banks 1988).

IMPLICATIONS

When African American children openly express pejorative terms about Africans and Blacks it seems apparent that the community needs to examine how the ideas and self-concepts of African American children are shaped. Their words sounded as if they were spoken by some nineteenth-century scientist justifying the inferiority of Africans and Blacks. Instead, these ideas were mouthed by children who had only been on this planet for little more than a decade. Why have these thoughts rolled so comfortably and confidently from the tongues of these youths?

When a subordinate population, in this case African American youths, accepts their inferiority and values the superiority of the dominant group, deculturation has occurred (Baker 1983, p. 37). Their identity then becomes firmly rooted in the social order which has been ascribed to them (Magubane 1987, p. 15). This phenomenon was clearly seen among the younger group members. The placement of two of the students in special education classes for the emotionally handicapped, perhaps, reinforced their belief in the inferiority of Blacks.

These children linked their concepts of blackness and Africanness to the television news. Would it be possible for an external force to have such influence over the minds of these children if their community affirmed a more positive message concerning Africans and Blacks? Research suggests that minority groups assist in perpetuating their inferiority once they have accepted a subordinate status (Magubane 1987, p. 15; Baker 1983, p. 37; Fanon 1970, p. 137).

The younger students' perception of Jesus implies that the church is complicitous in the oppression of African Americans. A depiction of Christ as white rather than Jewish suggests to African American youth that God is "white." James Cone (1969), an American theological scholar, argues that in America Christ is portrayed with "light skin, wavy brown hair, and sometimes— wonder of wonders—blue eyes" (p. 68). He agrees that such image "serves only to make official and orthodox the centuries-old portrayal of Christ as white" (p. 68). Cone (1969) concludes that the black church though spatially located in the community of the oppressed, "has not responded to the needs of its people. It has rather...condemned the helpless and have mimicked the values of whites" (p. 115). The acquiescence of black churches to symbols of racism conveys a stronger message of the subordination of African Americans than any religious sermon which expresses the equality of all humans.

A critical assessment by African Americans of their culture and how children are socialized into various roles is crucial to their survival. Answers to these question will offer insight into the enculturation that is needed to prepare African American children for the future. How successful can a child be in a society where he or she feels inferior? Why did the younger students have negative attitudes toward being African and Black? Were these concepts prevalent earlier in the older students but changed by time? What roles have schools and parents played in shaping the impressions of African American youth? Which messages do the social institutions convey to children? Are children socialized to assimilate? Did the events that occurred during their birth era make a difference? How can the community support students who seek greater awareness of themselves as cultural beings? The documentation of the social history of African Americans in St. Petersburg allows African Americans to examine historical patterns of socialization and their implications in assisting African American children in reaching their full potential. However, further exploration of these issues are needed.

Derrick Bell (1991) speaking of African Americans' quest for racial justice writes "we have attained all the rights we sought in law and gained none of the resources we need in life. Like the crusaders of old, we sought the holy grail of 'equal opportunity' and, having gained it in court decisions and civil right statutes, find it transformed from the long-sought guarantee of racial equality into one more device the society can use to perpetuated the racial status-quo." This analysis describes the paradox of education in the African American community.

African Americans perceived that the desegregation of schools would improve their condition. Instead they found the integrity of their culture threatened and the status of their children and community weakened because the school was no longer the core of the community. Although many of the facilities were still located in their neighborhoods, their children felt like intruders (Hacker 1992; Reed 1993). Their power to use school as a medium to transmit African American cultural values was significantly reduced. The community now had to depend upon the individual actions of concerned teachers. Discontinuity between the cultures of school, home, and community has seriously jeopardized the academic achievement of many African American children. This historical watershed in the legacy of St. Petersburg, twenty years later, would create a complex dilemma for African Americans. The issue is whether to pursue the current path of desegregation or return to a separate and "equal" system.

In retrospect, it appears that African Americans leaders did not understand the role of mainstream schools. One of the major goals of schools has been to rid ethnic groups of their ethnic characteristics and reinforce Anglo-Saxon values and behaviors as the standard (Banks 1984, p. 71). Ellwood Patterson Cubberly concluded that the task of the school "was to break up immigrant groups and their settlements, to assimilate or amalgamate them as part of the American race and to implant in their children as far as can be done, the Anglo-Saxon concept of righteousness, law, order, and popular government, and to awaken in them reverence for democratic institutions and for those things which we as a people hold to be of abiding worth" (Ibid., p. 474). Hence, as a social institution, school constitutes a machinery that helps to maintain the social structure and its continuity.

Schools served a similar role in the African American community but their message was different. Students were acculturated in the mainstream worldview and socialized into the African American perspective. They were nurtured to be proud of their "race" and be academically competent. A retired Gibbs high school history teacher described the former curriculum at the "all Black school." Students were the taught the classics, Latin, French and Shakespeare. Race pride was also instilled by inviting successful Negroes like Dr. Mary McCleod Bethune and New York Yankee player Elston Howard to talk to the students about their lives and the challenges they faced and overcame. This socialization was supplemented by organizing extra curricular activities like a school choir that would expose students to life outside of their community. To prepare their children to rise above their racially ascribed status, African Americans schooled their children to be conscious of their ethnicity and to understand how it is shaped by the mainstream society.

Multicultural education implies that the worldviews of diverse cultures are equally respected. In a society where respect is accorded in relation to power, African Americans must extend their struggle of multicultural education beyond the classroom. This venue allows children to be socialized in their heritage. More importantly, this process affirms the indigenous knowledge of African Americans and shows how the political economy perpetuates cultural hegemony against African American culture. Therefore, African Americans cannot afford to structure multicultural education around the concept of 'individual differences,' and advance an apolitical and fragmented model of culture that presumes an attitudinal explanation for ethnic conflicts (Olneck 1990, p. 147). This process should include social action that will transform the community economically, politically, spiritually, and socially (Sleeter and Grant 1988). African American young people need to learn to work collectively to challenge the structures and culture of racism and poverty that imprison them, and to develop the spiritual strength to undertake this work.

NOTES

I acknowledge funding from the Pride Fellowship of the University of South Florida. I would like also to thank Nancy Greenman, Ph.D., Susan Greenbaum, Ph.D., and Happy Dobbs who commented on earlier drafts of this chapter.

1. After St. Petersburg failed to secure the Giants, newspaper commentaries reminded the city of its earlier treatment of Bill White, president of National League. During the late 1950s and 1960s White was a ballplayer with the St. Louis Cardinals. Preseason training was held in St. Petersburg. This coastal resort town was a segregated during that time. Negro players, as they were called during those days, were not permitted to share social activities with their European-American cohorts during those days. In 1961 the St. Petersburg Chamber of Commerce held a "Salute to Baseball" breakfast banquet, but White and the other "Negro players" were not invited. White informed the press of this discrimination. The embarrassed chamber issued a last minute invitation to White, but he refused to attend. Newspaper journalists wondered if White was reminded of the incident when he visited St. Petersburg in 1992 during the summer. This time the city was divided by race on the hotly debated issue of the firing of the chief of police who is white by an acting city manager who is black (Gosier 1992).

2. One of the consequence of racial identity for oppressed people is an internalization of their oppressors' attitudes. Donald Baker (1983, p. 37) in *Race, Ethnicity and Power* argues that in racial relationships the cultural identity of subordinate groups is destroyed and an inferiority complex is instilled.

3. Pseudonyms are used for all of the pupils.

REFERENCES

Adair, B. (1991, March 6). Black population grows in cities. *St. Petersburg Times*, p. B.

Akbar, N. 1985. *The community of self.* Jersey City: New Mind Productions.

————. 1989. *Chains and images of psychological slavery.* Jersey City: New Mind Productions.

Albright, M. 1977. Module 16 members warned by city council. St. Petersburg: *Evening Independent*, August 8.

————. 1977. Off beat. St. Petersburg: *Evening Independent*, September 24.

Aronowitz, S. and Giroux, H. A. 1991. *Post modern education: Politics culture and social criticism.* Minneapolis: University of Minnesota Press.

Arsenault, R. 1988. *St. Petersburg and the Florida dream 1888–1950.* Norfolk: The Donning Company.

Asante, M. K. 1989. *Afrocentricity.* Trenton: Africa World Press.

Baal, S. 1992. Did we lose the Giants in the '60s? *Creative Loafing* 5 (37): 3–6.

Baker, Donald. 1983. *Race, ethnicity and power: A comparative study.* London: Routledge and Kegan Paul.

Banks, J. 1984. Multiethnic education in the U.S.A.: Practices and promises. In *Education in multicultural societies.* ed. Trevor Corner, pp. 68–95. New York: St. Martin's Press.

Banks, J. 1988. *Multicultural education: Theory and practice.* Boston: Allyn and Bacon.

Banks, J. A. and Lynch, J. 1986. *Multicultural education in western societies.* New York: Praeger.

Bell, C. and E. J. Jenkins 1990. Preventing homicide. In *The state of Black America 1990.* ed. J. Dewart, pp. 143–156. New York: National Urban League.

Bell, D. 1987. *And we are not saved: The elusive quest for social justice.* New York: Basic Books.

————. 1991 . The elusive quest for racial justice: The chronicle of the constitutional contradiction. In *The state of Black America.* ed. J. Dewart, pp. 9–24. New York: National Urban League.

Bennett, K. P. and LeCompte, M. 1990. *How schools work: A sociological analysis of education.* White Plains: Longman.

Cohen, Y. 1971. The shaping of mens's minds: Adaptations to imperatives of culture. In *Anthropological perspectives on education.* ed. Murray Wax, pp. 19–50. New York: Basic Books.

Cone, J. 1969. *Black theology and black power.* New York: Seabury Press.

Corner, T. 1984. *Education in multicultural societies.* New York: St. Martin's Press.

Cruse, H. 1987. *Plural but equal: A critical study of Blacks and minorities and America's plural society.* New York: William Morrow.

Davis, A. 1992. Schools see sharp rise in suspensions. *St. Petersburg Times*, July 5.

DeLoache, F. 1980. Desegregation: Many Blacks find it a burden but remain wary of the possible alternatives. In *To be Black and to live in St. Petersburg.* St. Petersburg: St. Petersburg Times.

Fanon, F. 1970. *Black skin, white masks.* London: Granada.

Florida Institute on Education. 1985. *The education condition of Black males in Florida: An exploratory study.* Tallahassee: Florida Board of Regents.

Foster, M. 1991 . Constancy, connectedness and constraints in the lives of African American women teachers: Some things change, most stay the same. *National Women's Studies Association Journal,* 3(2) :1–15.

Foster, M. 1991 . The politics of race: Through the eyes of African-American teachers. *Journal of Education* 172(3): 23–40.

Gibson, Patricia. 1987. Suspension and corporal punishment 1985–86. Pinellas County Schools. Unpublished manuscript.

Gibson, M. 1984. Approaches to multicultural education in the United States: Some concepts and assumptions. *Anthropology and Education Quarterly* 15(1): 94–118.

Goodenough, W. 1976. Multicultural education as the normal human experience. *Anthropology and Education Quarterly* 7(4): 4–6.

Gosier, E. 1992. Bad surprise at good school. *St. Petersburg Times,* April 25.

———. 1992. Sights come home to roost. *St. Petersburg Times,* November 23.

Hacker, A. 1992. *Two nations: Black and white, separate, hostile, unequal.* New York: Charles Scribner's Sons.

Harris, R. 1983. From inclusion to interpretation: Teaching Afro-American history in the 1980s. *The Social Studies* 74(1): 25–29.

Hillard, A. G. 1978. Equal educational opportunity and quality education. *Anthropology and Education Quarterly* 9(2): 110–126.

Juvenile Welfare Board of Pinellas County 1993. *Social indicator report.* 14(1) St. Petersburg, Florida: Juvenile Welfare Board.

Juvenile Welfare Board of Pinellas County October, 1988. *School dropouts in Pinellas county by race. Social indicator report.* St. Petersburg, Florida: Juvenile Welfare Board.

Kunjufu, J. 1984. *Developing positive self-images and discipline in Black children.* Chicago: African-American Images.

Magubane, B. 1987. *Ties that bind: African American consciousness.* Trenton: Africa World Press.

Martin, J. 1992. Dropout numbers still high. *St. Petersburg Times,* December 20.

Nixon, J. 1985. *A teacher's guide to multicultural education.* Oxford: Basil Blackwell.

Nobles, W. and Goddard, L. L. 1989. Drugs in the African-American community: A clear and present danger. In *The state of Black America.* ed. J. Dewart, pp. 183–192. New York: National Urban League.

Norton, W. 1992. Busing case returned to court. *St. Petersburg Times,* June 11.

Ogbu, J. U. 1990. Minority education in comparative perspective. *The Journal of Negro Education* 59(1): 45–57.

Ohaegbulam, F. U. 1990. *Towards an understanding of the African experience from historical and contemporary perspectives.* Lanham, Maryland: University Press of America.

Olneck, M. R. 1990. The recurring dream: symbolism and ideology in intercultural multicultural education. *American Journal of Education* 9 (2): 147–173.

Peterman, P. 1992. Reading, writing and retirement. *St. Petersburg Times,* June 23.

Reed, J. 1993. Should Gibbs return to its roots? *St. Petersburg Times,* January 10.

———. 1993. Big change suggested for busing in Pinellas. *St. Petersburg Times,* December 12.

Sacks, M. 1985. Without tradition you are blank: Ethnic heritage education in America today. *Ethnic Groups* 6: 249–273.

Serwatka, T., Deering, S. and Stoddard, A. 1989. Underrepresentation of Black students in classes for gifted. *Journal of Negro Education,* 58(4): 500–543.

Sleeter, C. and Grant, C. 1988. *Making choices for multicultural education: Five approaches to race, class and gender.* Columbus: Merrill Publishing.

St. Lawrence, T. and Singleton, J. 1975. Multiculturalism in social context: Conceptual problems raised by educational policy issues. *Anthropology and Education Quarterly* 7(4): 19–22.

Spears, A. 1978. Institutional racism and the education of blacks. *Anthropology and Education Quarterly* 9(2): 127–147.

Thomas, K. 1993. Pinellas school suspend more. *St. Petersburg Times,* January 10.

Van Sertima, I. ed. 1990. *Blacks in science: Ancient and modern.* New Brunswick, New Jersey: Transaction Books.

Vesperi, M. D. 1985. *The city of green benches: Growing old in new downtown.* Ithaca, NY: Cornell University Press.

Warfield-Coppock, N. and Harvey, A. 1989. *A rites of passage resource manual.* Washington, D. C.: United Church of Christ.

White, T. 1980. Ground breaking for multiservice center. *St. Petersburg Times,* June 22.

————. 1981. Finding a name for the center. *St. Petersburg Times,* February 26.

Wigginton, E. 1972. *The foxfire book.* Garden City, New York: Anchor Books.

Wigginton, E. 1986. *Sometimes a shining moment: The foxfire experience.* Garden City, New York: Anchor Books.

Williams, I. W. October 17, 1992. The vanishing African-American teacher: Part I. St. Petersburg, Florida. *The Weekly Challenger* 25 (6): 1.

Williams, I. W. October 24, 1992. The vanishing African-American teacher: Part II. *The Weekly Challenger 25(7): 1.*

Williams, I. W. November 21, 1992. The vanishing African-American teacher: Part III. *The Weekly Challenger* 25 (11): 1.

Woodson, C. G. 1919. Negro life and history in the schools. *Opportunity* 4(3): 273–281.

————. 1969. *The mis-education of the Negro.* Washington, D.C.: Associated Publishers.

Wurzel, J. 1988. *Toward multiculturalism: A reader in multicultural education.* Yarmouth, Maine: Intercultural Press.

15

JANINE PEASE-WINDY BOY ————————————————

Cultural Diversity in Higher Education: An American Indian Perspective

CULTURAL DIVERSITY AND THE WHOLE SYSTEM OF EDUCATION

From an American Indian perspective, the American system of education has given avalanches of attention to cultural diversity. The changing complexion of America's children has brought about debate and frustration, if not even a sense of uncertainty and threat, in the field of education. All too often, the mainstream educational institutions regard cultural diversity as a few learning units that are cosmetically brown or black in complexion or as a few festivals that celebrate the food, clothing, or dance of minorities. The concept of cultural diversity, in this light, is painfully peripheral if not superficial. The system has just a few soft spots where cultural diversity may alight.

For the American Indian communities across this country, the practice of educational cultural diversity is a practice that is systemic in nature. In twenty-seven tribally controlled colleges in the American West, American Indian people have built institutions reflective of the people they serve. In so doing, there are curricular structures that set tribal knowledge bases at the core of general studies requirements. The tribal value system has found its expression in administrative and budget structures. Cultural norms and respect systems have critically formed educational strategies and classroom methods. These systemic structures reflect a vital cultural community, particularly unique to the tribe/nation where the tribal college has been chartered.

THE AMERICAN INDIAN COMMUNITY TODAY

The American Indian population in 1990 totaled two million, 38 percent more than in the decade before. The tribal communities on federally recognized reservations number over 450, and are scattered across the West. Tribal colleges are located in just twenty-seven of these communities. The colleges serve approximately

399

15,000 American Indian students. The strength of tribal peoples has defied the odds, as these diverse nations have undergone cataclysmic economic, health, and social changes since the arrival of European immigrants on the continent. Today's distribution of the American Indian people is half urban (off reservation) and half reservation based. Another striking 1990 census statistic was the youthfulness of the population; 50 percent of the two million are under the age of twenty-one years. High school completion rates range from 40 percent to 61 percent, averaging only 50 percent (1990 U.S. Census).

LOCAL CONTROL AND ACCESS KEY PRECEPTS

The tribal colleges have a firm understanding of local control and equal access to education. While these are common and ordinary foundation blocks in American education, American Indians have only recently enjoyed the opportunity to partake of either of these cornerstones. The decision-making role in American Indian education has been dealt out to church groups, federal and state educational agencies, and, historically, even the military. In contrast, the congressionally enacted Indian Education Act of 1972 provided support for the services that uniquely and appropriately served Indian children in their schools. The funds were an entitlement, but their receipt was contingent on parental control of funded activities. The Kennedy, Johnson, and Nixon federal administrations were strong in programs to benefit the poor and disadvantaged. American Indians fell within that class of Americans and obtained funding for Headstart, the Indian Action Team, economic development, and housing and jobs training. All these were predicated on local control—American Indian control. Despite treaties that provide a foundation for tribal sovereignty, just twenty years ago, American Indian people were finally able to express decisions that reflected their own needs, images, and visions (Scheirbeck 1980; Wilkinson 1988). Local control is a concept long enjoyed by public schools across the country; American Indian access to this fundamental concept in education is only recent.

THE TRIBAL COLLEGE MOVEMENT

The tribal college movement is on its face both logical and acceptable to the education community at large, for the concepts of local control and educational access that are served there. Nevertheless, at a closer look, the tribal colleges have had intensive battles over curricular content, operational resources, control, quality evaluations, and operational values. From their inception, the tribal colleges each cooperated with a parent and mainstream institution, whose values, structures, and curriculum were well-established and somewhat (usually very) standardized. While there are animated claims throughout higher education about the range and variation among institutions of higher education, systemically they are very similar from a tribal American Indian perspective. The American Indian version of higher education, the tribal colleges, vary beyond the range of common higher education practice in many important ways. This essay will illustrate those systemic pressure points that must be culturally American Indian in nature and how they must be situated in the tribally controlled institution.

SURVIVABILITY A TEST OF TRIBAL KNOWLEDGE BASES

The nations around the world are all contemporary and appropriate to the present. They all are populated by the human species (no Neanderthals survived) and have successfully coped with daily challenges. All cultures and races of people have acquired volumes of information along the way, generating literature, history, sciences, and the arts to name a few areas of knowledge. The American Indian tribes have survived thousands of years, among which the last one hundred were a crucible of economic, health-related, and social upheavals (McNickle 1973). Still, the people have survived and are among the fastest growing population groups in the country.

STEREOTYPES CAST AMERICAN INDIANS INTO THE PAST

American Indians are uniquely typecast to the past. If you recall when and where you acquired knowledge of American Indians, your first response will certainly be "from the movies." The images we have of ourselves and each other have a great deal to do with how we conduct our lives. Images map out values, expectations, and behaviors. Can you imagine acting like the American Indians in the late night spaghetti westerns? Can you imagine a human being in 1993, or any other time, having a one or two word vocabulary? Can you imagine the men, going around together in packs? Can you imagine being just an extra among thousands, with no lines, ever? Can you imagine being confined at best to being a loyal, uncreative sidekick? Oh, you say, let us check the history books, for surely there are famous moments in history about American Indians. The normal American history text in eighth grade, junior year of high school, or in the university mentions American Indians at isolated junctures: in general, only when in contact or conflict with Euro-Americans as when Columbus landed, when the Pilgrims celebrated Thanksgiving, when the West was won over from the Indians, and, just maybe, when Ira Hayes helped secure Iwo Jima during the Second World War. These are mere fragments and scraps from which to build an image.

IMAGES HAVE REAL LIFE IMPACTS ON STUDENTS

American Indian students have scarcely had an opportunity to study the knowledge bases that brought their people across the millennia to the present. Clearly, the lives of American Indian people cannot be summarized by three or four windows into the past. The damage of fixing the American Indian with an image with a one word vocabulary, as an extra among other whooping or silent extras, or as a sidekick (never the brains)—all of these imply inferiority, inappropriateness, and even brainlessness. The museum industry has also made contributions to this distorted image and while there are exceptions, has usually characterized times and materials back in the eighteen hundreds and seldom go beyond the all too frequent curio displays of technologies—just technologies, no interrelationships, values, genuine vital intellects, human challenges, and intrigues.

Images and portrayals of one's past are crucial to the empowerment of any person (McLaren 1989). The American Indian has struggled with accessing an accurate past image and is bombarded by the media's contrived and inaccurate images...these intrude and damage individual visions of past, which so significantly influence "today."

TRIBAL COLLEGES AUTHOR THEIR OWN SYSTEM

Birthed in the community development era of the 1960s, the tribal colleges were founded by eminent tribal scholars, who indeed understood the challenges of the present and were familiar with appropriate knowledge bases. Tribal colleges each instituted a tribal studies curriculum that encompassed many disciplines and ranged from economics to legal issues of American Indians, to pre and post-white contact histories, to oral and written American Indian histories and literature, to music, art, and dance. The sciences have included herbal foods and medicines, astronomy, animal physiology, familial and relationship systems, language studies in series, and leadership profiles of visionaries and chiefs. The range is broad and far-reaching. Most tribal colleges have situated these courses among the general education requirements and have required the tribal language as a communications requirement. The tribal knowledge bases are a fundamental part of the core studies, comprising the general education purposes of the tribal community college.

LIBRARY, TEXTBOOKS AND EMINENT SCHOLARS

The tribal colleges had no collection of American Indian authored volumes, bearing the rich and extensive tribal knowledge bases. The tribal studies curricula housed this knowledge base area. Often interdisciplinary, the tribal studies courses are instructed by eminent tribal scholars. The available written tribal materials have been almost entirely authored by outsiders and non-Indian authors. By contrast the instructor, the eminent tribal scholar, has become the class textbook, as well as the lecturer and discussion leader. When research is required, students are encouraged to go interview community and family members—their library. The combination of instructor, textbook, and library is vital and unique to the nation/tribe and has no duplicate anywhere else. The tribal studies curriculum has also been supported by growing archival collections, where, in several of the tribal colleges, original manuscripts, audio and video tapes, photographs and maps are available to speak for themselves. In this regard, the students have role models from their contemporary community; they have a chance to observe and interact with the images of their people in the present (Vecsey 1987). With the past subsuming so much of the American Indian image, the present seldom gets a headline. The tribal colleges have acquired a method to present the present (Pease-Windy Boy Speech Transcript 1993).

TRIBAL STUDIES INTEGRALLY SITUATED

The central and integral location of the tribal studies programs in the general education core has attracted attention and review from the higher education community. This tribal studies approach varies remarkably from the peripheral ethnic studies programs offered at larger, mainstream institutions. These tribal studies courses are academic in nature and instill the critical thinking skills and abilities that the general core classes should instill. In 1987, an accreditation evaluator admonished the Little Big Horn College (LBHC), suggesting a more vocational approach would be more effective with the service population. But LBHC persisted in their mission which emphasized both "thinking and being" as well as "skills acquisition and doing." Further, this evaluator asked about the delivery of course work discussion in the Crow language. LBHC answered that the thinking processes for any human being work best in the individual's primary language—at LBHC that language is the Crow language. Including tribal studies in the core curriculum, the movement toward a curriculum that is more academic than vocational, and the development of thinking skills development in the primary language—all these were controversial decisions.

The tribal studies area has to do with the content and information in the tribal knowledge areas. Along with that content, values are delivered. The field of education has often characterized itself as a straightforward unbiased vehicle of information delivery. However, the juxtaposition of bodies of knowledge and their presence in the higher education implies and infers value. For the American Indian students, the absence of information about themselves has surely implied invisibility and unimportance. The tribal colleges have positioned the content in a place of importance—in fact, a valued and significant place, one with meaning to the students and their tribal world. In this way, education takes value positions on information and its assigned meaning in society (Freire 1985). From the American Indian perspective, the partisan presentation of information in the mainstream institutions is both blatant and discriminating. Values are indeed a crucial part of education's role in society.

CLASSROOM METHODS AND STRATEGIES CULTURALLY LADEN

The tribal colleges have made a commitment to accessible education. In so doing, the methods and strategies employed by faculty have also been selected and designed to provide tribal student access—in a cultural sense. In many fields and disciplines, the tribal colleges have not been able to retain tribal faculty members and have had the good fortune of finding excellent partners in faculty members from other cultural backgrounds. To acquire the tribal voice in the classroom, Salish Kootenai College trained their faculty members to videotape eminent tribal scholars in order to bring the tribal voice (subject appropriate) to the classroom (Salish Kootenai College Self Study 1989). The Oglala Lakota College Archives has a daily practice of video and audio taping tribal and community events and providing them to faculty members and students as library checkout items. Finally, going to the community to find the voice of the eminent scholars has been encouraged through recognizing oral sources as acceptable references in research papers. The tribal colleges have acquired the tribal voice in the curriculum, through simple video camera training of faculty and students. Further, an acquaintance with the community is paramount for identifying and for students and faculty to gain access to eminent community members. Paulo Freire (1970) calls this the naming process, finding the peoples' voice in describing life and ascribing value to its characteristics. Miles Horton, of the world renowned Highlander Institute in Kentucky, contended "the answers lie within the people" (Horton Interview 1988).

TIME-BASED LEARNING TARGETED

The American education system is replete with time based learning objectives. Students are crammed through materials regardless of readiness and competency. For some students, this time factoring knocks them out or pushes them out forever. American Indian students have frequently been damaged by time-based learning, and the tribal colleges have attempted to relieve the connections to time, particularly in the entry level courses in math, English, and science (Iverson 1987). LBHC removed the time factor from mathematics and unitized the concepts into one credit units. Concepts were isolated and correlated with a credit; where sequences were important, that was applied to the unitizing. Not all learning is sequential, however. Key concepts, then, are bundled into credits, and in small number of credits, students gradually self-pace their learning. The practice at LBHC also includes a "no-fail" or "always-pass" grading system. To qualify, the student must accomplish a 70 percent competency based on individual achievement, not on a comparative basis with a fellow student. The penalties in the education systems for timed learning are heavy baggage. The common criminal can serve a sentence for a convicted crime, but an American student who fails carries that powerful F throughout life. Lowered anxiety and incremental units of bundled concepts, have contributed to impressive access to mathematics at LBHC.

WHEN THE GOING GETS TOUGH, THE TOUGH COOPERATE

The tribal colleges have been founded on community cooperation and the sharing of vision and hard work. The classroom, however, is no stranger to this concept. The struggle to survive through hard winters and land losses (not to recount history) has engendered a time proven faith in cooperative learning models. At Little Big Horn College, the final project of core studies class in "Interpersonal Communications" is the organization of a class project. The classes have organized voter registration drives, children's art shows, a recognition dinner for college graduates, an awards ceremony dinner, and a science fair for children. In this project approach, the strengths and weaknesses of each class member are appreciated, the project is understood by its task, the tasks are carried out in the community, and the final production of the task is achieved. The faculty member observes the accomplished event and grades for effective communication. The grade is shared.

The mathematics lab at LBHC is driven in large part by cooperative study groups. A specially dedicated room has become the lab setting—encouraging group work, with the aid of slightly more advanced (in subject matter) bilingual tutors. In the sciences, partly due to space pressures and also due to the group involvement concept, classrooms are not separated from labs. The class/lab concept allows the faculty and students to move almost spontaneously to a lab when the moment of learning requires involvement with the content material.

The value of education is measured in part by the participation of the student with the information; the connection or engagement made by students with real life empowers and transforms (McLaren 1989). The cooperative learning projects in tribal colleges replicate real life situations, with problems to solve, innovations to implement, children to raise, elders to listen to, co-workers to understand, selves to manage, and so on. When the going gets tough, the tough cooperate—an important tribal value. (This attitude contrasts with individualized competition in the mainstream method of instruction.)

SECONDARY SCHOOLS SORT AND SIFT

Many states have recently adopted a selective system for admission to college, which emphasizes high school classes completed and grade point average. American Indian students in large percentages fall short of these measurements. The high school transcript reviews at Little Big Horn College for Crow students in the Crow Reservation area have indicated that large groups of students have been vocationally tracked. This tracking contributes to the 40 percent of the American Indian high school students who have left high school before graduation! In a voting rights litigation of a reservation border school with 40 percent Indian students, it was found in federal court, that tracking was formally applied to Indian students, even in 1986! The selection processes in our system of education are powerful and political sifters of human potential. For the American Indian, the educational sifting process has damaged the potentialities of those hundreds of American Indian people who attempted the educational gauntlet. In the fall of 1992, the college and university admissions officers in Montana met to discuss admission waivers. The author was present. Each unit retold how they were granted a number of admission waivers based on the total enrollment ceiling. Alas, none of these institutions had used their waivers, for few if any students (Indian and non-Indian) had applied for a waiver. Although convenient for the schools, this explanation indicated to the author that students in Montana have self-selected—that is, sorted and sifted themselves out of the system's reach. The political message of education's "sort and sift" has apparently been internalized and then has been personally applied to themselves (Giroux and McLaren 1989)!

VALUES ILLUSTRATED IN THE ADMINISTRATIVE STRUCTURE

The tribal colleges have organized themselves in a manner reflective of the tribal family and community organization. At Sinte Gleska University in Rosebud, South Dakota, the organizational chart resembles the Lakota extended family relationships. (Sinte Gleska Self Study 1983) At Little Big Horn College, the organization is a flat hierarchy and mirrors the level of interpersonal respect among Crow tribal adults. The Crow tribal value system holds that all the members of the community have an equal importance to the community as a whole. This organization is further reinforced by the budgetary commitments made to salaries across the institution—equal pay for equal work, regardless of professional assignment or gender. In this regard, the variation of salary between the president and a faculty member is negligible. In the past an accreditation team member seriously questioned the wisdom of this organizational structure, finding the flat hierarchy especially disrespectful to the president's reputation and position. This team member advised that interpersonal respect could be built instead in a two week retreat to a resort, like the annual retreat taken by this evaluator and his colleagues each fall. The values implied by organization and budget are significant and voice loud and clear the assignment of importance to position and interrelationship.

VALUES COMMUNICATED IN THE COLLEGE BUILDINGS

The tribal colleges have had to scour the countryside of their reservations for buildings even remotely suitable for education. The rural and impoverished communities on the reservation have few locations to offer. From their tribal backgrounds, the college leaders did not suffer from an "edifice complex" for they understood that education is interpersonal and personal with an environmental function. Education was, in other words, not a place or location but a relationship among tribal members, a sharing of knowledge, a problem recognized and solved, a topic researched, a group task accomplished under a tree or by the river, in a home around the kitchen table, in a lodge, in the ceremonial arbor, or on a mountain top. The lack of formidable "college looking buildings" was no barrier to configuring a tribal college.

The tribal colleges found mostly condemned and abandoned buildings. With cleaning and some reclamation, they became new homes for the college's activities. Yet another accreditation evaluator questioned the value of a building if it had not been built or purchased. Specifically, they searched for a cash value to attach to the tribal contribution toward the college's operations, and the value of an abandoned/condemned building eluded the evaluator, even though she was standing in the facility. LBHC was forced to estimate the rental costs for a similar facility in downtown Billings, Montana to establish the worth of our building. Consider the worth of an abandoned fish cannery in northern Michigan, one built entirely of cement and without windows; consider a century old brick military compound in North Dakota; consider a century old army barracks in North Dakota. All of these are examples of facilities that have been adopted for tribal college homes.

Almost half of the tribal colleges have organized building trades classes to accomplish two things: first, the training of tribal members in the building trades and second, the capacity to remodel, renovate, and in a few cases build college facilities. The tribal college leadership found useful fixtures from discarded federal equipment and furniture recovered from the neighborhood dumps. In fact, the federal government cannot give furniture away, although the surplus system could probably assist (at a distance of several hundred miles away). The local Bureau of Indian Affairs and Indian Health Service have discards that have proven to be useful furniture. In addition, the building trades classes have fashioned useful and tough furniture for far less than retail prices. The tribal colleges have had to invent ways to "make do" with limited cash. In addition, the students constructing buildings and furniture have developed proprietary ties with the tribal colleges, where control and ownership are in key precepts in the movement (Stein 1990).

Libraries Demonstrate Values, Too

The fledgling institutions, most less than twenty years old, have had a very real struggle to obtain library holdings. Books are very expensive, averaging $25 to $40 each, and reference volumes averaging $250 each. The librarians and college administrators have innovated and created ways to acquire valuable volumes without much of a cash outlay. At Oglala Lakota College, the librarian engineered a tax deductible truckload of books sight unseen from a major book publisher in New York City. Then, the LBHC librarian in tandem with several other librarians raised the money for transcontinental shipping. A truckload of books—a gold mine. Seconds stacks in libraries across the West have been important sources of books and materials for the colleges, and cooperation from within the librarians organizations has been instrumental in building the collections.

In Montana, the seven tribal colleges have assigned a book selector to the donation stacks at the Library of Congress in the nation's capital. Weekly, this selector (a college student) follows acquisitions lists and carefully selects books for the tribal colleges. The accreditation evaluators in 1987 told the LBHC Librarian that there was no measure of a used book holding, especially when the used books comprised 75 percent of the collection; there were only a few books in the library with a bill of sale or invoice. Once again, the value of budget percentages and commitments to the library were apparently measured in some unwritten but literally applied ratio: library acquisitions compared to overall college operations. The college had to devise a method of valuation in consultation with used book store dealers and the U.S. Internal Revenue Service to acquire a market value on the college's donated used book collection. Values in American education are conveyed in so many ways. Despite the exemplary college collection development and documented review performed in cooperation with the Montana state library, the accreditors' question persisted: "How many dollars did you spend on your collection?" The American higher education system values bills of sale to estimate collection worth, despite the documented exemplary collection of donated used volumes.

TUITION RATES SPEAK RESPONSIBILITY AND VALUE

Another fundamental question of value arose when still another LBHC evaluator questioned the comparatively low tuition rates. The college charged $10/credit hour (that was in 1986). The rate of charge was determined by community data such as an unemployment rate of 85 percent. The evaluator's analysis was that the college was implying that there was "no value" to the education delivered. The value of an education is what you pay for it, the evaluator advised. In his appraisal by setting a low tuition rate, the college was promoting irresponsibility among its students. The college, since its inception, has been committed to an open door policy with regard to access to education. Access meant two things: (1) locally available classes and tuition prices and (2) knowledge appropriate to tribal members. What possible sense can be made of charging inordinately high tuition rates of tribal members who have no means to afford tuition at any rate? Then and now, a Crow family of four receives $340/month on Bureau of Indian Affairs welfare. Eighty percent of the LBHC students are parents. For these students to make any tuition payment requires serious tradeoffs: no lights, no heat in subzero weather, no shoes for a growing child. What does the rate of tuition indicate, and to whom?

FACULTY SALARIES COMMUNICATE VALUE

The faculty/administration pay schedule was examined during the early accreditation visits (prior to full accreditation in 1990). LBHC has a small staff, administrators often assume faculty teaching loads as well. The small staff is determined by a severely constrained budget. The U.S. Congress appropriates a student allocation each year for tribal college support (which is another long and interesting story). The rate of allocation has averaged $2,500 per student over the past ten years, only 60 percent of the national average for community college allocations. The rate has generated a well founded "make do" attitude and practice among the faculty and staff in the tribal colleges. Salaries reflect this inadequate and low allocation rate. In 1989, Salish Kootenai College surveyed tribal college salaries and found them to be in a range of $15,000 to $25,000 per year for the faculty. The criticism of these low salary levels by the accreditation committee was a follows: "You are paid what you are worth." However, the tribal colleges are in economically impoverished rural areas. Compared with community income levels, the faculty salaries actually make those faculty members among the most wealthy individuals on the reservation. The community reflection on the tribal colleges is very immediate and literal. The community in tribal community colleges has the strongest "community" implications (Carnegie Foundation for the Advancement of Teaching 1989).

CONCLUSION

The concept of cultural diversity has a broad and deep significance to American minorities. The tribal colleges movement in America's Indian communities has located the systemic pressure points where culture raises its important presence and implies, if not demands, values and information. Further, the tribal colleges have applied and designed tribal systems that vary beyond the range of common educational practice. Reflective of their tribal cultures, these colleges have fashioned culturally appropriate curricular content and knowledge bases, administrative structures, budget commitments, and learning strategies. To achieve authentic cultural diversity, educators must critically analyze the educational system at all its vital pressure points, or the result will be superficial and without significant impact to a system steeped in the majority culture (whatever that culture may be).

The American people are undergoing a major face-lift and a major "cultural lift." The complexion of our American children, present and future, is rapidly becoming more and more brown and black. The prominence of mainstream, white, and middle-class cultural biases our educational systems must be critically examined. If education has the fundamental precept of empowerment, then systemic change is inevitable. The urgency of this consideration cannot be underestimated. Authentic cultural diversity is in remarkably short supply. To American higher education the tribal colleges movement may call attention to the deep-seated majority value systems that continue to damage American minority students. Somehow, educators who are accustomed to monocultural systems of education and monocultural lives must come to realistic terms with authentic cultural diversity as a concept and practice. The American education system must reflect the American people. Critical education speaks to the system and examines both the mission and the method.

Lives are wasting while American educators pay only superficial lip service to educational cultural diversity. The wages of this myopic neglect and cultural ignorance are great, a price our children (of all cultures) will bear in their lives and in the lives of their fellow citizens.

REFERENCES

Carnegie Foundation for the Advancement of Teaching. 1989. *Tribal colleges: Shaping the future of Native America.* Princeton: Princeton University Press.

Freire, Paulo. 1970. *Pedagogy of the oppressed.* New York: Herder and Herder.

———. 1985. *The politics of education: Culture, power and liberation.* South Hadley, Mass.: Bergin and Garvey.

Giroux, Henry A. and McLaren, Peter L. 1989. *Critical pedagogy, the state, and cultural struggle.* Albany: State University of New York Press.

Highlander Institute, Horton, Myles. Interview in Bozeman, Montana, July 1988.

Iverson, Peter. 1987. I may connect time. In *The American Indian and the problem of history.* ed. C. Martin. New York: Oxford University Press.

McLaren, Peter L. 1989. *Life in schools.* New York: Longman.

McNickle, D'Arcy. 1973. *Native American tribalism: Indian survivals and renewals.* New York: Oxford University Press.

Salish Kootenai College Self-Study. 1989. Tribally Controlled College of the Salish and Kootenai Confederated Tribes. Pablo, Montana.

Sinte Gleska Self-Study. 1983. Tribally Controlled College of the Rosebud Sioux of Rosebud, South Dakota.

412

Scheirbeck, Helen Maynor. 1980. *Education: Public policy and the American Indian.* Ed.D. diss., Virginia Polytechnic Institute and State University.

Stein, Wayne. 1988. *A history of the tribally controlled community colleges, 1968–1978. Diss.*, Washington State University.

Vecsey, Christopher. 1987. Envision ourselves darkly, imagine ourselves richly. In *The American Indian and the problem of history.* ed. C. Martin. New York: Oxford University Press.

Wilkinson, Charles F. 1988. The idea of sovereignty: Native people, their lands and their dreams. *Native American Rights Fund Legal Review.* 13 (4).

16

Christine E. Sleeter————————————————————————————

Reflections on My Use of Multicultural and Critical Pedagogy When Students Are White

Emancipation. Liberation. Social justice. What compelling ideals these are that undergird both multicultural education and critical pedagogy. Multicultural education advocates transformation of the entire process of education with the goal of "elimination of oppression of one group of people by another" (Sleeter and Grant 1993, p.209). Critical pedagogy seeks to reinvigorate democracy as a public process, as well as grappling with ethical issues of domination and control. It "would stress student participation in the learning process with the intention of enabling students to challenge the social order" (Stanley 1992, p. 102).

Those who work with critical pedagogy "ask how teachers can affirm the voices of marginalized students, engage them critically, while at the same time assist them in transforming their communities into sites of struggle and resistance" (McLaren and Hammer 1989, p. 41). While some critical pedagogy has been criticized as lacking much practical guidance for teachers, one can find a few descriptions of how teachers have used it. For example, Solorzano (1989) developed a Chicano Studies course on media analysis that worked with the three phases in Freire's (1973) teaching method: "1) identifying and naming the problem, 2) analyzing the causes of the problem, and 3) finding solutions to the problem" (p. 218). The great majority of his students were Chicano, from working-class backgrounds; historically marginalized, his course taught them skills of critique and action.

What if one's students occupy social positions of privilege? How might one prompt students to challenge the social order who largely stand to benefit from it as it exists? Is that even possible? For example, Kozol (1991) summed up a huge challenge:

> No matter what devices are contrived to bring about equality, it is clear that they require money-transfer, and the largest source of money is the portion of the population that possesses the *most* money. (223)

They also have the most power and authority. Now imagine what multicultural critical pedagogy might mean if one is teaching those with the most, rather than least. Banks (1988) recognized that curriculum for powerful groups needs to differ from that for oppressed groups. He explained that the "Enlightening Powerful Groups" model of curriculum should attempt "to modify the attitudes and perceptions of dominant ethnic groups so that they would be willing, as adults, to share power...and willing to take action to change the social system so it would treat powerless ethnic groups more justly" (p. 182). However, he expressed pessimism that one could achieve significant change by trying to educate powerful groups and saw more hope in strategies to empower oppressed groups.

While I agree with his emphasis on empowering oppressed groups, I believe there is value in attempting to educate others who (like me) are white and relatively secure economically. This is a challenge I have struggled with for several years. Early, I recognized an unsatisfactory but common dichotomy in pedagogical orientations that Elshtain (1976) described as the "coercive" classroom versus the "non-authoritarian" classroom. Teachers who wish to critique structural oppression want their students to learn to engage in the same form of critique. The greater the likelihood their students will find social critique threatening and foreign, the greater the tendency of the teacher to control the selection and flow of ideas, which many students experience as coercive rather than liberating. This coercive pedagogy contradicts the participatory mode of critical teaching. So, many teachers instead construct a non-authoritarian classroom in which students are invited to create knowledge by sharing their own perspectives and feelings— which often are not critical at all. For Elshtain, liberatory classrooms are neither nonauthoritarian nor coercive but involve shifting relations of power as students engage with ideas they may find threatening; the long-range goal is construction of "a theory of human liberation" that includes all of us (p. 110; see also Weiler 1988).

So again, how does one do that? How, for example, does one involve a class of male and female white students from mainly middle class backgrounds in a critique of various forms of oppression and at the same time help them to construct for themselves insights grounded in emancipation of *other people*?

Feminist poststructuralist work alerts us to complexities of this challenge. In raising questions about multiple identities within subjects and the interplay between rational thought and desire, such works probe subtle and often unanticipated dynamics that occur in classrooms in which critical or feminist pedagogies are employed. "Feminist poststructuralist discourse views the struggle over identity within the subject as inseparable from the struggle over meanings of identities and subject positions within the culture at large" (Orner 1992, p. 74). This does not mean that critical and feminist pedagogies are impossible but rather that they are more complex than often recognized (Lather 1992).

In the fall semester of 1992, I assigned a class of twenty-two undergraduate preservice students a paper, in which they were to ask a "why" question involving some aspect of race, social class, and/or gender that they genuinely did not understand. They were to attempt to answer the question from a perspective of the oppressed group(s) the question was about, with relatively little direct help from me. All of the students were white; sixteen were women and six were men. They ranged in age from about twenty-one to thirty-five; and in social class from about working to middle-class.

Their papers surpassed what I would have expected several years ago. In most preservice teacher education classes, if one poses a question such as why do children of poor families disproportionately not complete school? one is likely to receive answers that focus on inadequacies of their families and communities, changes in the moral climate among students over the past three decades, or the problem of gangs. My students learned to proceed quite differently. In this chapter, I will briefly frame the teaching problem I addressed in a theoretical context, describe what the students learned to do, describe my own teaching processes, and then discuss further complexities of this work.

REPOSITIONING PERSPECTIVE

Giddens (1979) advanced his analysis of social theory on the premise that "every social actor knows a great deal about the conditions of reproduction of the society of which he or she is a member" (p. 5). Considering Kozol's challenge above, for example, those who have the *most* money do not lack for theories about why others have less. It is very possible, in fact, to study the "other" and retain one's own ideas about justice and the existing social system. When multicultural education is reduced to teaching about "other" people, students are usually allowed to retain their perspective and theories about the workings of society.

Repositioning one's perspective requires recognizing that one is situated in an unequal context, and one's perspective grows partially out of one's situation. Many postmodern theorists would have us believe that our diverse experiences and subjective identities yield such a polyphony of narratives that one cannot meaningfully categorize and juxtapose them. I, as well as many others, do not share that view. Addressing the diversity of ideas and experiences of groups classified as "minorities," for example, JanMohamed and Lloyd (1987) explained that

> The theoretical project [of constructing a theory of minority discourse] involves drawing out solidarities in the form of similarities between modes of repression and modes of struggle which all minorities separately experience, and experience precisely as *minorities*..."[B]ecoming minor" is not a question of essence (as the stereotypes of minorities in dominant ideology would want us to believe) but a question of position. (p. 11)

It is this question of position, more so than that of difference, that anchors my approach to teaching.

Figure 1 juxtaposes two perspectives about the nature of society and the nature of "have not" groups which derive from different positions in an unequal social order. The dominant perspective holds that society is free and open to anyone who tries to advance, although one may encounter barriers one must work to overcome. To explain inequality, "deficiencies" of "have not" groups are highlighted: supposed deficiencies of language, effort, education, culture, family, and so forth. "Minority position" perspectives hold that society is unfair and rigged to favor groups with power. "Have not" groups are more accurately understood as

FIGURE 1

Perspectives about Inequality

	Dominant Position	"Minority Position"
Nature of Society	Fair, open	Unfair, rigged
Nature of "Have Not" Groups	Lack ambition, effort, culture, language, etc.	Strong, resourceful

oppressed; they may lack access to society's resources but culturally have generated a considerable reservoir of strengths.

My students, in many respects, hold membership in groups that are in dominant positions; they have also learned the dominant perspective very well. My challenge as a teacher is to help them learn to see issues through "minority position" perspectives. This is much more than an intellectual task, however, because perspective is strongly rooted in lived experience. Elsewhere I have argued that the life experiences of most white teachers, especially those who are women and those of working-class origin, provide them an experiential base and social location in which to construct an interpretation of society that is fairly conservative (Sleeter 1992a, 1992b). Their own personal and familial experiences with social mobility usually have taught them that the social system is open to those who work hard to lift themselves. Many couch this process of having worked their way up within their family's European ethnic immigrant experience. As women, many teachers have experienced prejudice and stereotyping, which they usually interpret as individual rather than structural: they locate sexism mainly in biased attitudes of individuals who limit the opportunities of others by treating them stereotypically. Most teachers (and most Americans) view the ideal of social equality as meaning equal opportunity for individual upward mobility and view barriers as effects of individual prejudices—imperfections in an otherwise just system (Kluegel and Smith 1986). The dominant discourse, as projected through the media as well as most school curricula, reinforces this interpretation of experience (van Dijk 1993).

White teachers' experiences with social mobility, European immigrant experiences, and teachers' interpretations of sexism provide a way of understanding other forms of inequality, including racial inequality. White teachers and preservice students grow up in different locations in the racial structure from Americans of color—often different geographic locations, always a different location of privilege. As a result, the theories they construct about racial inequality fit the dominant perspective and deny a "minority position" perspective. Whites generally resolve the contradiction between the ideal of equality and the reality of racial stratification "by minimizing racism" (Wellman 1977, p. 219), equating racism with individual prejudice and attributing inequality mainly to cultural deficiencies. Those who attempt to teach white teachers or preservice students about various forms of oppression encounter predictable defenses. For example, convinced that individual attitudes and stereotypes form the basis of racism and sexism, they try not to "see" color. They acknowledge stereotypes in texts but express great discomfort with African American intellectual thought, feminist thought, or critiques of capitalism. Many express interest in learning about groups such as the Amish or the Hmong but do not wish to hear about how white supremacy works.

The approach I will describe aims toward helping students learn that there is more than one perspective; from there they learn to use a "minority position" perspective to examine school issues. When attempting to teach "minority position" perspectives, teachers often bombard students with them, leaving intact the assumption that there is one correct interpretation of society: the teacher's interpretation. This creates what Elshtain termed the "coercive" classroom, which many students resist. Partly what students resist is the implication that the sense they have made of their lives is wrong. I have found them far more likely to entertain another perspective, as long as it is not presented as the only "correct" one.

Embedded within the project of attempting to reposition perspectives, however, is the recognition that students' perspectives are not singular. As feminist poststructuralists remind us, each student can learn to engage in a "minority position" perspective regarding some issues and in some circumstances but retain a dominant perspective in other situations. Further, to the extent that my pedagogical process is "liberating," it is not necessarily liberating my students. Rather, my work attempts to connect students with discourses that others find liberating, so that when they enter the classroom as teachers, they will recognize and hear (and, one hopes, begin to act with) the words and visions of disenfranchised people.

PRESERVICE STUDENTS CONSTRUCT MINORITY POSITION PERSPECTIVES

During their second semester with me, twenty-two preservice students posed "why" questions about a variety of issues. They formulated their questions on the basis of personal experiences or observations; most opened their "why" papers with very specific examples of the questions they had addressed. Most of their questions had to do with race and culture; some involved gender issues. Their sources of information were mainly interviews with people who are members of the group(s) their questions involved; papers also drew on scholarly articles written by members of such groups. I will share examples of their work, then discuss the teaching they had experienced.

Four young white women wondered why African American males experience difficulties in schools. Their papers explored a variety of factors; their conclusions differed but fit within the context of an observation one made:

> The "black male crisis" becomes reified in isolation and addressed outside the full cultural, historical, political, and economic contexts of African Americans' lives. Eurocentric formation of the issue defines it as a "black" issue, thus making it both the product and the responsibility of Black people.

One of the papers focused on black community self-help strategies, noting that white society, though creating problems that impact on the African American community, cannot be relied on to help. Another examined African American males' cultural coping mechanisms for racial oppression. Yet another white woman concluded that the greatest problem African American male students face in school is white female teachers who, afraid of them, refer them to remedial and special education programs in order to rid themselves of a "problem" they fear.

> So I feel the first main objective to help make a change for the young African American male is to work with the white female teacher and work to change their perceptions about the African American male.

Several papers examined facets of institutional racism. One of these concluded that social services for low-income Hispanic children in the local community are appallingly inadequate largely because of the indifference of the dominant community. Another asked why low-income Hispanic children do not attend school regularly even though their parents regard school as important; she concluded that schools are structured such that they force a choice between school versus family, requiring those who place family responsibility first to make "a choice they shouldn't have to make". A young woman who previously had not believed that institutional racism exists asked why many educational institutions that serve mainly people of color do not employ pedagogical strategies that would benefit the students. She concluded (with many specific examples she had observed) that schools were structured initially to reproduce society as it is; those who control schools are mainly white males, and many teachers in the schools are prejudiced. As a result, she asked:

> How many times have we heard teachers and administrators blame the failure of the students on their environment? Hardly ever do we hear of a teacher saying that his/her methods of teaching are not beneficial to students. Instead we are given explanations of students' deficiencies as being the source of failure.

Sleeter

A young woman asked why the omission of minorities from training videos in industry matters. She argued that, although it would be good business sense to produce material that reflects the diversity of the public, corporations are run mainly by white men who often do not do that. Her paper then raised the question of whether capitalism can reduce racism or supports it, noting W. E. B. DuBois's argument that capitalism is part of the problem of racism.

Two young men wondered why males exhibit more interest and success in math than females in secondary schools and higher education. One focused on adolescence and the dilemma young women face of trying to please the peer group, especially boys who do not like girls who seem "smarter than the average guy." He reflected personally on how the male peer culture suppresses displays of female academic achievement without placing similar restrictions on boys, realizing that boys learn early to blunt girls' aspirations. The other young man (a prospective math teacher) focused on the university level, uncovering more blatant sexism in math and engineering departments than he had previously recognized.

The rest of the papers addressed similarly interesting questions, such as why Spanish-speaking students use Spanish instead of English to communicate, even in an ESL (English as a Second Language) class; why complexion variation makes a difference within the African American community; why students of color drop out of school disproportionately more than white students; and why African American and Hispanic community groups experience difficulty coalescing to effect political change. Although their papers focused mainly on why patterns exist, most also recommended strategies for change—strategies that oppressed groups advance.

Readers may critique some of these examples for limits of their political analysis. However, I regard the great majority of them as successful in beginning to use a minority position perspective: they framed concrete observations of inequality in terms of institutional discrimination and uncovered strategies oppressed groups use to cope with or attempt to advance from a minority position. The students sought answers from members of oppressed groups themselves and recognized social change strategies that oppressed groups advocate.

PEDAGOGICAL STRATEGIES

I will discuss some teaching strategies I used in two sequential, required preservice courses. First, however, I must contextualize them within the entire teacher education program in the institution in which I taught these two courses, since my courses were only one site in which preservice students encountered "minority position" perspectives. The institution is located in a semiurban area, between two large metropolitan areas and serving two school districts that have very diverse populations. Over the past several years, the teacher education program has worked to develop a strong multicultural focus throughout the entire program. Part of this effort has been in hiring a diverse faculty; currently about half of the teacher education courses are taught by faculty of color. Most of the teacher education faculty have taught in inner city schools and lived in inner-city neighborhoods. To varying degrees, courses expose students to minority (primarily African American) intellectual thought, feminist thought, specific multicultural teaching strategies, and the repeated experience of learning and taking directions from a person of color. In addition, field experiences for methods courses are often in culturally diverse classrooms. Thus, the strategies I use were supported in various ways outside my courses, in a context rich with thought rooted in "minority position" perspectives.

Critical pedagogy questions the teacher's power over students in the classroom. Initially, some teachers interpret this as meaning that the teacher should exercise no more power than each student. Shor (1982) described a more helpful view, which he termed "the withering away of the teacher:"

> One goal of liberatory learning is for the teacher to become expendable. At the start and along the way, the teacher is indispensable as a change agent. Yet, the need to create students into self-regulating subjects requires that the teacher as organizer fade as the students emerge. (p. 98)

The process I will discuss is predicated on this transfer of power. Initially I use my power as teacher to make assignments, organize activities and discussions, present material, evaluate work, and so forth. However, over the two courses, spaces for student authority enlarged. I have organized the discussion that follows in relationship to five kinds of strategies, more so than to the order of their use (a chronological description of some of what follows appears in Sleeter, in press).

Graphic, Emotionally-charged Portrayals of Inequality

Social reconstructionism, multicultural education, and critical pedagogy rest on the assumption that society faces a crisis of grave proportions that impacts very disparately on different groups (Stanley 1992). Some students come to school aware of a crisis they experience in personal terms; many, however, come unaware of any major crisis in American life. As noted above, Americans who perceive themselves as relatively well-off construct a perspective that explains and legitimates their own experience by denying that groups differ in social position. So, I begin with a graphic portrayal of crisis and, throughout the two courses, provide real and vicarious experiences with disenfranchised groups.

The students' first assignment is to read *The Education of a WASP* (Stalvey 1988), which is an autobiography of a white middle class woman as she relearns how race in the U.S. worked for African Americans during the 1960s. It opens with the author's brief description of her life and her naive beliefs about the fairness and justice of American society. It then chronicles her experiences and the change in her perspective over a four-year period as she became increasingly involved with struggles within the African American community. She describes how she learned about institutional racism in a variety of areas: housing, schooling, media coverage, job opportunities, and so forth. Over the four years, Stalvey crossed a color line that most white Americans never cross, and learned first-hand how African Americans experience the U.S. from the other side of that color line. The book provides my students with a vicarious experience with racism as African Americans experience it and with a white reexamination of what racism is. Overwhelmingly students react strongly to the book. (Other books, such as Kozol's *Savage Inequalities* (1991), can provide similar vicarious experiences.)

This first experience should provoke an emotional jolt, clearly illustrate unequal conditions, and provide a range of concrete examples of structural inequality that can be used for analysis later. Initially students are caught up in their emotional reaction, and many do not identify any structural factors at all in the text; they will need help doing so later. I believe this first experience should not be fictional. If it challenges their thinking and provokes discomfort, many students try to dismiss the text (as dated, fictional, exaggerated, and so forth).

In the second course, students complete a fifty-hour field experience. I used to place them mainly in urban classrooms but now place most students in urban community organizations, such as community centers, field-based tutoring programs, or minority-run social service agencies. Placements are those in which the population being served as well as running the agency represent a low-income minority group. My students will have specific service work to do under the direction and supervision of a staff person, and their work will allow them to talk informally with some of the clients (usually children and youth). Here, students usually find themselves actually seeing many conditions Stalvey described. For example, several students assigned to help with one agency's food bank and energy assistance program have been shocked to realize the economic deprivation many people endure, the shortage of resources available, and the work ethic of many recipients of assistance. Students discover how piecemeal recreational and educational programs are for low-income children in the community. Many students experience successfully teaching academic skills and content to low-income children and begin to question whether their "learning problems" are really schooling problems. Questions for the papers they wrote emerged largely in this field experience, as did most of their answers. Students also develop personal relationships with people in the field. These relationships often gradually develop a trust level in which the university student can begin to ask questions some would not have dreamed of verbalizing earlier.

Other experiences throughout the courses, such as films that portray graphic poverty, readings, or listening to personal accounts of victimization, add to students' bank of vicarious experience. I highlighted the book and the field experience because both explicitly illustrate what oppression looks like from the bottom, both provide data for a structural analysis of oppression, and both provoke a strong emotional, as well as conceptual, reaction in students. A caveat: I do not view it as ethical to place a survivor of oppression in a situation of having to "spill guts." Consequently, I do not invite guest speakers or class members to do this unless an individual volunteers to do so. I also caution students not to ask individuals in their field experiences about personal issues that are inappropriate to the nature of their work there. In addition, I direct students to identify a community's self-help strategies in their field experiences rather than focusing entirely on the community's problems. My caveat is stated much more straightforwardly than actually occurs, but the ethics involved in asking others to speak about their lives cannot be underemphasized.[1]

Instruction in a "Minority Position" Perspective

By themselves, the experiences described above, especially when they are of limited duration, rarely lead one on one's own to construct a different perspective about society. Unmediated experience can, in fact, reinforce a "cultural deficiency" interpretation. Therefore, I explicitly teach a framework I expect students to practice, illustrated in Figure 2. It is predicated on an ideal that Americans share: that people should be able to achieve what they work for. (Important ethical issues are embedded in this ideal, such as, what is worth striving for? I do not begin using the framework by probing such issues, however; my intent is to focus first on other elements of the framework.)

The framework delineates three levels for analysis: the individual, institutional, and symbolic levels (see Collins 1993). At the individual level, one examines an individual's ability, effort, desire, and so forth. In dominant discourse, most explanations for inequality are drawn from this level (for example, in the assertion that few women are school administrators because women do not desire that career). At the institutional level, one examines the availability of rewards people work for (such as housing, jobs, good grades, and entry to college) and the social rules for distributing rewards. Social rules include both written and unwritten rules and procedures and organized

FIGURE 2

Analysis of Oppression

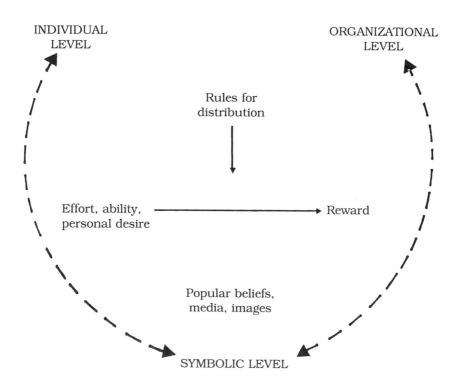

patterns of behavior. At the symbolic level, one examines social beliefs about society and diverse groups, and the encoding and expression of beliefs, particularly through various media. One also examines how media impact on individual behavior, connections between institutional structures and control, and media.

The Education of a WASP provides rich material to use with this framework. Americans who adhere to a dominant perspective assume that, for the most part, the rules for distributing social rewards work fairly for everyone. The book illustrates that, in the 1960s, they clearly did not: blacks and whites followed two different sets of institutional and social rules that were set by white society.

This is the crux of what I try to have students realize: Their own social reality and their interpretation of that reality is valid within limits. However, the entire social order is structured around boundaries that define different sets of rules for different categories of people. People are categorized socially on ascribed differences (that for the most part are visible, such as sex or skin color), with images of effort, ability, and desire projected repeatedly through media in such a way that the dominant society explains inequalities with reference to characteristics of people rather than the rules of institutions.

In *The Education of a WASP*, the author gradually discovers a wide range of informal as well as formal rules of society that apply differently to blacks and whites. She also discovers the degree to which her own ideas about race and about blacks as well as whites had been shaped by her absence of contact with blacks and persistent contact with highly distorted media imagery. After students have read the book, I have them analyze it in small groups, filling in the framework in Figure 2 with examples. We then discuss their difficulty in using this framework, and their reactions to it.

A simulation that helps illustrate this framework is Star Power. (Shirts 1969). In the simulation, students become divided into three groups based on points accumulated in a trading game, with the highest group eventually given power to make rules governing the game. Invariably, they use this power to further their own advantages; the other two groups use various coping and resisting strategies, such as cheating or refusing to play. In the discussion that follows, I try to help students move from their own experience in the simulation to broader issues of unequal power, rule-making, and social behavior. The simulation provides the class with a shared vocabulary and shared set of experiences that illustrate concepts in Figure 2, although they typically need help connecting these with real-life issues in the local community.

In the remainder of the first course, we practice using the frame-work, focusing on the institutional and symbolic levels of analysis. I tell students that my goal is to help them learn to pose questions and examine factors within the context of the framework. I explain that doing this will challenge much of their thinking, but it will also help them understand where other groups are "coming from." Ultimately, their own personal beliefs are their own business; as a teacher, my responsibility is to help them see a different perspective.

Tatum (1992) described her use of research on racial identity development to help students acknowledge and transcend their emotional reactions to learning about racism. This research postu-lates stages that whites and people of color experience when confronting racism and repositioning their perspectives. As students are confronted experientially and vicariously with inequality and "minority position" perspectives, many feel very threatened and use predictable strategies to deal with their feelings. I have found it very helpful to share this work with students, broadening the discussion to gender, social class, and other forms of oppression. Doing so vali-dates their discomfort, gives them a shared language to discuss their feelings, and provides a "roadmap" of growth they can anticipate.

I also use Figure 1 in class with students to contrast dominant and "minority position" perspectives. For example, after they have been in their community field experience for a period of time, students often become very upset about the living conditions of people about whom students have come to care. I ask the class to construct an interpretation of what they are seeing from a dominant perspective and a "minority position" perspective, filling in Figure 1 with examples. During this discussion some students begin to connect the language and interpretative frameworks used in class with the dominant ideology as it appears in textbooks, newspapers, and so forth, and with "minority position" discourse as articulated by groups such as Black Power advocates, feminists, and labor unions.

Reflective Writing

Those who use both critical and feminist pedagogies often discuss the benefits of reflective writing, especially journals (Bigelow 1990; Liston and Zeichner, 1987). Writing allows students to define issues, express feelings, and develop descriptive texts for analysis. In addition, "Creating personalized narratives is also a way of guarding against the rampant intellectual imperialism so prevalent in teaching, whereby outsiders provide the packaged and com-modified answers to the issues that are nonquestions for teachers" (Smyth 1992, p. 296–297).

Students in my courses complete two different kinds of reflective written work. In the first course, they are to keep a journal. I have structured the journal with specific assignments, although some students go much beyond that. The assignments mainly ask students to relate concepts or insights from the course to examples or incidents in their own lives. For example, I may ask them to reflect on a reading assignment and to write about any relationships they see between the text and their lives. I collect journals periodically and write comments or questions. Although a few students complete only a minimal amount of writing in the journal, most take it seriously; in some cases the journal develops into an active, personal dialog between me and the student.

The second form of reflective writing occurs in relationship to the field experience. I provide students with guides for conducting a wide array of miniethnographic investigations, such as suggested interview questions or guidance for observing language use. Students are to select three of these (or design their own) and collect data. When writing the assignment, they are to interpret and reflect on what they have learned, particularly focusing on what it means for them as a teacher. Quite often these assignments, too, become vehicles for personal communication between me and the student, as I write questions for thought and further work.

There is far more one can do with reflective writing than I have described here. For example, some teachers have students share their written texts for broader analysis. Still, most students tell me that the reflective writing described above is very helpful, mainly because it forces them to think and to seek connections between their own experience and ideas discussed in class.

Tapping into Sources That Bring Minority Position Perspectives

Commonly, students perceive ideas and sources of information (such as textbooks) that draw on dominant perspectives as "normal," and those that use "minority position" perspectives as biased and political. Commonly also, they have had little exposure to "minority position" discourse, with the exception of excerpts on the news. I try to help students to realize that no discourse is ideologically neutral, that "minority position" discourses are sophisticated and often richer with strategies for addressing social problems than dominant discourse, and that they can learn to access such discourses themselves.

Throughout the teacher education program, in addition to my courses, students are exposed to black intellectual thought and (to a lesser degree) intellectual thought of other groups. Thus, it is not incumbent on one course alone to attempt this huge teaching task. I engage students in explicit instruction and practice in accessing and using "minority position" sources to answer questions; at least one of my colleagues has engaged students in similar practice.

As students pose questions, ranging from the miniinvestigations they share with the class to the "why" papers they write, we talk about where one might go for information and why. Figure 3 illustrates distinctions I make when discussing sources of information. The two vertical columns distinguish between in-group and out-group members. The importance of this distinction can be illustrated by comparing two articles about the same event or issue, one written by an in-group and the other by an out-group member. I require that at least some sources for "why" papers be in-group members with respect to the question the student is investigating.

The three horizontal rows illustrate different perspectives one might encounter: a child's perspective, the perspective of an adult community member, and the perspective of a scholar who has studied an area of investigation. We discuss unique insights each of these perspectives might offer and fill in each cell of the figure with examples of sources. Then, in small groups, prior to their "why" paper investigations, students help each other generate a list of reasonable sources of information.

Before I worked with students on source selection, they typically sought answers to questions from in-group children and out-

FIGURE 3

	In-Group Member	Out-Group Member
Child		
Adult in community		
Scholar		

group adults (usually teachers) or scholars (such as textbooks or mainstream journal articles). The result was usually an elaboration of a dominant perspective. When challenged to seek information from in-group adults and scholars, students usually find themselves engaging with "minority position" perspectives. Initially, many find this threatening (a few try to circumvent such engagement) and difficult (few have ever read an African American or Latino journal). However, students also report finding more insights and potential solutions from in-group adults and scholars than from any other source.

Collective Knowledge Production

Ultimately, for critical pedagogy to be empowering, it must involve "a process of knowledge production" in which students work together to generate their own text (Gore 1992, p. 68). This is different from having students write traditional papers; papers are usually a private experience students share only with the teacher and require students to seek published knowledge from "experts" rather than actually creating their own interpretations. When working with peers to create text about social issues, students educate each other in ways that I cannot by sharing examples, disagreeing with each other, and building large ideas from their collective multiple examples. I structure collective knowledge production in a variety of ways.

First, after students have read *The Education of a WASP*, I divide them into three groups to conduct miniinvestigations on racism, poverty and social class, and sexism. Beginning with the racism group, I put Fig. 2 on the board and ask the class as a whole to generate as many questions as they can about possible examples of racism today at the institutional and symbolic levels. As they ask questions, I write them on the board, asking for ideas as to how questions might be investigated. Then the students who selected racism each volunteer to take a question; I give them a week or two to conduct their investigations. (I repeat the same process with the other two groups, a bit later in the semester.)

About ten students at a time share what they have found out, and usually considerable discussion follows. For example, with respect to poverty, one student acquired published information about available child care for low-income people, then pretended to be a single mother looking for childcare, and actually made the telephone calls specified; she found out that the printed descriptions can differ widely from the treatment low-income, single women may actually receive. Another assembled paperwork a woman must fill out to receive AFDC. Another looked into local homeless shelters and was shocked to discover how many homeless people the city has. I used to provide much of the information students now bring to class but realized that when they provide the information, they find it more believable and real, and they also learn where to locate such information for themselves.

A second form of collective knowledge production occurs in the context of ethnographies students read. This is a rather complex assignment, using jigsaw cooperative learning. Each student reads one ethnography of schooling; about ten or twelve different books are available to choose from. For discussion, I first group together students who have read the same or similar books, to make sure they understand the main ideas in their books. Then I mix students so that four or five books are represented by one student each, per group. I give the groups four to five questions to answer collectively, that require them to synthesize information and ideas in the books; I also encourage students to use their own personal experience. The questions connect Figure 2 with school issues in the books, such as asking students to examine who benefits most from tracking and why. Sometimes the groups put on a skit illustrating what they learned; other times they collectively write a short paper.

The culminating experience for these two courses is the production and use of a text about issues related to multicultural education. Students are to complete their "why" papers about half-way through the semester. I read them, give students feedback, and give them about two weeks to complete any revisions they wish to make. Then I collect their papers, organize them around common topics or themes, and have them duplicated and bound to form a text that the class uses for the remainder of the semester. At this point, students take control of the production and discussion of knowledge. I participate in discussions with the students but am no longer "in charge."

At the time of this writing, I had only actually turned students' "why" papers into a class text once, after having found that the papers were consistently strong enough to do this effectively. Of all the reading assignments I have ever given, students seemed to take this the most seriously. They told me that they wanted to find out what their peers learned and found important and that this had more meaning to them than any other reading assignment, no matter how interesting other reading assignments might have been.

Multicultural teaching is not simply a list of teaching strategies. Rather, it is an orientation to listening to oppressed people, including scholars, with the aim of learning to hear and understand what is being said, building dialog, and learning to share decision-making power with oppressed communities. The process of listening, engaging in dialog, and power-sharing is very difficult to learn. Educated whites are very accustomed to believing that we can construct good solutions to other peoples' needs, ourselves. I want students to leave my class having begun a process of listening and dialog; I deliberately reduce my own position as "the" source of information about multicultural teaching. While I do not know the extent to which students continue to seek out minority position perspectives for themselves from their students, students' parents, or professionals of color, at least they will have begun this process.

EPILOGUE

Shortly after the twenty-two students turned in their "Why?" papers, a protest erupted among students in the program— including some of the twenty-two—over an alternative certification program for prospective teachers of color. The program was created in collaboration with the local school districts in order to certify more teachers of color. Representatives from my institution participated in designing the program, which was a modified and somewhat shortened version of our standard program. The student protest centered mainly around some white students' perception that people of color were being given special privileges and an easier route into the profession, which they perceived as unfair. Some students were also angered by the implication that the multicultural teacher education they had experienced was not enough; in spite of the work it demanded of them, they were not perceived as prepared to teach everyone effectively.

This incident highlighted the difficulty and complexity of the project my teaching attempts. Students can learn to identify and use "minority position" insights to answer specific questions they encounter in specific situations. However, students also bring to teaching their personal life histories, personal struggles, and deep-seated feelings. I suspect that some students had submerged very real distrust of and anger at people of color throughout the entire teacher education program, which exploded when confronted with an issue that seemed to threaten them. Many students had become angry over the length of the teacher education program and resented the possibility that someone else might "get off" easier. Many students understand a crisis facing students of color in the schools at an intellectual level, not at a "gut" level.

When I teach, who am I trying to liberate? Construction of "a theory of human liberation" that includes all of us (Elshtain 1976, p. 110) sounds good but is very difficult. In a very real sense, I am not trying to liberate preservice students: I am trying to connect them with liberatory work of groups with whom they share at best partial membership and, to varying degrees, some, personal identity. Thus, their dominant ways of understanding issues are still those that are rooted in their own experience and social position.

The students were no longer in my class, so I had no organized way of addressing this issue. In informal interactions with a few, however, I suggested that they turn the issue into a "why" question and follow the same process they had learned to use to construct their papers. Whether they actually did or not, I do not know, but the suggestion reframed the issue into one of multiple perspectives the students do have the capability to understand. I believe they realized that.

As I reflect on my own life and learning process, it is evident to me that no single course, experience, or individual transformed my own way of understanding issues. Cumulatively, several experiences did jolt me out of the dominant perspective I had grown up taking for granted. I am still periodically painfully jolted. What I hope is that the teaching process described here serves as one such experience for the students I work with.

NOTES

1. On occasion I have seen classroom situations deteriorate into unintended emotional side-shows, in which the student or guest sharing painful personal experiences breaks down in tears or anger, and the class feels sorry for him or her. One cannot teach about oppression without representing pain, but I try to plan painful experiences in ways that do not violate privacy, as much as possible, such as through the use of films and videos, readings, or talks by individuals who have had some practice discussing painful experiences with a group.

REFERENCES

Banks, J. A. 1988. *Multiethnic education*, 2d ed. Boston: Allyn and Bacon.

Bigelow, W. 1990. Inside the classroom: Social vision and critical pedagogy. *Teachers College Record* 91(3): 437–448.

Collins, P. H. 1993. Toward a new vision: Race, class, and gender as categories of analysis and connection. *Race, Sex and Class* 1(1):25–46.

Elshtain, J. B. 1976. The social relations of the classroom: A moral and political perspective. *Telos* 97:110.

Freire, P. 1973. *Pedagogy of the oppressed.* New York: Seabury.

Giddens, A. 1979. *Central problems in social theory.* Berkeley. University of California Press.

Gore, J. 1992. What we can do for you! What can "we" do for "you"? Struggle over empowerment in critical and feminist pedagogy. In *Feminisms and critical pedagogy.* ed. C. Luke and J. Gore, pp. 54–73. New York: Routledge.

JanMohamed, A. and Lloyd, D. 1987. Introduction: Toward a theory of minority discourse. *Cultural Critique* 6: 5–12.

Kluegel, J. R. and Smith, E. R. 1986. *Beliefs about inequality: Americans' views of what is and what ought to be.* New York: Aldine de Gruyter.

Kozol, J. 1991. *Savage inequalities.* New York: Crown Publishers.

Lather, P. 1992. Post-critical pedagogies: A feminist reading. In *Feminisms and critical pedagogy.* ed. C. Luke and J. Gore, pp. 120–137. New York: Routledge.

Liston, D. P. and Zeichner, K. M. 1987. Critical pedagogy and teacher education. *Journal of Education* 169(3): 117–137.

McLaren, P. and Hammer, R. 1989. Critical pedagogy and the post-modern challenge: Toward a critical postmodernist pedagogy of liberation. *Educational Foundations* (Fall): 29–62.

Orner, M. 1992. Interrupting calls for student voice in "liberatory" pedagogy: A feminist poststructuralist perspective. In *Feminisms and critical pedagogy.* ed. C. Luke and J. Gore, pp. 74–89. New York: Routledge.

Shirts, G. 1969. *Star Power.* LaJolla, CA: Western Behavioral Sciences Institute.

Shor, I. 1982. *Critical teaching and everyday life.* Boston: South End Press.

Sleeter, C. E. 1992a. *Keepers of the American dream.* London: Falmer Press.

———. 1992b. Resisting racial awareness: How teachers under-stand the social order from their racial, gender, and social class locations. *Educational Foundations* (Spring): 2–32.

———. In press. Teaching whites about racism. In *Practicing what we teach.* ed. R. Martin. Albany, NY: State University of New York Press.

Sleeter, C. E. and Grant, C. A. 1993. *Making choices for multicul-tural education,* 2d ed. Columbus, OH: Macmillan.

Smyth, J. 1992. Teachers' work and the politics of reflection. *American Educational Research Journal* 29(2): 267–300.

Solorzano, D. G. 1989. Teaching and social change—Reflections on a Freirean approach in a college classroom. *Teaching Sociology* 17: 218–225.

Stalvey, L. 1989. *The education of a WASP*. Madison, WI: University of Wisconsin Press.

Stanley, W. B. 1992. *Curriculum for utopia*. Albany, NY: State University of New York Press.

Tatum, B. D. 1992. Talking about race, learning about racism: The applications of racial identity development theory in the classroom. *Harvard Educational Review* 62(1):1–24.

Van Dijk, T.A. 1993. *Elite discourse and racism*. Newbury Park, CA: Sage Publications.

Weiler, K. 1988. *Women teaching for change*. South Hadley, MA: Bergin and Garvey.

Wellman, D. T. 1977. *Portraits of white racism*. Cambridge, MA: Cambridge University Press.

AFTERWORD

KRIS D. GUTIERREZ

Although the United States has always been a multi-ethnic society with a wide range of cultural practices and beliefs, this country is currently entering the most extensive period of cultural diversity in its entire history. Our nation is further characterized by extreme racial, economic, and educational stratification and vast cultural and linguistic diversity. Yet, if we examine the ideological content of the narratives and metanarratives of everyday interactions and activities of institutional contexts, white racial hegemony continues to remain essentially unchallenged. Critical race theorists such as Goldberg (1993) propose that despite the demographic changes, the new discourse of multiculturalism both celebrates diversity and rationalizes hegemonic control of difference, power, access and the perpetuation of signifying systems and objects in which new forms of racism are manifest (p. 8).

In the past decade, for example, conservatives have appropriated the discussions of culture and multiculturalism and have declared culture the terrain upon which social, political, and ideological struggle is waged. These struggles have been most evident in the schools, their curricula and practices, as well as in efforts to weaken the civil rights and social welfare reforms gained in previous decades. This conservative agenda has reconstructed multiculturalism so that it reinforces the structures that preserve the power and interests of a specific few. Within this agenda, there is a call for cultural homogeneity and a premium placed on a shared common culture. However, the blatant racism and classism in English-only and anti-bilingual education and cultural literacy movements, for example, only reinforce hegemonic discourses, literacies, histories, and social practices that exclude particular communities. Similarly, schools and other public institutions promote the acquisition and maintenance of one particular kind of "literacy," not multiple literacies. Thus, the push for a

439

"shared" common language is not, in fact, about language or preserving languages; rather, it is about preserving particular language communities and cultures and marginalizing others. In particular, the anti-immigration backlash, such as the one evident in California, justifies discrimination and racism in its effort to protect a culture of exclusion, self-interest, and inequality.

Liberal multiculturalists take up cultural diversity and multi-culturalism in ways that sidestep conflict and ignore the critique needed to examine and expose the relationship between difference and power; thus, the norms remain unchallenged. Their educational pedagogies seek to gloss over difference and call for tolerance and harmony across class structures, ethnicities, races and cultures. Further, the reification of race as a category has allowed liberal multiculturalists to focus on remedying educational structures and social injustices through the use of token inclusions in the curricula, the texts, the larger academy, and the courts. In this way, the tran-scendent scripts of the larger society are neither challenged nor ruptured and transformed (Gutierrez, Kreuter, & Larson, 1994).

Within these various perspectives, difference is acknowledged without unmasking the ways in which current norms, values, social practices, and institutional structures are the result of Eurocentric domination. Moreover, discussions of race continue to center around bipolar and, often, essentialist notions of race and racial difference, i.e., black and white. Critical multiculturalists, exempli-fied by the authors in this volume, provide opportunities to rethink race, ethnicity, culture, and difference outside of the binary opposi-tions generally used to define these social constructs. However, as we engage in the process of re-envisioning political projects in a multicultural world, progressive educators must examine the ways in which they sometimes also define racial identities in very static or essentialist terms. Racial identity is still often characterized by one's physical, cultural, and linguistic practices; minority groups are still defined as homogenous groups. Instead, critical multiculturalism must call for contextualized and relational definitions of identity. Difference should be situated in structures of power, equality, justice, and access. These more situated beliefs of multiculturalism serve to challenge essentialist views of identity and culture.

We need to develop new perspectives on race and culture and ground our discussions in sociohistorical and sociocultural under-standings of culture and difference and processes of socialization. Moreover, we need a language that acknowledges the multicultural, multilingual, and multi-racialized nature of our present society. In short, we must combine critical multiculturalism with anti-racist and

social, cultural, and feminist theories so that we rewrite the relationship between theory and practice and cultural politics (Giroux, 1992).

As we rethink multiculturalism in school contexts, we must
also construct a new discourse and accompanying social practices
that encompass a much broader sociocultural and sociopolitical
terrain. In doing so, we must not hold sacred existing educational
and institutional practices, even those aligned earlier with progressive projects. Educational programs such as bilingual education
programs, for example, must be reexamined and critiqued to
insure that the ongoing social, linguistic, cultural, and political
needs of the students they serve are indeed met. Moreover, the
goals of such programs must be redefined so that the multiple
literacies students ultimately acquire serve as tools and vehicles of
empowerment and competence across contexts and institutions.
This requires a move from programs that emphasize bilingualism
to programs that insist on critical biliteracy. Programs that
promote biliteracy necessarily acknowledge the bicultural nature
of the lives of many school children and begin to help educators
reconsider notions of difference and identity and to challenge hegemonic perspectives of race, culture and difference.

Multiculturalism, then, is not about making the school
curricula more inclusive; multiculturalism, that is, critical multiculturalism, requires a transformation of the social relationships
in the contexts for learning and in the purposes for learning.
Hegemony needs to be understood not only as the product of the
larger social systems that define our society but also as the
product of the way individual classrooms and their social relations
are organized and constructed (Gutierrez & Larson, 1994). As we
struggle for social heteroglossia, we must insist on the commingling
of various sociocultural perspectives and curricula that have both
a political and sociocultural conscience. To do so requires access
to and participation in multiple public spheres in which people
with diverse values, beliefs, and practices jointly construct new
sets of relationships, interactional forms, and sociocultural understandings of race, culture, and diversity. The resulting pedagogies
of resistance postmoderism, such as those suggested by McLaren
(1994), will address the issue of difference "in ways that don't
replay the monocultural essentialism of the 'centrisms' (p. 213).

Ultimately, critical multiculturalism must challenge and reconstruct the hegemonic theories of multiculturalism so that issues of
representation, the unequal distribution of power, economic and
material resources, and access to educational institutions and sociopolitical spheres are taken up. This edition is an important beginning.

REFERENCES

Giroux, Henry (1992). *Border crossings: Cultural workers and the politics of education*. New York: Routledge.

Goldberg, David Theo (1993). *Racist culture: Philosophy and the politics of meaning*. Cambridge, MA: Blackwell.

Gutierrez, K. and Larson, J. (1994). Language borders: Recitation as hegemonic discourse. *International Journal of Educational Reform*, 3(1), pp. 22–36.

Gutierrez, K., Kreuter, B., and Larson, J. (1994). James Brown Vs. Brown vs. Board of education: Scripts, counterscripts and underlife in the classroom. Unpublished manuscript. University of California, Los Angeles.

McLaren, P. (1994). Multiculturalism and the postmodern critique: Toward a pedagogy of resistance and transformation. In H. Giroux and P. McLaren (Eds.), *Between Borders: Pedagogy and the Politics of Cultural Studies*. New York: Routledge, pp. 192–224.

CONTRIBUTORS

Carl Allsup is Associate Professor at University of Wisconsin-Platteville. He received his Ph.D. in American History from the University of Texas at Austin in 1976. His scholarship includes the first scholarly monograph/history of a Mexican-American organization, numerous articles on Mexican-American history, the teaching of ethnic/gender/class studies, the matrix of race, gender, and class analysis, with his current focus on the relationship between postmodernism, multiculturism, and feminism. Professor Allsup has been active in ethnic studies program development in the Midwest since 1975. His current pedagogical work includes the development and teaching of a university-required course on race, gender, and class issues in the U.S.

Antonia Darder is an Associate Professor of Education at The Claremont Graduate School and Scholar in Residence at the Tomas Rivera Center. Darder is the author of *Culture and Power in the Classroom* (Bergin and Garvey) and *Bicultural Studies in Education: The Struggle for Educational Justice* (Claremont Graduate School). In addition, she has two edited volumes in progress, *Culture and Difference: Critical Perspectives on the Bicultural Experience in the United States* (Bergin and Garvey) and a reader on Latino education entitled *In Search of the Dream: The Education of Latino Students in the U.S.* (Routledge). Darder's work primarily examines issues related to bicultural development and identity, the politics of education, and the manner in which sociopolitical forces impact the academic development of Latino students and Latino educators in this country.

Geneva Gay is Professor of Education and Associate with the Center of Multicultural Education at the University of Washington, Seattle. She is the recipient of the 1990 Distinguished Scholar Award, presented by the Committee on the Role and Status of Minorities in Educational Research and Development of the American Educational Research Association, and the 1994 Multicultural Educator Award, the first to be presented by the National Association of Multicultural Education. She is known nationally and internationally for her scholarship on multicultural education, particularly as it relates to curriculum design, classroom instruction, staff development, and the culture and learning of students of color. Her writings include over ninety articles and book chapters, the coeditorship of *Expressively Black: The Cultural Basis of Ethnic Identity* (Praeger 1987), and authorship of *At the Essence of All Learning: Multicultural Education*, a 1994 publication of Kappa Delta Pi.

Kris D. Gutierrez is an Assistant Professor in Curriculum in the Graduate School of Education at the University of California, Los Angeles. Her research interests include a study of the sociocultural contexts of literacy development, particularly the study of the acquisition of academic literacy for language minority students. Her research also focuses on understanding the relationship between language, culture, development, and pedagogies of empowerment.

Stephen N. Haymes is an Assistant Professor at Depaul University-Chicago in the School of Education, the social and historical foundations program. His theoretical interests currently include race urban cultural studies, and critical studies in pedagogy. He has recently completed his book *Race Culture and the City: A Pedagogy of Black Urban Struggle*, which will be published by the State University of New York Press, and is currently working on another book dealing with black critical pedagogy and social movement.

Joe Kincheloe teaches Cultural Studies and Pedagogy at Penn State University. He has written numerous books and articles on critical theory, educational research, and multiculturalism. These include *Teachers as Researchers: Qualitative Paths to Empowerment* (Falmer Press) and *Thirteen Questions: Reframing Education's Conversation*, with Shirley Steinberg (Peter Lang). His latest book is entitled *Toil and Trouble: Good Work, Smart Workers, and the Integration of Academic and Vocational Education* (Peter Lang).

Donaldo Macedo received an Ed.D. in Applied Psycholinguistics and Second Language Teaching and a Ph.D. in Language Behavior from Boston University. He holds a M.A. in Spanish literature from New York University. To study the literature and culture of Spain, he attended the Instituto Internacional in Madrid, Spain. Since his arrival in the United States from Cape Verde in 1966, Dr. Macedo has been directly involved in bilingual education. Professionally, he has been teaching at the University of Massachusetts as a linguist and bilingual educator. He has been honored in the field, including the departmental prize from the University of Massachusetts for undergraduate distinction in Spanish, and was nominated for the Metcalf Award for excellence in teaching at Boston University. Along with his pedagogical experience, Dr. Macedo has published extensively. He is the author of *Issues in Portuguese Bilingual Education*, for which he is the contributing editor. His most recent publications include *Literacy: Reading the Word and the World*, coauthored with Paulo Freire and *Literacies of Power: What Americans are not Allowed to Know*. Dr. Macedo has also presented numerous papers dealing with linguistics and bilingual education in major conferences in the United States, Portugal, and Brazil.

Cameron McCarthy teaches curriculum theory and cultural studies at the University of Illinois at Urbana in Champaign, Illinois. He has published widely on the topics of problems with neoMarxist writings on race and education, institutional support for teaching, and school ritual and adolescent identities in journals such as *Harvard Education Review, Oxford Review of Education, Educational Theory, Curriculum Studies, the Journal of Curriculum Theorizing, Education and Society, Contemporary Sociology, Interchange, the Journal of Education,* and *the European Journal of Intercultural Studies*. He is the author of *Race and Curriculum* (1990) published by Falmer Press. Along with Warren Crichlow of the University of Rochester, he is the coeditor of *Identity and Representation in Education* (1993) published by Routledge. He is also a coeditor of a special issue of *Cultural Studies* on Toni Morrison and pedagogy.

Carmen Montecinos is Assistant Professor in the Department of Educational Psychology and Foundations at the University of Northern Iowa. She conducts research on multicultural teacher education with an emphasis on the professional development of teachers of color.

Khaula Murtadha is Assistant Professor of Education at Indiana University. Her interest in African Centered education began with her years of working with Muslim schools in Washington, D. C. as a science teacher, preschool director, summer camp coordinator, and board member. A mother of six sons and one daughter, she is acutely aware of the problems facing those who are responsible for educating African American children. Parents who were deaf and active in the deaf community were the source of her commitment to social justice for marginalized people in this society.

Peter McLaren is formerly Renowned Scholar-in-Residence, Miami University of Ohio where he served as Director of the Center for Education and Cultural Studies. He is currently Associate Professor in the Graduate School of Education and Information Studies. University of California, Los Angeles. He is the author of the Canadian best-seller, *Cries from the Corridor: The New Suburban Ghettos*, (Methuen) and numerous scholarly books and publications, some of which include *Critical Pedagogy and Predatory Culture* (Routledge), *Between Borders*, (Routledge, coedited with Henry Giroux); *Critical Pedagogy, the State and Cultural Struggle*, (SUNY Press, coedited with Henry Giroux); *Paulo Freire: A Critical Encounter*, (Routledge, coedited with Peter Leonard); *Critical Literacy: Politics, Praxis and the Postmodern*, (SUNY Press, coedited with

Colin Lankshear); *Schooling as a Ritual Performance*, (Routledge) and *Life in Schools*, (Longman). His articles have appeared in *Social Text, Polygraph, American Journal of Semiotics, Cultural Studies, Strategies, Harvard Educational Review, Collective Literature, Philosophy and Social Criticism, Educational Theory, Journal of Education*, and numerous other journals. Professor McLaren is a faculty advisor to the Chicano Studies Research Center, UCLA and international editor of the journals *Taboo* and *The International Journal of Educational Reform.* He also edits a series for Westview Press with Joe Kincheloe and Shirley Steinberg called "The Edge: Critical Studies in Educational Theory." Two of Professor McLaren's books have been winners of the Critic's Choice Award, American Education Studies Association, for one of the most significant books published in education in the United States (1989; 1992).

Sonia Nieto is Professor of Education in the Cultural Diversity and Curriculum Reform Program, School of Education, at the University of Massachusetts in Amherst. Born and raised in Brooklyn, she was a teacher at P.S. 25 in the Bronx, the first bilingual school in the Northeast, as well as a junior high school teacher and college professor in the Puerto Rican Studies Department at Brooklyn College before moving to Massachusetts. She received her doctoral degree from the University of Massachusetts, concentrating in curriculum studies with a special emphasis in multicultural and bilingual education. Dr. Nieto's scholarly work has focused on multicultural and bilingual education, the education of Latinos and the role of parents, curriculum reform, and Puerto Rican children's literature. She has written numerous articles and book chapters on these issues, as well as a book, *Affirming Diversity: The Sociopolitical Context of Multicultural Education* (Longman, 1992). She has also edited a number of volumes and journals, the most recent being a co-edited volume with Ralph Rivera, *The Education of Latinos in Massachusetts: Research and Policy Consideration* (Boston: Gaston Institute, 1994). In addition, she has served on many commissions, panels, and advisory boards that focus their efforts on educational equity, including the Massachusetts Advocacy Center, the Facing History and Ourselves Program Committee, and National Scholarship Advisory Board for Girls, Inc., and California Tomorrow. She received the Human and Civil Rights Award from the Massachusetts Teachers Association in 1989 and the Outstanding Accomplishment in Higher Education Award from the Hispanic Caucus of the American Association of Higher Education in 1991.

D. Michael Pavel is an enrolled member of the Skokomish Indian Nation in Washington State. Formerly a faculty member in the Graduate School of Education, Division of Higher Education and Organization Change at the University of California, Los Angeles, Michael has recently accepted a faculty position at Washington State University. Before accepting the faculty position at UCLA, Michael was honored as the distinguished doctoral graduate at Arizona State University while receiving his Ph.D in education and was twice honored as the Carnation Dairies Teaching Incentive Award winner for outstanding service to the community while maintaining an excellent academic record. As a young scholar, Michael has published in leading educational journals and edited volumes of national circulation. More importantly, he has been instrumental in reviving and maintaining the traditional Skokomish culture and making the general public more aware about the importance of traditional culture to sustain Native American communities.

Janine Pease-Windy Boy is a member of the Crow Tribe of Indians of Montana. She has served as president of Little Big Horn College (Crow Agency Montana), the tribally chartered college of the Crow Tribe for the past twelve years. Since completion of her undergraduate degree in anthropology and sociology at Central Washington State University in 1970, Ms. Pease-Windy Boy has held adult and higher education positions in Washington, Arizona, and Montana. Beginning in 1982, Pease-Windy Boy has been a board member of the American Indian Higher Education Consortium (AIHEC) and was Consortium president from 1983 to 1985. Pease-Windy Boy offered lead AIHEC testimony in congressional committee hearings from 1983 to 1991. The National Indian Education Association named Pease-Windy Boy 1990 Indian Educator of the Year. She served as lead plaintiff in the 1986 federal Indian voting rights case *Windy Boy v. Big Horn County*. At home in Crow County, Pease-Windy Boy is a member of the Big Lodge Clan, the Nighthawk Dance Society, the Native Americans for Action Now and the First Crow Indian Baptist Church. She resides with her husband, John Pretty on Top, and teenage children Roses and Vernon in Lodge Grass, Montana.

Evelyn Newman Phillips is an applied anthropologist who teaches at Central Connecticut State College. She received her doctoral degree from the University of South Florida in Tampa. Her research interests include African American ethnicity, multicultural education, and the political economy of urban redevelopment. Her current experiences are supported by several years of experiences as a social worker and an international development worker.

Mary Simpson Poplin is a Professor on the faculty in education of the Claremont Graduate School in Claremont, California. After teaching elementary and special education students in north Texas for a number of years, she received her Ph.D. from the University of Texas at Austin in 1978. Her early work was in the field of special education. For the past ten years, she has concentrated on the preparation of teachers and teacher educators for multiethnic and multilingual urban environments.

During the spring of 1990, she also taught second language students every morning in an urban high school. Her professional publications center on the exploration of nonreductionistic pedagogies in diverse educational settings, including constructivist, critical or liberation, and feminine pedagogies. Professor Poplin is also the Director of Teacher Education and the Institute for Education in Transformation Claremont Graduate School. She is the author/editor of the Institute's national report on schooling, an eighteen-month intensive, qualitative study entitled *Voices from the Inside: A Report on Schooling from Inside the Classroom.*

Mary Ritchie, a member of the Forest County Potawatomi of Wisconsin, is the cofounder of the Kenosha-Racine Native American Council. She is a feminist, grandmother, beadworker, writer, public speaker, and researcher in issues regarding Native American women. Currently, she is doing research regarding leadership and gender as it pertains to the First People of the land we call Turtle Island, also known as North America.

John Rivera is a faculty member at San Diego City College and a research fellow in the Institute for Education in Transformation at The Claremont Graduate School. During the course of the study he was an ACE fellow at the Graduate School. Currently, he is actively involved in a number of participatory, community action research projects at both the local and national levels in the fields of business and education.

Christine E. Sleeter was formerly Professor of Teacher Education at the University of Wisconsin-Parkside and is now a Professor at California State University, Monterey Bay. She was formerly a learning disabilities teacher in Seattle. She received her Ph.D. from the University of Wisconsin-Madison in 1981. She has produced several books on multicultural education, including *After the School Bell Rings*, (with Carl Grant), Falmer Press; *Making Choices for Multicultural Education* (with Carl Grant), Macmillan; *Turning on Learning*, (with Carl Grant), Macmillan; *Empowerment Through Multicultural Education*, State University of New York Press; and *Keepers of the American Dream*, Falmer Press. She has also published numerous journal articles and book chapters on multicultural education. In 1993 she was awarded the UW-Parkside Excellence in Research and Creative Activity Award, and in 1994, the National Association for Multicultural Education Research Award.

Shirley Steinberg is an educational consultant and frequent lecturer on multiculturalism and children's popular culture. She is the coauthor with Joe Kincheloe of *Thirteen Questions*, and with Joe Kincheloe and Deborah Tippens of *The Stigma of Genius: Einstein and Beyond Modern Education*. She is presently finishing a book on social drama and education.

INDEX

education(al) (*continued*)
principles, 343; community,
400; democratic, 208;
disempowering, 213–14;
domestication, 81;
emnpowerment, 411; equal,
201, 206; equity, 159, 164, 182;
goals, 163, 200, 208;
humanistic, 236; multicultural
theory of, 271; process, 176,
333, 355; programs, 223, 425;
progressive, 56; public, 180;
purposes, 224, 233; racial
antagonism, 245; reality, 322;
reform, 159, 161, 262; role in
society, 404; transformation,
161; U. S., 168; value, 406, 409
education system, 152, 332, 364;
American, 405; higher, 311;
public, 136, 162; sifting process,
406; teacher, 136–37; transmission model, 205; U. S., 158
educators, conservative, 148, 223;
critical, 106, 200, 223, 226,
229–31, 236, 320, 329–30, 336,
411; democratic, 208; feminine,
235–36; multicultural, 208, 226,
229, 231–32, 236; white, 12
Educational Excellence Network,
133
educational opportunities, 157
elite/elitism 33, 36; academic,
309; cultural, 150; intellectual,
22; males, 269; populist, 61;
power, 99; whitemen, 140, 285
Elshtain, J. B., 416, 420, 433
empower/empowerment, 11, 44,
155, 157, 164, 174–75, 177–78,
192–93, 204–06, 211, 213, 323,
328–29, 345, 349, 358, 372–73,
406, 416; collective, 14, 326;
personal, 178, 181–82; process,
176. 178; social, 164–65;
student, 175, 178, 180, 333,
340
enculturation, 389

environmentalist, 36; cultural,
336; linguistic, 336; school, 285;
traditional educational, 335
equal access, 400
equality, racial, 390
equal opportunity, 390
Estrada, K., 60
ethnic/ethnicity, 11, 49, 50, 52,
142, 169, 173, 199, 202, 250,
292, 295, 297–98, 304–05,
349–50, 372–73; awareness,
372; conflict, 392;
consciousness, 358;
contributions, 170; factor, 160;
heritage schools, 377; identity,
377; minorities, 47, 158, 293;
non-white, 107; origin, 285;
peoples, 150; powerless, 416;
studies, 12, 149, 198–99, 229,
269, 285, 403; white, 108, 247
ethnocentric, 40, 43, 143, 149,
197, 211, 309
"Ethos of the Blues", 119–20
EuroAmerican, 112, 122, 150,
163, 196, 198–99, 228, 230,
236, 247, 312, 376–77, 392,
402
EuroAnglican, 167–68; ideology,
350
Eurocentric/Eurocentrism, 15, 25,
55, 57, 59, 119, 143, 145, 149,
152, 165, 171, 174, 176, 178,
211, 248, 250, 269, 272–73,
276, 279, 285–87, 320, 352–53,
361, 421; cultures, 46, 273,
297; curriculum, 350;
scholarship, 352
exotic Black, 117–19
expectations, 231, 233; assimilationist, 335; Latino teacher, 342;
lowered, 230, 239; negative,
230; student, 335; teacher, 320,
341; traditional, 320
experience, 41, 45, 109, 151, 155,
161, 169–71, 173–74, 195–96,
199, 204, 221, 229, 237, 260,